Handbook of Coaching Psychology

A guide for practitioners

Edited by Stephen Palmer and
Alison Whybrow

Routledge
Taylor & Francis Group

LONDON AND NEW YORK

First published 2008
by Routledge
27 Church Road, Hove, East Sussex BN3 2FA

Simultaneously published in the USA and Canada
by Routledge
711 Third Avenue, New York NY 10017

*Routledge is an imprint of the Taylor and Francis Group,
an Informa business*

Typeset in Times by
RefineCatch Limited, Bungay, Suffolk

Paperback cover design by Lisa Dynan

This publication has been produced with paper manufactured to
strict environmental standards and with pulp derived from
sustainable forests.

British Library Cataloguing in Publication Data
A catalogue record for this book is available from the British Library

Library of Congress Cataloging-in-Publication Data
Handbook of coaching psychology / edited by Stephen Palmer and
Alison Whybrow.
    p. cm.
  Includes bibliographical references and index.
  ISBN 978-1-58391-706-0 (hardback) –
ISBN 978-1-58391-707-7 (pbk.) 1. Personal coaching.
1. Palmer, Stephen, 1955– II. Whybrow, Alison, 1968–
  BF637.P36H36 2007
  158'.3 – dc22

                        2007016117

ISBN: 978-1-58391-706-0 (hbk)
ISBN: 978-1-58391-707-7 (pbk)

Printed and bound in Great Britain by
TJ International Ltd, Padstow, Cornwall

To Josh and Sam; to Maggie for her support on this project; to all my colleagues who supported the setting up of coaching psychology in the UK and around the world. (SP)

To my mum for making all things possible, my husband for his enduring support and of course Millie and Georgie. (AW)

Contents

Illustrations

Figures

Tables

Boxes

Notes on the editors and contributors

Stephen Palmer PhD is Founder Director of the Centre for Coaching and Centre for Stress Management, London, UK. He is an Honorary Professor of Psychology at City University and Director of its Coaching Psychology Unit, and also the UK's first Visiting Professor of Work Based Learning and Stress Management at the National Centre for Work Based Learning Partnerships, Middlesex University. He is a Chartered Psychologist, an APECS Accredited Executive Coach and Executive Coach Supervisor. He is President and Fellow of the Association for Coaching, Vice President and Honorary Fellow of the Institute of Health Promotion and Education, and Honorary Vice President and Fellow of the International Stress Management Association (UK). He has been past Chair of the Coaching Psychology Forum and in 2004 he became the first Chair of the British Psychological Society (BPS) Special Group in Coaching Psychology.

He is the UK coordinating co-editor of the *International Coaching Psychology Review*, executive editor of *Coaching: An International Journal of Theory, Research and Practice*, editor of the *International Journal of Health Promotion and Education*, co-editor of the *Rational Emotive Behaviour Therapist*, consultant editor of *The Coaching Psychologist*, consulting editor of *Counselling Psychology Review* and *Stress News*. He has written over 100 articles and authored or edited over 35 books including *Achieving Excellence in your Coaching Practice: How to run a highly successful coaching business* (with McMahon and Wilding, 2005). He edits a number of book series including *Essential Coaching Skills and Knowledge Series* (Routledge), *Stress Counselling* (Sage) and *Brief Therapies* (Sage).

Stephen received from the BPS Division of Counselling Psychology the Annual Counselling Psychology Award for 'Outstanding professional and scientific contribution to Counselling Psychology in Britain for 2000', and in 2004 he received an Achievement Award from the Association for Rational Emotive Behaviour Therapy. His interests include jazz, astronomy, walking, writing and art. Email: dr.palmer@btinternet.com

Alison Whybrow is a Chartered Occupational Psychologist, with significant experience as a consultant and coach. Along with her degree and PhD in Psychology from the University of Liverpool, she has completed a Foundation Course in Counselling Psychology with the School of Psychotherapy and Counselling at Regent's College, London.

Alison has worked with private and public sector organisations from the frontline to the board. As a coach and facilitator, Alison integrates phenomenological frameworks with expertise in Cognitive Behavioural Coaching. Alison has had significant involvement in the development of the coaching psychology profession, co-proposing the Special Group in Coaching Psychology within the BPS with Stephen Palmer. She has published papers on coaching, team working and change and reviewed articles and books for a number of journals and publishers.

Alison is a co-editor of the *International Coaching Psychology Review*, Consulting Editor of *The Coaching Psychologist*, sits on the editorial board of the *British Journal of Guidance and Counselling* and the editorial board of *Coaching: An International Journal of Theory Research and Practice*. With a range of interests, Alison spends most of her time when not working with her young family.

Julie Allan MSc, CPsychol has a passion for developing purpose and capability in individuals and organisations. Her primary areas of activity are organisational change management and leadership/top team development in the for-profit, governmental and charity sectors. She is co-author of *The Power of the Tale: Using narratives for organisational success* (with Fairtlough and Heinzen, 2002).

Hannah Azizollah, a Chartered Occupational Psychologist, has worked in the field of Assessment, Development, Organisational Development and Change for many years. Most of her current work involves coaching individuals and teams through a wide range of changes or transitions.

Tatiana Bachkirova PhD is a Chartered Occupational Psychologist working both as an academic at Oxford Brookes University and as a practitioner in coaching and coaching supervision. She is Course Leader for the postgraduate certificate in supervision for coaching and mentoring and co-editor in chief of *Coaching: An International Journal of Theory, Research and Practice*.

Helen Baron, a Chartered Psychologist, has over 20 years' experience in providing training and consultancy to organisations in formulating equal opportunities policy and promoting fairness in staff assessment and selection. In addition she designs and develops assessment tools.

Alan Bourne is a Chartered Occupational Psychologist specialising in assessment, development and change management with nine years' experience of developing and delivering value-adding solutions for clients. He has previously worked as an external consultant with SHL and Capital Consulting, internal consultant with Royal Mail Group and as an independent consultant with a variety of clients and consulting organisations. He is Director of Talent Q UK Ltd.

Halina Brunning is a Chartered Clinical Psychologist, Organisational Consultant and Executive Coach. She has worked in the British and Polish National Health Services and has published extensively on clinical and organisational issues. She edited a book *Executive Coaching: Systems-psychodynamic perspective* published by Karnac (2006).

Richard Bryant-Jefferies has worked as a primary care alcohol counsellor, has managed substance misuse services, and is currently an Equalities and Diversity manager for an NHS Mental Health Trust. He has written over 21 books on counselling themes. His first novel is *Binge!* (2007). www.bryant-jefferies.freeserve.co.uk

Michael Carroll PhD is a Chartered Counselling Psychologist and an Accredited Executive Coach. He is Visiting Industrial Professor at the University of Bristol and the winner of the 2001 BPS Award for Distinguished Contributions to Professional Psychology.

Elaine Cox PhD is the Director of Postgraduate Coaching and Mentoring Programmes at Oxford Brookes University. She is editor-in-chief of the *International Journal of Evidence Based Coaching and Mentoring*.

Kieran Duignan coaches leaders, managers and staff to figure out the best possible ways to accomplish their most important business goals by gathering, organising, evaluating, sharing and applying knowledge of their own, and of their employees, systematically. He applies personal construct psychology within an interpersonal reconstructive coaching model he has developed.

Annette Fillery-Travis is an academic, researcher and coach working in executive education and professional development at masters and doctorate level with the Professional Development Foundation. Her passion is in facilitating self-directed learners to realise their full capability.

Anthony M. Grant PhD, MAPS is a Coaching Psychologist and the Founder and Director of the Coaching Psychology Unit in the School of Psychology, University of Sydney, the world's first Coaching Psychology Unit. He is widely recognised as being a key figure in contemporary coaching psychology. Email: anthonyg@psych.usyd.edu.au

Bruce Grimley, a Chartered Occupational Psychologist, runs Achieving Lives Ltd and also Inner Game associates. As a psychologist he specialises in stress management and coaching, also running public level A psychometric training courses. He runs Inner Game independently from

Achieving Lives as he recognises NLP to be slightly different from psychology in many aspects, yet surprisingly similar in others. He enjoys the synergy and professional development afforded by having one foot in each camp. Websites: www.achieving-lives.co.uk www.innergame.co.uk

Susan Harrington works in Occupational Psychology at the University of Leicester following a business career as a manager within large organisations, and subsequently providing consultancy on issues such as bullying and harassment. Her PhD research is focusing on human resources (HR) decision-making, specifically on the issue of bullying, and how positive psychology may inform ethical decision-making within organisations.

Vic Henderson is a Chartered Occupational Psychologist with extensive internal and external consultancy experience and a passion for coaching, learning and development. She has a particular skill ensuring development initiatives are linked to both individual and broad commercial goals.

Caroline Horner DProf (Coaching Psychology), i-coach academy Ltd, specialises in helping organisations maximise their benefits from coaching; she coaches senior leaders and is a lecturer-supervisor to coaches evolving their own professional practice. Her approach draws on her appreciation of existential thinking, passion for learning and wide ranging international experience as a consultant and marketing director. Email: Caroline@ i-coachacademy.com

Stephen Joseph PhD, Chartered Health Psychologist, is Professor of Psychology, Health and Social Care in the School of Sociology and Social Policy, University of Nottingham. He is a senior practitioner member of the BPS Register of Psychologists Specialising in Psychotherapy, and Honorary Consultant Psychologist in Psychotherapy in Nottinghamshire Healthcare NHS Trust.

David Lane PhD, CPsychol, FBPsS, FCIPD is Research Director of the International Centre for the Study of Coaching and Professor at Middlesex University, Chair of the British Psychological Society (and EFPA) Register of Psychologists Specialising in Psychotherapy. He has worked worldwide as a coach and on standards setting/benchmarks for EMCC, WABC and SGCP. Email: David.Lane@pdf.net

Ho Law PhD, AFBPsS, ACMI is a Chartered Occupational Psychologist and Chartered Scientist, the Managing Director of Empsy Ltd and Research and Technical Director of Morph Group Ltd, an international practitioner in psychology, coaching, mentoring and psychotherapy, specialised in diversity and intercultural coaching. Email: ho.law@empsy.com, www.empsy.com, www.morphgroup.net

P. Alex Linley PhD is Director of the Centre for Applied Positive Psychology, Coventry, UK, where he dedicates his time to developing and delivering the benefits of applied positive psychology in work, education and health (see www.cappeu.org). His research and practice is specifically concerned with the identification, measurement, and applications of psychological strengths.

Alanna O'Broin is a Coaching Psychologist, Chartered Counselling Psychologist, and Honorary Treasurer of the BPS Special Group in Coaching Psychology. She runs a coaching and therapy practice. Her research interests include client and coach contributions to the coaching relationship and outcome.

Bill O'Connell is currently the Director of Training with Focus on Solutions Ltd, a training agency based in Birmingham. He is a Fellow of the BACP and an Accredited Counsellor. He is the author and co-editor of a number of solution-focused books. Email: focusonsolutions@btconnect.com

Jonathan Passmore is a Chartered Occupational Psychologist. He has board level experience having worked as a chief executive and company chair. More recently he has worked as a consultant with Pricewaterhouse Coopers Consulting, IBM and OPM, and also with the University of East London. He is auther of *Appreciative Inquiry for Organisational Change* and The Association for Coaching guides, *Excellence in Coaching* and *Psychometrics in Coaching*. Email: jonathancpassmore@yahoo.co.uk

Vega Zagier Roberts trained originally as a psychiatrist and psychotherapist, and has worked primarily as an Organisational Consultant and Coach since 1985. As Senior Organisational Analyst at the Grubb Institute, she has a special interest in leadership development, and works with managers and leaders across the UK and Europe. She is co-editor of *The Unconscious at Work: Individual and organisational stress in the human services* (1994). Email: v.roberts@grubb.org.uk

Ernesto Spinelli is a Professor of Psychotherapy and Counselling Psychology, a Fellow of the BPS and a BPS Chartered Counselling Psychologist. He maintains a private practice as a psychotherapist, executive coach and supervisor, and is Senior Fellow at the School of Psychotherapy and Counselling, Regent's College, London. Email: ESA@plexworld.com

Kasia Szymanska is a Chartered Psychologist, an accredited cognitive behavioural psychotherapist and an Associate Fellow of the BPS. She is editor of *The Coaching Psychologist* and book review editor of *The AC Bulletin*. She is a director of distance learning programmes and a coaching psychology supervisor at the Centre for Coaching in London. She also works as a trainer and has her own practice as a coach and psychotherapist in London.

Foreword

Traditions of coaching are truly ancient. They stretch back across not mere tens of years but hundreds and perhaps thousands. The image of the wise teacher, guiding the student through a series of learning experiences, combining encouragement with analysis and reflection, has formed the basis of legends. The journey from ignorance to knowledge, from doubt to confidence and from inexperience to achievement.

In an age where much store is set on maximising personal and organisational potential, it is not surprising to find a thriving industry has arisen offering a modern day equivalent. Abraham Maslow would have recognised this as the drive for 'self-actualisation'. Whether in the context of commerce, sport or just personal satisfaction, it is the urge to be the best that you can be.

Yet all teachers are not equal. How does the prospective 'student' decide which of the many paths to follow?

The emergence of coaching psychology provides some answers to that dilemma. Here opportunities are built on sound foundations of tried and tested psychological theory and practice. Drawing on psychological science, we can have confidence in approaches and techniques that have survived critical analysis and evaluation to provide a strong evidence base for their effectiveness.

Many branches of applied psychology have contributed to this discipline and a strength of coaching psychology within the British Psychological Society has been the recognition that it transcends professional practice boundaries. The methods are appropriate to, and found in, such diverse areas as clinical, educational and occupational settings.

So how has coaching psychology made a significant additional contribution? Martin Seligman, pioneer of the Positive Psychology movement, has criticised traditional applied psychology as starting from the basis of identifying and treating deficiencies, weaknesses or psychopathology. Many applied psychologists contest that view, believing that a major part of therapeutic intervention is about recognising and building on strengths. Nonetheless, there is some truth in the notion that many people access these services through routes such as healthcare or counselling where there is some implicit notion of dysfunction.

Coaching psychology has a different starting point. Rather than dysfunction, the implicit assumption is of a desire to grow, develop and improve: to gain new skills and to hone existing ones. It reaches out to a new clientele, offering the benefits of psychology to people and organisations wishing to make the most of the resources that lie within the individual.

The British Psychological Society often uses the strapline 'Bringing Psychology to Society'. Coaching psychology is achieving that goal. Readers of this handbook will have the opportunity to judge for themselves. A thorough analysis of its origins is backed up by clear descriptions of its rich theoretical underpinnings and explicit guidance on practice and implementation. It is a timely book for those seeking to explore and utilise the new opportunities: incorporating the best evidence-based practice as well as practice-based evidence. A wise teacher for both the discerning student and the experienced practitioner who wants further encouragement, analysis and reflection.

Ray Miller
Vice President, British Psychological Society

Preface

Why a *Handbook of Coaching Psychology*? Since 2000, when Dr Anthony Grant (2000) announced that coaching psychology had come of age, the coaching psychology movement in terms of the establishment of both the Australian Psychological Society Interest Group in Coaching Psychology (IGCP) and the British Psychological Society Special Group in Coaching Psychology (SGCP) has occurred. The IGCP has over 740 members and the SGCP has over 2000 members so both groups have quite substantial memberships in terms of the psychology community. In fact the IGCP were supportive of the setting up of the SGCP. In addition, the IGCP and SGCP collaborated to launch and edit an international peer-reviewed publication, the *International Coaching Psychology Review*. The SGCP also publishes *The Coaching Psychologist*. These journals have provided coaching psychologists and others with an outlet for articles focusing on coaching psychology research, theory and practice.

With the development of coaching psychology groups has been the advent of national coaching psychology conferences and symposiums too. In Australia this has included health coaching symposia. In December 2006, the First International Coaching Psychology Conference was held at City University, London, UK, and was organised by the SGCP. Other professional coaching psychology groups or bodies have also been set up in Switzerland and Denmark and we predict that we will see more collaborative work between all of the professional psychological bodies over the next few years (see page 450). There certainly has been ongoing collaboration between the coaching bodies at national, European and international levels.

Since 2000 university-based units have developed, including the Coaching Psychology Unit at the University of Sydney, Australia, the Coaching Psychology Unit at City University, London, UK and more recently the Coaching Psychology Institute at Harvard Medical School, USA. University accredited postgraduate and doctorate programmes in coaching psychology are run at a number of universities and external centres too.

This *Handbook* has been published at an exciting time in the fields of coaching and coaching psychology. The interface between the two arenas will further the development of evidence-based coaching. We hope that this *Handbook* will provide trainees and experienced practitioners with an insight into the theory and practice of coaching psychology.

Finally, we would like to thank The Australian Psychological Society, Interest Group in Coaching Psychology and the British Psychological Society, Special Group in Coaching Psychology for reproduction of their history, terms of reference, and definitions, taken from various sources. Their support has encouraged the growth of coaching psychology.

Stephen Palmer
Alison Whybrow
November 2007

Reference

Grant, A. M. (2000) Coaching psychology comes of age. *PsychNews* 4(4): 12–14.

Chapter 1

Coaching psychology

An introduction

Stephen Palmer and Alison Whybrow

This handbook was conceived at a point in time when coaching as a personal and organisational development activity was increasing in popularity, the developing professional bodies within the coaching industry were in their infancy and the understanding of coaching in general was limited (see Grant, 2001). The situation has shifted significantly at the time of going to press. As Cavanagh and Palmer (2006: 5) point out in their editorial for the second issue of the *International Coaching Psychology Review*, 'six months in the rapidly expanding field of coaching psychology really is a long time'. Thus, at the time of publication, it is likely that the field of coaching psychology will have continued to develop.

Against this ever changing background, the primary aim of this handbook is to support the development of the professions of coaching and coaching psychology. This is the first book in the field to draw together the range of approaches and broader practical considerations that provides psychologists, non-psychologists, coaching buyers and human resources professionals with a straightforward insight into coaching psychology. In the first instance we hope this book supports the development of coaching practitioners to address the situation that is clearly highlighted by the well-known coach, Sir John Whitmore:

> In too many cases they [coaches] have not fully understood the performance-related psychological principles on which coaching is based. Without this understanding they may go through the motions of coaching, or use the behaviours associated with coaching, such as questioning, but fail to achieve the intended results.
>
> (Whitmore, 1992: 2)

In this introductory chapter we consider what is coaching and coaching psychology, the origins of coaching pychology and the specific study of the psychology of coaching, and the gradual professionalisation of coaching psychology with the move towards coaching psychology becoming an applied area of psychology. Then we introduce the different parts of this handbook.

What is coaching and coaching psychology and is there a difference?

The generally accepted definitions or descriptions of coaching illustrate the difference between coaching and coaching psychology. Three well-known authors and practitioners describe coaching below:

- Coaching is unlocking a person's potential to maximise their own performance. It is helping them to learn rather than teaching them – a facilitation approach (Whitmore, 1992, based on Tim Gallwey, a tennis expert).
- Coaching is the art of facilitating the performance, learning and development of another – a facilitation approach (Downey, 1999).
- Coaching is directly concerned with the immediate improvement of performance and development of skills by a form of tutoring or instruction – an instructional approach (Parsloe, 1995).

However, definitions or descriptions of coaching psychology which have developed since the beginning of the new millennium usually include attention to psychological theory and practice:

- Coaching psychology is for enhancing performance in work and personal life domains with normal, non-clinical populations, underpinned by models of coaching grounded in established therapeutic approaches (Grant and Palmer, 2002).

This definition was developed as Anthony Grant and Stephen Palmer were co-authoring a paper and Palmer used it in a coaching psychology workshop he presented at a BPS Division of Counselling Psychology Annual Conference in 2002. This definition was subsequently used in the initial proposal to set up a BPS Special Group in Coaching Psychology. As the proposal went through the BPS system of committees, the working definition above for coaching psychology evolved over time. An attempt was made to make it more inclusive as psychologists from a variety of BPS subsystems such as occupational, educational, health, clinical and counselling psychology became involved in the process. In addition, the term 'non-clinical' was dropped after a meeting with the BPS Professional Practice Board. This recommendation by the Board does have repercussions in that coaching psychologists in the UK are not rigidly restricted to non-clinical work assuming they have received appropriate training. The SGCP working definition became:

> Coaching psychology is for enhancing well-being and performance in personal life and work domains underpinned by models of coaching grounded in established adult learning or psychological approaches.
>
> (adapted from Grant and Palmer, 2002)

The Australian Psychological Society's Interest Group in Coaching Psychology describes coaching psychology as follows:

> an applied positive psychology, draws on and develops established psychological approaches, and can be understood as being the systematic application of behavioural science to the enhancement of life experience, work performance and wellbeing for individuals, groups and organisations who do not have clinically significant mental health issues or abnormal levels of distress.
>
> (Australian Psychological Society, 2007)

The key difference between definitions of coaching and coaching psychology is that the latter include the application of psychological theory. Although the SGCP and IGCP definitions are similar, the IGCP definition states that it is 'an applied positive psychology'. Due to the diverse and varied backgrounds of the SGCP membership, this statement has not been included although there is an affinity between coaching psychology and positive psychology. We are unable to predict the future but definitions seldom remain static unless the area of psychology has stagnated.

In the light of feedback received from some SGCP members, in particular educational psychologists who coach children and young people, the most recent description or working definition is:

> Coaching psychology is for enhancing well-being and performance in personal life and work domains underpinned by models of coaching grounded in established learning theories and psychological approaches.
>
> (Adapted from Grant and Palmer, 2002)

No doubt other definitions will be developed but the different professional psychological bodies around the world will need to continue to provide a working definition or description that is relevant to practise in their own country.

Coaching psychology: the coming of age

In 2000, Anthony Grant announced that coaching psychology had come of age. A few years later Cavanagh and Palmer (2006: 5) asserted that 'the theory, practice and research base of coaching psychology is developing at a fast pace'. It does seem that coaching psychology appears to be a rapidly expanding area of applied psychology in both research and professional domains (Grant, 2005, 2006; Cavanagh and Palmer, 2006).

But how and where did coaching psychology evolve? There are various views on this question (see Chapter 2). It is generally agreed that the foundations of modern day coaching psychology developed from the Humanistic movement of the 1960s. The humanistic approaches to counselling particularly focused on affect, interpersonal relationships and phenomenally based cognitions about self (Dryden and Palmer, 1997). These can still be seen as crucial elements in life, personal and workplace coaching where the coach facilitates a client-centred goal-orientated process. However, in the 1960s cognitive behavioural therapies were also developing, with an emphasis on cognition, behaviour and imagery, relegating affect to a product of cognitive processing (see Dryden and Palmer, 1997).

For the hard-hitting world of business the cognitive behavioural approach, or more specifically, the rational emotive behaviour therapy version, was being adapted to the workplace largely by psychologists (e.g. Ellis and Blum, 1967; Ellis, 1972; DiMattia with Mennen, 1990; Palmer and Burton, 1996). The Humanistic approach did not put up barriers on who could practise client-centred or person-centred counselling or other forms of Humanistic therapies whereas the cognitive behavioural training centres in North America and the UK expected trainees to be qualified health professionals. In addition, the majority of members of the UK professional bodies for cognitive behavioural therapies had a core health-related professional qualification in psychiatry, nursing or psychology. This may highlight the divide between the approaches that coaching psychologists (or psychologists as coaches) and coaches practise in Australia, the USA and the UK. Non-psychologists are more likely to use the GROW model (**G**oal(s), **R**eality, **O**ptions, **W**ill or **W**ay forward) without having any underpinning psychological theory taught to them on their training programmes whereas coaching psychologists report using a wide range of therapeutic approaches that have been adapted to the coaching arena (see pages 11–12; Whybrow and Palmer, 2006a, 2006b). The GROW model or, to be more precise, framework to hold a conversation, with the addition of basic coaching skills such as listening and communication, is less likely to be effective when the practitioner needs to underpin their practice with a psychological model to help understand the coachee who is *not* achieving their coaching goals. So often GROW, which has many great strengths, is taught in a psychological vacuum. In the USA this may also reflect the legal issues on who can practise psychological methods and the American based International Coach Federation, which recognises courses internationally, but operates within the legal jurisdiction of the USA. In the UK there some signs that coaching training providers are lengthening their courses and including more theory as they obtain external university accreditation and recognition by professional bodies.

A psychology of coaching

Although modern-day coaching and coaching psychology has its roots back in the 1960s, the formal systematic study of the psychology of coaching goes back to the 1920s, if not earlier. The study of the psychology of coaching should be seen as distinct from the development of the profession of coaching psychology, which will be covered later.

As early as 1918, Coleman R. Griffith was making psychological observations about football and basketball. He studied at the University of Illinois and was awarded his PhD in 1920. His dissertation was on the vestibular system (Green, 2003). On graduating he was soon appointed as assistant professor at Illinois and offered psychology-based courses for athletes (Griffith, 1930). In 1925 Mr Huff, the Head of the University of Illinois, Department of Physical Welfare for Men, asked Griffith to establish a Laboratory for Research in Athletics. In the USA this research institute was the first of its kind (the first dedicated scientific athletics research laboratory was located in Berlin: see Green, 2003). Griffith (1926: vii) wrote that it was 'a special laboratory for the purpose of making an experimental and psychological study of men while they were engaging in the various forms of athletic competition'. Griffith became director and was invited to research three areas (Griffith, 1926: vii):

- toward the discovery of pure psychological fact and theory
- toward the discovery of facts about human behaviour that have a bearing upon athletic skill and athletic mindedness, and
- toward increasing the effectiveness of coaching methods.

Griffith believed a coach was 'more than an instructor. He is a teacher, in the ancient sense of the word . . . a character-builder; he molds personalities' (1926: 2). He believed that the coach should be an athlete, a physiologist and psychologist. In his book, *Psychology of Coaching* (Griffith, 1926) he covered many different aspects of coaching such as handling spectators, sports stars or jinxed players, or the problems of over-coaching teams, and included the laws and principles of learning. Also he questioned commonsense thinking such as 'practice makes perfect'.

Griffith was academically very productive and it is claimed that he published over 40 articles between 1919 and 1931, at least half of them on the psychology of sport (see Gould and Pick, 1995; Green, 2003). This helped to establish the psychology of coaching in this particular era. In 1932 the laboratory was closed but Green (2003) mentions Griffith's continued active involvement in sports research and the difficulties he encountered:

> In 1938, P. K. Wrigley, owner of the Chicago Cubs, hired him to help improve the team's performance. Griffith and an assistant filmed and measured the players' skills, attempting to build a 'scientific' training program for the team. Many of Griffith's subjects, most notably the managers, objected to his interference (as they saw it) and attempted to undermine his work. Griffith wrote more than 600 pages of reports on his work with the Cubs between 1938 and 1940.
>
> (Green, 2003: 267)

Griffith encountered difficulties working at the Chicago Cubs as the managers were resistant to applying his recommendations and by 1940 he left and finally stopped his coaching research. There is no evidence of doctoral students taking forward his research either. Thus the golden age of the psychology of coaching research within the sports field did not return for a couple of decades. However, his publications and work in the field were conveniently rediscovered in the 1960s by the sports psychology fraternity who were attempting to establish sports psychology as a discipline of psychology in America. Griffith's papers possibly added credence to their quest.

Griffith was probably the first professional psychologist to be employed by a major league sports franchise for an extended period of time (Green 2003). He is now thought of as the 'father' of the American discipline of sports psychology (Kroll and Lewis, 1978). His great contribution, which often goes unrecognised, was to emphasise the importance of the psychology in coaching.

Later others started to write about the psychology of coaching although the focus continued to be on the field of sports such as *Psychology of Coaching* by Lawther (1951). The first book to have coaching psychology in the title appears to be *Modern Coaching Psychology* by Curtiss Gaylord (1967). Again sports related, but it did suggest that the coach could be a health teacher. It also included evaluation questionnaires for coach and coachee. Later books included *The Psychology of Athletic Coaching* (Moore, 1970), *Psychology of Coaching* (Tutko and Richards, 1971) and *Motivation and Coaching Psychology* (Wilt and Bosen, 1971).

In their book, *Psychology of Coaching: Theory and application*, Llewellyn and Blucker (1982) discussed the different topics taken directly from psychology to underpin the practice of sports psychology. Nearly all of them are still relevant to present-day coaching and coaching psychology (Singer, 1976: 25):

- *Developmental:* optimal learning and performance years; heredity and experience; maturational processes; childhood, adolescence, maturity and ageing; disabilities.
- *Personality:* adjustment problems; self-concept; motivation, persistence, direction, effort; psychological attributes and success.
- *Social:* group and organisational dynamics; competition and cooperation; leadership and management; spectator effects; peer and culture effects; communication, social dimensions.
- *Learning and training:* learning processes and variables; factors influencing skill acquisition; administration of practice sessions; performance variables; ergonomics; instructional design; systems models, media usage, individualised learning approaches.
- *Psychometrics:* measurement; individual differences; group differences; abilities, aptitudes, and skills; personal selection, prediction of success.

Nowadays the link between business and sports is attractive to corporate clients, who may wish to identify and be associated with excellence and high performers (O'Broin and Palmer, 2006) and attending seminars or being coached by leading sports athletes is seen as a positive experience. Intuitively they can see a link between sports and performance; Robert Singer's (1976) overview of sports psychology really does highlight what psychology has to offer an employee who enters coaching with a practitioner whose practice is informed by a range of psychological theories and skills. Peltier (2001: 170) notes that 'counselling is associated with weakness and inadequacy, while coaching is identified with successful sports figures and winning teams'. In fact there is some research that indicates that employees would rather see a coach than a counsellor as a stigma is associated with counselling (Gyllensten et al., 2005).

However, the early developments in the psychology of coaching in the sports arena can be seen as a parallel but often separate developmental path whereby modern-day executive and life coaching has not necessarily applied or integrated the findings from sports psychology, although Peltier (2001: 170) notes that executive coaching has its roots in athletic and performance coaching. This is in stark contrast to the way coaching psychologists have adapted therapeutic approaches to the field of coaching (Whybrow and Palmer, 2006a, 2006b).

O'Broin and Palmer (2006) concluded with reference for future research:

> three areas of synergy between sport psychology and coaching psychology, those of performance psychology, positive psychology, and the coach-athlete and coach–client relationships are argued to offer opportunities for interested commentators and researchers to take forward.
>
> (O'Broin and Palmer, 2006: 21)

Grant (2005, 2006) looked at the development of coaching research by reviewing papers taken from the behavioural science and scholarly business databases. He focused on executive, workplace and life coaching papers. One of the earliest published scholarly papers Grant (2005) found was by Gorby (1937), who described how newer employees were coached by older employees to reduce waste and thereby increase profits which would maximise profit-sharing programme bonuses. This first paper crystallises one of the key interests that employers have in workplace coaching, the maximising of profits, and it makes commercial sense but can have possible benefits for the employee too.

Grant (2005) summarises the limited peer-reviewed research relating to executive, workplace and life coaching taken from the behavioural science literature (PsychInfo and Dissertation Abstracts International (DAI)). He states:

> Published peer-reviewed research has escalated since 1995. The first published peer-reviewed paper on coaching was published in 1937.

Between 1937 and March 2005 there were a total of 175 published papers. Between 1937 and 1994, 50 papers or PhD dissertations were cited in the PsychInfo and DAI databases. Between 1995 and 1999 there were 29 papers or PhD dissertations. Between 2000 and March 2005 there were 96; a total of 175. Between 1935 and March 2005 there were a total of 44 PhDs. Of these total 175 citations, 97 were articles which discussed coaching, theories of coaching or application of techniques, and there were 78 empirical studies. It is clear that there is a growing body of knowledge about workplace, executive and life coaching. Since 2000, there has been considerable growth in the number of PhDs, and peer-reviewed papers. However, the majority of empirical investigations are still uncontrolled group or cases studies, and more randomised controlled studies should be conducted. Although coaching-related research is still in its infancy, there is an emerging body of empirical support for the effectiveness of workplace and life coaching.

(Grant, 2005)

Grant (2006) in December 2005 conducted a literature search of the scholarly business databases for the use of coaching in organisations or the workplace to enhance executive development and work performance. The first relevant paper was published in 1955 and between 1955 and December 2005, 393 papers were published; 314 covered coaching, application of techniques and the theories of coaching articles, and the remaining 79 papers were empirical studies, of which 67 had been published since 2001. Grant concludes:

> Clearly, far more empirical research needs to be conducted. Such research should focus on the impact of coaching at both individual and organizational levels, as well as the establishment of validated, evidence-based coaching methodologies.
>
> (Grant, 2006: 369)

It is easy for us to conclude that more empirical research is required especially as currently relatively few papers have been published that establish that life coaching works. The claims or hyperbole of many coaching books, coaching training course literature or the training centre websites do not necessarily match up with the published coaching research (see Grant and O'Hara, 2006). Many teach their own proprietary trade-marked brands of coaching, essentially a framework or model with little published research underpinning its efficacy. Many do not teach a cognitive behavioural and/or solution-focused approach yet these are the approaches that recent research has indicated increase goal striving, well-being, hope, goal attainment, and reduce test anxiety and stress (e.g. Grant, 2003; Green et al., 2006). But in reality the evidence base is still limited.

Looking at the bigger picture, it is only since the mid-1990s that executive and personal coaching textbooks explicitly grounded in psychological theory have been published. So often it is good books that stimulate and inspire interest in a subject (e.g. Peltier, 2001; Neenan and Dryden, 2002; Skiffington and Zeus, 2003; Cavanagh et al., 2005; Stober and Grant, 2006) yet the vast majority of coaching books on the market do not even include academic references.

In the UK the psychotherapy profession has also encountered problems attempting to establish exactly what works, for whom, with what disorder. The National Institute for Health and Clinical Excellence (NICE, 2005) guidelines for psychological treatments seem to recommend cognitive behaviour therapy for a wide range of disorders such as anxiety, depression, post traumatic stress disorder and so on. Understandably, this has triggered much discontent among psychotherapists especially with the move towards statutory Health Professions Council Registration. In this handbook a range of therapeutic approaches are covered to enrich our understanding of how they have been adapted to the coaching.

What coaching approaches do coaching psychologists use?

During 2003, 2004, 2005 and 2006/7 annual surveys have been undertaken in the UK to research the views and experiences of coaching psychologists who are SGCP members (see Whybrow and Palmer, 2006a, 2006b). In the most recent survey of coaching psychology practice (2006/7) by Palmer and Whybrow, coaching psychologists are more likely to describe their approach as facilitational (67.9 per cent) rather than instructional (17.4 per cent). Many practitioners may see this as a position on a dimension, rather than an 'either/ or' approach. For example, one can have a predominantly facilitational style, yet this may not stop the coach appropriately providing input and information within the coaching framework.

The 2006/7 survey indicates that there are in excess of 28 different psychological models and approaches used by coaching psychologists. Figures 1.1 and 1.2 indicate the 23 approaches used by at least 10 per cent of survey respondents. Solution-focused (67.9 per cent) and cognitive behavioural coaching (60.6 per cent) approaches are reported to be the most frequently used. These approaches are followed by goal-focused (45.9 per cent), behavioural (45.9 per cent), cognitive (42.2 per cent) and person-centred (39.4 per cent).

Solution-focused, goal-focused, cognitive and behavioural approaches have been consistently more popular since the surveys started in 2003 (note, cognitive behavioural as an option was added only in this most recent survey). The view of whether these more popular approaches are more effective than others is not yet clear. Certainly the solution-focused and cognitive

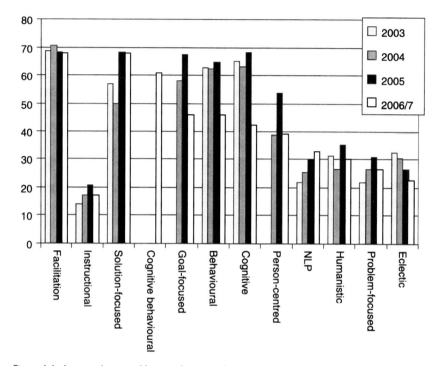

Figure 1.1 Approaches used by coaching psychologists.

behavioural approaches have been more readily identified as effective (e.g. Grant, 2003; Green et al., 2006).

Those approaches that are reportedly used by less than 10 per cent of survey respondents include narrative, transpersonal, action, psychosynthesis and psychoanalytical. It would be interesting to know whether coachees' experiences differ depending on the preferred psychological model of their coach.

This handbook details 10 of the 28 psychological approaches mentioned in the survey plus motivational interviewing. With little published literature on the application of the majority of the therapeutic approaches and how they are applied to the field of coaching and coaching psychology, this handbook marks a step forward in bringing these approaches together in the one publication.

The development of coaching psychology

The development of coaching psychology within an established profession of psychology took place in tandem in both Australia and the UK. We include details about them below.

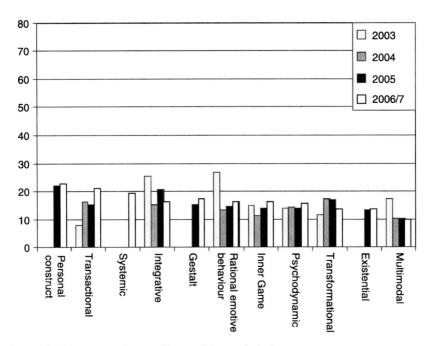

Figure 1.2 More approaches used by coaching psychologists.

Australian Psychological Society, Interest Group Coaching Psychology[1]

The Australian Psychological Society created the Interest Group in Coaching Psychology at its annual meeting in August 2002. The first National Committee met in January 2003 and has since sponsored state forums, panels and launches of the IGCP in Melbourne, Sydney, Brisbane, Adelaide and Perth. There are over 600 members, with state and territory groups in Victoria, NSW, South Australia, Queensland, Western Australia and ACT.

The Interest Group in Coaching Psychology facilitates the theoretical, applied and professional development of coaching psychology as an emerging theoretical and applied subdiscipline of psychology. Coaching psychology, as an applied positive psychology, draws on and develops established psychological approaches, and can be understood as being the systematic application of behavioural science to the enhancement of life experience, work performance and well-being for individuals, groups and organisations who do not have clinically significant mental health issues or abnormal levels of distress.

As a benchmark professional forum the IGCP is theoretically inclusive, independent of external commercial influences, promotes rigorous critical

1 Source of this section: APS IGCP website, retrieved 9 April, 2007.

thought and the development of applied coaching skills, and adheres to the highest levels of professional integrity and practice as reflected in the APS Code of Ethics and Ethical Guidelines.

Terms of reference

1   To enhance the professional identity of Coaching Psychology within the Australian Psychological Society and to establish and maintain a linking mechanism for researchers and practitioners throughout Australia.
2   To provide a forum for discussion and peer contact, and for information sharing between Interest Group and other APS members.
3   To facilitate discussion around the definition and nature of coaching psychology.
4   To promote development of appropriate ethical standards and guidelines for the practice of coaching psychology.
5   To foster publications and research into coaching psychology.
6   To organise and promote continuing education for APS members.
7   To promote best practice professional development within the psychology profession for coaching psychology.
8   To provide expert advice to the Australian Psychological Society on issues relating to the nature and practice of coaching psychology.

British Psychological Society, Special Group in Coaching Psychology

The BPS Special Group in Coaching Psychology was launched in December 2004 and, within a short space of time, became the third largest subsystem of the British Psychological Society with over 2000 members. Half of these members are Chartered Psychologists. A Special Group exists to represent groups of BPS members working in a particular field.

The aims of the SGCP are as follows (BPS, 2007):

2.1   To promote the development of coaching psychology.
2.2   To encourage the research and study of coaching psychology in a variety of personal, organisational and training contexts.
2.3   To promote the application of appropriate ethical standards and guidelines for the practice of coaching psychology.
2.4   To encourage the development of coaching psychology by facilitating workshops, symposia, conferences and publications.
2.5   To develop public awareness of the nature, aims and practical applications of coaching psychology.
2.6   To work closely with Sections, Special Groups and Divisions of the Society in pursuit of these aims and to collaborate appropriately with external agencies and organisations.

2.7   To promote the interests of members of the Special Group in their activities in coaching psychology.

2.8   To carry on all such activities as may be conducive to the foregoing Aims.

The origins of the Special Group in Coaching Psychology go back to the BPS Division of Counselling Psychology Annual Conference in 2002 when Stephen Palmer raised the issue of setting up a coaching psychology Special Interest Group within the Division of Counselling Psychology at the annual general meeting. He was given the go-ahead to run a coaching psychology workshop at the conference. At the workshop it was agreed by the participants to set up an internet forum so that the interested delegates would be able to keep in contact. The internet group was called the Coaching Psychology Forum (see Palmer and Whybrow, 2006). Unfortunately, it was discovered that the constitution of the Division of Counselling Psychology did not allow the setting up of Special Interest Groups.

The membership of the Coaching Psychology Forum (CPF) was growing and included members from occupational and clinical psychology in addition to the original counselling psychologists. At a meeting of CPF members held in London on 21 February 2003 at the IBM offices, it was decided to submit a proposal to the BPS for the setting up of a Special Group in Coaching Psychology. Although the proposal did encounter some difficulties at times, it did receive support from over 1200 BPS members by 31 August 2004. Then the entire BPS membership had the opportunity to vote for or against the proposal and the vote was declared in its favour on 16 October 2004. The inaugural meeting and inaugural conference were held on 15 December 2004 at City University, London, UK. Dr Anthony Grant from the Coaching Psychology Unit, University of Sydney, often considered as the father of modern coaching psychology, gave an invited keynote paper.

Other psychology bodies

As coaching psychology develops we predict that more coaching psychology related bodies will set up. Currently there is a Swiss Society for Coaching Psychology and as a part of the Danish Psychological Association, the Society for Evidence-based Coaching was launched in 2007 (see Appendix 1 for contact information). The development of these professional coaching psychology bodies that form part of a national psychology body does mean that codes of practice and ethical guidelines exist for their members who are coaching psychologists. Therefore they can practise within an ethical framework.

At the First International Coaching Psychology Conference held at City University, London, on 18 December 2006, a group of psychologists from around the world held a meeting and agreed to set up the International Forum for Coaching Psychology (IFCP). The proposed aims were as follows (IFCP 2007):

- create a network organisation of coaching psychologists that is across-communities and cultures
- accreditation of coaching psychologists
- collaboration between different countries
- cross-cultural research
- identify/bridge cultural gap
- identify what works.

To an onlooker, it could appear that coaching psychology has come from nowhere yet we hope it can be seen that there have been many influences in its development over decades and its growth is very likely to continue.

Introduction to the *Handbook of Coaching Psychology*

In this handbook, we outline the frameworks and psychological theories that have been developed, adapted and applied to coaching practice. Indeed, these frameworks and theories are argued to underpin and bring depth to the coaching relationship (Cavanagh, 2006).

Part I

In Part I the context is set with a personal reflection from Anthony Grant, who provides a perspective on the past, present and future of the profession. Following this, the natural partnering of positive psychology and coaching psychology is considered by Alex Linley and Susan Harrington. They explore the shared aspirations of the two movements in their endeavours to enhance well-being and performance. Annette Fillery-Travis and David Lane explore the research indicating the real value of coaching to individuals and organisations. With the broad definition of coaching practice, the range of approaches and the challenge of consistency of measurement, defining the real value is a particular challenge. However, through thoughtful reflections and redefinition of the question 'Does coaching work?', the chapter provides a useful framework from which to assess coaching interventions. This background and context provide a useful starting point from which to explore the psychological theories and models that fall within the body of knowledge and practice of coaching psychology.

Part II

Part II introduces a number of psychological theories and frameworks that are applied by coaching psychologists, and coaches who use psychological techniques in their coaching practice. This collection of approaches is not exhaustive. However, some of the more popular approaches are represented such as cognitive behavioural, behavioural and solution-focused coaching (Palmer and Whybrow, 2006). In addition, some of the less often practised approaches are also included, for example narrative coaching, existential and gestalt coaching (Palmer and Whybrow, 2006). The eleven psychological models and frameworks are presented in alphabetical order in Chapters 5 to 15.

Behavioural coaching, an approach that is likely to fit well in organisational contexts, is introduced by Jonathan Passmore. Stemming from the work of relatively famous psychologists such as Pavlov, Skinner, and Bandura, this chapter highlights that using this approach, coachees are ultimately creating their own motivating self-rewarding system of behaviours. Stephen Palmer and Kasia Szymanska introduce cognitive behavioural coaching as an integrative approach. Here the various frameworks and concepts underpinning this approach are discussed alongside the very practical methods for appropriate application with clients. Existential coaching is introduced by Ernesto Spinelli and Caroline Horner. As an approach that explicitly acknowledges and utilises its foundational philosophical assumptions, existentialism stands apart from other approaches. As ever, the authors provide an accessible and practical introduction to this potentially complex, philosophical approach to practice. Julie Allan and Alison Whybrow introduce a second existential area of coaching practice, gestalt coaching. This chapter outlines the gestalt therapy philosophy of which Fritz Perls is perhaps one of the better known figures, and provides insight into the application of this philosophy in coaching practice.

Jonathan Passmore and Alison Whybrow discuss Motivational Interviewing, a particular method of communication with the client that aims to enhance the client's intrinsic motivation towards personal change goals. Mapping onto the change cycle, the appropriate communication style and content is discussed to maximise client engagement with the coaching process and movement towards the client goal. Narrative coaching is introduced by Ho Law, an approach that is seen as particularly appropriate within a multicultural context. Based on storytelling, this approach raises individual and community awareness of the strengths, knowledge and skills that they possess through a process of active listening.

Coaching from a neuro-linguistic programming (NLP) framework is introduced by Bruce Grimley. Presented in a readable and straightforward manner, this chapter outlines the strong roots of NLP in existential phenomenology and gestalt psychology. Stephen Joseph and Richard Bryant-Jefferies discuss person-centred coaching, an approach that has a purely facilitational orientation. The assertion that people are their own best experts will come as no surprise to the coaching practitioner. However, the philosophical and theoretical depth of this assertion may be surprising to those who have unquestioningly accepted this rhetoric as part of the territory of coaching. Personal construct psychology (PCP) is presented by Kieran Duignan. PCP interweaves themes of constructivist, humanistic and contextual psychology with techniques of psychological measurement, soft systems methodology and behavioural reinforcement. This systemic coaching approach is discussed from a very practical perspective. Halina Brunning and Vega Zagier Roberts provide a great insight into psychodynamic and systems-psychodynamic coaching. A seemingly very individual, therapy-based framework is brought to life through the combination of the psychodynamic concepts with a systems approach. This integration lends itself to a very practical and useful coaching approach that is aimed at providing deeper insight for the client. In contrast, in the final chapter of Part II, Bill O'Connell and Stephen Palmer outline solution-focused coaching. This approach is unashamedly outcome oriented and competency based. Fitting well within the current and pervasive positive psychology paradigm, this approach gives centre stage to the existing skills, strengths, knowledge and experience of the client.

The expertise of the individual contributors in Part II is evident in the way that the conceptual and theoretical backgrounds are made accessible for the reader and by the ease with which the central concepts of each approach are brought to life in the case study material presented. Each of these chapters is a gift to the reader whether the approach is one that is congruent with their individual practice, or not. The clarity with which the approach is highlighted provides the reader with an invaluable insight into what might or might not be interesting to pursue as a coaching psychology practitioner.

Part III

Understanding relationships, diversity and development in coaching and coaching psychology encompasses the contributions in Part III. The coach–client relationship, a key aspect of one-to-one and indeed, one-to-many development work is thoughtfully explored by Alanna O'Broin and Stephen Palmer. With little specific research on the coaching relationship, they draw on the existing evidence, concepts and developments in related fields. A well-founded proposal regarding the important characteristics of a successful coaching relationship is put forward. Tatiana Bachkirova and Elaine Cox's chapter on a cognitive-developmental approach for coach development outlines the theories that underpin models of adult development, cognitive-reflective development and ego development. These theories are carefully applied to coach, coaching psychologist and mentor development, resulting in a model that can be used for coach development in a range of learning contexts.

The boundary between coaching and counselling is explored by Bachkirova in her second contribution to this handbook. As Bachkirova points out, 'This distinction is particularly important for newcomers to the field of coaching, counselling and coaching psychology, for potential clients and sponsors and also for those who are qualified and experienced as coaches and counsellors' (page 352). Helen Baron and Hannah Azizollah bring the thinking and concepts underpinning diversity to coaching. It is very clear reading the approaches in Part II that to be a good coach it is necessary to work from a diversity perspective, even if it is not labelled as such. This chapter discusses equal opportunities and diversity and provides a number of vignettes to promote reflection and exploration of the impact of our own values and norms on our work as a coach. Finally in Part III, Alan Bourne considers the role that psychometric measures can play within the coaching process, including the theory behind types of psychometric assessment and importantly, how to select an appropriate measure and provide feedback. Taking the contributions in Part III together, we would like to see that they engage the practitioner in broad and deep reflections about their own development and the development of their coaching or coaching psychology practice.

Part IV

Part IV of this handbook, focusing on sustainable practice, includes only two chapters. First, Alison Whybrow and Vic Henderson look at integrating and sustaining coaching in organisations. This chapter builds on a change management framework, considers how such a framework might be used to support a coaching intervention and highlights some of the underpinning psychological research that points to why certain practices are likely to smooth the change process. Second, in Michael Carroll's contribution on coaching psychology supervision, he explores the added value that supervision can give to coaching psychology using a model of supervision where the work of the coaching practitioner is the focus of the meeting between the supervisee and the supervisor.

From the outline of the contents alone the breadth and depth of the handbook can be appreciated. The effort of each individual contributor has been brought together within this text to provide the reader with a thoroughly practical, insightful and reflective read.

We conclude this chapter with an observation made by Llewllyn and Blucker (1982: 2):

> Mastery of the various aspects of coaching psychology is not a simple task.

References

Australian Psychological Society (2007) Definition of coaching psychology. Available www.groups.psychology.org.au/igcp/ (10 April 2007).
British Psychological Society (BPS) (2007) The aims of the Special Group in Coaching Psychology. Available www.sgcp.org.uk/coachingpsy/rules.cfm (9 April 2007).

Cavanagh, M. (2006) Coaching from a systemic perspective: a complex adaptive conversation. In D. R. Stober and A. M. Grant, (eds) *Evidence Based Coaching Handbook: Putting best practices to work for your clients.* Hoboken, NJ: Wiley.

Cavanagh, M. and Palmer, S. (2006) Editorial: The theory, practice and research base of coaching psychology is developing at a fast pace. *International Coaching Psychology Review* 1(2): 5–7.

Cavanagh, M., Grant, A. M. and Kemp, T. (2005) *Evidence Based Coaching.* Volume 1, *Theory, Research and Practice from the Behavioural Sciences.* Bowen Hills, Qld: Australian Academic Press.

DiMattia, D. J. with Mennen, S. (1990) *Rational Effectiveness Training: Increasing productivity at work.* New York: Institute for Rational-Emotive Therapy.

Downey, M. (1999) *Effective Coaching.* London: Orion.

Dryden, W. and Palmer, S. (1997) Individual counselling. In S. Palmer and M. McMahon (eds) *Handbook of Counselling,* 2nd edition. London: Routledge.

Ellis, A. (1972) *Executive Leadership: A rational approach.* New York: Institute for Rational-Emotive Therapy.

Ellis, A. and Blum, M. L. (1967) Rational Training: a new method of facilitating management labor relations. *Psychological Reports* 20: 1267–1284.

Gaylord, E. C. (1967) *Modern Coaching Psychology.* Dubuque, IA: W. C. Brown.

Gorby, C. B. (1937) Everyone gets a share of the profits. *Factory Management and Maintenance* 95: 82–83.

Gould, D. and Pick, S. (1995) Sport psychology: the Griffith era, 1920–1940. *The Sport Psychologist* 9: 391–405.

Grant, A. M. (2000) Coaching psychology comes of age. *PsychNews* 4(4): 12–14.

Grant, A. M. (2001) *Towards a Psychology of Coaching.* Sydney: Coaching Psychology Unit, University of Sydney.

Grant, A. M. (2003) The impact of life coaching on goal attainment, metacognition and mental health. *Social Behavior and Personality* 31(3): 253–264.

Grant, A. M. (2005) Workplace, executive and life coaching: an annotated bibliography from the behavioural science literature (March 2005). Unpublished paper, Coaching Psychology Unit, University of Sydney, Australia.

Grant, A. M. (2006) Workplace and executive coaching: a bibliography from the scholarly business literature. In D. R. Stober and A. M. Grant (eds) *Evidence Based Coaching Handbook: Putting best practices to work for your clients.* Hoboken, NJ: Wiley.

Grant, A. M. and O'Hara, B. (2006) The self-presentation and self-promotion of Australian life coaching schools: cause for concern? Unpublished paper, Coaching Psychology Unit, University of Sydney.

Grant, A. M. and Palmer, S. (2002) Coaching psychology workshop. Annual Conference of the Division of Counselling Psychology, British Psychological Society, Torquay, UK, 18th May.

Green, C. D. (2003) Psychology strikes out: Coleman R. Griffith and the Chicago Cubs. *History of Psychology* 6(3): 267–283.

Green, L. S., Oades, L. G. and Grant, A. M. (2006) Cognitive-behavioral, solution-focused life coaching: enhancing goal striving, well-being and hope. *Journal of Positive Psychology,* 1(3): 142–149.

Griffith, C. R. (1926) *Psychology of Coaching: A study of coaching methods from the point of view of psychology.* New York: Charles Scribner's Sons.

Griffith, C. R. (1930) A laboratory for research in athletics. *Research Quarterly* 1: 34–40.

Gyllensten, K., Palmer, S. and Farrants, J. (2005) Perception of stress and stress interventions in finance organizations: overcoming resistance towards counselling. *Counselling Psychology Quarterly* 18(1): 19–25.

International Forum for Coaching Psychology (IFCP) (2007) International perspectives: taking coaching psychology forward. Available www.freewebs.com/ifcp/inauguralmeeting2006.htm (9 April 2007).

Kroll, W. and Lewis, G. (1978) America's first sport psychologist. In W. F. Straub (ed.) *Sport Psychology: An analysis of athlete behavior* (pp. 16–19). Ithaca, NY: Mouvement.

Lawther, J. D. (1951) *Psychology of Coaching.* Englewood Cliffs, NJ: Prentice Hall.

Llewellyn, J. H. and Blucker, J. A. (1982) *Psychology of Coaching: Theory and application.* Minneapolis, MN: Burgess.

Moore, J. W. (1970) *The Psychology of Athletic Coaching.* Minneapolis, MN: Burgess.

Neenan, M. and Dryden, W. (2002) *Life Coaching: A cognitive-behavioural approach.* Hove: Brunner-Routledge.

NICE (2005) *Clinical Guidelines for Treating Mental Health Problems.* London: National Institute for Health and Clinical Excellence.

O'Broin, A. and Palmer, S. (2006) Win-win situation? Learning from parallels and differences between coaching psychology and sport psychology. *The Coaching Psychologist* 2(3): 17–23.

Palmer, S. and Burton, T. (1996) *People Problems at Work.* London: McGraw-Hill.

Palmer, S. and Whybrow, A. (2006) The coaching psychology movement and its development within the British Psychological Society. *International Coaching Psychology Review* 1(1): 5–11.

Parsloe, E. (1995) *Coaching, Mentoring, and Assessing: A practical guide to developing competence.* New York: Kogan Page.

Peltier, B. (2001) *The Psychology of Executive Coaching: Theory and application.* New York: Brunner-Routledge.

Singer, R. (1976) Overview of sports psychology. *Journal of Physical Education and Recreation,* September; 25.

Skiffington, S. and Zeus, P. (2003) *Behavioural Coaching: How to build sustainable personal and organizational strength.* North Ryde, NSW: McGraw-Hill.

Stober, D. R. and Grant, A. M. (eds) (2006) *Evidence Based Coaching Handbook: Putting best practices to work for your clients.* Hoboken, NJ: Wiley.

Tutko, T. A. and Richards, J. W. (1971) *Psychology of Coaching.* Boston, MA: Allyn and Bacon.

Whitmore, J. (1992) *Coaching for Performance.* London: Nicholas Brealey.

Whybrow, A. and Palmer, S. (2006a) Taking stock: a survey of Coaching Psychologists' practices and perspectives. *International Coaching Psychology Review* 1(1): 56–70.

Whybrow, A. and Palmer, S. (2006b) Shifting perspectives: one year into the development of the British Psychological Society Special Group in Coaching Society in the UK. *International Coaching Psychology Review* 1(2): 85.

Wilt, F. and Bosen, K. (1971) *Motivation and Coaching Psychology.* Los Altos, CA: Tafnews Press.

Discussion points

- Is there really a difference between coaching and coaching psychology?
- Is coaching psychology just a fad or is it here to stay internationally?
- Was there just one root to the origins of coaching psychology?
- Will the development of coaching psychology impact upon the field of coaching? If so, in what ways?

Suggested reading

Cavanagh, M., Grant, A. M. and Kemp, T. (eds) (2005) *Evidence Based Coaching. Volume 1, Theory, Research and Practice from the Behavioural Sciences.* Bowen Hills, Qld: Australian Academic Press.

Grant, A. M. (2001) *Towards a Psychology of Coaching.* Sydney: Coaching Psychology Unit, University of Sydney.

Passmore, J. (2006) *Excellence in Coaching: The industry guide.* London: Kogan Page.

Peltier, B. (2001) *The Psychology of Executive Coaching: Theory and application.* New York: Brunner-Routledge.

Stober, D. R. and Grant, A. M. (eds) (2006) *Evidence Based Coaching Handbook: Putting best practices to work for your clients.* Hoboken, NJ: Wiley.

Books on sport psychology

Cockerill, I. (2002) *Solutions in Sport Psychology.* London: Thomson.

Green, C. D. (2003) Psychology strikes out: Coleman R. Griffith and the Chicago Cubs. *History of Psychology* 6(3): 267–283.

Llewellyn, J. H. and Blucker, J. A. (1982) *Psychology of Coaching: Theory and application.* Minneapolis, MN: Burgess.

This chapter is dedicated to Coleman R. Griffith, who was one of the pioneers who introduced the Psychology into Coaching.

Part I

Perspectives and research in coaching psychology

Chapter 2

Past, present and future

The evolution of professional coaching and coaching psychology

Anthony M. Grant

Introduction

Coaching psychology can be understood as being the systematic application of behavioural science to the enhancement of life experience, work perform-ance and well-being for individuals, groups and organisations who do not have clinically significant mental heath issues or abnormal levels of distress.

In broad terms, coaching psychology sits at the intersection of sports, counselling, clinical, and organisational and health psychology. Where clinical and counselling psychologists tend to work with the client who is distressed and/or dysfunctional, coaching psychologists work with well-functioning clients, using theoretically grounded and scientifically validated techniques to help them to reach goals in their personal and business lives. Coaching is a robust and challenging intervention, is results driven, delivers tangible added value, is typically a short-term or intermittent engagement, and enables the attainment of high standards or goals.

Thus, in our education and training, coaching psychologists are looking for empirically validated ways to facilitate the growth and development of our clients. We are looking for effective means to help them reach goals in their personal and work lives, and for ways we can design and implement real-life interventions that allow us to understand the psychological mechanisms of human change and development.

Many of us, as psychologists-in-training, assumed that such issues were already being addressed within mainstream psychology, and would be covered in our undergraduate and graduate psychology degrees. Unfortunately, we were disappointed. Compared to the emphasis on areas such as psycho-pathology and neuro-psychology it was frustrating that so little was taught about the normal, well-functioning adult person, and even less about how to apply theory to practice. These frustrations gave impetus to the emergence of coaching psychology. This chapter presents a brief overview of a personal perspective on the past, present and possible future of coaching psychology.

Contemporary coaching psychology as a specific academic psychological subdiscipline can be considered to have come into being with the establishment of the Coaching Psychology Unit at the University of Sydney in 2000 and the offering of the world's first postgraduate degree in coaching psychology. The establishment in 2005 of a Coaching Psychology Unit at City University, London has been another important step in further developing the academic underpinnings of coaching psychology and in the near future we can expect to see a number of other universities worldwide offering postgraduate degrees in coaching psychology.

Past influences on contemporary coaching practice

Of course psychologists have been involved in coaching for many years (e.g. Filippi, 1968). The roots of coaching psychology stretch back to the humanistic traditions of psychology (e.g. Maslow, 1968) and are related to the factors underpinning the emergence of the Positive Psychology movement (e.g. Seligman and Csikszentmihalyi, 2000; Snyder and McCullough, 2000) and the forces underpinning the Human Potential Movement (HPM) of the 1960s.

As Spence (2006) has succinctly noted, the HPM surfaced during the 1960s and 1970s and drew heavily on the emerging humanistic-existentialistic psychologies. The 1960s and 1970s were a period of significant social, political and philosophical upheaval. A wide range of self-development methodologies and formats emerged, including encounter groups, personal growth workshops, and community living experiments (communes) where individuals systemically explored and deconstructed their sense of self and their understandings of social reality. In many ways the HPM was a multifaceted underground aspirational religion with its own mores, gurus, prophets and tribes.

The HPM was based on an 'anything goes' eclecticism, in which methodologies, techniques and philosophies from a wide range of perspectives were combined. Frequently the result was a conceptually incoherent smorgasbord of esoteric positions, methodologies and ideologies. Such eclecticism, an essential part of post-modernist approaches, was highly attractive to many people and continues to be so today.

Eclectic pragmatic utilitarianism, the 'use whatever works, and if it works, do more of it' philosophy, heavily influenced the early development of the contemporary commercial coaching industry. Although the diversity inherent in eclecticism has significant strengths, an unfortunate tendency towards an uncritical anti-intellectualism left the HPM closed to scientific and objective investigation. The result of this anti-intellectualism was that many HPM proponents were not prepared or able to engage in serious and rigorous debate about the coherence of their conceptual foundations, or participate in scientific evaluations of the outcomes of their adopted methodologies. Unfortunately, this anti-intellectualism and an accompanying suspicion of scientific debate or rigorous evaluation was a noticeable aspect of many early commercial proprietary life coaching schools, and this approach stands in stark contrast to the scientist-practitioner model of psychology.

In the early days of professional coaching the differences in these underpinning philosophies were manifest in a measure of tension between coaches who were psychologists and non-psychologist coaches. Some psychologists perceived non-psychologist coaches as providing para-psychological services and encroaching on their professional turf, while from the other perspective, some professional coaches saw psychologists as usurping their newly established business domains. I believe that such tensions have significantly diminished, and that as a greater sense of unified professionalism grows in the coaching industry, increasing emphasis will be placed on solid theoretical foundations, and an inclusive evidence-based approach to coaching will come to the fore. Clearly both psychologist and non-psychologist coaches have important roles to play in a establishing a vibrant and diverse professional coaching industry.

The nature of contemporary professional coaching

Definitions of coaching vary considerably (Palmer and Whybrow, 2005) and have been the subject of much debate (e.g. Mace, 1950; Kilburg, 1996; D'Abate et al., 2003). Central to most definitions are the assumptions of an absence of serious mental health problems (Bluckert, 2005), the notion that the client is resourceful (Berg and Szabo, 2005), willing to engage in finding solutions (Hudson, 1999) and that coaching is an outcome-focused activity which seeks to foster self-directed learning through collaborative goal setting, brainstorming and action planning (Greene and Grant, 2003). In this way coaches help clients enhance aspects of both their personal and professional lives. Coaching is, thus, collaborative, individualised, solution-focused, results orientated, systematic and stretching; it fosters self-directed learning, it should be evidence based and incorporate ethical professional practice.

Contemporary professional coaching is a cross-disciplinary methodology, used for promoting individual and organisational change, both personal or 'life' coaching, and workplace coaching with staff, managers and executives. The cross-disciplinary aspect of professional coaching is very important. One aspect of this is that no single industry or professional group 'owns' coaching. Indeed, in a study of 2,529 professional coaches Grant and Zackon (2004) found that coaches had come to coaching from a wide variety of prior professional backgrounds including (in order of magnitude) consultants (40.8 per cent), managers (30.8 per cent), executives (30.2 per cent), teachers (15.7 per cent) and salespeople (13.8 per cent). Interestingly, in that sample only 4.8 per cent of respondents had a background in psychology (note that percentages are not accumulative).

Such diversity is both strength and a liability. The diversity of prior professional backgrounds means that the coaching industry draws on wide range of methodological approaches to coaching, and a wide range of educational disciplines inform coaching practice. On the other hand, due to the diversity and sheer number of individuals offering coaching services, there is a lack of clarity as to what professional coaching really is and what makes for an effective or reputable coach (Sherman and Freas, 2004).

This diversity also means that there may be a wide range of perspectives about what constitutes best ethical and professional practice, and what is the proper focus of coaching. Most coaches do not have a background in psychology or behavioural science and most commercial coach training programmes are short courses based on proprietary models of coaching with little or no theoretical grounding, and finish with the granting of some kind of coaching 'certification'.

Not surprisingly, there have been concerns expressed that inappropriately trained coaches tend to conduct atheoretical one-size-fits-all coaching interventions (Kauffman and Scoular, 2004) and may cause harm to clients, particularly those who have unrecognised mental health problems (Berglas, 2002; Naughton, 2002; Cavanagh, 2005). Although coaching is aimed at non-clinical populations it may be that some individuals seek coaching as a more socially acceptable form of therapy. Indeed, recent studies have found that between 25 per cent and 50 per cent of individuals presenting for life coaching met clinical mental health criteria (Green et al., 2005; Spence and Grant, 2005).

Such issues have been of considerable concern to psychologists and mental health professionals. However, it is hard to find factual reports of such damage beyond occasional newspaper articles about the impact of failed therapy or counselling (e.g. Pyror, 2005) or social commentary articles decrying the rise of the self-help or coaching culture (e.g. Furedi, 2005).

One reason for the lack of such complaints may be because, at present, there are no registration or licensing requirements for coaches who are not psychologists. Thus, there is no accessible body for disgruntled members of the public to complain to. If such damage is in fact occurring then one assumes that reports of such harm will eventually surface. Of course it may be that coaching clients are in fact highly resilient and that little harm is being done by non-psychologist coaches. Interestingly, more common are newspaper reports of inadequately trained business coaches or the inappropriate franchising of coach businesses as 'lifestyle and wealth-creation opportunities' or the promotion of coach 'certification' programmes (Walker, 2004), and it may be that these issues are of greater threat to the long-term development of professional coaching and coaching psychology.

The current professional credibility of coaches

One area of concern is the hunger for credibility and credentialling by some sections of the coaching industry. This is an important issue. The general public are not well educated as to the worth of various psychological qualifications and accreditations (Lancaster and Smith, 2002) let alone coaching qualifications, and may rely on impressive sounding titles to guide them in their selection of a coach. Because coaching is an industry and not a profession, there are no barriers to entry, no regulation, no government-sanctioned accreditation or qualification process and no clear authority to be a coach; anyone can call themselves a 'Master Coach'. Worldwide there is a veritable industry offering a range of 'coach certification' programmes.

Some of these commercial coach training organisations appear to be little more than coach 'credentialling mills' where, following a few days' training and the payment of a suitable fee, one can become a 'Certified Master Coach'. Unfortunately, it sometimes seems as if 'every man and his dog' offer a coach certification programme, and the value of such certifications is highly questionable. Indeed, it may be that the majority of money made within the coaching industry is being made by commercial coach training organisations rather than through actual coaching by coaching practitioners.

Of course, organisations such as the Association for Coaching (AC), the European Mentoring and Coaching Council (EMCC) and the International Coach Federation (ICF) have put considerable effort into establishing credentialling processes and have done important work in beginning to define coaching competencies. The establishment of the Australian Psychological Society Interest Group in Coaching Psychology and the British Psychological Society Special Group in Coaching Psychology are very welcome and vital moves in the development of professional coaching as well as coaching psychology.

However, the credibility and professionalism of coaching is still tenuous. There are increasing media reports which question the credibility of unqualified life coaches who appear to have the lowest perceived levels of credibility (e.g. Salerno, 2005). In contrast, psychologists who are coaches are viewed in a far more credible light and this is particularly the case for executive developmental coaching (Seligman, 2005).

Looking to the future: raising the bar for coaching training

As the coaching market matures, the corporations who are the main consumers of coaching are demanding higher standards of qualifications from the coaches they employ, and postgraduate qualification in behavioural science is a key selection criterion for executive coaching (Corporate Leadership Council, 2003). Psychologists have increasingly and more publicly become involved in the coaching industry. The entry into the coaching arena by psychology, with its attendant rigorous educational programmes and professional ethos and qualifications has, I believe, noticeably raised the bar for the coaching industry in general.

The commercial training programmes that dominated the coaching market during the late 1990s tended to be atheoretical and drew heavily on HPM concepts and methodologies such as the Landmark Forum seminars. In contrast, there are now a number of universities that offer programmes in coaching.

However, the fact that a specific coach training programme is associated with a university is not in itself sufficient to guarantee its professional validity or evidence-base. This is because many coach training programmes have been offered by universities and business schools as part of non-degree continuing education programmes, and some of these programmes essentially offer a university-branded version of various atheoretical proprietary coaching systems.

In 2006, in at least two cases in the USA, such arrangements between universities and commercial coach training schools have led to unfortunate situations where the commercial coaching schools have inappropriately leveraged their association with a university, for example presenting marketing material and self-promotional claims as being university-authorised research or conference presentations. Clearly these are highly undesirable incidents which have the potential to significantly undermine the developing credibility of the academic foundations of coaching, and may well cause some universities to be more cautious in taking coaching seriously.

Fortunately, despite such issues, evidence-based, theoretically grounded postgraduate university degrees in coaching and coaching psychology are increasingly available worldwide. There are three Australian universities offering coach-specific education as part of postgraduate degree programmes (as of July 2007). All of these are offered by schools of psychology. At least seven UK universities offer coaching degree programmes. Only one of these is based within a psychology department, most others are offered by business schools or from within faculties of education. In the USA at least seven universities offer coach degree programmes and in Canada there are two postgraduate programmes in coaching. The majority of the North American programmes are offered from within business schools rather than schools of psychology. These developments represent welcome changes, and the involvement of graduate schools and universities will raise the standard of the general coaching industry.

The downside of the quest for credibility

However, as the bar gets raised within an increasingly demanding market, and in the quest for credibility and the subsequent commercial advantage, there has been a shake-up in the market. Coaches who do not have proper training in coaching or psychology are beginning to feel the pressure to present themselves in a more academic or professional light.

The temptation for these people is to inappropriately leverage affiliations and/or qualifications which are only tenuously connected to coaching practice. An example here might be the individual who holds a PhD in anatomy presenting themselves as holding doctoral qualifications relevant to coaching, or the unqualified part-time instructor in a university-based continuing education programme presenting themselves as an 'adjunct professor'.

The issue here is that the general public, when presented with impressive sounding qualifications and affiliations, may well attribute a level of credibility which is not warranted. In an applied area of practice such as coaching, this can be seriously problematic. This is of particular concern given that there is no one central regulating body to which dissatisfied clients can complain about unethical practices.

An emerging trend towards academic credibility in commercial coach training was confirmed by a study (Grant and O'Hara, 2006) which explored the self-presentation and the legitimacy of qualifications and certifications offered by the fourteen commercial schools that comprise the majority of the Australian Life Coaching training industry. The study found that five life coaching schools offered formal training qualifications that sat within the government-sanctioned Australian Qualifications Framework at Certificate IV and Diploma level.

This movement towards a more credible foundation to coach training is very welcome. However, Grant and O'Hara (2006) also found a number of concerning marketing claims made by a small minority of these coach training schools. For example, one school promoted its life coach training courses based on the claim that 'you don't need a university degree or possess any specific educational qualifications to be a life coach, all you need is determination, commitment and a willingness to learn', another claimed that 'the profession of coaching is similar to the practice of physician, attorney or psychologist'. Yet another claimed to offer a coaching 'qualification' (unspecified) sanctioned by a well-known American university.

What is the future place of coaching psychology?

Psychologists have several important factors which enhance both their suitability for coaching and their credibility as professional coaches. Psychologists bring to coaching a solid understanding of the psychology of human change, and the ability to develop coaching interventions based on theoretically grounded case conceptualisations using evidence-based processes and techniques. Further, psychology is a recognised profession with established academic qualifications and rigorous training, enforceable ethical codes and barriers to entry, and has government-sanctioned organisations which are in a position to police the profession.

Unfortunately, in the past psychologists have not been represented in the media as being uniquely competent coaching practitioners (Garman et al., 2000). Yet psychology has a genuine and important contribution to make to professional coaching in terms of adapting and validating existing therapeutic models for use with normal populations and evaluating commercialised approaches to personal development to ensure consumer protection and inform consumer choice (Starker, 1990; Grant, 2001). I believe that the emergence of a subdiscipline of coaching psychology can make psychology more accessible and attractive to the public.

It may be argued that psychology does not need another delineated subdiscipline, and that the work of coaching is already being conducted by psychologists. Indeed, there is evidence that there is considerable overlap between both the training and the actual practices of different established psychology subdisciplines. For example, Cobb et al. (2004) found that training programmes across three areas, clinical, counselling and school psychology, were more similar than different. Further, many applied, clinical and counselling psychologists already consider themselves to be acting as 'coaches' and continue to work with clinical clients long after their initial treatment objectives have been met. This is because clients frequently find such an ongoing performance-enhancing relationship to be highly beneficial.

Paradoxically, such observations also argue for the formal establishment of coaching psychology. The fact that some psychologists are already shifting to a coaching style once therapeutic aims have been met, suggests that there is a client demand for coaching by psychologists, and that clients value a coaching relationship with a psychologist that is focused on goal attainment and well-being, rather than being curative. Further, as Kauffman and Scoular (2004) note, the vast majority of individuals presenting for executive coaching are not remedial clients, but are seeking support in stretching and development. Thus interventions and helping relationships based on a clinical or medical model may be highly inappropriate.

Unfortunately in the public's mind, psychologists are often confused with psychiatrists and have long been seen by the public as being focused on therapy and clinical work (Webb and Speer, 1986), rather than being proactive facilitators of human or organisational change. There is a clear need for psychologists to present their skills in a way that the public finds attractive and accessible (Coleman, 2003). Further, many psychologists find coaching to be an appealing and personally rewarding alternative to therapeutic practice (Naughton, 2002).

Thus, rather than *act* as a coach, it makes more sense for psychologists to actually *be* a coach, to develop coaching skills and psychological frameworks that go beyond existing clinical or counselling frameworks and applications.

One future challenge for the emerging subdiscipline of coaching psychology will be to develop coaching interventions that utilise existing theory and technique, but do so in a way that is relevant and engaging for non-clinical populations. If we can rise to this challenge I believe that coaching psychology has tremendous potential to be a major force for the promotion of well-being, productivity and performance enhancement for the individual, for organisations and corporations and for the broader community as a whole. Further, coaching psychology can speed the development of established and emerging psychological approaches by acting as a real-life experimental platform from which to further develop our knowledge of the psychological processes involved in purposeful change in normal, non-clinical populations.

Coaching psychology and positive psychology

Regardless of preferred theoretical orientation (systemic, cognitive, psycho-dynamic etc.), psychology as an applied helping profession has traditionally focused on ameliorating distress and repairing dysfunctionality rather than enhancing the well-being and goal attainment of normal, well-functioning adults.

There have been long-standing calls for psychology to broaden its relevance to society in ways that would help the general public to use psychology in a positive manner in their daily lives (Miller, 1969). Indeed, the general public and business organisations have a thirst for techniques that enhance life experience and performance. The worldwide market for personal development material has grown significantly since the 1950s (Fried, 1994) and continues to grow. The American personal development and self-help book market alone is worth over US$600 million annually (Wyld, 2001). However, traditional psychology as a research discipline and an applied profession has not risen to the challenge of meeting the needs of consumers in the normal adult population (Fox, 1996; Laungani, 1999).

Since 2000 there has been considerable interest in a positive psychology that focuses on developing human strengths and competencies (Seligman and Csikszentmihalyi, 2000; Snyder and McCullough, 2000). The emergence of positive psychology is to be applauded and welcomed, and marks a shift in the research focus of applied psychology away from psychopathology. Positive psychology can be understood as 'the scientific study of optimal functioning, focusing on aspects of the human condition that lead to happiness, fulfilment, and flourishing' (Linley and Harrington, 2005: 13).

There has been considerable progress made by positive psychologists in developing theoretical frameworks for understanding human strengths (Snyder and Lopez, 2002). However, most of the work thus far within the positive psychology arena has been about investigating correlational relationships between various constructs (Lazarus, 2003), for example, the relationship between self-concordance, well-being, goal attainment and goal satisfaction (Sheldon and Elliot, 1999), the measurement of constructs such as well-being (Ryff and Keyes, 1996) or a taxonomy of human strengths (Peterson and Seligman, 2004) as an alternative to the DSM diagnostic manual (American Psychiatric Association (APA), 2000).

Despite some publications on the application of positive psychology (e.g. Linley and Joseph, 2004), to date there has been relatively little work within the positive psychology arena about how best to operationalise positive psychology constructs. Further, there have been concerns that over-enthusiasm for positive psychology may lead to ideological enmeshment, and that an over-simplistic dichotomous thinking about 'the positive' or 'the negative' is not helpful or accurate (Lazarus, 2003). We need to bring the promise of a positive psychology into fruition (see Ryff, 2003). One way to further develop the emerging field of positive psychology is to extend past cross-sectional or correlation work by designing interventions which use coaching as an experimental framework, and this may be an important future role for coaching psychologists.

The future: theoretically inclusive and technically sophisticated coaching

Although the links between positive psychology and coaching psychology are clear, coaching psychologists employ a wide range of theoretical perspectives in their work, not just positive psychological frameworks. These include psychodynamic and systemic (Kilburg, 2000), developmental (Laske, 1999), cognitive behavioural (Ducharme, 2004), solution-focused (Greene and Grant, 2003) and behavioural (Skiffington and Zeus, 2003); also see Peltier (2001) for a useful overview of a range of theoretical approaches to executive coaching.

The relative value and efficacy of different theoretical approaches has been debated long and hard in the clinical literature. It is generally accepted that a key factor in therapeutic outcome is the quality of the working alliance (Horvath and Symonds, 1991), and the alliance is as important as the specific theoretical orientation employed (Howgego et al., 2003). Every theoretical framework emphasises a different understanding and formulation of the presenting issue, and suggests different interventions.

Rather than try to fit a specific theoretical approach to the client, as is frequently the case in clinical work within the medical model, coaching should be collaborative and client centred. For some developmental coaching clients who are seeking in-depth explanations this will mean coaching based on a psychodynamic model. For others, who are seeking a more psycho-mechanical approach, a cognitive-behavioural formulation and intervention will be more appropriate. Similarly, for those with a defensive pessimism personality style, an over-emphasis on aspects of positive psychology may not be helpful (Norem and Hang, 2002).

Coaching psychology needs to be theoretically inclusive and I believe that the professional coaching psychologist should be able to draw on a range of theoretical frameworks, using client-congruent, theoretically grounded techniques in order to best help the client reach their coaching goals. Such client-centred theoretical flexibility brings with it significant challenges in terms of the coach's training and personal and professional development.

First, in order to become skilled in the use of a specific theoretical modality, practitioners tend to integrate the key tenets of the psychological framework into their personal worldview, and in a sense, they personally embody the core facets of their preferred theoretical approach in their own lived experience (Binder, 2004). Indeed, it has been argued that integration of one's sense of self with one's theoretical approach is essential in order to be a truly effective therapist (Norcross and Halgin, 2005). Thus, for example, the psychologist trained in a cognitive-behavioural approach will tend to make sense of the world, both personally and professionally, using cognitive-behavioural concepts. In order to be flexible in working with different theoretical perspectives, as best suits specific coaching clients, the coach needs to view the presenting issues from a range of theoretical perspectives and this may well be very challenging personally.

Second, coaches need to be highly skilled in dealing with mental health issues. It has been my experience that coaching psychology is sometimes regarded somewhat disdainfully by some clinicians, as if it is a soft version of 'real' clinical psychology. In fact I argue that the contrary is the case. Clinical clients frequently present for therapy with specific symptoms and an expectation of treatment. Coaching psychologists' clients on the other hand may not know that they have a mental health problem (if indeed they do have such problems), and may be far less willing to engage in a therapeutic relationship (if indeed they do need treatment). The coach thus needs finely attuned diagnostic skills, maybe even more so than the clinician, and the ability to consider psychopathological issues while engaging in the type of goal-focused fast-paced relationship that characterises coaching.

Third, the dynamics of the coaching relationship differ from the often overtly hierarchical relationship that is associated with consulting, clinical or counselling work. Applied and therapeutic psychologists tend to work from the position of being the expert who has access to a privileged knowledge position from which they diagnose problems and prescribe interventions or treatment (Carlson and Erickson, 2001). Clearly, psychologists do have skilled expertise and expert knowledge about the psychology of coaching that their clients do not have, otherwise there would be little reason for the client to employ them. Also, in addition to the expert knowledge that a coach holds about the psychology of coaching, it is important for coaches to have a good understanding of the clients' issues and context.

The role of expert knowledge in coaching

The issue here is about the role of expert knowledge in coaching, and how expert knowledge can be best utilised within the coaching relationship. There are various approaches to the use of expert knowledge in coaching. Expert knowledge in coaching can be understood as highly specialised or technical knowledge held by the coach, in an area where the coachee has less expertise than the coach, and where such knowledge is related to the coachee's goals. The notion of the 'coach as expert advice-giver' is somewhat controversial, and there is some difference of opinion as to the appropriate role of expert knowledge in coaching. For example, John Whitmore's (1992) work emphasises a non-directional ask-not-tell approach, and this stands in contrast to the more directive approach of Marshal Goldsmith (2000), which emphasises robust feedback and advice-giving.

The issue is not which of these approaches is right and which is wrong, but rather which best helps the client reach their goals, and which is the most apt at particular points in any specific coaching conversation. In essence this issue is about striking the right balance between process facilitation and content or information delivery, and this balance varies at different points in the overall coaching engagement and within individual coaching sessions. The skilful and experienced coach knows when to move across the ask-tell dimension, and knows when to promote self-discovery and when to give expert-based authoritative or specialised information.

The challenge for many applied psychologists is to master such flexibility in working with coaching clients. Coaching requires a sophisticated skill set and the ability to be able to draw on expert knowledge, while at the same time facilitating the self-directed learning which lies at the core of the coaching enterprise.

Future directions for coaching psychology

What is the future for coaching psychology? It will be useful to have detailed competencies and practices that mark coaching psychology from counselling, clinical and other applied psychological practices. However, this will not be an easy enterprise. Boundaries between and definition of existing subdisciplines are vague as they stand (Cobb et al., 2004). Although competencies and practices are useful heuristics to define the core functions of a subdisciple, they tell us little about the overlap between various subdisciple practice. Perhaps more important, as a future research agenda, may be the development and validation of psychologically based coaching methodologies that are effective and engaging for non-clinical populations and the emergence of specific areas of coaching psychology practice.

Although executive coaching, workplace coaching and life coaching have received the most media coverage to date, an important emerging trend for coaching psychologists to be aware of is health-related coaching. Examination of the academic literature indicates that health coaching is emerging as the fastest growing area of coaching, and the coaching outcome research that is published in the medical press (e.g. *Medline*) tends to be of better quality than the outcome research published in the psychology press (e.g. *PsycINFO*) or the business press (e.g. *Business Source Premier*). Much of the health-related coaching is being conducted by dieticians, nurses and other health professionals rather than psychologists, yet there is a clear role for coaching psychologists who have a background in the health sciences. Positive psychology will prove to be an important theoretical basis for many coaching psychologists, and this may particularly be the case in relation to health coaching, where the focus is on both physical and psychological well-being. Of course, the development of BPS, APS and APA accredited postgraduate programmes, including accrediting conversion courses for practising psychologists who wish to work as coaches will be important and such moves will further develop the professionalism, credibility and reputation of coaching psychologists.

Finally, an interesting and important matter will be how coaching psychologists interface and work collegially with coaches who are not psychologists. Fortunately, psychologists have a well-established tradition of working effectively with a wide range of non-psychology disciplines while maintaining their own professional identity, for example in the medical, organisational change and educational fields. As coaching psychologists we need to ensure that we work collaboratively with non-psychologists, using our theoretical frameworks and applied training to further develop the broad church of professional coaching through excellence in coaching research, theory and practice.

Conclusion

Coaching psychology has the potential to be a major force for the promotion of well-being and performance enhancement for the individual, for organisations and society as a whole. The emergence of a subdiscipline of coaching psychology can make psychology more accessible and acceptable to the public. Further, through virtue of their training and professionalism, psychologists are ideally placed to provide coaching services in addition to collegially contributing to the emerging profession of coaching. In addition, coaching psychology can contribute to the development of established and emerging psychological approaches by providing a methodology with which to further develop our knowledge of the psychological processes involved in purposeful change in normal, non-clinical populations. However, perhaps the most vital factor in the development of coaching psychology will be that we do outstanding work with our clients. They after all, are the most important focus of our professional endeavours.

Acknowledgements

This chapter is based on Dr Grant's keynote address at the First Annual Conference of the BPS SGCP in London, December 2004 and draws on the paper Grant, A. M. (2006) A personal perspective on professional coaching and the development of coaching psychology. International Coaching Psychology Review 1(1): 12–22. Published by the British Psychological Society.

References

American Psychiatric Association (APA) (2000) *Diagnostic and Statistical Manual of Mental Disorders: DSM-IV-TR*, 4th edition. Washington, DC: APA.

Berg, I. K. and Szabo, P. (2005) *Brief Coaching for Lasting Solutions.* New York: W. W. Norton.

Berglas, S. (2002) The very real dangers of executive coaching. *Harvard Business Review* June: 87–92.

Binder, J. L. (2004) *Key Competencies in Brief Dynamic Psychotherapy: Clinical practice beyond the manual.* New York: Guilford Press.

Bluckert, P. (2005) The similarities and differences between coaching and therapy. *Industrial and Commercial Training* 37(2): 91–96.

Carlson, T. D. and Erickson, M. J. (2001) Honoring the privileging personal experience and knowledge: ideas for a narrative therapy approach to the training and supervision of new therapists. *Contemporary Family Therapy: An International Journal* 23(2): 199–220.

Cavanagh, M. (2005) Mental-health issues and challenging clients in executive coaching. In M. Cavanagh, A. M. Grant and T. Kemp (eds) *Evidence Based Coaching.* Volume 1, *Theory, Research and Practice from the Behavioural Sciences* (pp. 21–36). Bowen Hills, Qld: Australian Academic Press.

Cobb, H. C., Reeve, R. E., Shealy, C. N., Norcross, J. C., Schare, M. L., Rodolfa, E. R., et al., (2004) Overlap among clinical, counseling, and school psychology: implications for the profession and combined-integrated training. *Journal of Clinical Psychology* 60(9): 939–955.

Coleman, S. K. (2003) Furthering professional development: an assessment of psychologists' awareness of how they are understood by the public. Unpublished doctoral dissertation, University of Hartford, CT.

Corporate Leadership Council, (2003) *Maximising Returns on Professional Executive Coaching.* Washington, DC: Corporate Leadership Council.

D'Abate, C. P., Eddy, E. R. and Tannenbaum, S. I. (2003) What's in a name? A literature-based approach to understanding mentoring, coaching, and other constructs that describe developmental interactions. *Human Resource Development Review* 2(4): 360–384.

Ducharme, M. J. (2004) The cognitive-behavioral approach to executive coaching. *Consulting Psychology Journal: Practice and Research* 56(4): 214–224.

Filippi, R. (1968) Coaching: a therapy for people who do not seek help. *Zeitschrift Fuer Psychotherapie und Medizinische Psychologie* 18(6): 225–229.

Fox, R. E. (1996) Charlatanism, scientism, and psychology's social contract – 103rd Annual Convention of the American Psychological Association: Presidential address (1995, New York). *American Psychologist* 51(8): 777–784.

Fried, S. (1994) *American Popular Psychology: An interdisciplinary research guide.* New York: Garland.

Furedi, F. (2005) The age of unreason. *The Spectator* 19 November: 2–3.

Garman, A. N., Whiston, D. L. and Zlatoper, K. W. (2000) Media perceptions of executive coaching and the formal preparation of coaches. *Consulting Psychology Journal: Practice and Research* 52: 203–205.

Goldsmith, M. (2000) Coaching change. *Executive Excellence* 17(6): 4.

Grant, A. M. (2001) Grounded in science or based on hype? An analysis of neuro-associative conditioning. *Australian Psychologist* 36(3): 232–238.

Grant, A. M. and O'Hara, B. (2006) The self-presentation and self-promotion of Australian life coaching schools: cause for concern? Unpublished paper, Coaching Psychology Unit, University of Sydney.

Grant, A. M. and Zackon, R. (2004) Executive, workplace and life coaching: findings from a large-scale survey of International Coach Federation members. *International Journal of Evidence Based Coaching and Mentoring* 2(2): 1–15.

Green, S., Oades, L. G. and Grant, A. M. (2005) An evaluation of a life-coaching group program: initial findings from a waitlisted control study. In M. Cavanagh, A. M. Grant and T. Kemp (eds) *Evidence Based Coaching. Volume 1, Theory, Research and Practice from the Behavioural Sciences* (pp. 127–142). Bowen Hills, Qld: Australian Academic Press.

Greene, J. and Grant, A. M. (2003) *Solution-focused Coaching: Managing people in a complex world.* London: Momentum Press.

Horvath, A. O. and Symonds, B. (1991) Relation between working alliance and outcome in psychotherapy: a meta-analysis. *Journal of Counselling Psychology* 38(2): 139–149.

Howgego, I. M., Yellowlees, P., Owen, C., Meldrum, L. and Dark, F. (2003) The therapeutic alliance: the key to effective patient outcome? A descriptive review of the evidence in community mental health case management. *Australian and New Zealand Journal of Psychiatry* 37(2): 169—183.

Hudson, F. M. (1999) *The Handbook of Coaching.* San Francisco, CA: Jossey-Bass.

Kauffman, C. and Scoular, A. (2004) Towards a positive psychology of executive coaching. In P. A. Linley and S. Joseph (eds) *Positive Psychology in Practice* (pp. 287–302). Hoboken, NJ: Wiley.

Kilburg, R. R. (1996) Toward a conceptual understanding and definition of executive coaching. *Consulting Psychology Journal: Practice and Research* 48(2): 134–144.

Kilburg, R. R. (2000) *Executive Coaching: Developing managerial wisdom in a world of chaos.* Washington, DC: American Psychological Association.

Lancaster, S. and Smith, D. I. (2002) What's in a name? The identity of clinical psychology as a specialty. *Australian Psychologist* 37(1): 48–51.

Laske, O. E. (1999) An integrated model of developmental coaching. *Consulting Psychology Journal: Practice and Research* 51(3): 139–159.

Laungani, P. (1999) Danger! Psychotherapists at work. *Counselling Psychology Quarterly* 12(2): 117–131.

Lazarus, R. S. (2003) Does the Positive Psychology movement have legs? *Psychological Inquiry* 14(2): 93–109.

Linley, P. A. and Harrington, S. (2005) Positive psychology and coaching psychology: perspectives on integration. *The Coaching Psychologist* 1(July): 13–14.

Linley, P. A. and Joseph, S. (2004) *Positive Psychology in Practice.* Hoboken, NJ: Wiley.

Mace, M. L. (1950) *The Growth and Development of Executives.* Boston, MA: Harvard Business School, Division of Research.

Maslow, A. H. (1968) *Towards a Psychology of Being.* New York: Wiley.

Miller, G. (1969) Psychology as a means of promoting human welfare. *American Psychologist* 24: 1063–1075.

Naughton, J. (2002) The coaching boom: is it the long-awaited alternative to the medical model? *Psychotherapy Networker* July/August(42): 1–10.

Norcross, J. C. and Halgin, R. P. (2005) Training in psychotherapy integration. In J. C. Norcross and M. R. Goldfried (eds) *Handbook of Psychotherapy Integration*, 2nd edition (pp. 439–458). New York, NY: Oxford University Press.

Norem, J. K. and Hang, E. C. (2002) The positive psychology of negative thinking. *Journal of Clinical Psychology* 58: 993–1001.

Palmer, S. and Whybrow, A. (2005) The proposal to establish a Special Group in Coaching Psychology. *The Coaching Psychologist* 1(July): 5–11.

Peltier, B. (2001) *The Psychology of Executive Coaching: Theory and application*. New York: Brunner-Routledge.

Peterson, C. and Seligman, M. E. P. (2004) *Character Strengths and Virtues: A handbook and classification*. Washington, DC: American Psychological Association.

Pyror, L. (2005) Call to end free rein for therapists. *Sydney Morning Herald* 19 September: 22.

Ryff, C. D. (2003) Corners of myopia in the positive psychology parade. *Psychological Inquiry* 14(2): 153–159.

Ryff, C. D. and Keyes, C. L. M. (1996) The structure of psychological well-being revisited. *Journal of Personality and Social Psychology* 96(4): 719–727.

Salerno, S. (2005) Qualifications needed to be a life coach: er . . . none [electronic version]. *Time On Line*. Available www.timesonline.co.uk/article/0,,7-1726677,00.html (19 December 2005).

Seligman, M. (2005) The corporate chill pill. *New Zealand Management* 52(6): 64–66.

Seligman, M. E. and Csikszentmihalyi, M. (2000) Positive psychology: an introduction. *American Psychologist* 55(1): 5–14.

Sheldon, K. M. and Elliot, A. J. (1999) Goal striving, need satisfaction, and longitudinal well-being: the self-concordance model. *Journal of Personality and Social Psychology* 76(3): 482–497.

Sherman, S. and Freas, A. (2004) The Wild West of executive coaching. *Harvard Business Review* 82(11): 82–90.

Skiffington, S. and Zeus, P. (2003) *Behavioral Coaching*. Sydney: McGraw-Hill.

Snyder, C. R. and Lopez, S. J. (eds) (2002) *Handbook of Positive Psychology*. London: Oxford University Press.

Snyder, C. R. and McCullough, M. E. (2000) A positive psychology field of dreams: 'If you build it, they will come . . .'. *Journal of Social and Clinical Psychology* 19(1): 151–160.

Spence, G. B. (2006) On the professionalisation of the coaching industry and evidence-based coaching practice. Unpublished paper, Coaching Psychology Unit, University of Sydney.

Spence, G. B. and Grant, A. M. (2005) Individual and group life-coaching: initial findings from a randomised, controlled trial. In M. Cavanagh, A. M. Grant and T. Kemp (eds) *Evidence Based Coaching*. Volume 1, *Theory, Research and Practice from the Behavioural Sciences* (pp. 143–158). Bowen Hills, Qld: Australian Academic Press.

Starker, S. (1990) Self-help books: ubiquitous agents of health care. *Medical Psychotherapy: An International Journal* 3: 187–194.

Walker, J. (2004) Business-class coaches. *Business Review Weekly* 1st July: 15–18.

Webb, A. R. and Speer, J. R. (1986) Prototype of a profession: psychology's public image. *Professional Psychology: Research and Practice* 17(1): 5–9.

Whitmore, J. (1992) *Coaching for Performance*. London: Nicholas Brealey.
Wyld, B. (2001) Expert push. *Sydney Morning Herald* 15 August: 4.

Discussion points

- What is your own definition and understanding of coaching psychology?
- What is the role of expert knowledge in coaching?
- What are some of the issues that might impact on how coaching psychologists work with non-psychologist coaches?
- Should coaching be regulated? If so, why? What are some of the potential pitfalls of regulation?

Suggested reading

Fitzgerald, C. and Berger, J. G. (2002) *Executive Coaching: Practices and perspectives*. New York: Davies-Black.
Linley, P. A. and Joseph, S. (2004) *Positive Psychology in Practice*. Hoboken, NJ: Wiley.
Newton, J., Long, S. and Sievers, B. (2006) *Coaching in Depth: The organizational role analysis approach*. London: Karnac.
Stober, D. and Grant, A. M. (eds) (2006) *Evidence Based Coaching Handbook: Putting best practices to work for your clients*. New York: Wiley.

Chapter 3

Integrating positive psychology and coaching psychology

Shared assumptions and aspirations?

P. Alex Linley and Susan Harrington

Introduction

The end of the second millennium marked a contradictory time for western societies and their priorities. For decades, it had been assumed that economic progress could be taken to equal human progress, that the growth in industrial production would inevitably lead to more wealth, and more wealth to greater well-being. Yet the data simply did not bear this out. While wealth was increasing, happiness remained flat (Myers, 2000), and the prevalence of depression was even on the increase (Lane, 2000). Suddenly, the focus on 'the mighty dollar' as the solution to the needs of humanity seemed, at least in part, like an empty promise, and people began to turn their attention elsewhere. At the macro-level, governments started to take an interest in well-being (Donovan and Halpern, 2001), and psychologists (Diener and Seligman, 2004), economists (Kahneman et al., 2004) and policy think tanks (Shah and Marks, 2004) began to pose the question of how governmental priorities might be organised if well-being, rather than money, were the desired outcome. In parallel, at the micro-level, more attention was focused in the psychological sciences on what psychologists should do in terms of their research and practice, with the ever-growing recognition that as a discipline, we had made great strides in treating mental illness, but had often neglected the topic of human wellness. It was in this climate that positive psychology and coaching psychology, as we now know them, were born.

Coaching psychology arose, one might argue, from the arena of coaching – and especially executive coaching – more generally. This, in turn, had grown out of the field of sports coaching, with leading sports people realising that their talents could also be translated to the world of business to great effect. Indeed, the founding fathers of coaching as it is known in the UK were all originally sports people and sports coaches (Downey, 1999; Gallwey, 2002; Whitmore, 2002). However, these coaching approaches – while often based on excellent psychological principles – typically did not make these psychological principles explicit in their work or training. Coaching psychology came about as a means of recognising and celebrating the psychological foundations of coaching, and building a science of coaching that was solidly based on good psychological principles. In common with positive psychology, it draws from a wide range of psychological disciplines, both academic and applied, including clinical, cognitive, counselling, educational, occupational, social, and sports psychology. As such, through the development of coaching psychology in the UK, the following definition was developed:

> Coaching psychology is for enhancing well-being and performance in personal life and work domains underpinned by models of coaching grounded in established adult learning or psychological approaches.
> (Palmer and Whybrow, 2005: 7; adapted from Grant and Palmer, 2002)

There are two elements of this definition that we believe merit particular consideration, since they inform our consideration below of the relationship between coaching psychology and positive psychology. First, coaching psychology is for 'enhancing well-being and performance'. It would be easy to skip by this without much further consideration, but these few words contain a powerful objective that stands in sharp relief with much of the work of psychologists to date. Arguably, much of psychology to date has been about relieving psychological distress and alleviating mental illness, while being focused on errors and problems. There are very good reasons for this 'negativity bias' because negative events are more contagious, that is, more likely to multiply, and more resistant to elimination (see Rozin and Royzman, 2001), and because the evidence shows incontrovertibly that on many occasions 'bad is stronger than good' (e.g. bad emotions, bad parents and bad feedback have more impact than good ones; bad information is processed more thoroughly than good information; bad impressions and bad stereotypes are quicker to form and more resistant to disconfirmation; see Baumeister et al., 2001). We do not dispute this predisposition towards negativity, although we also note that there is evidence to suggest that positive emotions can undo the effects of negative emotions (Fredrickson and Levenson, 1998; Fredrickson et al., 2000). We do dispute that the negative should be the *only* remit of the psychologist, whether academic or applied. Hence, the explicit focus of coaching psychology on 'enhancing well-being and performance' speaks clearly to the aspiration to move 'beyond the zero point' (Peterson, 2000). Rather than our work being only about the alleviation of suffering (i.e. returning people to zero on a figurative −10 to +10 scale), we are also concerned with facilitating people to move further up through the positive poles of the scale (whatever the scale may be). This effectively doubles – or more – the psychologist's remit, and ensures that rather than considering our work is done when people are symptom-free, we might now consider that we have a role in facilitating their more optimal health, well-being and performance – just as sports coaches have done with regard to athletes and sports people for generations.

The second element of this definition to which we call attention is the grounding of coaching psychology in 'established adult learning or psychological approaches'. This clearly locates the remit of the coaching psychologist as being founded on psychology and psychological principles, rather than a 'box of tricks'. It further emphasises the oft-lamented need for further research in coaching and coaching psychology (Grant, 2001; Kauffman and Scoular, 2004). In this regard, positive psychology has much to offer. As the science of optimal human functioning, positive psychology has a research basis which can underpin and help validate much of what coaching psychologists do, a notion which in turn suggests the need for closer collaboration and integration between the two professions.

Hence, we consider that positive psychology and coaching psychology are natural partners with shared aspirations in their endeavours to enhance well-being and performance, and one might even argue that coaching psychology provides a core delivery means for the applications of positive psychology. The fact that both 'psychologies' have arisen around the same time, and thus in a similar socio-historical-cultural context, suggests that the zeitgeist, that is, the 'spirit of the times', is right for them both. In this chapter, then, we will go on to provide a more formal introduction to positive psychology, with a brief consideration of its remit, historical development, and likely future directions. We will then examine the fundamental assumptions that might be taken to characterise positive psychology, and explore the implications of them for coaching psychology, before moving on to consider the foundations, practices and aspirations of research within coaching psychology and positive psychology. These considerations lead us to adopt a more holistic view of human nature than is typically taken within modern psychology, but one which can be traced back to the work of Karen Horney and Carl Rogers. The final section of the chapter then examines what this view means for the agenda of coaching psychology research and practice, and demonstrates that it is yet another example of the shared assumptions and aspirations of positive psychology and coaching psychology. First, however, we will introduce positive psychology.

Positive psychology: a brief introduction

Positive psychology is concerned with the scientific study of optimal functioning, focusing on aspects of the human condition that lead to happiness, fulfilment and flourishing, with core positive psychology research topics including happiness, wisdom, creativity and human strengths.

The advent of 'positive psychology' as we now know it can be traced back to Martin E. P. Seligman's 1998 Presidential Address to the American Psychological Association (Seligman, 1999). Following an epiphanic moment when gardening with his daughter Nikki (Seligman and Csikszentmihalyi, 2000), Seligman realised that psychology had largely neglected the latter two of its three pre-Second World War missions: curing mental illness, helping all people to lead more productive and fulfilling lives, and identifying and nurturing high talent. The advent of the Veterans Administration (in 1946) and the National Institute of Mental Health (in 1947) had largely rendered psychology a healing discipline based upon a disease model and illness ideology (see also Maddux, 2002; Maddux et al., 2004). With this realisation, Seligman resolved to use his APA Presidency to initiate a shift in psychology's focus toward a more positive psychology (Seligman, 1999).

This presidential initiative led to the establishment of the Positive Psychology Steering Committee (Mihaly Csikszentmihalyi, Ed Diener, Kathleen Hall Jamieson, Chris Peterson and George Vaillant), which was designed to drive and inform the development of positive psychology. There followed the first Positive Psychology Summit in Washington, DC, a special issue of the *American Psychologist* on positive psychology to mark the new millennium, the establishment of several regional positive psychology networks, numerous books and journal articles, and many journal special issues dedicated to positive psychology, most recently with the launch of the *Journal of Positive Psychology* (see Linley et al., 2006, for a fuller history and bibliography). Within the UK, a special edition of *The Psychologist* (Linley et al., 2003) was devoted to the topic, and the First European Positive Psychology Conference was held in Winchester in June 2002.

However, we should be clear that positive psychology did not simply 'begin' in 1997, or 1998, or 1999, or 2000 (see also McCullough and Snyder, 2000). Research into positive psychology topics has gone on for decades, and might even be traced back to the origins of psychology itself, for example, in William James' writings on 'healthy mindedness' (James, 1902). In broad terms, positive psychology – and also coaching psychology – has common interests with parts of humanistic psychology, and its emphasis on the fully functioning person (Rogers, 1961), and self-actualisation and the study of healthy individuals (Maslow, 1968). Indeed, we note that in the mid-1950s, Maslow lamented psychology's preoccupation with disorder and dysfunction:

> The science of psychology has been far more successful on the negative than on the positive side. It has revealed to us much about man's shortcomings, his illness, his sins, but little about his potentialities, his virtues, his achievable aspirations, or his full psychological height. It is as if psychology has voluntarily restricted itself to only half its rightful jurisdiction, and that, the darker, meaner half.
>
> (Maslow, 1954: 354)

Just as positive psychology is now striving to reclaim the study of people in their completeness, so too, we believe, is coaching psychology. This is a theme that we consider in much greater depth below, but first we shall answer the question that may be foremost in the minds of some readers, that is, 'what is positive psychology?'

What is positive psychology?

As will become clear from our answer, positive psychology can be understood and interpreted both pragmatically, that is, as 'the topics of study of positive psychologists', and also at a meta-theoretical level, that is, as 'its aims and vision'. We believe that each level of understanding positive psychology has implications for its integration with coaching psychology, as we go on to show. The following definitions of positive psychology are all taken from authoritative positive psychological sources, and give a good flavour of what positive psychology is about:

> The field of positive psychology at the subjective level is about valued subjective experiences: well-being, contentment, and satisfaction (in the past); hope and optimism (for the future); and flow and happiness (in the present). At the individual level, it is about positive individual traits: the capacity for love and vocation, courage, interpersonal skill, aesthetic sensibility, perseverance, forgiveness, originality, future mindedness, spirituality, high talent, and wisdom. At the group level, it is about the civic virtues and the institutions that move individuals toward better citizenship: responsibility, nurturance, altruism, civility, moderation, tolerance, and work ethic.
>
> (Seligman and Csikszentmihalyi, 2000: 5)

> What is positive psychology? It is nothing more than the scientific study of ordinary human strengths and virtues. Positive psychology revisits 'the average person,' with an interest in finding out what works, what is right, and what is improving . . . positive psychology is simply psychology.
>
> (Sheldon and King, 2001: 216)

> Positive psychology is the study of the conditions and processes that contribute to the flourishing or optimal functioning of people, groups, and institutions.
>
> (Gable and Haidt, 2005: 104)

However, we believe that there are two primary ways in which positive psychology can be defined (see Linley et al., 2006, for a fuller consideration of these definitional issues). First, positive psychology can be understood at the meta-theoretical level. By 'meta-theoretical level' we mean that level at which we understand the *aims* of positive psychology, and the way in which it offers a 'grand vision'. The *aims* of positive psychology can be understood from the meta-theoretical perspective:

> The aim of positive psychology is to begin to catalyze a change in the focus of psychology from preoccupation *only* with repairing the worst things in life to *also* building positive qualities.
>
> (Seligman and Csikszentmihalyi, 2000: 5; emphasis added)

Second, it can be understood at the pragmatic level, that is, with reference to the topics of interest to positive psychologists (see Linley et al., 2006). Hence, a positive psychological perspective is that the focus of scientific research and practical application should be on understanding the entire breadth of human experience, from loss, suffering, illness, and distress through connection, fulfilment, health and well-being. Applied to coaching psychology, this raises the question of where our clients might fall on a continuum of human functioning. Do we restrict ourselves to people who are functioning above the fiftieth percentile, that is, those who we might consider to be reasonably 'well', thereby seeking to raise them from 'plus 2' to 'plus 6'? Or are we interested in working with people wherever they might fall on the continuum, because our models and assumptions are equally applicable in all cases, allowing us to both repair weakness and build strength, to relieve ill-being simultaneously as we facilitate well-being? This is a fundamentally important consideration, since it rests on how we understand the nature of ill-being and well-being, and by extension, determines our client base. Simply put, we can dichotomize ill-being and well-being into categories of 'normal' and 'abnormal' as the biomedical model is so inclined to do (see Maddux et al., 2004), or we can adopt a more holistic, integrative perspective that sees 'normality' as just a point on a continuum (and one that will be likely to vary between individuals according to a host of different biological, psychological, social and cultural influences), rather than a categorical difference (see Joseph and Linley, 2004; Maddux et al., 2004; Joseph and Worsley, 2005).

The humanistic psychology tradition, in which coaching psychology might arguably be considered to have at least some of its philosophical roots, was typically adamant about the over-medicalisation of psychological phenomena, with theorists including Carl Rogers providing alternative conceptualisations for how we understand the nature of ill-being and well-being. This is a perspective that has been infused with new life by positive psychologists, and one that provides a potentially valuable philosophical bedrock for coaching psychology's theoretical basis (cf. Joseph and Linley, 2004; Joseph and Worsley, 2005).

As such, the first part of defining positive psychology is its meta-theoretical value position: that the study of health, fulfilment and well-being is as meritorious as the study of illness, dysfunction and distress, and equally, that the study of human strengths and virtues is a topic that should be central to a psychology of the human condition, rather than one that is 'defined out' of psychological study, as Allport (1937) did, in his seminal definition of what constituted the psychological study of personality (cf. Cawley et al., 2000).

A second facet of this meta-theoretical perspective lies in positive psychology's providing a different lens through which to understand human experience, and perhaps most importantly, beginning the creation of a shared language and understanding that locates the study of positive states, traits and outcomes in relation to each other. Positive psychology has begun to provide a framework in which researchers and practitioners, across a range of psychological and social science disciplines, with different interests and agendas, are better able to communicate with each other, and locate their findings within a broader classificatory context.

At this pragmatic level, we can consider what positive psychologists *do* in terms of their research and their practice, rather than what their objectives may be. Here, we have previously distinguished between four levels of analysis for positive psychology (Linley et al., 2006).

The *wellsprings* of interest to positive psychology may be defined as the precursors and facilitators of the *processes* and *mechanisms*. They include things such as the genetic foundations of well-being, and the early environmental experiences that allow the development of strengths and virtues. The *processes* of interest to positive psychology may be defined as those psychological ingredients (for example, strengths and virtues) that lead to the good life, or equally the obstacles to leading a good life. The *mechanisms* of interest to positive psychology may be defined as those extra-psychological factors that facilitate (or impede) the pursuit of a good life. For example, these mechanisms may be personal and social relationships, working environments, organisations and institutions, communities, and the broader social, cultural, political and economic systems in which our lives are inextricably embedded. The *outcomes* of interest to positive psychology may be defined as those subjective, social and cultural states that characterise a good life. Here we may think of factors such as happiness, well-being, fulfilment and health (at the subjective level), positive communities and institutions that foster good lives (at the interpersonal level), and political, economic and environmental policies that embrace diversity, and promote harmony, citizenship and sustainability (at the social level).

On the basis of these considerations, Linley et al. (2006) defined positive psychology as follows:

> Positive psychology is the scientific study of optimal human functioning. At the meta-psychological level, it aims to redress the imbalance in psychological research and practice by calling attention to the positive aspects of human functioning and experience, and integrating them with our understanding of the negative aspects of human functioning and experience. At the pragmatic level, it is about understanding the *wellsprings, processes* and *mechanisms* that lead to desirable *outcomes*.
>
> (Linley et al., 2006: 8, original italics)

Integrating positive psychology and coaching psychology

Having provided what we hope is a solid introduction to positive psychology, we now consider the possible integration of positive psychology and coaching psychology. Given the very early stage of development of these disciplines, we do not propose specific integrations by approach or target population (these will emerge as both disciplines grow), but restrict our consideration to the meta-level issues that we see as important, that is, the nature of our fundamental assumptions and the foundations, practices and aspirations of our research endeavours.

Fundamental assumptions

As we have briefly noted (Linley and Harrington, 2005a), positive psychology has challenged us to consider the fundamental assumptions that we hold about human nature (see also Joseph and Linley, 2004, 2006; Linley and Joseph, 2004). In a nutshell, there are three possible assumptions that we may hold: we may believe that people are by nature destructive, and thus need to be controlled. Or we may believe that people have the propensity for both good and evil, and thus we need to keep down the evil and promote the good. Or we may believe that people are motivated by socially constructive directional forces, and that we need therefore to provide the right environmental conditions to allow them to flourish.

These assumptions are set out more fully by Karen Horney (1951) in her views on a *morality of evolution*, where she delineated these three possible positions in trying to understand core human nature. The first position was that people are by nature sinful or driven by primitive instincts. This first perspective accords with the 'rotten to the core' view that is considered by many to pervade modern psychology. This view has been described as the 'ghost in the machine' of Sigmund Freud and his implicit influence on our psychological thinking (Hubble and Miller, 2004), and has also been presented as

> a profound obstacle to a science and practice of positive traits and positive states: the belief that virtue and happiness are inauthentic, epiphenomenal, parasitic upon or reducible to the negative traits and states. This 'rotten-to-the-core' view pervades Western thought, and if there is any doctrine positive psychology seeks to overthrow it is this one.
>
> (Seligman, 2003: 126)

The second position was that inherent within human nature was both something essentially 'good' and something essentially 'bad', sinful or destructive. From this second position, the goal of society is to ensure that the 'good' side of human nature triumphs over the 'bad' side.

The third position was that inherent within people are evolutionary constructive forces which guide people towards realising their potentialities. Horney (1951) was careful to note that this third position did *not* suggest that people were inherently good (since this would presuppose knowledge of what constitutes good and bad). Rather, the person's values would arise from their striving towards their potential, and these values would thus be constructive and prosocial in their nature (and hence may be considered 'good'). From this third position, the goal of society is therefore to cultivate the facilitative social-environmental conditions that are conducive to people's self-realisation. When people's tendency toward self-realisation is allowed expression, Horney argued that:

> we become free to grow ourselves, we also free ourselves to love and to feel concern for other people. We will then want to give them the opportunity for unhampered growth when they are young, and to help them in whatever way possible to find and realize themselves when they are blocked in their development. At any rate, whether for ourselves or for others, the ideal is the liberation and cultivation of the forces which lead to self-realization.
>
> (Horney, 1951: 15–16)

Arguably the most influential psychologist to share this perspective was Carl Rogers (see Thorne, 1992, for a biography) who also proposed the view that human beings are organismically motivated toward developing to their full potential:

> I have little sympathy with the rather prevalent concept that man is basically irrational, and thus his impulses, if not controlled, would lead to destruction of others and self. Man's behavior is exquisitely rational, moving with subtle and ordered complexity toward the goals his organism is endeavoring to achieve.
>
> (Rogers, 1969: 29)

Deep within us, Rogers proposed, human beings are striving to become all that they can be. Rogers referred to this directional force of becoming as the actualising tendency:

> This is the inherent tendency of the organism to develop all its capacities in ways which serve to maintain or enhance the organism. It involves not only the tendency to meet what Maslow terms 'deficiency needs' for air, food, water, and the like, but also more generalised activities. It involves development toward the differentiation of organs and of functions, expansion in terms of growth, expansion of effectiveness through the use of tools, expansion and enhancement through reproduction. It is development toward autonomy and away from heteronomy, or control by external forces.
>
> (Rogers, 1959: 196)

Rogers (1959) was conceptualising the basic directionality of the actualising tendency as toward the development of autonomous determination, expansion and effectiveness, and constructive social behaviour. The actualising tendency, Rogers argued, was the one natural motivational force of human beings and which is always directed towards constructive growth:

> It is the urge which is evident in all organic and human life – to expand, extend, to become autonomous, develop, mature – the tendency to express and activate all the capacities of the organism, to the extent that such activation enhances the organism or the self.
>
> (Rogers, 1961: 35)

We have argued elsewhere (Linley and Joseph, 2004; Joseph and Linley, 2006) that positive psychology has implicitly adopted this third fundamental assumption about human nature. Here, we would argue that coaching psychology raises these same questions, and that by considering their own fundamental assumptions about the nature of human beings and what it means to be human, coaching psychologists may gain a greater insight on how these assumptions may impact on their practice.

Practice

Any practice of coaching psychology rests on our fundamental assumptions about human nature. These assumptions may be deep seated, but they are also easily seen in our choice of words, the agendas that we may or may not hold for our coaching psychological practice and our clients, and the very ways in which we choose to work. Our assumptions as coaching psychologists reflect our own personalities and preferences, and are likely forged through our own life experiences and training. They do not lend themselves to straightforward empirical inquiry, and hence may be considered as questions of value and morality – and thus individual ethics and preference. Further, it is because our assumptions are typically implicit, and therefore seldom consciously challenged, that they can often become accepted without critical reflection when we become trained in a particular model and a particular way of working, and become used to doing things in a particular way. It is precisely because of this that our fundamental assumptions are so often taken for granted and unchallenged, assuming the position of the status quo.

This being the case, we suggest an important element of the integration between positive psychology and coaching psychology is the invitation that positive psychology offers for us to consider and reflect upon our fundamental assumptions about human nature. This is especially important when we are dealing with questions of 'enhancing well-being and performance', since traditional models (and by extension, fundamental assumptions) are often found wanting on this issue, being unable to account for the *presence* of human health and well-being as well as they might be considered to account for the *absence* of human illness and ill-being (see Keyes, 2005).

To extend an earlier analogy, traditional models might well be able to explain how to get us back to zero, but not how to get us up to plus eight. However, the assumption of a tendency toward self-realisation, or actualising tendency, provides a holistic, integrative model of both ill-being and well-being that accounts more completely for the totality of human experience. It is notable that substantial evidence is now beginning to accrue that attests to this constructive directional tendency (see Joseph and Linley, 2004; see Joseph and Linley, 2006, for a review; see Sheldon et al., 2003, for an experimental illustration), supporting the claims of earlier humanistic psychology theorists through the use of more recently advanced experimental and statistical techniques (Sheldon and Kasser, 2001).

Overall, then, we argue that there is compelling evidence for the fundamental assumption of a constructive directional tendency within human nature, and we suggest that coaching psychologists would do well to consider these issues regularly as part of their continuing personal and professional development. However, let us be explicit that we would not wish to impose this view on others, respecting the diversity of opinions and the eclecticity of methods that should define any psychological endeavour, and recognising the subjective and personal nature of these assumptions. As research progresses, however, we suggest that these 'big picture' questions provide a rich – if challenging – topic of inquiry, and we would do well to remember that the absence of evidence does not automatically translate to the falsification of the hypothesis, especially if methodologies are as yet inadequate for the research question.

Research

The call for more research to underpin coaching and coaching psychology is not new (Grant, 2001; Kauffman and Scoular, 2004). There are increasing signs that it is being heeded, and the establishment of the joint British Psychological Society Special Group in Coaching Psychology and Australian Psychological Society publication, the *International Coaching Psychology Review*, should do much to facilitate this. However, in considering the nature of coaching psychology broadly, with its defined foundation as being grounded in established psychological approaches, and the integration of positive psychology and coaching psychology specifically, one can easily ascertain that there is already a research foundation on which coaching psychology can begin to be built. As indicated above, we will not consider here the specific blocks of this foundation, but restrict ourselves to some meta-level considerations about why, how and where we should conduct coaching psychology research.

However, before we proceed with these considerations, it is worth noting the very broad foundation – of both research and application – from which coaching psychology has emerged, and from which it might be expected to draw its evidential and theoretical bases. Coaching psychology has roots in each of clinical, counselling, educational, occupational and sports psychology (Palmer and Whybrow, 2005) and as such has a broader heritage than its relatively recent appearance might suggest. With positive psychology allied to this heritage, its foundation is even broader, since positive psychology similarly is not a 'new discipline', but rather a new way of looking at established disciplines, a change in perspective, as we described above (see also Linley et al., 2006).

So, *why* should coaching psychologists conduct research? It is axiomatic that research should lead to better practice, since this is the central tenet that underpins the model of 'evidence-based practice' to which most of us subscribe. However, we suggest that coaching psychology has much to contribute to 'practice-based evidence', that is, research findings that emerge through live applications in real world settings rather than through experimental designs in the laboratory or through the results of surveys completed by the ubiquitous psychology undergraduate! Simply, research allows us to understand more about what works, how it works, and why it works, so that we might then be able to ask more specific questions about when it works and with whom. The effectiveness and efficacy of our practice as coaching psychologists will ultimately determine our success in both academic kudos and applied value-added, and research is the underpinning arbiter of this judgement.

How should coaching psychology research be conducted? Readers of *The Coaching Psychologist* will be familiar with our exchange with John Rowan on this topic (Linley and Harrington, 2005b). In essence, we argued that there is a place – and an important place – for *both* quantitative and qualitative approaches within coaching psychology research. While we acknowledge the different epistemological and ontological assumptions of quantitative and qualitative approaches, we suggest that it is misleading to assume that their methodological approaches are mutually exclusive, but instead encourage coaching psychologists to recognise the value of each approach within the context of different research questions. This is especially important, because 'an appropriate combination may enhance productive and *practically* applicable research through complementary methods of data collection, analysis and interpretation, depending on the overall purpose of the research' (Linley and Harrington, 2005b: 19, original italics).

It is likely that these problems arise because of the disjunction between the needs of the psychological scientist (e.g. academic researcher) and the needs of the psychological practitioner (e.g. coaching psychologist). The academic pressures faced by psychological scientists (i.e. academics) push them to strive for publication in leading research journals, where editors and reviewers typically demand large Ns and tight experimental, statistical methods. The result of these endeavours is nomothetic research that may generalise across people, but may lose the subtle idiographic nuances that are often valued by the practitioner. In contrast, practitioners are often interested in findings that they can apply, immediately and appropriately, in their work. This requirement demands an idiographic approach that is at odds with the agenda of the academic researcher, since while it offers great depth and richness about the specific individual, it arguably cannot be more broadly generalised (and hence is less appealing to a high-status research journal).

The two agendas described here are thus divergent, and may be one cause of the much lamented academic–practitioner divide, with academics conducting research that is ever more detail-oriented and detached from the needs of the real world (i.e. *pedantic* research; Anderson et al., 2001), while practitioners are pushed towards research with popular market value but in a market that does not have the patience or the resource for necessary academic rigour (i.e. *popularist* research; Anderson et al., 2001). In thinking about how to conduct research, we suggest that coaching psychologists would do well to strive to combine the needs for both high impact relevance and academic rigour in their work, thus meeting the call for more *pragmatic* science that genuinely serves the needs of researchers and practitioners while also adding to our knowledge corpus and advancing the research agenda (Anderson et al., 2001).

Toward a positive coaching psychology?

A first key issue here is with regard to the question of 'whose agenda?' (see Linley, 2006). This question of 'whose agenda' is one that underpins everything we do as psychologists, indeed as people, and yet it is a question that is hardly asked as much as it might be. Simply, the agenda we follow determines the activities of our practice, and as such it is an issue of which we suggest we should all strive to be more mindful. It is a theme that recurs throughout our work (see e.g. Linley and Joseph, 2004; Linley, 2006) and one that has important implications for the integration of coaching psychology and positive psychology, as we shall go on to discuss.

When we speak of agendas, the real issue is one of power and control. Those who exercise the power and control are those who set the agenda that is followed, and as such, we should always be mindful of our own agendas and how they fit, or not, with the agendas of others. As we have described elsewhere, the question of the positive psychological agenda is an important one, which largely shapes how positive psychology moves forward in the future (see Linley, 2006; Linley et al., 2006). In essence, our view is that positive psychology should strive to inform, be informed by, and integrate with psychological disciplines and approaches more broadly. In this way, we have described 'the counselling psychology agenda for positive psychology', rather than vice versa. Similar initiatives pertain to positive clinical psychology

(Maddux et al., 2004), and the growth of positive organisational scholarship (Cameron et al., 2003a) as a branch of what might be considered positive occupational and organisational psychology.

A key consideration here is how we understand the 'territory' that is to be occupied by different psychological practitioners. Generally, positive psychology challenges us to adopt a more holistic perspective on human experience that accounts for the plus side of human functioning as much as it does the negative side of distress and disorder. In the context of positive clinical psychology, Maddux et al. (2004) proposed the adoption of a continuum model of human functioning that does away with the false dichotomisation of people into 'well' and 'not well', recognising that all of us are to some greater or lesser extent simultaneously both 'well' and 'not well'. Positive organisational scholarship argues that occupational and organisational psychologists should become focused equally on the positive deviance in organisations, as much as they are on the negative deviance (Cameron et al., 2003b).

Explicitly, coaching psychology defines its remit as being to enhance 'well-being and performance' (Palmer and Whybrow, 2005), thus implicitly advocating that the remit of the coaching psychologist lies at the more positive end of human functioning. But the central theme that unites all of these perspectives, whether informed by an explicit positive psychological approach or not, is that we should move away from understanding human experience as being neatly dichotomized into positive and negative, well and ill, healthy and unhealthy, strength and weakness. These are false dichotomies, and ones that were rejected by our humanistic psychology ancestors, who instead proposed a more holistic approach to understanding what it means to be human (Joseph and Worsley, 2005). The convergence of these perspectives around this uniting theme suggests that we might be seeing the beginning of a perspective shift in modern psychology. In time, positive psychology and coaching psychology might both be seen as forces that forged a more complete understanding of the human condition.

References

Allport, G. W. (1937) *Personality: A psychological interpretation*. New York: Holt.

Anderson, N., Herriot, P. and Hodgkinson, G. P. (2001) The practitioner-researcher divide in industrial, work and organizational (IWO) psychology: where are we now, and where do we go from here? *Journal of Occupational and Organizational Psychology* 74: 391–411.

Baumeister, R. F., Bratslavsky, E., Finkenauer, C. and Vohs, K. D. (2001) Bad is stronger than good. *Review of General Psychology* 5: 323–370.

Cameron, K. S., Dutton, J. E. and Quinn, R. E. (eds). (2003a) *Positive Organizational Scholarship: Foundations of a new discipline*. San Francisco, CA: Berrett-Koehler.

Cameron, K. S., Dutton, J. E. and Quinn, R. E. (2003b) Foundations of positive organizational scholarship. In K. S. Cameron, J. E. Dutton and R. E. Quinn (eds),

Positive Organizational Scholarship: Foundations of a new discipline (pp. 3–13). San Francisco, CA: Berrett-Koehler.

Cawley, M. J., Martin, J. E. and Johnson, J. A. (2000) A virtues approach to personality. *Personality and Individual Differences* 28: 997–1013.

Diener, E. and Seligman, M. E. P. (2004) Beyond money: toward an economy of well-being. *Psychological Science in the Public Interest* 5: 1–31.

Donovan, N. and Halpern, D. (2001) *Life Satisfaction: The state of knowledge and implications for government*. London: Downing Street Strategy Unit. Available www.strategy.gov.uk/2001/futures/attachments/ls/paper.pdf

Downey, M. (1999) *Effective Coaching*. London: Orion.

Fredrickson, B. L. and Levenson, R. W. (1998) Positive emotions speed recovery from the cardiovascular effects of negative emotions. *Cognition and Emotion* 12: 191–220.

Fredrickson, B. L., Mancuso, R. A., Branigan, C. and Tugade, M. M. (2000) The undoing effect of positive emotions. *Motivation and Emotion* 24: 237–258.

Gable, S. L. and Haidt, J. (2005) What (and why) is positive psychology? *Review of General Psychology* 9: 103–110.

Gallwey, T. (2002) *The Inner Game of Work: Overcoming mental obstacles for maximum performance*. New York: Texere.

Grant, A. M. (2001) *Towards a Psychology of Coaching*. Sydney: Coaching Psychology Unit, University of Sydney.

Grant, A. M. and Palmer, S. (2002) Coaching psychology workshop. Annual Conference of the Division of Counselling Psychology, British Psychological Society, Torquay, UK, 18 May.

Horney, K. (1951) *Neurosis and Human Growth: The struggle toward self-realization*. London: Routledge and Kegan Paul.

Hubble, M. A. and Miller, S. D. (2004) The client: psychotherapy's missing link for promoting a positive psychology. In P. A. Linley and S. Joseph (eds), *Positive Psychology in Practice* (pp. 335–353). Hoboken, NJ: Wiley.

James, W. (1902) *The Varieties of Religious Experience: A study in human nature*. New York: Longman, Green.

Joseph, S. and Linley, P. A. (2004) Positive therapy: a positive psychological theory of therapeutic practice. In P. A. Linley and S. Joseph (eds), *Positive Psychology in practice* (pp. 354–368). Hoboken, NJ: Wiley.

Joseph, S. and Linley, P. A. (2006) *Positive Therapy: A meta-theory for positive psychological practice*. London: Routledge.

Joseph, S. and Worsley, R. (2005) A positive psychology of mental health: the person-centred perspective. In S. Joseph and R. Worsley (eds), *Person-centred Psychopathology: A positive psychology of mental health* (pp. 348–357). Ross-on-Wye, UK: PCCS Books.

Kahneman, D., Krueger, A. B., Schkade, D. A., Schwarz, N. and Stone, A. A. (2004) Toward national well-being accounts. *American Economic Review* 94: 429–434.

Kauffman, C. and Scoular, A. (2004) Toward a positive psychology of executive coaching. In P. A. Linley and S. Joseph (eds), *Positive Psychology in Practice* (pp. 287–302). Hoboken, NJ: Wiley.

Keyes, C. L. M. (2005) Mental illness and/or mental health? Investigating axioms of the complete state model of mental health. *Journal of Consulting and Clinical Psychology* 73: 539–548.

Lane, R. (2000) *The Loss of Happiness in Market Democracies*. New Haven, CT: Yale University Press.

Linley, P. A. (2006) Counseling psychology's positive psychological agenda: a model for integration and inspiration. *The Counseling Psychologist* 34: 313–322.

Linley, P. A. and Harrington, S. (2005a) Positive psychology and coaching psychology: perspectives on integration. *The Coaching Psychologist* 1(1): 13–14.

Linley, P. A. and Harrington, S. (2005b) Coaching psychology and positive psychology: a reply to John Rowan. *The Coaching Psychologist* 1(2): 18–20.

Linley, P. A. and Joseph, S. (2004) Toward a theoretical foundation for positive psychology in practice. In P. A. Linley and S. Joseph (eds), *Positive Psychology in Practice* (pp. 713–731). Hoboken, NJ: Wiley.

Linley, P. A., Joseph, S. and Boniwell, I. (eds). (2003) In a positive light (special issue on positive psychology). *The Psychologist* 16(3).

Linley, P. A., Joseph, S., Harrington, S. and Wood, A. M. (2006) Positive psychology: past, present, and (possible) future. *Journal of Positive Psychology* 1: 3–16.

McCullough, M. E. and Snyder, C. R. (2000) Classical sources of human strength: revisiting an old home and building a new one. *Journal of Social and Clinical Psychology* 19: 1–10.

Maddux, J. E. (2002) Stopping the madness: positive psychology and the deconstruction of the illness ideology and the DSM. In C. R. Snyder and S. J. Lopez (eds), *Handbook of Positive Psychology* (pp. 13–25). New York: Oxford University Press.

Maddux, J. E., Snyder, C. R. and Lopez, S. J. (2004) Toward a positive clinical psychology: deconstructing the illness ideology and constructing an ideology of human strengths and potential. In P. A. Linley and S. Joseph (eds), *Positive Psychology in Practice* (pp. 320–334). Hoboken, NJ: Wiley.

Maslow, A. H. (1954) *Motivation and Personality*. New York: Harper.

Maslow, A. H. (1968) *Toward a Psychology of Being*. New York: Van Nostrand.

Myers, D. G. (2000) The funds, friends, and faith of happy people. *American Psychologist* 55: 56–67.

Palmer, S. and Whybrow, A. (2005) The proposal to establish a Special Group in Coaching Psychology. *The Coaching Psychologist* 1: 5–12.

Peterson, C. (2000) The future of optimism. *American Psychologist* 55: 44–55.

Rogers, C. R. (1959) A theory of therapy, personality and interpersonal relationships, as developed in the client-centered framework. In S. Koch (ed.) *Psychology: A study of a science*. Volume 3, *Formulations of the Person and the Social Context* (pp. 184–256). New York: McGraw-Hill.

Rogers, C. R. (1961) *On Becoming a Person*. Boston, MA: Houghton Mifflin.

Rogers, C. R. (1969) *Freedom to Learn*. Columbus, OH: Merrill.

Rozin, P. and Royzman, E. B. (2001) Negativity bias, negativity dominance, and contagion. *Personality and Social Psychology Review* 5: 296–320.

Seligman, M. E. P. (1999) The president's address. *American Psychologist* 54: 559–562.

Seligman, M. E. P. (2003) Positive psychology: fundamental assumptions. *The Psychologist* 16: 126–127.

Seligman, M. E. P. and Csikszentmihalyi, M. (2000) Positive psychology: an introduction. *American Psychologist* 55: 5–14.

Shah, H. and Marks, N. (2004) *A Well-being Manifesto for a Flourishing Society*.

London: New Economics Foundation. Available www.neweconomics.org/gen/
uploads/21xv5yytotlxxu322pmyada205102004103948.pdf

Sheldon, K. M. and Kasser, T. (2001) Goals, congruence, and positive well-being: new
empirical support for humanistic theories. *Journal of Humanistic Psychology* 41:
30–50.

Sheldon, K. M. and King, L. (2001) Why positive psychology is necessary. *American
Psychologist* 56: 216–217.

Sheldon, K. M., Arndt, J. and Houser-Marko, L. (2003) In search of the organismic
valuing process: the human tendency to move towards beneficial goal choices.
Journal of Personality 71: 835–886.

Thorne, B. (1992) *Carl Rogers.* London: Sage.

Whitmore, Sir J. (2002) *Coaching for Performance*, 3rd edition. London: Nicholas
Brealey.

Discussion points

• Do coaching psychology and positive psychology share the same fundamental assumptions about human nature? Is it possible to work within
these disciplines having different fundamental assumptions about human
nature?

• How can a positive psychology approach best be deployed within a
coaching psychology relationship?

• What are the biggest learnings that positive psychology and coaching
psychology can take from each other?

• What is the biggest contribution to human fulfilment that positive psychology and coaching psychology could make, and how should they go
about doing so?

Suggested reading

Joseph, S. and Linley, P. A. (2006) *Positive Therapy: A meta-theory for positive psychological practice.* London: Routledge.

Kauffman, C. (2006) Positive psychology: the science at the heart of coaching. In
D. R. Stober and A. M. Grant (eds), *Evidence Based Coaching Handbook: Putting
best practices to work for your clients.* Hoboken, NJ: Wiley.

Linley, P. A. and Kauffman, C. (eds) (2007) Editorial – Positive coaching psychology:
integrating the science of positive psychology with the practice of coaching
psychology. *International Coaching Psychology Review* (special issue on positive
psychology), 2(1): 5–8.

Linley, P. A., Joseph, S., Harrington, S. and Wood, A. M. (2006) Positive psychology:
past, present, and (possible) future. *Journal of Positive Psychology* 1: 3–16.

Chapter 4

Research: does coaching work?

Annette Fillery-Travis and David Lane

Introduction

With a global spend estimated at over US $2 billion (Sanghera, 2004) coaching is clearly not a niche market but an accepted contribution to the executive's development portfolio. It is unsurprising therefore that the buyers of coaching, both individuals and organisations, are starting to ask what can they expect to achieve from a coaching engagement, what approach or model is right for them and how can they get the best from the interaction. The market is, in effect, maturing.

However, a quick scan of the literature reveals that the term 'coaching' covers a multitude of interventions, undertaken by coaches with a range of training, to achieve a variety of aims. Coaches can describe themselves as executive coaches concentrating upon their client's role and behaviour within the work place with the aim of enhancing performance. Alternatively, a life coach may consider they also impact upon a client's work life but through consideration of more personal and generic life goals. It quickly becomes clear that to provide answers to the market's questions we need to consider coaching within a framework of practice based upon the needs of the client or organisation.

This framework should encompass the coaching mode and role as well as the supervisory relationships that exist. But at the heart of the framework should be the purpose of the coaching. In a review of the research literature on coaching effectiveness (Fillery-Travis and Lane, 2006) we identified that only when we have clarity as to the purpose of the coaching – i.e. the coaching agenda – can we identify appropriate criteria to measure coaching effectiveness.

In this chapter we summarise our work on the development of such a framework and identify briefly the research addressing effectiveness of coaching for each mode of coaching. We have not sought to provide a definitive list of all the research in this field. Indeed we have purposefully not covered the growing literature on the process of coaching. Our focus has been on research into whether coaching is delivering on its aims. While undertaking this review it became clear that evidence was beginning to emerge within the literature as to what were the factors which contributed to the perceived success of the coaching. We will look at these factors in more detail and how they can inform both our practice as coaches and how coaching is applied within organisations.

How is coaching being used within organisations?

Since 2001 there has been a plethora of surveys (Carter, 2001; Kubicek, 2002; Chartered Institute of Personnel and Development (CIPD), 2006) looking at how coaching is being used by organisations. The modes of coaching currently employed can be categorised as: external or executive coaching, internal and manager coaching. There is an embryonic literature on Team Coaching which is outside the remit of this chapter and we refer the interested reader to Diedrich's (2001) review. The differentiation between these modes bears some discussion as they can be confused.

The journal literature identifies that external coaches are being recruited by organisations for one of two tasks:

- The coaching of a senior executive to their own agenda – this may be part of an induction process within a new role or it may be as extra support for an individual identified for promotion but with a need for development prior to taking on the new role. Alternatively, a coach may be commissioned by an individual, on a private basis, as part of their own development plans. In both these cases, the agenda will, in general, be wide ranging and defined purely by the client. It will usually encompass organisational issues but may address fundamental questions within adult development such as identity and the change in perspective and motivation with maturity.
- The coaching of managers after training to consolidate knowledge acquisition and facilitate behaviour change to a specific organisational agenda. It is clear that the coaching agenda in this case is well defined and restricted to pre-set organisational goals.

Thus, the external coach can be working at a variety of levels of engagement. Categorisation of these levels has been part of the literature for some time (Peterson, 1996; Witherspoon and White, 1996; Grant and Cavanagh, 2004). The continuum ranges from skills coaching – focused on changing specific behaviours – through to developmental coaching where the coach is dealing with intimate, professional and personal questions – 'therapy for the people who don't need therapy'.

It is apparent that coaching draws substantially upon psychological perspectives to underpin its practice. However, these are not necessarily made explicit in many models. As Cavanagh and Grant (2006) argue, coaches are practising from a number of bases not informed by the psychological research (or even that of adult learning) and may use proprietary frameworks of dubious validity. Hence coaches are engaged often on a psychological enterprise without a background understanding of the psychology used. This is particularly worrying for open agenda coaching where the demands can be very detailed, intimate and touch upon fundamental belief systems for the client.

It follows that a high level of competency is required of the coach operating within this arena and various professional bodies have taken some time in defining what constitutes this level of professional mastery. See the European Coaching and Mentoring Council's website and the International Federation of Coaching and Worldwide Association of Business Coaches for a fuller description of this work.

The other two coaching modes, internal and manager coaching, are generally carried out by individuals within an organisational structure. Internal coaching has been defined by Frisch (2001) as follows:

> a one-to-one developmental intervention supported by the organisation and provided by a colleague of those coached who is trusted to shape and deliver a program yielding individual professional growth.
>
> (Frisch, 2001: 242)

The internal coach will have coaching as part of their job description but will generally be outside the line management of the client. The coaching agenda will be driven by organisational goals and is generally not as 'free' or open as that found for external coaching although there may be some exploration of the underpinning aspects of the behaviour or change under discussion.

The internal coach will not require as extensive a range of skills as the external coach and, in developing best practice, would expect to be supervised by an external or senior coach. Within our own study (Jarvis et al., 2006) the majority of internal coaches were senior human resources (HR) professionals. It has been argued that senior HR professionals have always had an internal coach role and many welcome the formalisation of this part of their profession. Indeed one expanding task of the internal coach has been to take over the 'training support' role of the external coach, particularly in the development of manager coaches. In working in this arena HR professionals are able to draw upon experience and theoretical frameworks from adult learning.

With regard to manager coaching, most organisations will also say their managers are coaching and that they support them in the role (Kubicek, 2002). The agenda of manager coaches is the most restricted of all and is usually solely concerned with the requirements of the organisation. It will tend to be focused on achieving operational goals and will concentrate on skills coaching. In contrast to the other modes this type of coaching has a direct mutual benefit for both coach and client. The employee is able to achieve their agreed outputs and the manager is able to delegate appropriately and confidently. With such a restricted agenda the competencies required of the coach are also correspondingly narrow. Their training will, in general, be short and focused commonly on a single model of practice. However, there is evidence that coaching skills can be learnt within such training (Graham et al., 1993). Supervision is, as always, pivotal to the ethical application of this mode of coaching and increasingly this task is being carried out by an internal coach.

Thus, in summary, the framework of practice can be represented schematically in Figure 4.1. The role and agenda of the coach will become more determined by the individual client as we go up through the pyramid. Correspondingly, the aims and objectives become more person-centred and less directly related to operational outputs. This has a significant impact on how we measure success of coaching throughout these levels and it is to this question that we now turn.

Does coaching work?

Coaching, whether internal or external, is a significant investment for the individual and the organisation. It is not surprising then that within the commercial world there is a growing demand for a return on investment figure as a measure of success. Research to date has had only limited success in providing it.

If we consider the framework in Figure 4.1, it is clear that different coaching modes will have different criteria for success. At the executive coaching level the coaching agenda can be focused on underpinning issues and the executive themselves will be of sufficient seniority that their impact will be at the strategic not the operational level. Correspondingly, the impact of

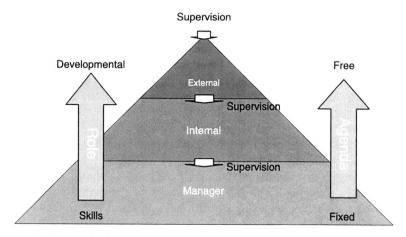

Figure 4.1 Framework of practice.

coaching on the bottom line will be indirect, prone to contributing factors such as market changes and usually operating at a longer timescale than a research study. The design of a measure to provide a return on investment (ROI) is therefore challenging and it is not surprising that only two studies have sought to quote a ROI measure (McGovern et al., 2001; Philips, 2004). The ROIs quoted are 5.7 and 2.2 respectively. These figures may provide a useful starting point but McGovern et al.'s study relies on the client's own estimates of ROI without consistent criteria across the study and the Philips study has yet to be peer reviewed.

It can be argued that coaching at this level is addressing the overarching skills of the executive, such as self-efficacy and interpersonal skills, and thus research should look directly at whether these skills have improved and assume the subsequent impact upon the bottom line. This has, in general, been the strategy of the majority of investigators. For example, some studies have looked at the impact of coaching on multisource feedback (Thach, 2002; Luthans and Peterson, 2003; Smither et al., 2003). These have found a consistent improvement in the performance rating of the coached managers in areas such as goal setting, seeking feedback to improve performance, interpersonal skills and leadership effectiveness.

Other studies have looked to the perception of the client themselves of the value of the coaching (Harder and Company Community Research, 2003; Dawdy, 2004; Dingman, 2004). Each study concentrated upon different specific behaviours, e.g. communication style, interpersonal support or self-efficacy, so direct comparison of the results cannot be possible but again there was consistent agreement by clients that the coaching had impacted favourably upon their performance.

It is where the coaching agenda is focused on behaviours of direct impact to operational performance that the ROI figure will become more directly accessible. This will occur at the internal and manager coach levels where organisational goals will be explicit within the coaching agenda. Unfortunately research studies on internal modes of coaching are still rare. One study was undertaken within a public sector agency (Olivero et al., 1997) on internal coaches and this attempted to measure the productivity of the client before and after the coaching. The measures they chose were appropriate to the manager's role and quantifiably of benefit to the organisation. Managers underwent a training programme and a sample also underwent coaching. An increase of 88 per cent in the productivity of the coached individuals compared favourably to a 22 per cent increase for the non-coached individual. Although this may seem clear cut the authors suggest that there are a number of factors which were not fully addressed in the study design and the interested reader is referred to their discussion.

Studies investigating the impact of manager coaching on key business indicators are difficult to find. The research flounders on the very pragmatic approach taken by companies. In our study of over 30 HR directors or buyers of coaching services (Jarvis et al., 2006) we explored the organisation's strategy for coaching and their perception of its effectiveness. We found internal monitoring was rarely pursued rigorously. The respondents justified this lack of monitoring by virtue of the fact that they could clearly see improvement in the manager and the staff and therefore they did not need to waste resource measuring it directly.

The School of Coaching study (Kubicek, 2002) also found that only 27 per cent of companies formally evaluated their coaching skills initiatives. Where evaluation happened the measures used were varied with 360-degree feedback (52 per cent) being the most preferred. Performance against specific objectives was used by 44 per cent, opinion survey by 32 per cent, and evaluation by direct reports was used by 28 per cent.

This restricts the conclusions that can be drawn but there is a wealth of individual case studies reported within the professional journals. For example, coaching as part of a move from command and control to a respect and empowerment culture was identified as highly effective by Vodafone (Eaton and Brown, 2002). The move from a heads down command and control culture to one based on coaching is identified as a significant contribution to Vodafone's turnaround from slipping behind BR Cellnet and Orange to regaining top market position.

It is clear that we do not have sufficient information to provide the empirical data on ROI for coaching at the levels where it is most appropriate i.e. the internal and manager coach. But the studies which have been undertaken provide some insight into what factors impact upon the perceived success of coaching and we will consider them next.

Factors impacting upon coaching effectiveness

We have grouped the generic factors arising from our review under four headings: see Figure 4.2. Obviously there is a degree of overlap and interaction between these factors but the headings serve as a useful label for discussion.

We will take each of these in turn, look at the evidence for their impact and the possible ways they can be considered within a coaching programme.

Coach attributes

There has been a range of discussions (Kilburg, 1996) on the important attributes of a coach. As identified before, there are a number of initiatives currently underway to identify the competencies required of a coach. We have not the space to explore these in detail and the interested reader is referred to the websites of the EMCC, WABC and the ICF for a full discussion of their work in this area. In this chapter we will simply look at those attributes which have been identified within research studies. Dingman (2004) categorises the attribute under three main headings:

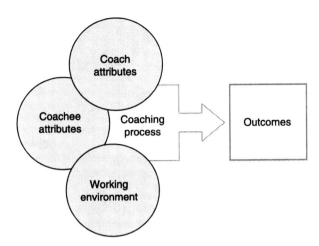

Figure 4.2 Generic issues influencing perceived outcomes within a coaching interaction.

- *interpersonal skills:* empathy, encouragement, genuineness, authenticity, approachability, compassion, intelligence
- *communication skills:* tact, listening/silence, questions, playful exchange
- *instrumental support:* creativity, dealing with paradox, self-knowledge, positive regard, tolerance for interventions made, stimulation to think, feel and explore new ideas and behaviours, working on resistance to change.

One factor coming through in practitioner publications is the issue of the coach's own agenda and how that can hamper delivery of the coaching. Specific mention is made of the coach who is too concerned with 'proving' their model of practice even if it is not appropriate to the organisation's culture or development agenda. This is addressed within the practitioner literature by Saporito (1996) the development of his model of practice.

Coachee attributes

Overwhelmingly the published work by coach practitioners points to the willingness by the client to change as the primary determinant of the success of the interaction. Interestingly this is less well covered in the empirical research where clients are viewed as a more homogeneous entity, i.e. no studies to date have identified either the readiness of the client for change or whether there is a performance issue prior to commencement of the study or even at its conclusion.

This aspect has been further developed by Kilburg (1997), who looked at the contributor factors which may give a negative outcome for a coaching intervention. Adapting the factors identified by Mohr (1995) as having a negative influence on outcomes from psychotherapy, Kilburg identifies lack of motivation, unrealistic expectations and lack of follow through alongside the more obvious ones of psychopathology and severe interpersonal problems. The issues surrounding the identification and referral of clients to therapeutic interventions is expanded upon in more detail by Grant (2001).

Other authors have thrown the net wider and suggested specific population groups can benefit directly from coaching. A US doctorate thesis (Dawdy, 2004) looked at whether personality type was a factor in the success of the intervention. Sixty-two managers within a large engineering firm received coaching for at least six months from one coaching firm. Although 90 per cent perceived the coaching as valuable there was no difference in this or other measures of outcomes between differing personality types. The population examined here was restricted and no information was available about the spread of managers across personality types so it is not clear how generic these conclusions are.

One study has considered the alpha male as potentially benefiting from coaching as 'their quintessential strengths are also what makes them so challenging, and often frustrating to work with' (Ludeman and Erlandson, 2004). In terms of gender there is an identification that traditional methods of leadership development can be overly geared towards male needs and learning requirements. According to Belenky et al. (1986), female careers are more discontinuous (i.e. staged) than the linear male model. It is argued that this difference requires a variety of support and opportunity for learning (Vinnicombe and Singh, 2003). Coaching and mentoring are identified as contributing to such a portfolio approach.

The duration of the coaching has also attracted comment on a number of studies. Durations of four to six months are considered appropriate while as identified before durations of one year and beyond are thought to yield decreasing returns (Harder and Company Community Research, 2003). Some studies have looked at a single coaching session to address the outputs of 360-degree feedback and have yielded good results (Luthans and Peterson, 2003).

Working environment

The respondents of our survey (Jarvis et al., 2006) were unanimous in identifying the buy-in of senior managers as the most effective support of a coaching programme. It is the organisation's culture which sets the tone for learning and hence has the potential to greatly affect the success of a coaching programme. There has been a great deal of research into how organisational culture influences the way people behave at work. A familiar example is Argyris's (1994) book on organisational learning. In it he argues that the rules, rituals and assumptions that exist in an organisation define its culture and dictate how its employees behave, what behaviour is expected and what is seen to be rewarded and recognised.

The academic literature also agrees with this view. Kilburg (2001) argues that without the support of the client's working environment, coaching efforts may have little bearing. But what do we mean by a coaching culture? Unsurprisingly, a number of definitions exist, including:

- 'a culture where people coach each other all the time as a natural part of meetings, reviews and one-to-one discussions of all kinds' (Hardingham et al., 2004: 184).
- 'coaching is the predominant style of managing and working together, and where a commitment to grow the organisation is embedded in a parallel commitment to grow the people in the organisation' (Clutterbuck and Megginson, 2005a: 45).

The extent to which an organisation has a coaching culture in place is likely to have an impact on the success of coaching in the organisation. A new model of the culture has been produced (Clutterbuck and Megginson, 2005b) that identifies six characteristics of a coaching culture:

- Coaching is linked to business drivers.
- Being a client is encouraged and supported.
- Provide coach training.
- Reward and recognise coaching.
- Adopt a systemic perspective.
- The move to coaching is managed.

The degree to which an organisation's culture conforms to these characteristics is likely to determine how supportive it will be of coaching activities. This, in turn, will impact on the results that coaching delivers to the organisation and the individuals involved

The CIPD's (2006) learning and development survey found 80 per cent of respondents using coaching claimed their organisations aspired to develop a coaching culture, and 75 per cent report investing time, resources and effort into achieving this aim. When organisations have a framework for coaching with a clear definition (including an agreed purpose), they are more likely to be able to gain buy-in and support for coaching within the organisation as their approach will look well-thought-through and researched.

Coaching process

Several authors have tried to categorise the published models of practice and identify their generic elements. These have been surprisingly successful and clearly identify that although coaches tailor their coaching in different ways depending on the specific individuals' needs, many coaching relationships follow a relatively simple structure. Dingham (2004) compared a series of different coaching processes and identified six generic steps or stages in coaching:

1   Formal contracting.
2   Relationship building.
3   Assessment.
4   Getting feedback and reflecting.
5   Goal setting.
6   Implementation and evaluation.

Within all the coaching models in the literature there is clearly an emphasis on the initial stages of the process   specifically contracting and relationship forming. The reason for this is not hard to find: the most consistently identified factor argued as contributing to the success of a coaching engagement is the 'fit' between coach and client. This mirrors findings from a range of therapeutic engagements – the relationship between client and practitioner is the primary factor in a successful outcome.

To the extent that there is mirroring of the findings from the therapeutic literature in coaching research the question is raised as to whether we should also be considering the same dilemmas. Lane and Corrie (2006) draw attention to the following areas of that debate:

- The debate on evidence-based practice (should we rely only on actuarial evidence of effectiveness based on standardised interventions or allow for professional discretion) has hardly touched coaching so far.
- How do we decide what issues should (or not) be addressed by coaching? (And what by therapy, training, or left alone entirely.)
- Should we be researching outcomes from the different stakeholders' perspectives (and consequently who decides what counts as critical evidence)?
- Should we be equally concerned with researching process in coaching – what happens (how does change happen, if at all, and what is down to the relationship and what to other factors)?

For coaching the issue of the client–coach relationship is identified not only within the practitioner publications but has also been explicitly tested with the research literature. So we have some data as identified below, but the broader questions which are a feature of the therapeutic and counselling psychology literature are not being extensively addressed. (Perhaps this will emerge as a major contribution from coaching psychology to the general coaching literature, to make explicit some of these interconnected questions.)

Two examples of attempts to develop an understanding of the relationship elements are found in the work of Wasylyshyn (2003) and Dingman (2004). In the survey of coaching clients (Wasylyshyn, 2003) the highest scoring personal characteristic of an effective coach was being able to form a strong connection with the client. In a study looking at the influence of coaching in conjunction with 360-degree feedback (Thach, 2002) on leadership development the correct 'matching' of the coach with the client was identified as required by the participants.

One study (Dingman, 2004) has tried to go further and test how far the quality of the relationship impacts on levels of self-efficacy and job-related attitudes such as job satisfaction, organisational commitment and work–life balance. The hypothesis that the quality of the relationship impacted upon job satisfaction was positively shown. Overall it was found that the quality of the coaching and the process of being coached both impacted upon self-efficacy and through that to job-related outcomes.

Conclusion

The aim of our review here was to consider the type of studies which have been undertaken by academics and practitioners into whether coaching works. It is clear that to answer this question we have to be clear about the original purpose of the coaching and the mode of coaching used. Both of these factors will impact upon the criteria for success and how it should be researched. There is a clear consensus that clients enjoy being coached and believe it is enhancing their professional life. This belief is shared with their organisations.

Research is now needed into the how, what works, and for whom questions which will develop coaching practice. How these questions will be formulated and the extent to which they will be informed by a psychological understanding of research or coaching, and draw upon critiques of the therapeutic research remains to be seen. It would be unfortunate if coaching research (and coaching psychology in particular) went down some of the less useful alleys that therapy research followed. We have seen that already research is identifying the factors of influence and these can inform not only the practice of individual coaches but also the way organisations seek to use coaching.

The market and, some would say the profession, of coaching is maturing. As yet the research literature has not kept complete pace with practice. But this presents the whole coaching community with the opportunity to not suffer from the academic/practice divide which afflicts most professions but for academic and practitioner researchers to continue to learn and work together to develop best practice for the profession.

References

Argyris, C. (1994) *On Organisational Learning*. Oxford: Blackwell.

Belenky, M., Clinchy, B., Goldberger, N. and Tarule, J. (1986) *Women's Ways of Knowing*. New York: Basic Books.

Carter, A. (2001) *Executive Coaching: Inspiring performance at work*, Volume Report 379. Falmer, UK: Institute for Employment Studies, University of Sussex.

Cavanagh, M. J. and Grant, A. M. (2006) Coaching psychology and the scientist-practitioner model. In D. A. Lane and S. Corrie (eds) *The Modern Scientist-Practitioner: A guide to practice in psychology*. London: Routledge.

CIPD (2006) *Learning and Development 2006*. London: CIPD.

Clutterbuck, D. and Megginson, D. (2005a) How to create a coaching culture. *People Management* 11(8): 44–45.

Clutterbuck, D. and Megginson, D. (2005b) *Making Coaching Work: Creating a coaching culture*. London: CIPD.

Dawdy, G. N. (2004) Executive coaching: a comparative design exploring the perceived effectiveness of coaching and methods. Unpublished doctorate, School of Education, Capella University.

Diedrich, R. C. (2001) Lessons learned in – and guidelines for – coaching executive teams. *Consulting Psychology Journal: Practice and Research* 53: 238–239.

Dingman, M. E. (2004) The effects of executive coaching on job-related attitudes. School of Leadership Development, Regent University.

Eaton, J. and Brown, D. (2002) Coaching for a change with Vodafone. *Career Development International* 7: 284–287.

Fillery-Travis, A. and Lane, D. (2006) Does coaching work or are we asking the wrong question? *International Coaching Psychology Review* 1: 23–36.

Frisch, M. H. (2001) The emerging role of the internal coach. *Consulting Psychology Journal: Practice and Research* 53: 240–250.

Graham, S., Wedman, J. F. and Kester, B. G. (1993) Manager coaching skills: development and application. *Performance Improvement Quarterly* 6: 2–13.

Grant, A. M. (2001) Towards a psychology of coaching. Paper presented at the Fourth Annual Oxford School Coaching and Mentoring Conference, Heythrope Park, Oxford.

Grant, A. M. and Cavanagh, M. (2004) Toward a profession of coaching: sixty-five years of progress and challenges for the future. *International Journal of Evidence Based Coaching and Mentoring* 2: 7–21.

Harder and Company Community Research (2003) *Executive Coaching Project: Evaluation of findings*. Harder and Company Community Research.

Hardingham, A., Brearley, M., Moorhouse, A. and Venter, B. (2004) *The Coach's Coach: Personal development for personal developers*. London: CIPD.

Jarvis, J., Lane, D. and Fillery-Travis, A. (2006) *Does Coaching Work?* London: CIPD.

Kilburg, R. R. (1996) Toward a conceptual understanding and definition of executive coaching. *Consulting Psychology Journal: Practice and Research* 48: 134–144.

Kilburg, R. R. (1997) Coaching and executive character: core problems and basic approaches. *Consulting Psychology Journal: Practice and Research* 49: 281–299.

Kilburg, R. R. (2001) Facilitating intervention adherence in executive coaching: a model and methods. *Consulting Psychology Journal: Practice and Research* 53: 251–267.

Kubicek, M. (2002) Is coaching being abused? *Training Magazine* May: 12–14.

Lane, D. A. and Corrie, S. (2006) *The Modern Scientist-Practitioner: A guide to practice in psychology*. London: Routledge.

Ludeman, K. and Erlandson, E. (2004) Coaching the alpha male. *Harvard Business Review* 82: 58.

Luthans, F. and Peterson, S. J. (2003) 360-degree feedback with systematic coaching:

empirical analysis suggests a winning combination. *Human Resource Management*, 42: 243–256.

McGovern, J., Lindemann, M., Vergara, M., Murphy, S., Barker, L. and Warrenfeltz, R. (2001) Maximizing the impact of executive coaching. *Manchester Review* 6: 1–9.

Mohr, D. C. (1995) Negative outcomes in psychotherapy: a critical review. *Clinical Psychology: Science and Practice* 2: 1–27.

Olivero, G., Bane, K. and Kopelman, R. E. (1997) Executive coaching as a transfer of training tool: effects on productivity in a public agency. *Public Personnel Management* 26: 461–469.

Peterson, D. B. (1996) Executive coaching at work: the art of one-on-one change. *Consulting Psychology Journal: Practice and Research* 48: 78–86.

Philips, J. (2004) Measuring ROI in business coaching. Available www.roiinstitute.net/websites/ROIInstitute/ROIInstitute/.

Sanghera, S. (2004) I went in for coaching, but couldn't stay the course. *Financial Times* (London) 5 July: 8.

Saporito, T. J. (1996) Business-linked executive development: coaching senior executives. *Consulting Psychology Journal: Practice and Research* 48: 96–103.

Smither, J. W., London, M., Flautt, R., Vargas, Y. and Kucine, I. (2003) Can working with an executive coach improve multisource feedback ratings over time? A quasi-experimental field study. *Personnel Psychology* 56: 23.

Thach, E. C. (2002) The impact of executive coaching and 360 feedback on leadership effectiveness. *Leadership and Organization Development Journal* 23: 205–214.

Vinnicombe, S. and Singh, V. (2003) Women-only management training: an essential part of women's leadership development. *Journal of Change Management* 3: 294–306.

Wasylyshyn, K. M. (2003) Executive coaching: an outcome study. *Consulting Psychology Journal: Practice and Research* 55: 94–106.

Witherspoon, R. and White, R. P. (1996) Executive coaching: a continuum of roles. *Consulting Psychology Journal: Practice and Research* 48: 124–133.

Discussion points

- What are the evaluations which are meaningful for our practice as individual coaches and does this link coherently to our purpose and mode of practice?
- Should we be considering outcomes and impact from a variety of stakeholder's perspectives?
- How can we leverage our knowledge of effectiveness factors within the coaching engagement?
- Within the framework of practice presented here there are delineations between modes of practice; manager, internal and external whereas the reality of the coaching agenda for each mode is less determined. How should this influence training and development of coaches?

Suggested reading

Grant, A. M. and Cavanagh, M. (2004) Toward a profession of coaching: sixty-five years of progress and challenges for the future. *International Journal of Evidence Based Coaching and Mentoring* 2: 7–21.

Jarvis, J., Lane, D. and Fillery-Travis, A. (2006) *The Case for Coaching*. London: CIPD.

Lane, D. A. and Corrie, S. (2006) *The Modern Scientist-Practitioner: A guide to practice in psychology*. London: Routledge

Smither, J. W., London, M., Flautt, R., Vargas, Y. and Kucine, I. (2003) Can working with an executive coach improve multisource feedback ratings over time? A quasi-experimental field study. *Personnel Psychology* 56(1): 23–44.

Part II

Coaching psychology: approaches

Chapter 5

Behavioural coaching

Jonathan Passmore

Introduction

Behavioural coaching is a structured, process driven relationship between a coach and coachee, or group which includes: assessment, examining values and motivation, setting measurable goals, defining focused action plans, and using validated tools and techniques to help coachees develop competencies and remove blocks to achieve valuable and sustainable changes in their professional and personal lives (Skiffington and Zeus, 2003: 6).

Behavioural based coaching is possibly the most popular of the coaching models used by UK coaches in the form of the GROW model (Whitmore, 2002). While GROW and its flood of associated models (Caplan, 2003; Macintosh, 2003; Hardingham et al., 2004) has become the dominant model, few coaches recognise the behavioural based roots of the model, or reflect on the implications of this for their practice.

In this chapter the foundation stones contributing towards behavioural coaching models are illustrated and how practitioners, both psychologists and coaching practitioners, can use these as building blocks in their practice is discussed.

Development of behavioural coaching

The development of behavioural coaching has its roots in the work of Pavlov, Watson, Skinner and Bandura. Unfortunately, these generic roots have almost been lost to some of what are now considered 'non-psychological' coaching models. These behavioural based models, based on rewards and punishment, form the core of business practice. As coaching has developed within organisations, it too has primarily followed this behavioural based approach.

The most popular of the behavioural coaching models is the GROW coaching model. GROW is a four-stage coaching model developed by Graham Alexander in the 1980s. Coaches work through four stages: identifying the *Goals*, reviewing the *Reality*, generating *Options* and agreeing a *Way forward*. The approach has spawned a host of similar models, at whose heart is a focus on incremental performance improvement through new learning and adjustments to individual behaviour.

Alongside these simple models are more sophisticated behavioural coaching frameworks (Skeffington and Zeus, 2003) which take many of the GROW concepts and integrate these with the evidence-based research from behaviourist traditions, around human learning and behaviour.

Theory and basic concepts

Behaviourism's popularity is rooted in the 1920s with the work of Pavlov (1927). Pavlov uncovered the concept of conditioned reflex – a response to a situation which is an adaptation to environmental conditions. In Pavlov's classic experiment the salivation of a dog was produced not by food, but by the sound of a ringing bell. The dog was initially observed salivating at food (the unconditioned stimulus). A neutral stimulus (in this case a bell ringing) is then associated with the food. At first the bell had no effect on the dog. After consistently ringing the bell every time food appeared, the dog learned to associate the ringing bell with food. The association between the food and the bell ringing was so strong that the ringing bell alone would make the dog salivate even without the production of food. Pavlov concluded that conditioned responses could be produced in dogs or humans by creating similar kinds of associations between behaviour and rewards or punishment.

This view informed much of subsequent management writing during the pre- and post-war period, with a belief that with an appropriate stimulus behaviour change could be brought about. Much of this writing has not acknowledged its behavioural basis.

Behaviourism remained the dominant force in psychology during the 1960s and into the 1970s, developing through the work of Skinner (1974), who distinguished between two types of behaviour. One he called respondent behaviour. This followed Pavlov's classic conditioning model, in which the dog or person learns to associate a new response (such as salivation) to an existing stimulus (a ringing bell). The second type Skinner called operant behaviour. In this learning the individual tries a new behaviour, possibly through trial and error, and the behaviour is reinforced through a successful outcome.

From this, Skinner argued that both reinforcement (reward) and punishment could be used to encourage learning. The reinforcement such as a reward for behaviour would encourage repetition of that behaviour. Punishment could also be used to produce desired behaviour. This could take the form of punishment by application of a sanction immediately after the behaviour. It could also be through removal of a positive reinforcement, such as withholding a performance bonus payment. Skinner's ideas have been instrumental in organisational development.

In management today, the growth of performance related pay and appraisals are a direct link back to a belief that individual behaviour can be modified through reward and punishment, whether financial or psychological such as praise. Additionally, performance management, goal setting and the use competency frameworks all have links back to behavioural thinking.

Bandura's (1969) work took behavioural thinking into a new arena by adding social learning to the mix. He argued that behaviourism, as observed by Pavlov and Skinner, may be appropriate for lower order species, but for humans with the powers of abstract thought, learning can also take place without reinforcement. In the work of Pavlov and Skinner, the individual had to experience the stimulus or response. They had to gain the reward or punishment, and recognise its clear relationship to the behaviour.

Bandura argued that learning could also take place by observing others' successes and failures. This learning, he argued, occurs in two ways. First, through observing behaviour and imitating it, for example seeing that when other employees smile at customers a sale is a likely outcome, a person copies that behaviour. Second, the behaviour can be observed and learned, and displayed only when a reward is linked to the display of the behaviour. For example, an individual may know that smiling increases sales, but will smile only when sales targets are linked to a sales bonus. Additionally, Bandura argued, individuals were able to observe and learn from others' mistakes, for example that colleagues who argue with the boss experience an increased likelihood of personal negative outcomes at work.

Perhaps the most interesting concept Bandura proposed is that of self-efficacy – a person's belief in their own abilities. The concept is based on self-perception, and is based on how well people perceive they perform a task. Bandura argued that people with high self-efficacy perform better, as they are able to persevere longer without corresponding increases in stress. Subsequent research (Locke and Latham, 1990; Gist and Mitchell, 1992) has shown a strong relationship between high self-efficacy and high work performance.

The behavioural concepts above have contributed considerably to our thinking and practice in management, human learning and more recently, coaching. Most often the behavioural underpinnings of our thinking go unquestioned, they are so integrated into our cultural approach.

Practice

How have coaching models been influenced by behavioural concepts? The behaviourist roots of much of the current management thinking about learning and development have led us towards using 'carrot and stick' management techniques. First, we focus on observing behaviours and more recently to measuring these through competencies. Second, subsequent performance is then rewarded (or punished) through pay and appraisal schemes. Third, learning is encouraged through mentoring and role modelling.

Behavioural based coaching models encourage the coachee to design their own ways of operating to create learning and growth. Coachees are encouraged to design their own performance assessment systems and observe the impact of their behaviour on achieving their targets. Aspects that most people find satisfying – achievement, control and growth – are embedded within the behavioural based coaching models. Thus, coachees are ultimately creating their own motivating, self-rewarding system of behaviours.

GROW model

The GROW model is perhaps the most well known coaching model. GROW has four stages, and is traditionally viewed as a non-psychological model, suitable for coaches without psychological training. Using this approach, the coach adopts a Socratic learning style. Open questions help the coachee move through the four action-focused stages (see Table 5.1). The four stages are designed to assist the coachees to identify the specific behaviours that will lead to improved performance or achievement of a specific, stated goal.

Identifying the goals

The first stage in GROW involves the identification of a goal. If the aim of the coaching relationship is both to develop the individual and to assist them to enhance their work performance, what types of goals are most effective for

Table 5.1 A sample of open questions to facilitate the GROW process

Stage	Possible questions
Goal(s)	• What do you want to achieve? • What do you want from this meeting? • What do you need to know about . . .?
Reality	• What is happening? • Why is it a problem? • What do you mean by that? . . . can you give me an example? • What have you tried? . . . what happened? • How do you feel about that?
Options	• What options do you think there are? • What have you tried? • What are the pros and cons of this? • Is there anything else you could do?
Way forward	• Can you summarise what you going to do and by when? • What obstacles and objections do you expect? • How will you overcome them? • Who will you get support from? • What resources do you need? • When should we review progress?

realising these aims? Evidence from a wide range of workplace studies gives us clear guidance in this area.

First, the goal should be as challenging as possible, while remaining realistic (Locke and Latham, 1990). In practical terms goals can be made highly challenging as long as the coachee is committed to achieving them and they have the ability to do so.

Second, the goal set should be highly specific (Locke and Latham, 1990). The more precisely the goal is defined the more effectively the coachee can assess their capability to achieve the goal and know when it has been achieved. The level of specificity that is helpful is a quantifiable measure of performance on a specific task, by a due date. Additionally, greater clarity enables a better understanding between coach and coachee.

Third, the coachee has to be committed to the goal. Goals should have meaning and be motivating for the coachee. If goal commitment is not evident, the coach can work to support the coachee to tease out the likely benefits of the goal. This process of discussion within the coaching session leads to more intense cognitive processing, which in turn results in a higher likelihood of the goal being realised (Gollwitzer et al., 1990).

Fourth, the coachee has to believe in their ability to achieve the goals they set. This belief needs to be realistic, based on: an understanding of the coachee's past performance, their awareness of their own ability, understanding of the skills required for successful completion of the task and an understanding of the time required to develop any necessary new skills. Clarity regarding the dynamics of the wider business or personal environment is also important.

Fifth, short- and longer-term achievements need to be built into the coaching goals. Long-range goals impact on the degree of commitment over time (Lerner and Locke, 1995). By establishing goals, with milestones at medium-term intervals progress can be tracked and the system of self-motivating self-rewarding behaviours can be maintained. Short- and medium-term goals need to be woven together to create a longer-term vision.

Reviewing the reality

The next step in the process is exploring the reality for the coachee and how their goals fit within this. The reality of a situation is tested by drawing on current performance, coachee capability and the personal and work dynamics that impact on the current context. This process may involve self-reflection by the coachee, gathering quantitative data from the coachee on their performance, inviting the coachee to complete a 360-degree competency questionnaire or other such assessment (for example a psychometric test). The output from these activities provides a useful framework for discussion about the reality of achieving a particular goal. The output encourages reflection about different behaviours and whether these different behaviours could support the achievement of the stated goal.

Once a clear view is held about current performance, and how this is informed by behaviour, the gap between the desired performance and current performance can be seen. Using this information, the coach and coachee can together explore whether the goal is indeed realistic, especially where the gap between desired and current performance is more significant. This may result in adjusting the timeframe for achieving the goal. The outcome may be a restatement of the goal, or the creation of a series of sub-goals that build towards the final goal.

Generating options

The behaviours that can be pursued to achieve the goals and sub-goals identified are explored as part of the GROW process. The coach will draw on problem-solving skills and creative techniques to encourage the generation of multiple ideas and options to achieve the goals. The more realistic options are then identified through critical evaluation. The coach may encourage the coachee to generate clear criteria against which to evaluate the different options. The range of options is likely to include behavioural adjustments that lead to alternative ways of managing alignment with the required organisational or cultural behaviours or personal values. Through careful questioning, the coach works with the coachee to ensure balanced evaluation of the options and full exploration of the possible consequences associated with a particular course of action.

Agreeing a way forward

The final element is to identify a way forward. This may be a single course of action, but is more likely to be a series of elements which will be tested and reviewed by the coachee. The trial and error nature of testing what works has echoes of Skinner's work, but is embedded in the complexity of our work and personal lives, where in one context a behavioural adjustment may work in another it may not.

The coachee, rather than the coach, summarises the future action plan and agrees with their coach a time when progress can be reviewed. Through subsequent coaching sessions, progress is reviewed. What worked and why? What has not worked? Why not? The coachee is then able to identify further actions to test, and to continue behaviours which appear to have a positive impact on goal achievement.

The GROW model thus moves the coachee forward, towards their goals. It uses a trial and error testing of behaviours to see what works. The coachee may draw their learning from personal previous experience, observation of others or simple here and now testing. A competency framework or any other relevant behavioural framework may be used to identify desirable behaviours. While a sequential description of the elements of GROW has been presented, in reality the coach and coachee will move backwards and forwards through the element of GROW as the focus of the session requires. At the core of GROW remains the belief that the coachee can attain their goal, through developing and deploying the right behaviours.

Behavioural four-stage coaching model

Building on the GROW process, other behavioural writers have developed their own behavioural coaching models. The four-stage behavioural model is a good example (Skiffington and Zeus, 2003).

Skiffington and Zeus use four stages and seven steps (see Table 5.2). The stages of reflection, preparation and action echo much of GROW. A preliminary step is added that includes the contracting element of the coaching relationship and the initial scoping of the coaching assignment. Further, a formal maintenance stage is included, which is an important but missing element from GROW. This four-stage model integrates the aspects of goal setting, reality testing, option generation and action, creating a linear behavioural coaching process that can be more easily accessed by less experienced coachees.

The model presented by Skiffington and Zeus (2003) has elements that might be considered cognitive elements by more traditional behaviourists. It encourages coachees not only to reflect on behaviour, but also to enter the 'black box' of beliefs and emotions.

It can be argued that coaching practice in reality integrates a range of different models and processes. Thus, the behaviourist coach uses humanistic elements to build rapport, create empathy and operate non-judgementally towards their coachee. They may equally draw on cognitive coaching elements; encouraging the coachee to reflect on the beliefs which enhance or inhibit their performance. The coach may also challenge client motivation, or encourage reflection on past experiences and bring into conscious awareness issues from the unconscious.

Which clients benefit most?

Behaviourally based coaching offers a positive and, on the surface, simple framework which fits intuitively with the western philosophy of development held by managers in the workplace and most people in their lives. Managers respond to its no-nonsense, process-based pseudo-scientific framework. There are several elements that are particularly appealing, including:

- setting goals to inspire high performance
- reviewing current and past performance using behavioural frameworks to identify gaps for improvement
- brainstorming ideas, and drawing on the successes and failures of others' experiences as well as their own

Table 5.2 Four-stage model

Stage	Step	Possible questions
1 Reflection	(a) Education	• Tell me about the change model which you use? • Are you aware of the processes, boundaries and benefits of coaching? • What are your organisation's and your personal objectives? • What forces are supportive and which stand in your way to achieving your objectives? • What would a success look like at the end of this coaching intervention?
2 Preparation	(b) Data collection	• What information have you obtained from key stakeholders? • What competencies would help you address this goal? • What feedback have you received from others on your performance (behaviour) at work?
	(c) Planning	• What behaviours will help you most to achieve your goal? • What other behaviours might support this? • What events trigger the reported behaviour? • What are the consequences of the behaviour? • Who do you consider is successful in achieving this goal (acting this way)? • How do you plan to monitor your progress?
3 Action	(d) Behavioural change	• How can you acquire the skills in this new behaviour?
	(e) Measurement	• What evidence are you collecting to measure the impact of the new behaviour?
	(f) Evaluation	• How does the new behaviour impact on the initial goal which you set?
4 Maintenance	(g) Maintenance	• How can you make this new skill part of your day-to-day behaviour? • What action will you take to continue to develop these skills? • What action will you take if this behaviour does not continue to achieve the goal you set?

Source: adapted from Skiffington, S. and Zeus, P. (2003) *Behavioural Coaching: How to build sustainable personal and organisational strength.* North Ryde, NSW: McGraw-Hill Australia, Table 1.1.4, with permission.

- evaluating options against a set of criteria, agreeing an experimental action plan and reviewing how this has worked out.

In client terms behavioural based coaching approaches fit well with the already dominant behavioural traditions in western organisations. The goal setting element of behavioural based coaching supports the drive for planning, achieving performance targets and continuous improvement. These themes are everyday aspects of current management practice. Almost all managers have personal targets that are integrated into wider business and organisational goals and strategies. For the manager concerned about making positive improvements in performance, behavioural coaching offers a ready-made framework.

The behavioural models have a strong and explicit learning component. This focus is supported by the ongoing learning debates about creating learning organisations (Senge, 1994). For the manager the model offers a space to reflect and learn through observing others.

In summary, behavioural based coaching models not only feel right to those operating within the dominant western organisational culture, but also echo much of what managers do on a day-to-day basis.

Behavioural coaching approaches alone may be less suitable for working with managers with more complex issues, such as where belief systems adversely impact on behaviour or where managers lack the motivation to make a change. It is not always possible to assume that the manager is aware of the issue, acknowledges the issue as an impediment to their performance or is motivated to do something about it. In these cases, coaching psychology approaches that enable exploration of the underpinning beliefs and values that drive an individual's behaviour may provide a more effective coaching intervention.

Case study

Christine is a high performing local authority education director. At the time of our first meeting she was new to the role. I was invited in to coach Christine following her appointment as part of the organisation's commitment to support new senior manager appointments. The organisation's HR department contracted for six two-hour sessions, spaced at four to six week intervals, to support Christine through her first six months in post. The HR client agreed a confidentiality clause ensuring confidentiality of the issues discussed in the coaching relationship.

Prior to her appointment Christine had worked as assistant director in a neighbouring council and was credited with turning round the education service over a six year period. In her new role, the education service was failing and the council had been severely criticised by inspectors. Christine's appointment was seen as a step towards redressing the problems.

Session one was a fact finding and relationship building session. Could I establish a trusting working relationship with the coachee? Was the coachee willing to disclose information? What were the key issues from the coachee's perspective? What help could I as a coach offer them? What were the consistencies and inconsistencies with their assessment of the situation? What supporting evidence was there to confirm or challenge their view?

In the first meeting with Christine we focused on building our relationship. I invited Christine to tell me about her career to date, its successes and low points, the appointment process and her first 40 days since taking up the post. The message was consistently positive. A track record of success, starting with a background in teaching, progressing into education policy and then senior management positions. Christine had spent six years as assistant director in her last council role, and her move was stimulated by a head-hunter's telephone call pointing her to the job advertisement. Christine had also had some challenging times, with difficult politicians and managers, but had survived these experiences by delivering her objectives and staying focused on the task.

Christine was keen to make an impact in the post and at 51 saw this as her last job, with a desire to be in post for seven to ten years. She recognised that senior posts were exposed and that on occasions, changes in politics or a chief executive led to changes across the top team, however effective individuals may be.

Christine's main concerns were about resolving a staffing issue in her team, and to manage her time demands more effectively. Christine reported that she was working a 75 hour week, arriving at 7am and working through until 8pm before travelling home. She had periodic late meetings which would finish at around 11pm. On nights when she was home by 8pm, she would eat dinner and then maybe do further work, reading council papers before bed. She worked at weekends, for four to five hours each day. As a woman with children this had implications for both her partner and her home life.

Christine had completed a personality profile as part of the selection process. I reviewed this as part of our initial discussion and explored relationships with key stakeholders and her team.

This initial phase of the discussion took about 50 minutes. It provided good background data and meant that we had a common story which could be referred to during subsequent sessions.

I summarised the issues raised by Christine and offered an agenda for the first discussion focused around three items: staffing, time management and work–life balance. The staff issue was urgent as a probation interview was due the following week. It was clear that the time management and work–life balance issues were related and would run throughout our six sessions. I have focused on the time management issue below as one example of how we explored issues using the behavioural coaching framework.

I invited Christine to tell me about the issue as she perceived it. Christine described how due to work pressure she was working long hours. She had started to make some changes such as shortening the weekly departmental management team meeting, but these had had a limited effect. I asked Christine what she wanted to achieve. How would she know when she had improved time management? What would success look like?

Christine defined this as feeling as if she was not wasting time. My challenge was then around the work–life balance; would this look different too? Christine felt in her job she should be working about 60 hours on an average week. Again I challenged what this was based on. Christine drew on her previous experience of the hours worked by her last director. I challenged what the effect of this might be on home life, and long-term sustainability. Christine felt this was OK. Lastly I encouraged Christine to gather evidence around this time goal; what did her partner think? What did her children feel about it?

We moved on to reflect on the behaviours which she was currently working on, and how successful they had been. I challenged Christine, encouraging her to reflect on the implications of these behaviours; how might others perceive her when she took work to a meeting? I invited Christine to generate other options for creating more time in her day, and to reflect on what would be an appropriate investment of time in the role and what time would be appropriate at home with family.

One of the issues that had emerged from the initial discussion and review of Christine's personality profile was her lack of reflection about her or others' behaviours. She was strongly task focused, and rarely thought about the behaviours of others. I encouraged her to think about how others perceived her behaviour. What message was she sending to her staff? What message to her family? What discussions had she had with either about the current working hours and how this might change in the months ahead?

Christine identified a selection of new behaviours to test out; more delegation of work and adopting more of a quality assurance role on some elements. She would attend meetings where she had something to contribute, and prioritise activities each day, spending some time to create a long-term plan which assisted with assigning priority. She identified the consequences of not undertaking tasks and letting the less important tasks go. From this, Christine created an action plan.

My objective during the session had been first to build a relationship, second to gain an understanding about Christine as a person and as a manager. With these building blocks in place, I had moved in to address Christine's priorities as she saw them. I was keen to create some time for reflection and to review the output from the reflection, particularly given Christine's behavioural bias towards action.

Towards the end of the session, I invited Christine to summarise the action plan she had developed. I made some notes on the plan of action to form the basis for a review at our next meeting. The final step was an invitation to Christine to evaluate the session.

References

Bandura, A. (1969) *Principles of Behavior Modification*. New York: Holt, Rinehart and Winston.

Caplan, J. (2003) *Coaching for the Future*. London: CIPD.

Gist, M. and Mitchell, T. (1992) Self efficacy: a theoretical analysis of its determinism and malleability. *Academy of Management Review* 17(2): 183–211.

Gollwitzer, P., Heckhausen, H. and Ratajczak, K. (1990) From weighing to willing: approaching a change decision through pre or post decisional mentation. *Organisational Behaviour and Human Decision Processes* 45(1): 41–65.

Hardingham, A., Brearley, M., Moorhouse, A. and Venter, B. (2004) *The Coach's Coach: Personal development for personal developers*. London: CIPD.

Lerner, B. and Locke, E. (1995) The effects of goal setting, self efficacy, competition and personal traits on the performance of an endurance task. *Journal of Sports and Exercise Psychology* 17(2): 138–152.

Locke, E. and Latham, G. (1990) *A Theory of Goal Setting and Task Performance*. Englewood Cliffs, NJ: Prentice Hall.

Macintosh, A. (2003) *Growing on Grow: A coaching model for sales*. Available www.pmcscotland.com.

Pavlov, I. (1927) *Conditioned Reflexes*. Oxford: Oxford University Press.

Senge, P. (1994) The leader's new world: building learning organisations. In C. Mabey and P. Iles (eds) *Managing Learning*. London: Pitman.

Skiffington, S. and Zeus, P. (2003) *Behavioural Coaching: How to build sustainable personal and organisational strength*. North Ryde, NSW: McGraw-Hill.

Skinner, B. F. (1974) *About Behaviourism*. London: Jonathan Cape.

Whitmore, J. (2002) *Coaching for Performance: Growing people, performance and purpose*. London: Nicholas Brealey.

Discussion points

- Due to its no-nonsense approach, behavioural coaching is ideal for commercial settings: discuss.
- Does the GROW model lack sophistication?
- Behavioural coaching is not suited for clients who are unable to develop clear goals: discuss.
- Is the GROW model really a framework for having a coaching conversation with a client?

Suggested reading

Peltier, B. (2001) *The Psychology of Coaching: Theory and application*, Chapter 4. London: Routledge.

Skiffington, S. and Zeus, P. (2003) *Behavioural Coaching: How to build sustainable personal and organisational strength.* North Ryde, NSW: McGraw-Hill

Starr, J. (2002) *The Coaching Manual: The definitive guide to the process and skills of personal coaching.* New York: Prentice Hall.

Whitmore, J. (2002) *Coaching for Performance: Growing people, performance and purpose.* London: Nicholas Brealey.

Chapter 6

Cognitive behavioural coaching
An integrative approach

Stephen Palmer and Kasia Szymanska

Introduction

Cognitive behavioural coaching is an integrative approach which combines the use of cognitive, behavioural, imaginal and problem-solving techniques and strategies within a cognitive behavioural framework to enable coachees to achieve their realistic goals. It can improve performance, increase psychological resilience, enhance well-being, prevent stress and help to overcome blocks to change.

It is a dual systems approach as it uses problem-solving, solution-seeking and cognitive behavioural methodology to help clients overcome practical problems and deal with emotional, psychological and behavioural blocks to performance and goal achievement. An important aspect of cognitive behavioural coaching is the principle of parsimony, i.e. applying the least effort to achieve the most benefit (also known as the principle of Occam's razor).

Development of cognitive behavioural coaching

The development of cognitive behavioural coaching is intrinsically linked to the development of the cognitive behavioural and problem-solving therapies in the USA and UK. Both countries have taken a different path which will be illustrated in this section.

Historically, cognitive therapy and coaching concepts can be traced back to the philosopher Epictetus, who in the first century AD stated that individuals 'are not disturbed by things but by the view they take of them'. More recently at the beginning of the twentieth century Dr Paul Dubois, a professor at the University of Berne, developed Rational Therapy. In *The Influence of the Mind on the Body* (1906) he wrote:

> Often in some days, almost always in some weeks, they [sick people] succeed in altering their point of view, in seeing things from another angle. In proportion as they recover their mental calm under the empire

of healthy reflections, functional troubles disappear, sleep returns, the appetite arises, the body becomes stronger, and the success of this mental treatment demonstrates the supremacy of the mind over the body.

(Dubois, 1906: 58)

The behavioural psychologist, John Broadus Watson (see Watson and Rayner, 1920) is known as the 'father' of the behavioural approach. However, many years later it was other researchers and practitioners, such as Dr Joseph Wolpe, Dr Hans Eysenck, Dr Arnold Lazarus, Dr Jack Rachman, Dr John Teasdale and Dr Isaac Marks, who were more responsible for the behavioural theory being used within the therapeutic context (see Wolpe and Lazarus, 1966; Marks, 1969; Rachman and Teasdale, 1969; Lazarus 1971, 1981).

Psychiatrist Alfred Adler reintroduced the importance of cognitions in his book, *What Life Should Mean to You* (1931, 1958). He wrote: 'Meanings are not determined by situations, but we determine ourselves by the meaning we give to situations' (Adler, 1958: 14). During the 1950s, psychologist and psychoanalyst Dr Albert Ellis (1962) developed rational emotive therapy which later was renamed as rational emotive behaviour therapy (REBT). He is credited for developing the well-known ABC model of emotional disturbance. In parallel cognitive therapy was developed in the 1960s by Dr Aaron Beck (1967, 1976) while later Dr Donald Meichenbaum (1977, 1985) emphasised the relevance of self-talk in what he described as cognitive-behaviour therapy and stress inoculation training.

In the UK, during the 1980s and 1990s gradually there was a fusion of cognitive therapy with behaviour therapy and this developed into cognitive behaviour therapy (CBT) (see Curwen et al., 2000). However, rational emotive behaviour therapy had also been used with non-clinical client groups as a part of organisational rational training or stress management programmes (Ellis and Blum, 1967; Ellis, 1972; DiMattia with Mennen, 1990; Palmer, 1992; Kirby, 1993; Lange and Grieger, 1993; Richman, 1993; Palmer, 1995; Palmer and Ellis, 1995; Ellis et al., 1998). Practitioners working in private practice and undertaking organisational consultancy or training assignments started to adapt cognitive behavioural, rational emotive behavioural, problem-solving and multimodal therapies to the needs of the clients in non-clinical settings.

Cognitive behavioural coaching that has developed since the early 1990s integrates the theoretical concepts and strategies applied in cognitive behaviour, rational emotive behaviour, problem and solution-focused approaches, goal setting theory, social cognitive theory (see Falloon et al., 1984; Wasik, 1984; Bandura, 1986; D'Zurilla, 1986; Hawton and Kirk, 1989; Zimmerman, 1989; Locke and Latham, 1990; Dryden and Gordon, 1993; Palmer and Burton, 1996; Palmer, 1997a, 1997b, 2002, 2007a, 2007b; Milner and Palmer, 1998; O'Hanlon, 1998; Palmer and Neenan, 2000; Szymanska and Palmer, 2000; Neenan and Palmer, 2001a, 2001b; Anderson, 2002; Kodish, 2002;

Neenan and Dryden, 2002; Smith and Kjeldsen, 2004; Edgerton and Palmer, 2005; Auerbach, 2006; Neenan, 2006; Palmer and Gyllensten, 2008).

When comparing the development of cognitive behavioural coaching in the UK and the USA the key difference is that in the UK its practice has focused on personal, life, business, executive, stress management and health coaching arenas whereas in the USA Cognitive Coaching[SM], developed by Costa and Garmston (2002) in 1985, has focused on supporting the pursuit of excellence in teaching (Sawyer, 2003). Its main premise is that teachers who are able to think at higher levels will produce students who are better problem-solvers, higher achieving and more cooperative. It is a supervisory or peer coaching model that focuses on and enhances the teacher's cognitive processes.

There have been many research studies into Cognitive Coaching[SM] (see Edwards, 2004). Researchers have found that Cognitive Coaching[SM] increases teacher efficacy (e.g. Dutton, 1990), increases satisfaction with the teaching profession (Edwards et al., 1998), improves collaboration (Alseike, 1997) and increases teacher reflection (Smith, 1997). Although Cognitive Coaching[SM] has been primarily used in the field of education it could be used with other client groups and settings too.

As cognitive behavioural coaching has been applied to a wider range of settings and client groups than Cognitive Coaching[SM], the rest of this chapter will focus on the cognitive behavioural approach.

Theory and basic concepts

There are two basic premises of cognitive behavioural coaching: a person may have underdeveloped problem-solving skills or may not apply those skills they already have successfully when under pressure or stress; the way a person feels or behaves is largely determined by the beliefs they hold and their appraisal of the particular situation or problem. In addition, the resulting negative emotions such as anxiety can interfere with their performance. The approach aims to help individuals to improve their problem-solving skills, become aware of their thinking and to support them in modifying beliefs that are performance interfering, stress inducing and goal blocking. Cognitive behavioural coaching helps coachees to develop action plans for the future with the ultimate goal in helping individuals to become their own self-coaches. These plans may include solution-seeking strategies. Within work contexts, the approach often focuses on enhancing or maximising perform-ance under pressure.

Five interactive modalities: SPACE

There is reciprocity between four modalities, Physiology, Action, Cognitions, Emotions (known as **PACE**) and the external environment, the Social context.

Cognitive behavioural coaching may target these five areas for change in helping coachees to achieve their goals. Edgerton created a convenient acronym **SPACE** (see Edgerton and Palmer, 2005):

- Social context
- Physiology
- Action
- Cognitions
- Emotions.

The **SPACE** model or framework can be used as an educational tool to highlight the link between the modalities, for assessment purposes and the development of a coaching programme. For example an individual who is going for a job interview (Social context) may perceive that the situation is going to be difficult (Cognition/appraisal). This negative appraisal is likely to trigger anxiety (Emotion), their physical response to anxiety may be an increase in sweating and bodily tension (Physiological) and they may start to pace up and down the waiting room (Action/behaviour). This can be noted down in a diagrammatic format on paper or a whiteboard using the SPACE framework.

Assessment

A key feature in cognitive behavioural coaching is assessment and case conceptualisation which commences in the first coaching session and if required is revised throughout the course of the coaching. Essentially, biographical data together with information about the coachees' reason for attending and their goals are collected and conceptualised within the cognitive framework and shared with the coachee. In brief coaching often SPACE, ABCDEF framework and/or the seven-step PRACTICE solution-seeking framework can serve as a simple case conceptualisation (Palmer, 2002, 2007a). A cognitive behavioural case conceptualisation helps to connect theory with practice, and provides a guide or template for the appropriate use of techniques and strategies applied in a systematic manner. In coaching there is no need for an in-depth assessment and case conceptualisation unless a particular problem or issue is difficult to resolve. Generally the conceptualisation is developed and shared with the coachee as it aids collaboration and provides the coachee with the opportunity to understand their issues from a cognitive behavioural framework and thus ultimately become their own self-coach (also see Wills and Sanders, 1997).

Problem-solving and solution-seeking framework: PRACTICE

Due to the problem-orientated, goal and solution-focused nature of cognitive behavioural coaching, time is not spent on in-depth cognitive assessment and interventions if these are considered unnecessary by the coach and coachee. This reflects the dual systems approach, focusing on either or both the psychological and practical issues involved in an attempt to help the coachee achieve their goals. Therefore a practical solution-seeking framework such as **PRACTICE** (Palmer, 2007a) may be used instead at some stage during coaching. The steps are described below.

Steps	Questions/actions
1 **P**roblem identification	What's the problem or issue?
	What would you like to change?
	Any exceptions when it is not a problem?
	Any distortions or can the problem or issue be viewed differently?
2 **R**ealistic, relevant goals developed (e.g. SMART goals)	What do you want to achieve?
3 **A**lternative solutions generated	What are your options?
4 **C**onsideration of consequences	What could happen?
	How useful is each possible solution?
	Rating scale: 1–10
5 **T**arget most feasible solution(s)	What is the most feasible solution(s)?
6 **I**mplementation of **C**hosen solution(s)	Go and do it (use manageable steps).
7 **E**valuation	How successful was it?
	Rating scale: 1–10
	What can be learnt?
	Can we finish coaching now?

If the proposed solution has been successful, then the person can select another problem he or she wishes to tackle and follow steps 1–6 again. It is important to tackle methodically one major problem at a time rather than several problems simultaneously. However, if the client had become stuck at a particular step in the framework due to an emotional or psychological block, for example, very anxious about implementing the agreed strategy, then the coach would probably use the ABCDEF model to help assess and then deal with the block to change.

Neenan and Palmer (2001a, 2001b) suggest that once coachees become adept at using the seven-step model, they may want to use a shorter model to quicken the problem-solving process. For example:

- **STIR**: **S**elect problem; **T**arget a solution; **I**mplement a solution; **R**eview outcome
- **PIE**: **P**roblem definition; **I**mplement a solution; **E**valuate outcome.

These shorter models of problem-solving are usually used for rapid process-ing of a problem in order to deal with a crisis or make a quick decision. With these shorter models, deliberation is exchanged for speed, so a less satisfactory outcome may be experienced by the person.

PRACTICE case study

Neenan and Palmer (adapted from 2001a) describe a coaching case study using the seven-step framework instead of immediately using the cognitive framework:

Step 1: Problem identification

Brian (not his real name) was presenting an important paper at a conference in a few weeks' time and was feeling anxious about it. The 'it' needed to be explored in order to make the problem clear and precise:

Coach: What exactly is the 'it': presenting the paper or something else?

Brian: It's the shaking. The audience will see my hands shaking and think I'm a nervous wreck. I won't be able to control the shaking.

Coach: You state the problem as if there is nothing you can do about the shaking. How could you restate the problem in ways that suggest change is possible?

Brian: Presently, I find it difficult to control my shaking when speaking to audiences.

Step 2: Realistic, relevant goals developed

Coach: What would you like to achieve with regard to your shaking?

Brian: To control it so my hands shake less or not at all.

Coach: And if neither of those goals could be achieved by the time of the conference?

Brian: To accept the shaking without getting too worried about it.

Step 3: Alternative solutions generated

Brian was encouraged to come up with as many solutions as possible to his problem no matter how stupid or ludicrous they initially sounded; in other words, to brainstorm. The coach can suggest some solutions if the person has difficulty generating them. The solutions proposed by Brian were:

(a) 'Keep my hands in my pocket the whole time if possible.'

(b) 'Not present the paper. Pretend I'm ill.'
(c) 'Mention my nervousness to the audience to justify the shaking just before I give my paper. Get it out of the way.'
(d) 'Take tranquillisers.'
(e) 'Accept that my hands shake. So what?'
(f) 'Make a joke every time my hands shake.'
(g) 'Give the paper and see what happens rather than automatically assuming the conference will turn out badly for me.'

Step 4: Consideration of consequences

This involved Brian considering the advantages and disadvantages of each solution generated from the brainstorming session. Brian rated the plausibility of each possible solution on a 0–10 scale (0 = least plausible to 10 = most plausible).

(a) 'I would look pretty stiff and awkward if I did that. I can't avoid using my hands while presenting the paper.' 2
(b) 'That sounds good initially but that would be running away and make it much harder to go before an audience at a later date. A non-starter.' 0
(c) 'That might release some tension but it might also suggest I'm asking for their sympathy. A double-edged sword.' 3
(d) 'I don't want the chemical way out. I might come across as somewhat dulled.' 4
(e) 'I like the sound of this one very much and can see the benefits I would reap.' 9
(f) 'This might bring too much unwanted attention to my shaking.' 3
(g) 'This is a reasonable way to approach the conference.' 7

Step 5: Target most feasible solution(s)

Brian chose steps (e) and (g) though he said if these steps were unsuccessful he might choose the tranquillisers (step d) as a last resort. How, he enquired, was he supposed to learn to accept the fact that his hands shook when he usually demanded 'they must not shake'? (a performance interfering thought or PIT).

Coach: What happens when you say that to yourself?
Brian: It just continually reminds me that I can't control the shaking, I get worried and then my hands shake even more.
Coach: So in order to gain control over your shaking, what do you need to give up?

Brian: Stop demanding that my hands must not shake. Just let it happen and don't get alarmed about it.

Coach: Exactly. What happens when you try to hide it from others?

Brian: I feel awkward and self-conscious. So try and be natural around others. My shaking is part of me, that sort of thing. But what happens if people smirk at me or think I'm a nervous wreck? How do I control that?

Coach: Well, what can you control and what can you not?

Brian: I can't control their smirking or what they might think about me but I can control or choose how I respond to it and how I think about myself.

Coach: That's it in a nutshell.

Brian: Let's get going then.

Step 6: Implementation of Chosen solution(s)

In the next few weeks, Brian said he no longer tried to hide or control his hands shaking and explained to others that he got nervous in front of audiences both large and small – 'My first step towards accepting the problem and myself for having it'. He said he would like to have a 'rehearsal' before the actual conference. The coach arranged with his colleagues for Brian to present a paper to them. Feedback was given regarding his performance such as not gripping the lectern too tightly and having more sips of water to avoid his voice cracking. A video of the rehearsal was made so Brian could see both his strengths and weaknesses and also re-evaluate more accurately his overall performance: 'Not as bad as I thought. It's hard to be objective about yourself when you're actually doing the talk and thinking you are coming across as a nervous wreck,' he concluded.

Step 7: Evaluation

Brian said that the strategies of 'giving up demands for control in order to gain control and striving for self-acceptance had worked a treat' (he never did resort to tranquillisers). While he had been nervous and his hands did shake at times, his major focus had been on presenting the paper rather than his own discomfort. On the lectern was a message encapsulating his new outlook: 'If I shake, so what?'

The ABCDEF coaching model

Albert Ellis (1962) developed the ABC model of emotion in which 'A' represents the activating event or adversity, 'B' represents beliefs about the event and 'C' the emotional, physiological and behavioural consequences. Ellis asserts that the key disturbance creating beliefs at B are usually rigid, inflexible, non-empirical, illogical and not functional. He called these 'irrational beliefs' and distinguishes between them and inferences people make about situations (the latter being of less importance in his opinion). The job interview example can be represented in ABC terms:

A (Activating event)
- Job interview

B (Beliefs about A)
- This job interview will be difficult and possibly awful
- I must perform well at the job interview
- I could not stand failing the interview

C (Consequences)
- High anxiety (emotion)
- Paces up and down waiting room; reduced performance in interview (behaviour)
- Sweats, palpitations, tension in back and shoulders (physiological).

In practice, during the session the coach would work collaboratively with the coachee and note down this cognitive behavioural assessment of the coachee's problem on a whiteboard or flipchart to aid the coachee's conceptual understanding of the cognitive model. Often at the beginning stage of coaching the intellectual insight for the coachee is that it is their thinking which largely contributes to their emotional distress and under-performance, not the situation itself. However, emotional or 'gut' insight takes more time to develop as the coachee needs to put into practice newly formed helpful, stress ameliorating and performance enhancing thoughts and beliefs and then observe how their own level of distress decreases and their performance increases. The term 'irrational beliefs' is not used within a coaching context as coachees can sometimes view 'irrational' as pejorative or even as an insult. Thinking errors and performance interfering thoughts (PITs) are preferable terms.

Dr Ellis's ABC model of disturbance includes two additional stages, 'D' representing disputation and modification of the unhelpful beliefs and 'E' for the effective new approach to dealing with the Activating event. Palmer (2002) added a further stage for the coaching arena, 'F', which represents the future focus on personal or work goals and the learning from the ABCDE process which may enhance future performance and may protect against future stress. Thus they gradually shift from intellectual to emotional insight. Returning to our illustrations, examples of questions and responses are added below:

D (Disputation)
- Will the job interview really be awful? Realistically the interview may be difficult but hardly awful.

- Why must you perform well? It's strongly preferable to perform well, but I don't have to.
- Is it true you can't stand failing at tasks? I'm living proof I've survived everything in my life so far although I may not like some of the things.

E (Effective new approach)
- Goal focused beliefs focusing on the interview; feels concern and not anxiety; stops pacing room; reduced physiological responses, e.g. less tense.

F (Future focus)
- Focus remains on achieving work goals. Learns to be less anxious attending interviews. Becomes less rigidly perfectionistic and learns not to demand that 'I must perform well'.

The full model includes the initial development of specific Goals which leads to G – ABCDEF. In coaching the G – ABCDEF model is often referred to as a model of stress, performance, resilience and well-being (Palmer, 2007b). This takes the original model beyond just dealing with clinical conditions into the workplace by focusing on the positive such as enhancing performance.

Unlike Ellis's ABCDE model of emotional disturbance described above, the cognitive approach based on the work of Beck (see Curwen et al., 2000) asserts that there are three levels of cognitions which may need to be addressed:

Automatic thoughts
- 'pop-up' thoughts or images: *I might make a mistake*

Intermediate beliefs
- Attitudes: *I couldn't stand making mistakes*
- Rules: *I must not make mistakes*
- Assumptions: *If I make a mistake it proves I'm stupid*

Core beliefs
- Usually formed in childhood or early adolescence and may be rigid: *I'm stupid*.

Therefore, the actual cognitive behavioural approach the coach uses will influence their assessment and practice of coaching. A key cognitive behavioural coaching text has incorporated both the theory driven deductive Ellis approach and the inductive Beckian approaches although this would not be obvious to the untrained reader (Neenan and Dryden, 2002). Others are more explicit in the cognitive behavioural approach they are using, such as, Palmer et al. (2003), who describe multimodal self-coaching.

It is worth noting that while cognitive behavioural coaching is predominately ahistorical and focuses on the present and the future, it does take into account, when relevant, the impact of developmental experiences. These may be important as often core beliefs which are deep-seated beliefs usually developed as a result of childhood or adolescent experiences or significant life events, under certain circumstances influence the individual's conscious belief systems and behaviours. For example, the chief executive officer (CEO) of a multinational company may, as a result of childhood parental criticism and high expectations, have developed perfectionist intermediate beliefs and a core belief associated with failure, which in many ways generally impacted on their career progression in a positive way and led to them being described as 'driven' and 'ambitious'. However, to meet their high standards the CEO may work an 80-hour week and their work–life balance is poor. The CEO is sensitive to criticism and poor business performance can trigger one of their intermediate beliefs, in this case an underlying assumption, 'If I don't do a perfect job then I'm a failure' and thereby activating their core belief, 'I'm a failure'. Understandably this may result in the CEO feeling clinically depressed and reducing their work performance even further.

The effectiveness of cognitive behavioural coaching

The efficacy of cognitive behavioural therapy has been firmly established for a range of clinical disorders such as depression and anxiety (Dobson, 1989; Gloaguen et al., 1998; National Institute for Health and Clinical Excellence (NICE), 2005). This is in contrast to the evidence base for the efficacy of solution-focused cognitive behavioural coaching which has only recently started to increase as the use of cognitive and behavioural strategies within the coaching arena is relatively new. Grant's (2001) research found improvements in mental health, self-regulation and self-concept with cognitive-based coaching whereas behavioural coaching improved academic performance. A combination of both cognitive and behavioural coaching led to enhanced performance which was maintained over time and enhanced well-being. Grant also demonstrated that cognitive interventions alone did not necessarily lead to increased academic outcomes. Simply put, cognitive insight alone may not lead to desired behavioural outcomes without the skills training or practice. Other research has found an improvement in the quality of life and improvement in goal attainment (Grant, 2003); increase in goal striving, well-being and hope (Green et al., 2005, 2006); reduction of stress using a self-help manual based on a cognitive behavioural self-coaching approach for managers; significantly reduced stress (Grbcic and Palmer, 2006a, 2006b, 2007); enhanced a male finance executive's sales performance, core self-evaluation, and global self-ratings of performance (Libri and Kemp, 2006).

Practice

Goals of cognitive behavioural coaching

The overall goals of cognitive behavioural coaching are

- to help the coachee achieve their realistic goals
- to ameliorate and resolve difficulties or problems
- to help the coachee acquire new skills and constructive coping strategies
- to help the client modify thinking errors, stress inducing thinking (SIT), performance interfering thoughts (PITs), negative automatic thoughts (NATs) and, when necessary, intermediate and core beliefs
- to help the client develop thinking skills, stress alleviating thinking (SAT), performance enhancing thoughts (PETs) and, when necessary, realistic and helpful intermediate and core beliefs
- to help the coachee become their own 'self-coach'.

Structure of coaching session and in-between session assignments

A structured approach similar to the session format used in cognitive behaviour therapy can be useful as it allows the coachee to negotiate a working agenda for the session with the coach so that the time available is maximised (Curwen et al., 2000). Both are able to raise issues that they think are relevant to the current session and the overall coaching programme (Palmer and Dryden, 1995). It also reflects the solution-focused nature of cognitive behavioural coaching. The structure is as follows:

1 Briefly check client's present state, e.g. 'How have you been recently?'
2 Negotiate an agenda for the session, e.g. 'What would you like to put on the session agenda today?'
3 Review in-between session assignment(s), e.g. 'How did you get on with the task last week?'
4 Target issue or problem, e.g. 'Let's now tackle the agenda item for today.'
5 Negotiate in-between session assignment(s).
6 Session feedback, e.g. 'Any feedback on today's session?'

The word 'homework' is generally avoided in coaching sessions as often it has negative memories for many coachees. The terms 'assignment' or 'in-between session assignment' are preferable. Reviewing the in-between session assignment(s) that were negotiated in the previous session is a crucial aspect of coaching. If this is overlooked, then the key message the coachee will learn is that undertaking assignments is unimportant so why bother doing them. The cognitive behavioural coach may remind the client how important the other 167 hours outside the coaching hour are for putting action plans, techniques and strategies into action. Important information can often be discovered focusing on how the assignments were undertaken. Problems encountered or assignments not undertaken are all 'grist to the mill' and are useful learning points in coaching.

Problem acquisition and maintenance

Cognitive behavioural theory sees problem development as multifactorial and contributing factors include life events, such as marital problems, redundancy, bullying, bereavement, illness; social factors, such as loneliness, poor housing, poor work–life balance and inadequate or unhelpful coping strategies such as increased alcohol consumption, aggressive behaviour, cognitive and behavioural avoidance; work problems such as work-related stress, an increase in work hours to manage workload, poor performance at work; and environmental stressors such as noisy workplaces. Skills deficits, genetic factors and childhood experiences may all contribute or exacerbate problems. At an individual level, although some of these problems may be amenable to coaching, due to the level of distress triggered by some of the above, professional counselling may be a more appropriate intervention.

Problems are often maintained by avoidance in dealing with the issues concerned; by skills deficits; stress inducing and performance interfering thoughts, thinking errors, intermediate and core beliefs that block the person from achieving realistic goals. These can become the focus of cognitive behavioural coaching or for disturbed clients with clinical disorders, therapy would be recommended.

Typical structure of a course of cognitive behavioural coaching

Palmer (adapted from 2007a) suggests a typical structure to a coaching programme:
Sessions:

1–2 Simple dual systems case formulation (e.g. SPACE, ABCDEF, PRAC-TICE), goal-setting and intervention. Probable focus on achieving SMART goals (see Locke and Latham, 1990; Locke, 1996). (Sessions could be of 60 to 120 minutes' duration.)
2–4 Some continuing assessment, if necessary, otherwise coaching focuses on working on achieving goals.
2–6 Focus on psychological blocks if these are impeding goal or task progress. Requires full assessment specific to a particular problem.
1–8 Coaching likely to finish with most clients reporting that it was effective (Gyllensten and Palmer, 2005).

The length of sessions may be between 30 and 120 minutes depending upon the time urgency to deal with a work-related issue, whereas life or personal coaching is more likely to be of 60 minutes' duration. Coaching may be for only a few sessions in total. The marketing of rigid coaching programmes of a specific number of sessions to organisations and employers is not advocated as it is contrary to what an employee may actually require to enhance their performance.

Cognitive techniques and strategies

There are a wide range of cognitive techniques and strategies. In this section we will cover the main ones.

Identifying thinking errors

Originally called 'cognitive distortions' in cognitive therapy (Curwen et al., 2000) they are more commonly known as thinking errors in cognitive behavioural coaching and training settings (Palmer et al., 2003). These are errors of processing in which the person cognitively focuses on insufficient or inappropriate data and draws illogical conclusions, makes inaccurate inferences or bases predicted outcomes upon little or no empirical evidence. A handout or a cognitive behavioural self-coaching book (e.g. Palmer et al., 2003; Palmer and Cooper, 2007) is usually given to the coachee to help them understand and recognise the different thinking errors they commonly use.

Thinking errors include the following:

- *Mind reading/jumping to conclusions*: jumping to a foregone conclusion without the relevant information, e.g. 'If I don't work overtime I'll get sacked.'
- *All-or-nothing thinking*: evaluating experiences on the basis of extremes such as 'excellent or 'awful', e.g. 'She always arrives late.'
- *Blame*: not taking responsibility and blaming somebody or something else for the problem, e.g. 'It's all her fault. She should have reminded me to post the letter.'
- *Personalisation*: taking events personally, e.g. 'If our team presentation is rejected, it's my fault.'
- *Fortune-telling*: assuming you always know what the future holds, e.g. 'I know I'll be made redundant next week.'
- *Emotional reasoning*: mistaking feelings for facts, e.g. 'I feel so nervous; I know this merger with fall apart.'
- *Labelling*: using labels or global ratings to describe yourself and others, e.g. 'I'm a total idiot' or 'As I failed my exam this proves I'm a complete failure.'
- *Demands*: peppering your narrative with rigid or inflexible thinking such as 'shoulds' and 'musts': making demands of yourself and others, e.g. 'He should have made a better job of that project.'
- *Magnification or awfulising*: blowing events out of all proportion, e.g. 'That meeting was the worst I've ever attended. It was awful.'

- *Minimisation*: minimising the part one plays in a situation, e.g. 'It must have been an easy exam as I got a good mark.'
- *Low frustration tolerance or 'I can't stand it-itis'*: we lower our tolerance to frustrating or stressful situations by telling ourselves, e.g. 'I can't stand it'.
- *Phoneyism*: believing that you may get found out by significant others as a phoney or impostor, e.g. 'If I perform badly, they will see the real me – a total fraud.'

Thinking skills

There is a range of thinking skills coaches can use to help coachees to tackle their thinking errors. Palmer and Strickland (adapted from 1996) summarise them as follows:

Writing down your thinking errors

When you are underperforming, procrastinating or feeling stressed, ask yourself what thinking errors you are making and note them down. You will then be in a better position to avoid them.

Befriend yourself

If a friend or colleague made a similar mistake, would you be as critical or harsh as you are towards yourself? Turn your internal critical voice around and do not ignore your positive aspects.

Relative thinking

If you are viewing a situation or outcome in absolute terms, such as awful versus excellent, attempt to find some middle ground. This will help you to keep the situation in perspective. Generally, situations and people are too complex to view in such extreme terms.

Look for the evidence

Sometimes our assessment of a situation is flawed. If you believe your performance was poor, ask others for feedback, rather than making assumptions which may be inaccurate. If you do not believe that you can stand staying in a situation, test it out, stay a few minutes longer.

De-labelling

Avoid globally rating yourself or others. We are too complex to be rated a 'total idiot' or 'complete failure'. As soon as you label people or yourself by a particular behaviour, question the validity of the label. For example, if you call yourself or a colleague 'a complete fool' because a deadline was not reached, does this one failing justify the label? You may wish to consider learning self-acceptance, literally accepting yourself, warts and all, with a strong preference to improve, but you do not have to.

Thinking more coolly

Emotive language, such as the 'musts', 'shoulds', 'oughts', 'have tos', 'it's awful' and 'I can't stand it', tends to increase stress levels and interfere with performance. Less emotive expressions should help us to remain cool: 'It's preferable', 'it's strongly desirable', and so on. This thinking skill needs to be practised on a daily basis, not just when a major difficulty arises. Practise this thinking skill regularly, but be careful you are not suppressing your feelings in the process.

Broaden the picture

When you feel that you are totally responsible for a situation or problem, write a list of all the other aspects involved and clarify whether you really are 100 per cent to blame. A pie chart can be drawn and divided up into the responsibility of each person or aspect.

If you totally blame others, you can repeat this process and include all the other relevant factors involved. Rarely are others totally to blame either.

Guided discovery and Socratic questions to examine thinking and challenge performance interfering thoughts (PITs)

Guided discovery is a process where the coach and coachee work collaboratively to view the world or particular problem differently. It uses questioning based on the systematic questioning and inductive reasoning developed by the fifth-century philosopher, Socrates. It is used to help PIT identification and modification. Some of the common Socratic questions the coach uses to examine the validity of PITS are listed below (adapted from Palmer and Dryden, 1995; Leahy and Holland, 2000; Palmer et al., 2003):

- Where is the evidence for your belief?
- What impact is this way of thinking having on you?
- Are you jumping to conclusions?
- Is there any evidence to disprove your belief?
- Are you concentrating on your weaknesses and neglecting your strengths?
- What are the pros and cons of thinking this way?
- Are you taking things too personally?
- Are you thinking in all-or-nothing terms?

- Are you using double standards?
- Are you overestimating the chances of something bad happening?
- Are you predicting the outcome instead of experimenting with it?
- Are you mind reading here?
- Are you expecting total perfection?
- What practical strategies can you adopt to convince yourself of the inaccuracy of your thinking?

Beck describes a dialogue with a student with fear of exams who is using all-or-nothing thinking and labelling. He demonstrates the use of Socratic dialogue to aid guided discovery (Beck, 1993: 363):

Client:	I feel terrible today.
Therapist:	Why?
Client:	I feel like a failure. I really blew the exam.
Therapist:	What do you think you got?
Client:	A really bad score?
Therapist:	50, 60, 70?
Client:	80, I guess.
Therapist:	Does that mean you failed?
Client:	No, but I didn't do as well as I wanted.
Therapist:	What did you want?
Client:	At least 90 per cent.
Therapist:	So anything less than a 90 is a failure?
Client:	Sounds silly, but I guess that's right . . . OK, I didn't blow it, but I wish I had done better.

By this process the client can start to perceive their world differently by gently examining their beliefs and perceptions.

Survey method

To avoid making assumptions or mind reading the coachee is encouraged to conduct a survey of other people's opinions such as colleagues or friends in order to confirm or refute their thinking.

Use of forms

Forms can be used to focus on, evaluate and replace PITs with adaptive performance enhancing thoughts (PETs). These PIT/PET forms used in cognitive behavioural coaching were developed by Neenan and Palmer at the Centre for Coaching. There are two-column and five-column versions (see case study). These forms have been adapted and can be used in coaching when coachees are feeling stressed about a specific situation. The focus is on modifying stress inducing thinking (SIT) to stress alleviating thinking (SAT).

Downward arrow

The process for uncovering underlying assumptions or core beliefs is known as the downward arrow technique. It was developed by Burns (1990) and involves articulating the implications of the coachee's negative automatic thoughts (NATs). They are temporally assumed to be true and their meaning sought.

Coachee: I know that I'm going to fail this promotion interview.
Coach: Let's suppose that happens, what does that mean to you?
Coachee: That I will be stuck in this job forever, with nowhere to go.
Coach: And if that was the case, what would that mean to you?
Coachee: I'm just not good enough, even a promotion is impossible for me.

In the above example, the core belief is 'I'm not good enough'. Having elicited the core belief, the coach can then go on to work with the coachee to modify it (see below).

Inference chaining

When undertaking an ABCDEF assessment and intervention as described previously, the coach may undertake a technique known as inference chaining to discover what aspect of the problem or activating event (A) the client is really troubled about, the critical 'A'. Often the initial problem noted is not the real underlying fear. In inference chaining the client's fears are not challenged, and temporarily, it is assumed that they could occur. The coach reinforces B–C thinking (i.e. the link between beliefs and the emotional consequences) and avoids using A–C language (i.e. the link between an activating event and emotional consequences). An example is given in the case study.

Although this technique is similar to the downward arrow, it is focusing on eliciting the critical 'A' or critical aspect of the activating event that is the greater concern to the client and then eliciting the associated beliefs whereas the downward arrow is seeking the underlying assumption and core belief.

Cost-benefit analysis of core beliefs

David Burns (1990) suggests that doing a cost-benefit analysis of a core belief highlighting the advantages and disadvantages of holding on to it before going on to revise the schema is a useful tool. In addition Greenberger and Padesky (adapted from 1995) have outlined a simple three-step process for changing schema:

1 Listing experiences which indicate that the core belief is not 100 per cent true.
2 Writing down a revised belief and then underneath it listing experiences that support the revised belief.
3 Finally rating confidence in the revised belief on a regular basis.

Bibliotherapy and bibliotraining

Bibliotherapy is the use by coachees of relevant self-help manuals, books, videos, DVDs, audiotapes and websites, at the coach's suggestion, in order to gain knowledge about their particular problem. However, in coaching and training settings, as the term includes the word 'therapy', often practitioners change it to bibliotraining or bibliocoaching instead (see Palmer and Burton, 1996).

Imagery techniques

Key imagery techniques that cognitive behavioural coaches use include motivation imagery, coping imagery, time projection imagery, imaginal exposure, positive imagery, mastery imagery, guilt reduction imagery, anger reduction imagery, rational emotive imagery (see Lazarus, 1984; Palmer and Dryden, 1995; Ellis et al., 1998; Palmer et al., 2003; Palmer and Puri, 2006).

Motivation imagery

Motivation imagery is in two parts (Palmer and Neenan, 1998). Initially coachees are encouraged to visualise the rest of their lives without tackling their particular problem and not achieving their desired goal (inaction imagery). Then they imagine how their future unfolds without the particular problem after having worked hard to deal with it (action imagery). This technique is used to motivate coachees who are reluctant or ambivalent about addressing problems or issues in their lives.

Coping imagery

Coachees are encouraged to visualise themselves coping with a problem or situation they are stressed and anxious about (Palmer et al., 2003). It includes imagining how they would deal with predicted problems that they fear might arise such as arriving late for an important meeting. Coping imagery should not be confused with mastery imagery in which the person envisions doing everything perfectly.

Behavioural strategies

Cognitive behavioural coaches use an array of behavioural strategies to support coachees in the management of psychological problems and to test out their PETs and core beliefs. Examples of some of the more common strategies are listed in this section.

Time management strategies

Poor time management skills are a common problem encountered in cognitive behavioural coaching. Together with tackling the PITs associated with procrastination (e.g. 'This is just too hard, I'll do it later') individuals are educated in applying effective time management strategies such as prioritising, list making and so on.

Assertion training and communication skills

Assertion is often mistaken for aggression in the minds of coachees and features strongly in cases of bullying. Cognitive behavioural coaching educates coachees on the differences between the two, elicits and evaluates PITs or blocks to assertion and uses role play and/or experiments to reinforce new behaviour.

Relaxation

Relaxation strategies are commonly used to decrease physical arousal. Relaxation scripts can be narrated in session or coachees are encouraged to invest in good relaxation tapes and CDs which outline the process of progressive muscle relaxation.

Behavioural experiments

Behavioural experiments are a key component of cognitive behavioural coaching. They can be applied within the coaching session or outside with friends or in the workplace as part of the coachee's in-between session task or assignment. The experiments are designed in a collaborative manner, recorded and reviewed. For example, a coachee who believes their voice will dry up when giving a presentation (prediction) plans an experiment which involves giving a mock presentation to colleagues at work and records the outcome.

The process of change

The process of change involves a number of steps for coachees:

1   The acquisition and refinement of both practical and emotion-focused problem-solving and solution-focused skills.
2   Identifying, challenging and changing of their inflexible performance interfering and stress inducing thinking, attitudes and beliefs.
3   Development of a flexible style of thinking to have performance enhancing and stress alleviating thinking, attitudes and beliefs.
4   Development of high frustration tolerance, greater self-acceptance and increased physiological resilience.

Which clients benefit most?

Cognitive behavioural coaching based on the cognitive behavioural, practical problem-solving and solution-seeking methodologies have benefited clients who wish to enhance or improve workplace or scholarly performance, public speaking, well-being, time management, decision-making, problem-solving, emotional and anger management. It can assist in overcoming procrastination, lack of assertiveness, career change indecision, stress and anxiety such as presentation anxiety. The approach can be used with children, adolescents, adults and older people, and applied in individual, group, school, health and work settings (see Palmer, 2007c).

Failures with coachees in cognitive behavioural coaching (adapted from Neenan and Palmer, 2000: 217) can be due to coachees:

- not accepting *emotional responsibility* – thereby blaming other factors (e.g. their manager, job or partner) for causing their problems and expecting that these other factors should change before they do, and/or
- not accepting *coaching responsibility* – they avoid or resist the hard work required of them to tackle their practical and/or emotional problems or blocks to change, and/or
- having a *clinical disorder(s)* – some clinical disorders such as depression can considerably reduce motivation and goal-focused behaviour.

Case study

Mark was a consultant, 35 years old, married with two children. He had just been offered promotion within a large petroleum company. He was keen to accept the post. However, there was a work-related problem he wanted to tackle. He will need to give presentations to the top team at head office on a monthly basis. Although he usually can do presentations without encountering much difficulty, he is becoming anxious about this task.

Engagement

As Mark was keen to take the job, he decided to have coaching in order to deal with his presentation anxiety. Initial contact was by email via HR. The coaching psychologist and Mark met in Mark's current office. It was noted that Mark had counselling previously but did not find it particularly helpful. Dealing with workplace presentation anxiety could come under the remit of coaching.

They agreed to review progress after three coaching sessions each lasting two hours. Additional sessions could be negotiated if necessary.

Presentation anxiety

On listening to Mark describe the problem it became apparent within the first ten minutes that he was reasonably skilled at giving presentations and his levels of stress were more likely to be due to his thinking about the presentation and not his abilities and skills to give it. In applying the principle of parsimony, the coaching psychologist concluded that there was no need to use the PRACTICE model at this stage of coaching.

The coaching psychologist completed a SPACE diagram with Mark to show the relationship between the modalities (see Figure 6.1).

Mark was able to see the connections between the four modalities and the social context. However, Mark was unable to access his beliefs easily. As part of the assessment to ensure that they were focusing on the most relevant problem and cognitions, they undertook an inference chain:

Coach: I suspect that when you are feeling stressed about the presentation you have additional thoughts on your mind that are possibly relevant. It would be really useful for us to discover what these are and also to see if we are focusing on the correct issue. Are you OK about me asking you a few more questions to see if we elicit this information?

Mark: Fine.

Coach: Once you get your new job, how do you feel emotionally about giving a presentation to the top team? (Clarifying the emotion.)

Mark: Pretty anxious.

Coach: Let's assume that you start to give the presentation to the top team, what are you anxious about? (Staying focused on the relevant emotion targeted for change.)

Mark: I'll screw up.

Coach: Let's assume for the moment you do screw up. You may find it easier if you close your eyes and really imagine you are screwing up. Can

SPACE

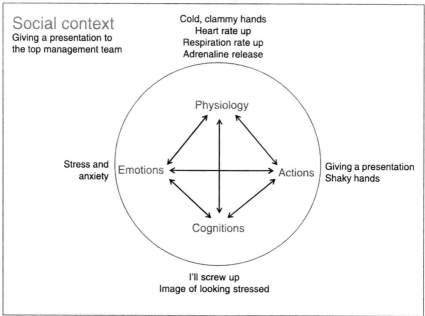

Figure 6.1 Space model.

you see it happening? (Helping the client to access his thoughts in the situation being discussed.)

Mark: Yes.

Coach: Now what are you most anxious about then?

Mark: They will think I'm useless?

Coach: And if they did think you were useless, then what?

Mark: I suppose I could jeopardise my new job?

Coach: Let's just assume for the moment that you did jeopardise your job what would you be anxious about then?

Mark: The financial repercussions could be bad as I'm mortgaged up to the hilt and I could lose everything.

Coach: Is there anything else you think may be relevant?

Mark: No.

Coach: Let me summarise your key inferences. (Coach starts to write on whiteboard.) You are anxious because:

1   'I'll screw up'
2   They will think I'm useless.

3   I could jeopardise my job.

4   The financial repercussions could be bad.

5   I could lose everything.

       When you are getting yourself anxious about doing the presentation to the top team, of the points one to five, what are you most anxious about?

Mark: Frankly I don't really think I'm going to lose everything. I've had tough times before and so have some of my friends but we haven't lost everything. I really want this job and I want to keep it once I get it. I've had my eye on it for some time. I think I'm stressed about doing anything that jeopardises my job.

Coach: Now we've probably found the critical 'A' or aspect associated with giving the presentation you are most anxious about, let's find out what beliefs you have about it. In your mind's eye, can you now imagine that you are screwing up your presentation thereby jeopardising your job? (Using imagery to elicit the 'hot' cognitions.)

Mark: Yes.

Coach: As you imagine you are jeopardising your job what's going through your mind now?

Mark: I mustn't lose this new job.

Coach: And if you did?

Mark: It would be awful. They would think badly of me.

Coach: What do you think they are actually thinking of you?

Mark: I'm totally useless?

Coach: And would you agree with them?

Mark: Yes!

Coach: Is the thinking 'I'm totally useless' associated with your presentation skills deficits or with you in the new role? (Clarifying question.)

Mark: Both, but it's how they see me in the new job that is important.

Coach: OK. So the key stress-inducing beliefs are (writing them on the whiteboard):

B: Beliefs

1   I mustn't lose this new job.

2   It would be awful!

3   I'm totally useless.

       If you hold these beliefs are you going to remain stressed or become relaxed? (To highlight the link between his thoughts and how he feels.)

Mark: I'm going to stay stressed.

Coach: Will that hinder or help your presentation? (Question to highlight the link between the fear about losing the job and how he may act or behave at the presentation.)

Mark: Make it far worse!

Coach: What do you suggest you could do about being so stressed? (Solution-seeking question.)

Mark: I could decide not to accept the new job, avoid the presentation which won't be possible or perhaps I suppose I could change my thinking.

Coach: As you want to keep this job, what would you prefer to do?

Mark: Change my thinking.

As there was sufficient time left in this session the coach introduced performance enhancing forms.

Coach: To help my clients recognise and then develop new performance enhancing thoughts which we call PETs for short, I usually suggest we complete a performance enhancing form. Do you want to give it a go?

Mark: Yeah.

The coach and Mark completed the first three columns of the performance enhancing form with the information they had elicited from earlier in the session. They also added additional PITs that directly related to the presentation. They then developed performance enhancing thoughts to counter the performance interfering thoughts in the second column and wrote these down in the fourth column. Mark found it useful to include some of the questions the coach asked him in the fourth column so he could use them after the session. Finally they completed the last column (see Table 6.1).

In-between session task

Near the end of the first session it was agreed that Mark would note down any additional PITs or PETs he may have regarding the presentation and possibly jeopardising his job between now and the next session. He was given a cognitive behavioural self-help book to read and asked to focus on reading Chapter 2, 'Changing your thinking to conquer stress', which covered recognising thinking errors and developing thinking skills and imagery skills (see Cooper and Palmer, 2000). The coaching session was audiotaped so that Mark could listen to the session again.

In the second coaching session Mark gave feedback on some of the thinking errors he recognised he regularly used. They returned to the SPACE diagram

Table 6.1 Performance enhancing form

Target problem (A)	Performance interfering thoughts (PITs) (B)	Emotional behavioural reaction (C)	Performance enhancing thoughts (PETs) (D)	Effective and new approach to problem (E)
Giving a poor presentation to the top team will jeopardise my job. *Goals* Give a reasonable presentation. Stay focused on the presentation and not on what they might be thinking of it or me.	1 I mustn't lose this new job. 2 It would be awful! 3 I'm totally useless 4 I must perform well and give a perfect presentation	Anxiety Very anxious Depressed Anxiety	Realistically I could lose this job but unlikely if I screw up just one presentation. Will it be awful? It may be a pain if I lost this job but I know it wouldn't be the end of the world. How can I ever be totally useless? I would need to be useless at everything which does not add up. Why must I perform well? Realistically I don't. Where is holding on to this thought getting me? It's making me more stressed and less likely to perform well. Is there such a thing as a 'perfect presentation' or are my expectations far too high? I will focus on giving a good enough, but not perfect presentation.	I will accept the new job. I will ensure I'm well prepared for the presentation and practise speaking out aloud. I will not mind-read others when giving the presentations. I will read about coping imagery on page 48 of the book.

© Centre for Coaching, 2001

and discussed the possibility of using the Benson relaxation technique to feel more relaxed prior to and during the presentation. This technique was covered in the self-help book. This would need to be practised on a daily basis so it would become 'second nature'. Although coping imagery was noted down previously on the performance enhancing form, there had been no time to discuss it in depth. However, the coach encountered some initial difficulty when he raised it in this session:

Coach: We said in our last session that we would consider using the coping imagery technique. Did you read it in the book?

Mark: Yes. But I don't really see it working as I don't use imagery.
(There was a few seconds' silence as the coach reflected upon the last session.)

Coach: I recall that you play golf.

Mark: Yes I do.

Coach: When you drive to the golf course, do you just listen to the radio or play your music or do you picture or visualise playing your next game of golf?

Mark: It's funny you mention it, but I do go over in my mind the difficult holes.

Coach: I've found that many of my clients do this with golf and other sporting activities. In what way does visualising help you?

Mark: I see myself practising the difficult shots and I think about how I'm going to do them.

Coach: So in fact you do use imagery to practise and enhance your golf?

Mark: Yes.

Coach: Coping imagery is no different except in this case you will be applying it it to your work situation by seeing yourself coping with the presentation.

Mark: It now makes sense.

Coach: Are you now happy to use it to enhance your performance when you give your next presentation?

Mark: Yes.

The coach then discussed in more detail using coping imagery to tackle the presentation. This included Mark seeing himself using his hands expressively when talking instead of them shaking and hovering above his laptop, and also dealing with difficult questions. It is worth noting that often coachees will say that they do not visualise but in fact they do when it comes to sporting activities.

The third and last session was by telephone although there had been some email contact between the sessions. The presentation had gone well and he had not jeopardised his job.

Reflections

Coaches and coachees often do not see the benefit of using imagery but it is a powerful method for assessment and skills rehearsal and can quickly help to build up confidence.

In one of the authors' (SP) experience, trained cognitive therapists who have subsequently become coaches sometimes neglect the principle of parsimony. They undertake in-depth, time-consuming cognitive case conceptualisations for non-clinical coaching populations when the problem or issue to be addressed does not warrant an in-depth assessment. If the coaching is not proving effective, an in-depth assessment may then be necessary as it is for most clinical disorders.

References

Adler, A. (1958) *What Life should Mean to You* (ed. A. Porter). New York: Capricorn. (Originally published 1931.)

Alseike, B. U. (1997) Cognitive Coaching[SM]: its influences on teachers. Doctoral dissertation, University of Denver, 1997. *Dissertation Abstracts International* 9804083.

Anderson, J. P. (2002) Executive coaching and REBT: some comments from the field. *Journal of Rational-Emotive and Cognitive-Behavior Therapy* 20(3/4): 223–233.

Auerbach, J. E. (2006) Cognitive coaching. In D. R. Stober and A. M. Grant (eds) *Evidence Based Coaching Handbook: Putting best practices to work for your clients.* Hoboken, NJ: Wiley.

Bandura, A. (1986) *Social Foundations of Thought and Action: A social cognitive theory.* Englewood Cliffs, NJ: Prentice Hall.

Beck, A. T. (1967) *Depression: Clinical, experimental, and theoretical aspects.* Philadelphia, PA: University of Pennsylvania Press.

Beck, A. T. (1976) *Cognitive Therapy and the Emotional Disorders.* New York: International Universities Press.

Beck, A. T. (1993) Cognitive approaches to stress. In P. M. Lehrer and R. L. Woolfolk (eds) *Principles and Practice of Stress Management*, 2nd edition. New York: Guilford Press.

Burns, D. (1990) *The Feeling Good Handbook.* New York: Plume.

Centre for Coaching (2001) *Completed ABCDE Form.* London: Centre for Coaching.

Cooper, C. and Palmer, S. (2000) *Conquer your Stress.* London: Chartered Institute of Personnel and Development.

Costa, A. L. and Garmston, R. J. (2002) *Cognitive Coaching: A foundation for Renaissance schools.* Norwood, MA: Christopher-Gordon.

Curwen, B., Palmer, S. and Ruddell, P. (2000) *Brief Cognitive Behaviour Therapy.* London: Sage.

DiMattia, D. J. with Mennen, S. (1990) *Rational Effectiveness Training: Increasing productivity at work.* New York: Institute for Rational-Emotive Therapy.

Dobson, K. (1989) A meta analysis of the efficacy of cognitive therapy for depression. *Journal of Consulting and Clinical Psychology* 57(3): 414–419.

Dryden, W. and Gordon, J. (1993) *Peak Performance: Become more effective at work.* Didcot, UK: Mercury Business Books.

Dubois, P. (1906) *The Influence of the Mind on the Body* (trans. L. B. Gallatin). New York: Funk and Wagnalls.

Dutton, M. M. (1990) Learning and teacher job satisfaction (staff development). Doctoral dissertation, Portland State University, 1990. *Dissertation Abstracts International 51/05-A*, AAD90–26940.

D'Zurilla, T. J. (1986) *Problem-solving Therapy: A social competence approach to clinical intervention*. New York: Springer.

Edgerton, N. and Palmer, S. (2005) SPACE: a psychological model for use within cognitive behavioural coaching, therapy and stress management. *The Coaching Psychologist* 2(2): 25–31.

Edwards, J. (2004) Cognitive coaching: research on outcomes and recommendations for implementation. In I. F. Stein and L. A. Belsten (eds), *Proceedings of the 1st ICF Coaching Research Symposium* (pp. 20–32). Mooresville, NC: Paw Print Press.

Edwards, J. L., Green, K., Lyons, C. A., Rogers, M. S. and Swords, M. (1998) The effects of Cognitive Coaching[SM] and nonverbal classroom management on teacher efficacy and perceptions of school culture. Paper presented at the Annual Meeting of the American Educational Research Association, San Diego, CA.

Ellis, A. (1962) *Reason and Emotion in Psychotherapy*. New York: Lyle Stuart.

Ellis, A. (1972) *Executive Leadership: A rational approach*. New York: Institute for Rational-Emotive Therapy.

Ellis, A. and Blum, M. L. (1967) Rational training: a new method of facilitating management labor relations. *Psychological Reports* 20: 1267–1284.

Ellis, A., Gordon, J., Neenan, N. and Palmer, S. (1998) *Stress Counselling: A rational emotive behaviour approach*. New York: Springer.

Falloon, I. R. H., Boyd, J. L. and McGill, C. (1984) Problem-solving training. In *Family Care of Schizophrenia*. New York: Guilford Press.

Gloaguen, V., Cottraux, J., Cucherat, M. and Blackburn, I. (1998) A meta-analysis of the effects of cognitive therapy in depressed patients. *Journal of Affective Disorders* 49: 59–72.

Grant, A. M. (2001) Coaching for enhanced performance: comparing cognitive and behavioural approaches to coaching. Paper presented at the Third International Spearman Seminar, Extending Intelligence: Enhancement and New Constructs, Sydney.

Grant, A. M. (2003) The impact of life coaching on goal attainment, metacognition and mental health. *Social Behavior and Personality* 31(3): 253–264.

Grbcic, S. and Palmer, S. (2006a) A cognitive-behavioural self-help approach to stress management and prevention at work: a randomized controlled trial. Paper presented at the National Conference of the Association for Rational Emotive Behaviour Therapy in Association with the Association for Multimodal Therapy, London, 24 November.

Grbcic, S. and Palmer, S. (2006b) A cognitive-behavioural manualised self-coaching approach to stress management and prevention at work: a randomised controlled trial. Paper presented at the First International Coaching Psychology Conference, City University, London, 18 December.

Grbcic, S. and Palmer, S. (2007) A cognitive-behavioural self-help approach to stress management and prevention at work: a randomised controlled trial. *Rational Emotive Behaviour Therapist* 12(1): 21–43.

Green, L. S., Oades, L. G. and Grant, A. M. (2005) An evaluation of a life-coaching group programme: initial findings from a waitlist control study. In M. Cavanagh, A. M. Grant and T. Kemp (eds) *Evidence Based Coaching.* Volume 1, *Theory, Research and Practice from the Behavioural Sciences.* Bowen Hills, Qld: Australian Academic Press.

Green, L. S., Oades, L. G. and Grant, A. M. (2006) Cognitive-behavioral, solution-focused life coaching: enhancing goal striving, well-being and hope. *Journal of Positive Psychology* 1(3): 142–149.

Greenberger, D. and Padesky, C. (1995) *Mind over Mood: A cognitive therapy treatment manual for clients.* New York: Guilford Press.

Gyllensten, K. and Palmer, S. (2005) The relationship between coaching and workplace stress: a correlational study. *International Journal of Health Promotion and Education* 43(3): 97–103.

Hawton, K. and Kirk, J. (1989) Problem-solving. In K. Hawton, P. Salkovskis, J. Kirk and D. Clarke (eds) *Cognitive Behaviour Therapy for Psychiatric Problems: A practical guide.* Oxford: Oxford University Press.

Kirby, P. (1993) RET counselling: application in management and executive development. *Journal for Rational-Emotive and Cognitive-Behavior Therapy* 11(1): 51–57.

Kodish, S. P. (2002) Rational emotive behaviour coaching. *Journal of Rational-Emotive and Cognitive-Behavior Therapy* 20: 235–246.

Lange, A. and Grieger, R. (1993) Integrating RET into management consulting and training. *Journal for Rational-Emotive and Cognitive-Behavior Therapy* 11(1): 19–32.

Lazarus, A. A. (1971) *Behavior Therapy and Beyond.* New York: McGraw-Hill.

Lazarus, A. A. (1981) *The Practice of Multimodal Therapy.* New York: McGraw-Hill.

Lazarus, A. A. (1984) *In the Mind's Eye.* New York: Guilford Press.

Leahy, R. and Holland, S. (2000) *Treatment Plans and Interventions for Depression and Anxiety Disorders.* New York: Guilford Press.

Libri, V. and Kemp, T. (2006) Assessing the efficacy of a cognitive behavioural executive coaching programme. *International Coaching Psychology Review* 1(2): 9–20.

Locke, E. A. (1996) Motivation through conscious goal setting. *Applied and Preventative Psychology* 5: 117–124.

Locke, E. A. and Latham, G. P. (1990) *A Theory of Goal Setting and Task Performance.* Englewood Cliffs, NJ: Prentice Hall.

Marks, I. M. (1969) *Fears and Phobias.* London: William Heinemann.

Meichenbaum, D. (1977) *Cognitive-behavior Modification: An integrative approach.* New York: Plenum Press.

Meichenbaum, D. (1985) *Stress Inoculation Training.* New York: Pergamon.

Milner, P. and Palmer, S. (1998) *Integrative Stress Counselling: A humanistic problem focused approach.* London: Cassell.

Neenan, M. (2006) Cognitive behavioural coaching. In J. Passmore (ed.) *Excellence in Coaching: The industry guide.* London: Kogan Page.

Neenan, S. and Dryden, W. (2002) *Life Coaching: A cognitive-behavioural approach.* Hove: Brunner-Routledge.

Neenan, M. and Palmer, S. (2000) Problem focused counselling and psychotherapy. In S. Palmer (ed.) *Introduction to Counselling and Psychotherapy: The essential guide.* London: Sage.

Neenan, M. and Palmer, S. (2001a) Cognitive behavioural coaching. *Stress News* 13(3): 15–18.

Neenan, M. and Palmer, S. (2001b) Rational emotive behaviour coaching. *Rational Emotive Behaviour Therapist* 9(1): 34–41.

NICE (2005) *Clinical Guidelines for Treating Mental Health Problems*. London: National Institute for Health and Clinical Excellence.

O'Hanlon, W. (1998) Possibility therapy: an inclusive, collaborative, solution-based model of psychotherapy. In M. F. Hoyt (ed.) *The Handbook of Constructive Therapies: Innovative approaches from leading practitioners*. San Francisco, CA: Jossey-Bass.

Palmer, S. (1992) Stress management interventions. *Counselling News* 7: 12–15.

Palmer, S. (1995) A comprehensive approach to industrial rational emotive behaviour stress management workshops. *Rational Emotive Behaviour Therapist* 1: 45–55.

Palmer, S. (1997a) Problem focused stress counselling and stress management training: an intrinsically brief integrative approach. Part 1. *Stress News* 9(2): 7–12.

Palmer, S. (1997b) Problem focused stress counselling and stress management training: an intrinsically brief integrative approach. Part 1. *Stress News* 9(3): 6–10.

Palmer, S. (2002) Cognitive and organisational models of stress that are suitable for use within workplace stress management/prevention coaching, training and counselling settings. *Rational Emotive Behaviour Therapist* 10(1): 15–21.

Palmer, S. (2007a) Cognitive coaching in the business world. Inaugural lecture given at the Swedish Centre for Work Based Learning, Goteburg, Sweden, 8 February.

Palmer, S. (2007b) Stress, performance, resilience and well-being: the 'fit' vs 'unfit' manager. Paper given at the Institution of Safety and Health National Conference, Telford, UK, 27 April.

Palmer, S. (2007c) PRACTICE: A model suitable for coaching, counselling, psycho-therapy and stress management. *The Coaching Psychologist* 3(2): 71–77.

Palmer, S. and Burton, T. (1996) *People Problems at Work*. London: McGraw-Hill.

Palmer, S. and Cooper, C. (2007) *How to Deal with Stress*. London: Kogan Page.

Palmer, S. and Dryden, W. (1995) *Counselling for Stress Problems*. London: Sage.

Palmer, S. and Ellis, A. (1995) Stress counselling and management: Stephen Palmer interviews Albert Ellis. *Rational Emotive Behaviour Therapist* 3(2): 82–86.

Palmer, S. and Gyllensten, K. (in press) Can cognitive behavioural coaching prevent mental health problems? *Journal of Rational Emotive and Cognitive Behavioural Therapy*.

Palmer, S. and Neenan, M. (1998) Double imagery procedure. *Rational Emotive Behaviour Therapist* 6(2): 89–92.

Palmer, S. and Neenan, M. (2000) Problem-focused counselling and psychotherapy. In S. Palmer and R. Woolfe (eds) *Integrative and Eclectic Counselling and Psycho-therapy*. London: Sage.

Palmer, S. and Puri, A. (2006) *Coping with Stress at University: A survival guide*. London: Sage.

Palmer, S. and Strickland, L. (1996) *Stress Management: A quick guide*, 2nd edition. Dunstable, UK: Folens.

Palmer, S., Cooper, C. and Thomas, K. (2003) *Creating a Balance: Managing pressure*. London: British Library.

Rachman, S. and Teasdale, J. (1969) *Aversion Therapy and Behaviour Disorders: An analysis*. London: Routledge and Kegan Paul.

Richman, D. R. (1993) Cognitive career counselling: a rational-emotive approach to career development. *Journal for Rational-Emotive and Cognitive-Behavior Therapy* 11(2): 91–108.

Sawyer, L. (2003) Integrating cognitive coaching^{SM} with a framework for teaching. In J. Ellison and C. Hayes (eds) *Cognitive Coaching: Weaving threads of learning and change into the culture of an organisation* (pp. 151–156). Norwood, MA: Christopher-Gordon.

Smith, K. A. and Kjeldsen, R. (2004) Kognitive Coaching. *Erhvervspsykologi* 2(4): 38–49.

Smith, M. C. (1997) Self-reflection as a means of increasing teacher efficacy through Cognitive Coaching^{SM}. Master's thesis, California State University at Fullerton, 1997. *Masters Abstracts International* 1384304.

Szymanska, K. and Palmer, S. (2000) Cognitive counselling and psychotherapy. In S. Palmer (ed.) *Introduction to Counselling and Psychotherapy: The essential guide.* London: Sage.

Wasik, B. (1984) Teaching parents effective problem-solving: a handbook for professionals. Unpublished manuscript, University of North Carolina, Chapel Hill, NC.

Watson, J. B. and Rayner, R. (1920) Conditioned emotional reactions. *Journal of Experimental Psychology* 3: 1–4.

Wills, F. and Sanders, D. (1997) *Cognitive Therapy: Transforming the image.* London: Sage.

Wolpe, J. and Lazarus, A. A. (1966) *Behavior Therapy Techniques.* New York: Pergamon.

Zimmerman, B. J. (1989) Models of self-regulated learning. In B. J. Zimmerman and D. H. Schunk (eds) *Self-regulated Learning and Academic Achievement.* New York: Springer-Verlag.

Discussion points

- In what way is the principle of parsimony important in coaching? Did the case study reflect this principle?
- Cognitive behavioural coaching is superficial: discuss.
- In coaching, not developing an in-depth cognitive behavioural case conceptualisation is lazy and possibly unethical: discuss.
- Recommending that clients read self-help material is patronising and unhelpful: discuss.

Suggested reading

Costa, A. L. and Garmston, R. J. (2002) *Cognitive Coaching: A foundation for Renaissance schools.* Norwood, MA: Christopher-Gordon.

Milner, P. and Palmer, S. (1998) *Integrative Stress Counselling: A humanistic problem-focused approach.* London: Cassell.

Neenan, S. and Dryden, W. (2002) *Life Coaching: A cognitive-behavioural approach.* Hove: Brunner-Routledge.

Palmer, S. and Burton, T. (1996) *People Problems at Work.* London: McGraw-Hill.

Chapter 7

An existential approach to coaching psychology

Ernesto Spinelli and Caroline Horner

Introduction

Existential coaching psychology is centred upon the structured exploration of clients' way of being as expressed through both the meanings which they generate and the relations they adopt in the world. Arising directly from its philosophical grounding, an existential approach argues that human experience is unavoidably uncertain and thereby always open to novel and unpredicted possibilities.

All approaches to coaching rest upon various philosophical underpinnings and postulates, even if in many cases they remain implicit and covert to coaching practitioners. An existential approach to coaching, however, initially stands out from others precisely because it acknowledges explicitly and utilises overtly its foundational philosophical assumptions.

At the same time, it is not so much *that* it is philosophically grounded but rather *the particular set of philosophical suppositions which it espouses* that distinguishes the existential approach to coaching from the various competing alternative models currently in existence. In this way, an existential approach presents a radical challenge to many of the fundamental assumptions brought to the theory and practice of contemporary coaching psychology.

Theory and basic concepts

As various authors have argued, the existential approach has no single founder or authoritative source. Rather, it is best understood as a 'rich tapestry' of intersecting practices which focus on a shared concern – that of human existence (Cooper, 2003). Much of the literature on the existential approach to coaching comes from applications in the fields of psychology and psychotherapy (Peltier, 2001; Sieler, 2003).

For us, the most significant foundations to existential thought and practice in general and to existential coaching in particular lie in the following key ideas:

The inter-relational foundation

Stated succinctly, the key idea proposed by existential thought argues that the baseline, or foundational condition, for all reflected experiences of being is *inter-relation*. As Merleau-Ponty expressed it: 'The world and I are within one another' (Merleau-Ponty, 1962: 123).

Whereas dominant views of philosophy, psychology and therapy impose a separateness or distinction between subject and object (or between 'self' and 'other'), the existential approach denies this distinction and proposes a view that everything we are, or can be aware of, is inter-relationally derived.

Meaning

Existential theory argues that humans are 'meaning-making' beings. We *interpret* the world via the human process of constructing meaning of those 'things' which impinge themselves upon our experience and with which we are in relation. We are disturbed by the lack or loss of meaning, and can go to great lengths to avoid or deny those instances and experiences that challenge our meanings.

As several key existential theorists have highlighted, every act of meaning interpretation not *only* constructs, or reconstructs, the object of our focus. Just as significantly, the inter-relational stance and meaning of the constructing being (i.e. the focusing 'subject', or, more broadly, the 'self') is also simultaneously constructed or re-constructed in and through the act (Merleau-Ponty, 1962; Ihde, 1977; Spinelli, 2005, 2007). Our attempts to make meaning of the world reveal an interdependent, co-constitutional foundation through which both 'subject' and 'object,' or 'self' and 'other', are mutually and simultaneously made meaningful (Heidegger, 1962). As such, an individual's experience of and given meanings to existence can no longer be considered in isolation but rather must be placed in an inevitable inter-relational context.

As a consequence of the above conclusion, human experience is placed in an uncertain relativistic realm of being wherein whatever meaning is generated can no longer be permanently fixed and certain. Our meanings now emerge as being subject to constant flux rather than fixed or fully definable.

In like fashion, meaning as well as being uncertain and unfixed, can also be seen to be unique and never fully sharable, since the variables that make up each human being's experience of the world are not accessible in any complete or final manner to those of any other human being.

Anxiety

As beings who reveal a persistent tendency to 'fix' or 'capture' meaning in spite of its inter-relational basis, our experience of the inescapable uncertainty and uniqueness in the meanings we generate is one of unease and insecurity, often referred to as *existential angst or anxiety*.

In our attempts to avoid or diminish angst we seek out and assert fixed truths, facts, statements and deny or dissociate those instances in our experience that cast doubt or challenge our assertions of certainty and fixed meaning. This denial has been referred to as *inauthenticity* (Heidegger, 1962) or *bad faith* (Sartre, 1956) and its frequency and appeal lies precisely in that it serves to allay the unease and uncertainty of being-in-the-world (Yalom, 1980; Cohn, 1997; Spinelli, 2005, 2007).

In a related fashion, the existential notion of *death anxiety* has often been misunderstood as meaning 'a fear of death'. All human beings become aware of their temporal nature and their inevitable 'movement towards death'. At the same time, the conditions for death's occurrence (such as when and how it will occur, or what will kill us) remain uncertain and unpredictable. Each individual responds to the certainty of, and uncertainties associated with, death in a unique fashion. Existential theory argues that this death anxiety permeates *all* of our relations with self, others and the world in general. As can now be understood, death anxiety is more expressive of a human being's ongoing overall response to existence within its uncertain and finite context.

Although our conflicts and dilemmas can be seen to be based in our experience of, and relation to, anxiety, the existential perspective recognises that anxiety in general and death anxiety in particular are not *only or even necessarily* 'bad' or problematic presences that must be reduced or removed. The feeling of anxiety can also be stimulating, can put us in touch with our sense of being alive, and is the source to all creative and original insight and decision-making. A life that was anxiety-free would be empty of meaning, enthusiasm, curiosity and the urge to advance itself.

The possible solutions to our problems therefore do not hinge upon the eradication of anxiety but rather rest upon the search for more beneficial ways to 'live with' it.

Choice

The existential idea of choice has often been misunderstood to suggest that we possess unlimited freedom to choose how and what 'to be' or 'to do'. This view is incorrect. The choices that we are free to make arise within an inter-relational context which *situates* our freedom to choose. Rather than being free to choose what we want, when we want it, we are rather free to choose our *response* to the contextual situation in which we find ourselves. In this sense, as Sartre argued, it may be more accurate to state that we are *condemned* to choose (Sartre, 1956).

Human choice is interpretive, not at the event, or stimulus, level. And even then, the range of interpretations we might be able to generate is dependent upon an inter-relational temporal context – that is to say, when, where and how each of us 'is' within such contextual factors as time, culture and biology.

As can be ascertained, many of the problems that clients are likely to bring to coaching originate from the unwillingness to choose the choices which are available rather than insist that other, unavailable, choices are an option. The difference between 'choosing that which is there for me' as opposed to deceiving myself that any imaginable choice option is available is both significant and profound at every level of our experience (Spinelli, 1997, 2005, 2007). Quite simply, we are our choices.

Conflict and change

From an existential perspective, conflict is viewed as an inevitable condition of human existence. Conflict can express the existence of a gap or dissonance between that which one believes and/or claims to adopt and the *actual* stance or way of being that one adopts. Alternatively, conflict can emerge as a direct consequence and expression of the inter-relational stance that one both believes in and adopts.

The first type of conflict can be resolved only through the re-constitution of one's divided or dissonant inter-relational stance – which may be expressed as 'change' in one's relations with self and/or others or the world in general. The second type of conflict is an expression of the consequences of an undivided and coherent stance. It is that conflict which arises *because* we choose. The possible resolution of this type of conflict has less to do with issues of overt change and is more focused upon the embracing and acceptance of the presenting inter-relational stance in a more complete way such that one embraces its uneasy or unwanted consequences as well as those that one deems to be desirable and/or necessary.

This distinction is of central import to the coaching-focused goals and strategies that are to be negotiated with clients. At the same time, in both cases, no individual *alone* is in complete control of the emergence or reduction of conflict since it is always the case that the role of the world, and the stance it takes towards either the person or the problem itself, remains beyond an individual's full authority.

Most importantly for existential theory, every conflict that presents itself can be seen to be an attempt to 'live with' anxiety to a degree that remains tolerable or desirable. If one removes the presenting problem without sufficiently understanding its relation to that stance, one might also be removing a solution that is far more important in its impact upon the person than is the presenting problem.

Unfortunately for coaches, at present the impact of directive attempts at conflict resolution cannot be predicted with perfect accuracy. As a consequence, it is wise for coaches to bear in mind that, sometimes, the change solutions that are offered can create far greater distress and unease in living than did the presenting problem.

In addition, existential theory argues that change in any *one* aspect or expression of a person's behaviour or performance will alter *the whole* of his or her worldview. In terms of our current understanding of the impact of directive change, it remains uncertain as to how subtle or radical this alteration may be for any particular client.

Viewed in this way, an existential approach to a conflict-resolving focus in coaching is neither solely about nor predominantly concerned with alteration in behaviour. Instead, it suggests that the coach's focusing upon, and connecting more accurately with, the worldview that shapes and defines the client's behaviour is likely to provoke a noticeable shift in the worldview. Such a shift may provoke either alterations in behaviour or a new-found relation to existing behaviour.

Practice

Unlike other coaching perspectives that focus upon broadly positive, self-actualising qualities and possibilities for each client, the existential approach recognises and gives equal emphasis to the divided stances, aims and aspirations that may well exist as competing values and beliefs held by each client. The approach helps clients to clarify and reconsider the meanings and values given to the various inter-relations that make up their personal and professional lives and how the relational stances that they adopt impact upon the quality and enjoyment of their own lives as well as those of others.

Part of the existential approach to coaching therefore expresses a commitment to assist clients to arrive at personal decisions and life change that are grounded in an inter-relationally attuned awareness and understanding.

The approach emphasises *a way of being in the world* as opposed to focusing principally upon change-focused 'doing' interventions. It does not rely upon a unique set of tools and techniques. While there are various 'skills' associated with an existential approach, their value depends upon the 'being focused' grounding from which they emerge. An existential approach to coaching relies upon the coach's and client's experience of being in relation with one another and how this experience illuminates the whole of the client's worldview as its primary 'tool' or 'skill'.

Centrality of the coaching relationship

The existential approach to coaching advocates the descriptive exploration of the client's worldview as a pivotal factor for beneficial interventions. As such, coaching is centred on the attempted entry into the currently lived world of the client as it is being embodied and experienced so that it can be more adequately investigated in such a way that the presenting problems and conflicts can be understood as aspects and expressions of that worldview rather than treated as alien or tangential to it.

The success of such explorations depends upon the establishment of a trustworthy coaching relationship. This view is slowly beginning to be acknowledged by other coaching modalities and parallels conclusions regarding the centrality of the relationship arrived at by psychotherapy research (Cooper, 2003; Spinelli, 2005, 2007).

While setting goals or planning change strategies are valued as central to effective coaching, an existential approach focuses upon these in relation to the specific structure of, and meanings contained in, the client's worldview. As such, existentially speaking, the coach's willingness to assist the client in the descriptive disclosure of the worldview as it manifests itself in the client's wider inter-relations and in the specific inter-relation with the coach is pivotal to the coaching enterprise.

Via the relationship itself, the existentially informed coach attempts to open up and make explicit the embedded and largely implicit inter-relational tensions that exist within the client's worldview. Below, two central 'skills' related to the exploration of the client's worldview are briefly summarised.

The phenomenological method

One powerful way to assist the coach in remaining attuned to the currently lived worldview of the client is to apply what has become known as the phenomenological method of investigation. There are three descriptive 'steps' in this process (Ihde, 1977; Spinelli, 2005, 2007).

Step 1: The rule of epoché

Step 1 urges the coach to set aside his or her initial biases and prejudices, to suspend expectations and assumptions – in short, to *bracket* all presuppositions regarding the client as far as is possible. The rule of epoché urges the coach to attune his or her focus to what presents itself as it presents itself so that the client's currently lived worldview can be more adequately disclosed and, in turn, so that any subsequent reconstructions of it fit its meanings and values.

Step 2: The rule of description

The essence of Step 2 is: 'Describe, don't explain'. Rather than attempt to immediately analyse or transform the client's concerns on the basis of the coach's preferred theories or hypotheses, the rule of description urges the coach to remain initially focused on that information which arises from a concretely based descriptive exploration of the client's worldview. The focus of this rule centres more on the 'what and how' of a client's experience than it does on the 'why'.

Step 3: The rule of horizontalisation

Step 3 in the phenomenological method is known as the rule of horizontalisation. This rule further urges the coach to avoid placing any initial hierarchies of significance or importance upon the items of description, and instead to treat each as having initially equal value.

In the attempt to describe while avoiding any hierarchical assumptions, the coach is better able to access the client's worldview with far less prejudice and with a much greater degree of adequacy so that, as far as is possible, he or she can avoid making immediate misleading hierarchically based judgements that may significantly misunderstand significant aspects of the client's worldview.

As phenomenologists themselves have pointed out, no final or complete adherence to, or fulfillment of, each of the three steps in the phenomenological method is possible, nor should we trust any claim to have done so (Merleau-Ponty, 1962). Even so, while it remains impossible for coaches to fully achieve bracketing, pure description or total horizontalisation, they are certainly capable of *attempting* each and, by so doing, become more aware of their biases at each step of their investigation. What is more, it can be argued that the act of recognition of bias is itself likely to lessen its impact by invoking for the coach a greater degree of caution in adhering too closely or uncritically to the immediate prejudices that he or she may have imposed upon an investigation from its earliest stages.

It should now be clearer that each 'step' in the phenomenological method is, more accurately, a particular point of focus that is taken rather than an entirely independent activity that can be wholly distinguished from the remaining two.

The inter-relational realms of discourse

A second means by which the client's worldview can be clarified centres upon the exploration of four inter-relational realms, or focus points, of discourse (Spinelli, 2005, 2007).

I-focus

The I-focused realm of encounter attempts to describe and clarify 'my experience of being "myself" in any given relationship'. It asks, in effect, 'What do I tell myself about my current experience of being me in this encounter?' The use of the I-focus permits the client to express to both him or herself and to the coach that which is currently being experienced regarding *self in relation to self.*

You-focus

The You-focused realm of encounter attempts to describe and clarify 'my experience of "the other" being in relation with me'. Its focus is on the question: 'What do I tell myself about the other's experience of being with me in any given encounter?' The use of the You-focus permits the client to express to both him or herself and to the coach that which is currently being experienced regarding self in relation to others via the particular present other who is the coach.

We-focus

The We-focused realm of encounter attempts to describe and clarify each participant's experience of 'us' being in relation with one another. It asks: 'What do I tell myself about the experience of being *us* in the immediacy of this encounter?'

While all three of the above realms help the coach to access and explicate the client's currently lived experience, the We-focused realm of encounter is treated with particular importance in the existential approach since it is char-acterised by its immediacy. It is concerned with, and expresses, that which is being experienced 'in the moment' of engagement with the other from a person-to-person standpoint. As such, it expresses explicitly that inter-relational grounding that exists (and is more implicitly expressed) in I-focused and You-focused statements.

They-focus

The They-focused realm of encounter attempts to describe and clarify my experience of how those who make up my wider world of 'others' (extending beyond the other who is the coach) experience their own inter-relational realms in response to my current way of being and, as well, to the novel ways of being that may have begun to present themselves as possibilities to me as a result of coaching (Spinelli, 2005, 2007).

The exploration of this fourth relational realm is likely to be particularly significant when the client has reached a point of considering and making choices about new-found alternative 'ways to be'.

It asks: 'What do I tell myself about the meaning and impact that my new stance is having or will have upon my relations with those others who have been singled out by me as being significant?' Further, the They-focus also asks: 'What do I tell myself about the meaning and impact that my decision is having or will have upon each of those others' relations with one another?'

The intent behind They-focused exploration is neither to alter nor prevent the client's decision, nor to impose either the coach's or the others' own moral stance upon the client's perspective, nor to expose the actual views of these 'others' in the client's world. Rather, its consideration serves to implicate the client's newly chosen way of being in such a way that it includes his or her lived experience of the world and the others who exist within it rather than permits a 'world-excluding' possibility.

At the heart of both of the skills summarised above lies the attempt to ensure the client's experience of 'being heard' accurately both at the level of what is being stated overtly and, as significantly, at the level of exposing those underlying, implicit and covert values, beliefs and assumptions that both give rise to and inform the client's overt statements.

This attempt on the part of the coach creates the conditions that permit clients to 'hear themselves' accurately and non-defensively through their inter-relation with the coach.

In this sense, the focus is not on the relative rationality or irrationality of values and beliefs held by the client. Rather, the enterprise centres upon the disclosing of areas of coherence and incoherence within the client's worldview and the consequent experience of disturbance, unease and conflict that such provoke.

Through such, the presenting problems and conflicts, as well as their possible resolution, can be addressed from the context of the client's worldview. Considered as direct expressions of inter-relational quandaries either within, or arising from, the client's worldview, presenting problems can no longer be disconnected from the whole of the client's worldview nor dealt with in isolation but rather are reconsidered from that inter-relational grounding which serves as a critical distinguishing feature of an existential approach to coaching.

Which clients benefit most?

It is our view that the existential approach is amenable to every form of coaching. However, the approach is particularly useful when working with those in transition – particularly life stage transition such as mid-life and retirement, or progression and advancement in work, where dilemmas are often about regaining meaning at work, or dealing with lost possibilities and legacy. Clients who are open to an approach which is reflective, exploratory and deeply challenging will warm to this system. Those seeking certainty, and who wish to use coaching to drive towards a fixed outcome, may struggle with the ambiguity it embraces.

The approach is, in our view, most appropriate for those who are competent and successful, and who are open to the challenge of grappling with complex and paradoxical issues. It is less about developing an immediate shift in specific behaviours and performance than it is about extending clients' understanding of their individual stance to life and developing skills via a more open and truthful assessment of the relational stances being adopted and how these impact upon their behaviour and, in turn, upon the quality and enjoyment of their lives.

Outcomes from this approach include individuals being more congruent with their lived experience, and thereby becoming clearer about who they are and who they are not; the accessing of skills for managing complexity, ambiguity and anxiety; and the enhancement of attitudes of self-responsibility and ownership of choice within an inter-relational context.

Some have argued that the existential perspective leads to a kind of individualism that is thoughtless or empty of direction and which, in turn, does not work very well either in real life or in organisations as its focus tends away from equally balancing the influence of the system on the individual (Peltier, 2001). We have attempted to demonstrate that such views express a distortion of the most basic existential assumption: the inter-relatedness of being. As such, rather than foster an individualistic ethos that separates self from others, or the client from his or her life and work context, the existential approach is foremost among approaches in asserting the necessity to acknowledge and place oneself in an inter-relational context. In practice terms, the exploration of the client's worldview encourages a stance that takes responsibility for personal responses to the system as opposed to the tendency to externalise ownership to an environment 'outside of one's control'.

Major potential limitations in the approach include its tendency to avoid direct exploration of data in the system or organisation as experienced by others; its sceptical stance toward the use and value of assessment tools and techniques which, often behaviourally derived, are seen to conflict with the inter-relational emphasis on the direct encounter between client and coach; and the limited experimental data regarding the effectiveness of existentially focused coaching .

Overall, the approach's emphasis on 'being qualities' and meaning exploration as opposed to the development and refinement of the coach's 'doing' skills and repertoire runs counter to current dominant assumptions and emphases within coaching as a whole. Whether this divergence will eventually prove to be the existential approach's greatest strength or weakness remains to be seen.

Case study

Marianne has held a senior position in an established and well-regarded UK market research organisation for over four years. Although she has established a strong presence and revealed many desirable qualities, Marianne has, from the start of her employment, maintained poor relations with both her team and her line manager. As a result, she has been passed over for promotion on two separate occasions even though various structured assessments suggested that she has skills and potential that are consistent with those identified by the organisation to establish their long-term strategy. In an attempt to retain Marianne and create an opportunity for promotion, the company offered Marianne coaching to develop her interpersonal skills. Marianne considered a few coaches before selecting one of the authors (ES) and highlighted the relationship established in the preliminary session as the rationale for her selection. A total of eight fortnightly face-to-face sessions each of 90 minutes was arranged and a contract specifying their frequency, duration and fees was agreed, as were specific points dealing with matters of confidentiality from the viewpoints of multiple stakeholders.

At the start of her first formal session, Marianne stated that she had come to coaching because she wanted to prove herself to be the most capable and respected member in the organisation so that she would either be promoted or, if necessary, so that the company would feel the significance of her loss should she decide to leave. Marianne then announced her expectation that the coach identify specific outcome-focused goals and suggest ways as to how she was to implement them.

In reply, the coach expressed his unwillingness to identify specific goals at the start of their sessions on the grounds that he had no adequate sense as to how Marianne's stated outcomes related to her overall worldview as well as the expectations of leadership behaviour in the organisation. Instead, he proposed that, together, they could begin to address these so that any outcome goals could be tested for their coherence with them. Marianne's immediate reaction was one of anger, dismissal of the value in such an enquiry, a questioning of the coach's competence and a threat to sever the relationship then and there and find someone far more capable as a replacement.

Instead of arguing with her or attempting to alter her view, the coach urged Marianne to consider whether her response to his 'stupid' request for clarification might be in any way resonant with her response to other 'stupid' suggestions and requests by members of her team. This comment surprised Marianne, her irritation subsided and she began to seriously consider the challenge. Overall, she decided, there were very close parallels. As such, the coach suggested that they look at the issue of conflict as it arose in the coaching relationship since it was immediate and present between them and then consider whether what they discovered of this might be applicable to Marianne's wider inter-relational conflicts.

This discussion revealed that Marianne's strong reaction was generated by her assessment of her own stupidity for not having immediately understood the point and value of the coach's statement. Her response to this felt stupidity and inadequacy was to accuse the coach of the same.

The coach then repeated Marianne's conclusion: 'When I feel stupid and inadequate, I accuse the other of being stupid and inadequate.' What, if anything, did hearing this statement provoke for Marianne? Marianne considered this and, surprising both herself and the coach, revealed that were she to understand and accept the other's comments as being valid and appropriate, she would somehow 'lose' since she would be conceding defeat to others' views and demands on her – even if these made sense and held value. To complicate matters further, Marianne now saw as well that if the coach had gone along with her demand to set goals and provide strategies, she would probably have never returned since to go along with him would also have been tantamount to 'losing'. Why so? Because it would have revealed the coach as someone who had no ideas of his own, who simply went along with her views, who was himself 'a loser' and that by choosing him, so was Marianne.

In brief, Marianne realised that her stance of verbal criticism and dismissal, whether of the coach or her work team, served, oddly enough, as a means to *avoid* 'losing'. Did it provide a sense of 'winning'? Interestingly, it didn't. In Marianne's worldview, 'winning' was a potential outcome available only to others.

At the start of her second session, Marianne clarified that whenever something that ought to feel like winning happened, she actually felt nothing and, indeed, always explained 'win outcomes' as the result of chance or some other external agent for which she had no responsibility or control. In contrast, 'losing', always came about because of Marianne's doing.

With further exploration, it emerged that Marianne's worldview maintained that 'winning' was equated with 'being good' but also feeling cut off, unreal, and amorphous, while 'losing' meant 'being bad' but also feeling connected, real and substantive.

With this dichotomy in mind, Marianne began to explore her relations with various others: her work team, her father, and two significant past romantic partners. In all cases, she connected to her felt sense of 'losing' but at the same time realised that this sense of loss, as well as the associated judgement of 'being bad', also provided her with a powerful experience of 'being real'. If relations appeared to be progressing in an appropriate way (i.e. approached 'winning'), Marianne theoretically 'felt good' but in actuality, felt increasingly disengaged, empty, and dissociated from her self.

At this point, Marianne, not surprisingly, wondered aloud as to why she had to be this way. What had led her to this fixed view of herself and inter-relational stance toward others? The coach assisted her in addressing these questions not by encouraging her to focus upon past events from early points in her life in order to expose an originating cause, but rather by encouraging her to remain focused upon her current living with the effects of unknown past causes through a descriptive focus upon her body state and any emotions or judgemental statements that accompanied such. In attempting this, Marianne began to expose recurring fixed attitudes, beliefs and assumptions regarding self, others and the inter-relations between self and others which resonated with her body feelings, emotions and behaviours. Marianne practised this descriptive process both in the sessions with the coach and on her own between sessions.

Since Marianne had identified that the area likely to have the most immediate impact in relation to her leadership potential was by delivering through others, she and the coach agreed to focus upon her relations with her work team in the remaining coaching sessions.

This exploration began with an exercise that prompted Marianne to explore descriptively her perceptions of the various others' perceptions of her. This was then followed by Marianne's descriptive exploration of these perceptions from the standpoint of her own perceptions of her self. Out of this, Marianne realised that in both cases the perceptions that emerged were highly critical in that everyone, Marianne included, emerged as being both 'bad and a loser'. And 'real'? Yes, Marianne conceded, at least they were all 'real'.

Here, once again, the coach urged Marianne to focus on her experience of the immediate coaching relationship. Did she perceive it as real? Yes. As bad? No. And did she feel she was 'losing'? No, the very opposite in fact. So what was so different about this relationship that it broke the fixedness of her worldview regarding self, others and the inter-relations between them?

Among the various significant variables that Marianne expressed was that of *styles of communication*. She realised that in her wider-world interactions with others, as well as with her self, she could identify various elements such as her angry voice, her tense body, her desire to maintain emotional distance, her being constantly alert to subtle critical messages. Equally, she concluded that her communications, whether to others or to herself, were typically telegraphic in nature, unclear, open to confusion. And, at the same time, Marianne saw that her ability to hear accurately others' responses to her statements was hampered because of all of these identified factors. In contrast, the coaching sessions provoked a much 'easier, connected and understandable' series of communications.

Because it stood out as a readily manipulable variable among those she had identified, the coach and Marianne focused on practising with each other the un-telegraphing and de-confusing of statements. The experience provoked a response from Marianne whose significance she recognised immediately: she laughed heartily and unguardedly. And along with the laughter she felt 'good, real and a winner'.

At the start of the following session Marianne reported that she had tried out what she had learned with her team and that, as a result, the interactions between them had started to improve to such an extent that others, including her line manager, had commented on the change in her. And how did Marianne experience all this? Not well; in fact, close to awful.

This truthful disclosure permitted Marianne and the coach to return to the experience of difference that Marianne experienced in the coaching relationship. Via this discussion, Marianne realised that while she continued to feel 'real and good and a winner' – all of which she valued greatly – she also felt extremely exposed and open, perhaps too open some of the time. Once again, a clear link was made between this experience and that sense of 'close to awful' that had been provoked through her novel inter-relations with her team. Being 'real and good and a winner' came with a price. Was the price worth paying as far as Marianne was concerned?

That question became the focus of discussions for the remainder of the sessions. The details of these far extend the limits of this discussion. At the end of the eight sessions, Marianne had a deeper understanding of her emotional reactions and felt empowered to choose her response when in relation with her work team. She continued to apply the skills she had learnt in coaching and within four months was offered a promotion. Marianne currently engages ES in a personal capacity to support her through the transition to step up to this more complex leadership role which requires her to develop a wider repertoire of influencing skills.

References

Cohn, H. W. (1997) *Existential Thought and Therapeutic Practice.* London: Sage.

Cooper, M. (2003) *Existential Therapies.* London: Sage.

Heidegger, M. (1962) *Being and Time* (trans. J. Macquarrie and E. Robinson). New York: Harper and Row.

Ihde, D. (1977) *Experimental Phenomenology: An introduction.* Albany, NY: State University of New York (1986).

Merleau-Ponty, M. (1962) *The Phenomenology of Perception* (trans. C. Smith). London: Routledge and Kegan Paul.

Peltier, B. (2001) *The Psychology of Executive Coaching: Theory and application.* New York: Brunner-Routledge.

Sartre, J. P. (1956) *Being and Nothingness: An essay on phenomenological ontology* (trans. H. Barnes). London: Routledge (1991).

Sieler, A. (2003) *Coaching to the Human Soul: Ontological coaching and deep change.* Blackburn, Vic.: Newfield Australia.

Spinelli, E. (1997) *Tales of Un-knowing: Therapeutic encounters from an existential perspective.* London: Duckworth.

Spinelli, E. (2005) *The Interpreted World: An introduction to phenomenological psychology*, 2nd edition. London: Sage.
Spinelli, E. (2007) *Practising Existential Psychotherapy: The Relational World*. London: Sage.
Yalom, I. D. (1980) *Existential Psychotherapy*. New York: Basic Books.

Discussion points

- An existential approach to coaching places pivotal emphasis upon the coaching relationship itself and seeks to foster an experiential immediacy between coach and client. How does this stance compare and contrast with the one that you currently uphold? How would your approach to coaching change if you were to adopt this existential focus?
- As an exercise in practising the phenomenological method discussed in this chapter, work together with a partner. Take turns in exploring a specific event that has recently occurred in your life by opening up its personal meaning through the three 'steps' of the phenomenological method. When you have completed the exercise, discuss what value, if any, you experienced from this method of enquiry.
- Consider the idea of two forms of conflict being proposed by existential theory. Looked at from the standpoint of your clients, what value might this view have for your understanding of the impact that your coaching work has had upon their presenting areas of focus?
- When you consider the case of Marianne that is presented in this chapter, what are the key points in it that, for you, express an existential approach to coaching psychology? What stands out for you in this case study that has challenged your current way of working as a coach?

Suggested reading

Cooper, M. (2003) *Existential Therapies*. London: Sage.
Sieler, A. (2003) *Coaching to the Human Soul: Ontological coaching and deep change*. Blackburn, Vic.: Newfield Australia.
Spinelli, E. (2005) *The Interpreted World: An introduction to phenomenological psychology*, 2nd edition. London: Sage.
Spinelli, E. (2007) *Practising Existential Psychotherapy: The Relational World*. London: Sage.
Yalom, I. D. (2001) *The Gift of Therapy*. London: Piatkus.

Chapter 8

Gestalt coaching

Julie Allan and Alison Whybrow

Introduction

Gestalt coaching concerns a process of becoming fully aware and turning that awareness into action. Gestalt coaching has a relatively short history, yet an increasing body of coaches access this approach in some way, perhaps particularly in executive and leadership work and for those whose time is spent drawing on their own generative and creative abilities. Practitioners draw on their understanding of gestalt psychology and gestalt psychotherapy, both of which preceded the arrival of the gestalt coaching label.

There is a curious dilemma when describing gestalt coaching, in line with Resnick's (1984) challenge in relation to gestalt therapy:

> Every Gestalt therapist could stop doing any gestalt technique that had ever been done and go right on doing gestalt therapy. If they couldn't, then they weren't doing Gestalt therapy in the first place. They were fooling around with a bag of tricks and a bunch of gimmicks.
>
> (Resnick, 1984: 19).

So what might gestalt coaches do? How would gestalt coaching be experienced? Why might a client choose it and benefit from it?

At the moment in time when this sentence was written, the person writing it experienced some anxiety, a concern at how the apparent lack of definition might be received, and wanted to make the explanation a little more concrete. She chose the following words:

> Gestalt coaching concerns a process of becoming fully aware and then turning that awareness into action. The coach and coachee will attend to each emerging focus in such a way that a positive cycle of resolution and emergence of the next focus is created.
>
> In gestalt coaching, the coach will specifically draw on their own awareness (thoughts, feelings, sensations) during sessions and feed this back into the process in order to challenge, support and enquire. In particular

they do this in service of promoting movement wherever they believe the coachee is in some way blocking their experience and potential and failing to move through complete cycles of experience. There may be more emphasis on 'what is going on right now', rather than 'what happened there and then'. A useful analogy is the process of breathing, which sustains life and is generally most effective if one can breathe fully in and also fully out, to allow the next inhalation.

Having written those words, the author felt that some reasonable explanation had been made and her attention was attracted to how it would be possible to link this with some basic theory and in particular with more concrete examples of gestalt in action. In gestalt terms, she had attended to one 'figure' that had emerged from the 'ground' and was free to start to address the next thing that asked for attention.

Development of gestalt coaching

Gestalt psychology was pioneered by Max Wertheimer (1880–1943), Wolfgang Köhler (1887–1967) and Kurt Koffka (1886–1941). Gestalt means a unified or meaningful whole. Fritz Perls (1893–1970) was the, sometimes controversial, originator of gestalt therapy, developing his ideas through the 1920s and onwards. His wife Laura was also actively involved and both have written on the subject. Gestalt coaching might differ from Perls' practice, as indeed might gestalt therapy these days, in that Perls had a very rigorous and perhaps uncompromising attitude to how 'authentic' the therapist needed to be in the relationship with their client. However, the intention of a very 'full' experience of the coachee, the coach and the relationship between them in the 'here-and-now' of their sessions, is a part of a gestalt coaching framework.

The approach in general, based around individual active awareness, differs from two other main strands of psychology that grew up in the early twentieth century, these being the behaviourist or cognitive-behavioural approach, concentrating on learning mechanisms (see chapter 6), and the psychoanalytic (initially Freudian) tradition concentrating on biological drives.

Perls believed that the Freudian approach reduced the person to a set of basic drives, and found this an insufficient way of regarding human development. Through the 1930s, 1940s and 1950s Perls and his colleagues continued with their regard for the person as a whole and in context (holism), incorporating gestalt movement understandings about perception, individual sense-making and resolution/closure. The term holism was originally coined by Smuts (1936). The individual level work was also developed into group settings and, from the 1960s, organisational settings. So here, if it had not done so before, gestalt entered a corporate context.

In recent years, different emphases have come about through different practitioners and approaches to practice, including the growth of gestalt as a coaching approach. It is in the nature of gestalt to evolve, and so it continues to do so in a way that prohibits the exposition of 'the' gestalt way but does, if only just, allow some exposition of common themes.

Theory and basic concepts

Drawing on gestalt psychology and gestalt psychotherapy, gestalt coaching attends to awareness-raising and the ways in which we organise or perceive the world around us. It may, like its therapeutic cousin, be held to be humanistic, existential and phenomenological.

A gestalt psychological view is that what we see and how we perceive things is not an objective reality but the result of who we are at one moment in time. What makes sense (becomes figure) in a particular context (ground) changes momentarily. In an attempt to organise the dynamic complexity of experience, we tend to arrange things in a way that makes sense according to our current thinking, prior experience or preoccupations. We are also predisposed to look for symmetry and equilibrium or 'closure'. Experiments with our visual process give us some understanding of the way our perception of the world is self directed.

In the faces/candlestick picture, we can experience either the faces or the candlestick becoming figure and the other ground, perhaps then reversing this perception. In another picture, we see three unconnected lines as a connected triangle – we fill in the gaps to create the whole (see Figure 8.1).

We also have a tendency to favour similarity, seeing patterns, grouping similar items together and differentiating them from others. For example, the diagonal line of O's stands out from the horizontal lines of X's in Figure 8.1.

Additionally, we reinterpret our world in some way in the light of new experiences and thus our understanding of who we are through our experiences is continually shifting. An aim in gestalt coaching is to explore this subjective world in a way that enables the coachee to access a wider range of choices and make the most of their capacities. In Rogerian terms this is the equivalent of actualising one's potential.

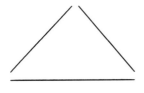

```
OXXXXXX
XOXXXXX
XXOXXXX
XXXOXXX
XXXXOXX
XXXXXOX
```

Figure 8.1 Patterns of perception.

It is apparent that we are predisposed to perceive the world in ways that reframe any objective reality. Here we further explore phenomenology, and using a case study example, highlight how we might become more fully aware. Specific blocks to awareness in the cycle of experience are discussed and highlighted.

Phenomenology and the three defining principles

Phenomenology is the practice of seeking to understand situations through reference to the immediately obvious in-the-present phenomena. For example then, as I eat an orange I am doing so fully aware of the experience in the here and now: of the smell, the sight of the orange, the feel of the skin, the taste of the orange and the sound of it crunching. I am aware of the orange through all senses without distraction from previous or future events. I would not be fully aware of the orange if I ate it while focusing on something else, another thing or 'figure'. In a phenomenological approach, while the past and the future exist, and will no doubt be explored, full attention to the present is required in order to access the most immediate, potent information possible to help promote awareness of and, ultimately, decide on action. In a coaching setting, the coachee may expect the coach to pay detailed attention to feelings, physical movements and postures and so forth that actually occur within the session and enquire into them or reflect them back. Gestalt coaching is lively and alive because the coach will always be seeking to uncover what has to be changed right here and now in this room so that change can happen effectively outside it and at another time.

Phenomenology, according to Yontef (1980; cf. Clarkson, 1999) is one of the three defining principles of gestalt therapy. According to this principle of phenomenology, gestalt coaching would have awareness as its only goal and as its methodology.

The second principle states that gestalt is based wholly on dialogic existentialism. In the coaching setting this refers to the 'here-and-now' coach–coachee dialogue. Isaacs (1993) referred to the ongoing, shared inquiry into the processes, assumptions and certainties that make up day-to-day experience. In dialogue, from the Greek *dia* and *logos* (meaning flowing through), the attention to the relationship and the spirit of enquiry means that something new can emerge that was not in the minds of either party when the dialogue started. It is in this potentially very creative way that something completely appropriate for the current situation is generated. The focus on 'now' makes sense in gestalt terms because of the underpinning assumption of holism – that is, the coachee will show their behaviour patterns and the patterns of their context outside the session, within the session. So in-the-moment dialogue can effectively make a difference to the system.

The third principle is that gestalt's conceptual foundation is gestalt – based on holism and field theory. We exist within a context or 'field', and we understand ourselves in relation to that field, so we cannot be understood without reference to the field. Applied to coaching, this principle highlights the importance of the coach–coachee relationship. The coach cannot *not* be in the field. The coach and coachee are part of each other's fields or contexts, bringing the relationship between the coach and coachee into focus. Yontef (1980) saw these three principles as interlinked and, when fully understood, encompassing each other.

Against the 'ground' of these principles, gestalt coaching facilitates us becoming aware of what is stopping us engaging fully in our everyday experiences. A traditional gestalt therapeutic view is that as individuals we are responsible for our decisions and actions, or indecisions and inactions (existentialism). Identification, exploration and potentially removal of any 'blocks to awareness' enable us to exercise greater choice in our behaviour and function more effectively or healthily.

Perls (1969) saw self-awareness in the here-and-now being the key to people becoming healthy, as self-awareness creates the circumstances in which individuals have greater response-ability for who they are, transcending from environmental support to mature self support (not to be confused with isolated self-absorption) where individuals become fully themselves, engaging with life to their full potential. In coaching terms, the awareness creates the conditions in which the coachee has access to a wider range of possible behaviours, giving greater choice and capability in action and relationship. In gestalt coaching one first place of experiment and rehearsal is with the coach within the coaching relationship.

Traditionally, the gestalt view holds that the relationship between people, as human beings, can be developmental without need of a shared theism of any sort (humanistic). That said, those who identify themselves with the gestalt tradition include people of various spiritual traditions or those who would acknowledge the presence of what might be referred to as the spiritual or the transpersonal. In the early days of gestalt it was Zen that had an influence.

An application case study

A senior executive was responsible for brokering an effective partnership with another company, through interaction with his counterpart. He had spoken by telephone and was going to meet this woman. But he didn't feel at all comfortable and wasn't sure why, so he wanted help to prepare for the meeting . . .

Coach: You say you don't feel comfortable. Tell me more about that.
Exec: Well, I just get the sense that she doesn't want to meet me. (Hands are held in front of him, palms outwards, heels of the hands down and

fingers up; coach makes a subtle mimic of that posture as a part of her way of listening fully, exec nods.) . . .

Coach: You don't feel comfortable and if I'm understanding correctly there's some sense of backing away but only slightly and then a kind of . . . (Coach mimics the posture again and moves her body slightly backwards and forwards, which is what she had observed.)

Exec: Yes, yes (crosses legs and puts arms across stomach); it's a bit worrying.

Coach: You feel worried. (Facial expression of enquiry.)

Exec: Yes . . . I'm on the spot here to get it right and if she doesn't want to talk to me then I have a problem.

Coach: (Coach is now attending to body posture and 'on the spot', 'get it right' and 'if'.) What else do you feel?

Exec: Fear, actually. I might fail.

Coach: (Notes move from 'uncomfortable' to acknowledgement of fear of failure; chooses to engage client's positive capacities and mimics client's hand position.) So you fear you might fail and I notice that you look to be protecting your stomach a bit and you have a sense of being on the spot.

Exec: Just general anxiety I suppose.

Coach: and your anxiety is in your stomach. (Facial expression of enquiry.)

Exec: Yes.

Coach: You feel fear and you have anxiety in your stomach. That's good to be clear about. Shall we think about how you might make a really effective connection with this person even if you are holding anxiety in your stomach?

Exec: (Smiles, sits up, moves hands.)

Coach: That seems to be a thought that allows you to move.

Exec: Yes, I thought I wouldn't be able to . . . well that's funny really . . .

Coach: That's funny?

Exec: Actually I imagine she might be quite anxious too . . . we might both be anxious (smiles).

Coach: It's funny that you're both anxious (also smiles). How do you feel now?

Exec: A bit excited actually.

Coach: Excited . . . where excited?

Exec: I don't know really, just, well, sort of warmer towards the situation

Coach: Warmer towards the situation . . . and the situation's name is . . .? (smiling)

Exec: Andrea (laughs).

The coaching then continues addressing how the client can make an effective connection, including how to relate to emotions or physical reactions that they experience as adverse.

In terms of gestalt thinking, this case study includes:

- Dialogue in the 'here-and-now'.
- A presenting issue, or 'figure'.
- A process of using phenomenology to gain real clarity or 'contact' with that figure, the full contact allowing a degree of resolution on one part of the overall picture, allowing another figure to emerge.

This cycle, the gestalt cycle of experience, can be travelled many times within a session and there will be cycles within the overall picture. Aspects of humanism and existentialism at work are demonstrated in that the client had managed to separate himself from the human condition, his feelings, so separating himself from the potential for good contact with another person.

Key concepts

The contact boundary phenomenon is based on the gestalt concept of 'self' being a process of relating to the environment – of distinguishing what is self and what is not-self. The contact boundary is the actual point at which the self is distinguished from the not-self (Perls, 1957), and changes from moment to moment as our understanding and awareness of our self changes. In the case study, attending to phenomenology assisted the process of connecting the client with himself as a person and his capacity for connecting with others. It also helped the client distinguish between anxiety he has and anxiety that another may (or may not) have, again giving the potential for a better meeting place.

The paradoxical theory of change (Beisser, 1970) holds that in order to transition from A to B, it is first necessary to fully engage with A. Clarkson (1999) is among those who have forwarded a gestaltist view that whatever is said fully and completely, the opposite also begins to be true. In other words, once you are fully aware of what 'A' is, you then become aware of the opposite situation and any number of alternatives in between (B_1, B_2, ... B_x). A gestalt coach helps the coachee very fully raise and explore awareness of the state they are in (in this example, their anxiety about the forthcoming meeting) because with this sharpness or intensity of experience there also comes an ability for the coachee to become mobilised.

Our attention to our awareness is informed by and informs the cycle of experience. This seven-stage cycle is described by a number of writers (e.g. Zinker, 1978; Clarkson, 1999). Applied to the example above, the cycle might start with the client feeling not 'at all comfortable' (sensation) and 'fear, actually. I might fail', with anxiety held in their stomach (awareness), understanding how they might make a really effective connection with the person even though they are holding anxiety in their stomach (mobilisation), realisation that 'she might be quite anxious too' (action), 'excited' about the meeting (final contact), 'warmer towards the situation' (satisfaction) and finally, rest (withdrawal), before the cycle begins again. At any point, a cycle can feed into many other cycles, as awareness leads to greater awareness.

Blocks to awareness

Seven blocks to full awareness of ourselves and our environments as they truly are are described in gestalt therapy. While the seven-point cycle of experience might also be considered somewhat reductionist, we outline the blocks and the cycle stages in Table 8.1.

Of the boundary disturbances or defence mechanisms outlined in Table 8.1, Introjection and Retroflection are particularly relevant to the coach in terms of dealing with self-critical thought patterns and unfinished business. Imagine an executive returning after maternity leave. She is a section head and is exploring job sharing with another section head.

Back at work, feeling obliged to prove her value, she may engage in desensitisation to feelings of tiredness, anxiety, even hunger. When a project goes really well she will (quite possibly as she did before) attribute the success to her team making up for her not being there, or the contribution of her jobshare. This deflection cuts her off from the beneficial impact of the acknowledgement and the encouragement that would help her take credit for, and gain beneficial learning from, her effective behaviours in her workplace setting.

She may have a number of introjections or shoulds that are guiding her choice in returning part time – such as 'Women in our family stay at home and look after the children', 'You shouldn't try to work and be a mother.' If she leaves those introjections unaddressed, she is clearly setting herself up for a time of great strain and potentially poor performance. Retroflections could also be contributing to her actions. She may have wanted her own mother to work part time rather than full time and so chooses to do this for her own children instead; she hasn't really considered her own view on her own current situation.

Through the philosophical, theoretical and conceptual ideas presented above, it's easy to see that from the gestalt perspective the person's worldview changes moment by moment. As Perls (1969) succinctly described it, we never step in the same river twice.

The phenomenon of self is interesting here. Using the language of field theory, we can think of the self as making up the field. We are constantly, although not explicitly, engaged in understanding how to frame reality at a

Table 8.1 Blocks to awareness

Block to awareness and the part of the cycle it interrupts	What that means for the client
Desensitisation – interrupts Sensation	Sensations or feelings are diluted, disregarded or neglected. Pain or discomfort is kept from coming to mind (becoming figural). At a low level, desensitisation might be healthy in order to meet a short-term objective but over the longer term, becomes unhealthy and unsustainable (for example, drinking insufficient fluids, going without sleep, taking painkillers and other interventions that prevent the sensations from being perceived).
Deflection – interrupts Awareness	Where a person turns aside from direct contact with another person or a situation. The conversation subject may be subtly changed or reformed, for example: in response to 'How did you feel to receive such a positive accolade for the project you completed?' the person responds, 'I did nothing, it was the team that enabled the project to succeed.' Instead of sharing direct feelings with their full emotional intensity, abstract language that waters down the enquiry is chosen or eye contact may be avoided. Habitual deflection means the person fails to gain good feedback from themselves, others or the environment. Some deflection could be a healthy choice.
Introjection – interrupts Mobilisation, preventing the person taking appropriate action to meet their needs.	What we 'take in'. What do we chew over and fully prepare for digestion, or what do we swallow whole, barely noticing what it is? Introjects are often a legacy of childhood when we may not have had the means to be discerning about what was being fed to us: 'You must always work hard', 'You must not show your feelings', 'You are stupid', 'All the women in our family have stayed at home and brought up their families in the right way.' These become inflexible, totalitarian, internalised 'you should always . . .' ideas. Introjections may assist with learning certain skills but later need to be re-examined to investigate whether they still apply.
Projection – interrupts Action	This involves seeing in others' personality or behaviour what you don't acknowledge or see in yourself. For example, you might experience others as critical or judging towards you when, instead, it is you who is critical and judgemental of yourself (or of others). Projection presents an area for exploration and work for the coachee. It can also assist in planning and anticipating future situations, in being creative.
Retroflection – this may specifically interrupt the final contact phase of the awareness cycle	There are two types of retroflection. First, when you do to yourself what you want to do to or do with someone or something else. For example, rather than expressing negative feelings, anger, hurt to others, you turn the aggression on yourself: 'It's no wonder I'm being bullied when I'm just so useless.' Never allowing yourself to express your hurt or rage isn't usually a recipe for health.

Continued Overleaf

Table 8.1 Continued

Block to awareness and the part of the cycle it interrupts	What that means for the client
	The second type of retroflection is when you do to yourself what you want or wanted to have done for you by others. This can be a form of self-support, it can also interfere with getting genuine interpersonal needs met in the present. For example in response to the question 'What would you like to achieve from this meeting' you respond 'Oh I'm happy just to take part', rather than voice your real needs, perhaps 'I need to feel included', or 'I have a lot of good ideas on the issue and I'd like you to listen to them.'
Egotism – interrupts Satisfaction	Characterised by the individual stepping outside themselves and becoming a spectator or commentator on themselves and their relationship with the environment. The person can understand what's going on but doesn't act on that understanding, with the result that they can seem lacking in empathy and don't benefit from the satisfaction of a more hands-on involvement. So a boss notices a stressed employee and makes a mental note of the stress without extending a hand towards the person, as if the noticing was sufficient.
Confluence – interrupts Withdrawal	This is where the person is not differentiated from their environment or another person – the boundaries are blurred. The phrase 'We think this, don't we?' indicates confluence in a relationship. Confluence also appears in 'groupthink'. In this state of affairs, consideration of boundaries, conflict or disagreement is experienced as a threat to important relationships, even to 'survival'. In organisations, you may hear 'It's important not to rock the boat', 'stick one's head above the parapet', or any number of other phrases. To attend to boundaries and allow conflict is seen as a threat to the organisation and its survival. Confluence can assist in promoting empathy and life enrichment, in healthy contact, there is then a letting go with confidence that such moments can recur. If there is no 'letting go', development is prevented. A coachee may be confluent with their occupation, so they don't distinguish themselves from their job role.

Source: adapted from Clarkson, 1999: 51–57, with permission from Sage Publications.

particular moment; how to arrange our 'life space'; how to organise our experience. We do these things by organising (or configuring) the field according to particular meanings, a personal process in which certain parts of our total experience become figural and other parts are organised around them, as ground. This process can be construed as the self at work or in Latner's (1986) phrase, 'us-in-process'. The self is therefore (as in all gestalt theories of the self) a process and not a static abstract mental entity; it provides a way of describing an ongoing, evolving and transforming process in which we continuously engage, configuring the experiential field, or choosing our reality (Parlett, 1991). Houston (2003: 6) points out that 'nothing or no one is truly separable from their context'.

All these elements – the self, our experience, what is figure and what is ground – are distorted by the process of perception and our assumptions, stereotypes and subsequent expectations of our world. We do not actually experience anything as it 'truly' is, we experience life through the 'worldview' that we personally hold. We don't see things as *they* are. We see them as *we* are (Nin, 1973). We are predisposed to see what we expect.

The process of gestalt coaching is to work to sharpen individual experience, to become aware of our assumptions and stereotypes and to challenge them in order to see what is taking place more clearly and therefore respond to what is actually happening, not what we think is happening.

Through a process of dialogue, in the coach–coachee relationship, the aim is to raise awareness in such a way that new thinking can emerge because the coachee is prompted to uncover, or discover (and maybe to recover from) unexamined organisational and individual patterns of meaning making that have stopped being useful, but still remain unquestioned and often invisible.

It might be useful to end this part of the chapter with a quote from Smith. 'I consider this blend of existential and Zen philosophy, this organismic personality theory, and this phenomenological experiential style of working to be the necessary and sufficient conditions to define the Gestalt approach' (Smith, 1976: 74).

Practice

The goal of gestalt coaching is to enable coachees to fully engage with their experiences (of themselves, others, their context . . .) in such a way that they are able to generate and carry forward what they want to be doing in a beneficial and satisfying manner. Awareness is key.

How is this achieved? As Smith (1976) indicates, the gestalt approach is not defined by techniques. It is perhaps also worth recalling our statement from Resnick at the start of the chapter:

> every Gestalt therapist could stop doing any gestalt technique that had ever been done and go right on doing gestalt therapy. If they couldn't, then they weren't doing Gestalt therapy in the first place. They were fooling around with a bag of tricks and a bunch of gimmicks.
>
> (Resnick, 1984: 19)

With this in mind, the following material offers possibilities not prescriptions. There are at least as many possibilities as there are coach–coachee relationships, each unique yet each with the same purpose in view. This exquisite attention to creativity and generative potential, starting from fundamental principles each time, requires that the coach

- has a full understanding of the theoretical and practical history of gestalt,
- has an ability to responsibly use phenomenology in the service of others, and
- subscribes to appropriate standards of practice and ethics.

Fooling around with a bunch of gimmicks and a bag of tricks is hardly appropriate.

In the gestalt coaching space the coachee is encouraged to engage with themselves, their thoughts, their context, and their relationships through all five of their senses. Physical movement and play (for example, through modelling and drawing) may be part of the coaching. A comfortable space with room for this expression of experience is useful.

The gestalt coach brings themselves to the coaching relationship. They are present, authentic and part of the coachee's context. What the coach experiences in the coaching space is part of the coaching process. The central issues the coach detects are presented thoughtfully with good timing. It is the coaching relationship that is the major 'tool'. The development of trust, self-awareness and the creative experimentation that enables the coachee to develop a healthier worldview are enabled through the existence of an authentic relationship between coach and coachee.

Dialogue

One viewpoint that helpfully informs gestalt coaches is that through dialogue covert patterns are made overt as they are happening and some new understanding can emerge. Attending to behavioural patterns or language use that indicate interruptions enables further attention and reflection from the coachee.

Through dialogue the coach encourages the coachee to uncover assumptions and patterns for themselves. The coachee's awareness of how they use language is raised and they are encouraged to use language that reflects their control over themselves and identifies their responsibility for their thoughts, feelings and actions. The coach assists the coachee, as they become more aware and able to 'call out' patterns they had previously taken as read. The coachee is assisted in adopting this same approach beyond the coaching sessions.

Engaging with the full sensory impact of what is happening, the coachee learns to become more aware of themselves and their changing experience from moment to moment in the coaching session and through this, in their broader life and work context. One experiment in a coaching relationship might be receiving positive or negative feedback without deflecting it, and fully experiencing the thoughts, feelings, bodily sensations that go with it.

Experimentation

Experimenting, key to the gestalt approach, is closely associated with the action phase of the cycle of experience although, in reality, experimenting underpins the whole cycle of experience. The coachee is encouraged to try out new thoughts, beliefs or actions within the safety of the coaching relationship.

Creativity and timing are required on the part of the coach to identify the moment to suggest or enable creative experimentation by the coachee. Experiments might include polarisation, where the differences between positions (e.g. values, beliefs, the self-critical part of the coachee, and so on) are drawn out or accentuated and explored. Raising awareness of the values, assumptions and beliefs that the coachee holds is an important area for shaking off self-limiting thoughts, feelings and behaviours. Facilitating this through encouraging the coachee to hold a conversation with the critical part of themselves, or the absent other from whom these beliefs, assumptions and values were learned or gobbled up is a way of drawing out these underlying patterns of perception. The coachee, once aware of these patterns, can re-examine the moral imperatives that guide their thoughts, feelings and behaviour and make a conscious choice about what to retain and what to let go. This releases the coachee from the 'tyranny' of internalised values and prejudices (Clarkson, 1999). A number of techniques, such as 'two-chair work', 'meta mirror' or 'enactment', are examples of this element of gestalt work.

Visualisation may be used to experiment, with the coachee encouraged to visualise themselves in any number of ways that are different from the way they are, perhaps having achieved their identified goal, perhaps considering what it might be like to be the person they want to become. This provides a wealth of possibilities for experimentation and exploration for the coachee.

Storytelling and metaphor could be used as a means of experimentation, encouraging the coachee to create a story that can be used to reflect their own actual or desired personal story. Rehearsing potentially difficult situations before they occur is a further experiment that assists the coach to build their own personal resources beyond the coaching sessions. The experiments that are devised between the coach and coachee can be worked out within the coaching session, given as homework or both.

The coaching relationship

The coaching relationship is key to the effectiveness of gestalt coaching and the coach remains in a coachee's field whether they are physically present or not. It seems a mix of face-to-face and other forms of interpersonal contact would be appropriate for gestalt coaching. Attention to different elements of information (such as intonation or what specific language was used) is necessary in telephone coaching sessions, as the opportunity to attend to all five senses is diminished compared to face-to-face contact. Media such as video conferencing may overcome some of the challenges to telephone coaching using a gestalt approach. There is such little opportunity for contact between the coach and the coachee when using email, it may be better used as a limited medium, perhaps for discrete tasks when using a gestalt approach.

Application and process

Gestalt coaching can be used when working with groups. Skilful use of the gestalt approach, philosophy and concepts assists in raising the group's awareness of what is taking place in the group from moment to moment. What are they focusing on? What are people talking about? Are the patterns in this group replicated in the wider field?

The format of a gestalt coaching session is likely to contain elements of practice discussed above. You will not be surprised to hear that a standard format does not exist, rather what is brought to the coaching relationship by the coachee generates the format of the session. A full range of ways of working can be encompassed in any one session as the approach is about being fully present and fully raising awareness.

Which clients benefit most?

Gestalt coaching is potentially most suitable for those who are inclined towards regarding themselves holistically as 'the equipment for the job', and have an interest in using their own presence as a catalyst for change, rather than seeing themselves as somewhat separate from the application of their knowledge or skills base.

Senior executives and those in leadership positions (perhaps at whatever organisational level) frequently are in this group because it's about overall effective ways of being rather than (necessarily) the closing of a performance gap. They are also frequently individuals who are interested in systemic viewpoints, which is also a feature of gestalt coaching. Those with a very strong action orientation towards a defined future condition may not find attending fully to the present very appealing. This may be overcome by focusing on the huge potential for behaviour change that emerges through addressing blocks to awareness and in this way changing some habits or beliefs that are no longer appropriate. Gestalt approaches might not appeal to or be chosen by those people who would like a more strictly gap-analysis based and/or cognitive-behavioural approach rather than an overtly holistic, systemic approach.

Case study

A gestalt case study presents a challenge. If the ethos of the 'lively present' is to be honoured (shall we not say conserved or preserved, like pickle or jam) and it can take a thousand words to (fail to?) explain that moment of time in which the world came to be differently viewed, and in any event we are writing about a person, not a case, how might we proceed from this point? And if the whole is greater than the sum of the parts, yet in studying this case we are drawn to split it into bits in order to explain each part, and believing that the reconstitution is unlikely to match the original . . . it's a relief to know that readers will create the meaningful whole they need in order to gain value for themselves.

Carina is a senior executive in a large corporation that has recently undergone a merger and is in the process of creating its new organisational forms. Her former managing director, with whom she has an unproductive relationship, has remained MD. She is one of a selected group at her managerial level who were offered coaching support before the merger was announced because they were regarded as having potential for directorship (two steps above) or at least head of section (one step above). At lower levels some people have had to apply for their own jobs and there have been voluntary redundancies as well as involuntary exits. Her area has performed well overall, however there are some serious morale issues for her team and for herself, and some performance issues in her area (overseen by her senior team). Carina has been through a 360-degree feedback process and has six-monthly appraisal meetings with her manager. Owing to staff changes her recent appraisal was with a new manager (post merger) and the 360-degree process took place before the merger. Before her first coaching meetings she reports the need to address two areas:

- She is required to be seen as more strategic in her leadership.
- On a personal front she's had enough of the disruption, which she thinks has forced her to be more hands-on than ever, which she thinks might not be strategic even though necessary.

At her first session Carina reiterates the first aim and spends a lot of time speaking about her negative work experiences, wondering whether she even wants to stay in the company at all.

Session 1

Extract: exploring how things are for the coachee

Carina smiles on meeting, clasps her hands together and generally seems slightly awkward, standing in a position that's half turned to the door and half to a desk in one corner. She apologises for the wait the coach had in reception, for the slight difficulty in gaining a space away from her office and therefore the utilitarian nature of the meeting room and, explaining what she has been trying to finish this morning in order to be at the meeting, apologises because she feels unprepared. She speaks quickly, repeats herself and her shoulders are rounded.

Coach is aware of Carina's flushed face and slightly turned-away stance; a curiosity about why some facts that might be seen as unimportant are linked with a great deal of concern; the thought that she feels she's arrived at a coffee morning rather than a business meeting; a reactive concern to put a frame on proceedings.

Coach actions: to make a good greeting and attend to Carina, to accept hospitality offered and then to contract around the general remit for the coaching and the requirements of the particular session from the organisation's point of view, just to check for understanding. And then to ask the following question.

Coach: What is important for you at the moment for us to spend time on today?

Carina: Well, I'm told I need to be better at strategic leadership and probably no doubt I do, so probably that.

Coach: Hmmm? Strategic and leadership can have all sorts of different meanings ... or none ... I wonder what they mean for you, or for your work, and also what's important for you about them. Let's spend time on what's important for you at the moment.

Carina: Yes, well, quite. I do wonder what they mean by it.

Coach: What they mean ... Is there anything in writing that helps?

Carina: Not really. Just the usual descriptions.

Coach: And who's the 'they'?

Carina: (still speaking quickly, moving around in seat, eyes frequently raising to the ceiling) Well, it's the company and really at the end of the day it's how I'm seen by the board ... they want us all to be more strategic.

Coach: (pauses) Do you know, I'm starting to feel a bit rushed and some sense of confusion around all this. I've noticed your tone of voice when you mention the board and an interesting expression on your face when you say the word strategic ...

Carina: (is nodding) Hmmm. I've been spotted haven't I? Very good.

Coach: Well, perhaps you have ... what's it like to be spotted?

Carina: OK. Well it's just that I don't know if I want to do what's being asked and well, you see, I'm not like them.

Coach:	You're not like 'them'. So how are you? What are you like? (Coachee leans sideways on chair, swivels chair, leans on the back of the chair with one arm and supports her head with that hand, looks down, looks to one side, clears her throat, exhales audibly.)
Carina:	I'm not at all sure I fit.
Coach:	And what's important to you about this fit?
Carina:	It seems to me that the people who do well just spend their time unjustifiably promoting themselves and I just don't do that.
Coach:	You don't unjustifiably promote yourself?
Carina:	(smiles) No. Well, obviously I wouldn't *unjustifiably* promote myself . . . I see what you mean . . . well it just isn't me.
Coach:	Justifiably promoting yourself?
Carina:	I shouldn't have to promote myself. Good work is self-evident.
Coach:	And you have done good work.
Carina:	Yes, but it's just what I expect of myself. You shouldn't have to go around telling people.
Coach:	Says who?

Notes

Here the coach noted 'Good work is self-evident . . . it's just what I expect of myself . . . You shouldn't have to . . .' and the question 'Says who?' was slightly playfully stated and functioned as the beginning of an interlude in which potential introjects were checked and explored.

The coach has used phenomenology as a source of information – attending to the coachee's physical state and to their own – and is following what seems to become 'figure' against the ground for the coachee. The coach is also reflecting back certain uses of language to the coachee.

At any point there may be many choices of response, and the coach is holding lightly to one side the choices not taken so that they don't interfere with the current avenue. Lightly because in gestalt coaching there is the expectation that if something is important and remains unresolved, it will become figural once more. It's just useful to double-check over time any tendency to deflection that has emerged in the coach–coachee pattern and which might offer an avenue of enquiry relevant to the coachee's everyday situation.

The coach is always considering where the coachee might be on a contact cycle (or cycles), checking that out, and creating the opportunity for full contact in order that the next figure may emerge. Here, the main areas were Sensation and Awareness (with their attendant desensitisation and deflection) plus important information about introjects that seemed to be limiting the coachee's options for action (Mobilisation). The conversation about this raised uncomfortable emotions for the coachee as the whole area of 'shoulds' was explored in relation to the coachee raising their own profile (or not), accusing others of unjustifiable self promotion and feeling righteously indignant that they were not fully appreciated if they didn't behave that way. This system of sense-making was preventing action and contact; in the session full contact with the potential self-limiting aspects was achieved without the coachee retroflecting (thinking they were 'bad' or 'stupid', for example). They came to a useful realisation about 'what they are like'.

Homework

The coachee simply agreed to notice things and not try to change them. This suggestion was based around increasing the potential for sensation and aware-ness while avoiding attendant interruptions. And also links with Beisser's paradoxical theory of change – the more fully one becomes 'A' the more likely it is that being 'not-A' can just happen. The coachee decided to notice her response to 'giving themselves credit when it was due' or believing that others hadn't given them due credit, and her response to requiring their team to deliver what she asked of them without spending time on doing the work herself.

Session 2

Extract: making connections, some reframes

During this session Carina reported great success in being clear with her expectations of her team – the awareness had been all it took to amend her behaviour helpfully, and the team had responded. She also reported a series of interactions with one individual leading to Carina going home and bursting into tears when her partner asked how her day had gone.

Coach: As you think about it now, can you identify a point at which you became furious?

Carina: Well, I was doing fine although a bit bored really, given it was the fourth time, until I said that there wasn't room to accommodate what he was suggesting, at which point he said, 'That's what you said before' . . . and I said, 'Yes, three times and I've now had enough of not being heard. I have a meeting now. Please report back to me on Thursday.'

Coach: (Coach sits quietly, maintains eye contact, is aware of feelings of sadness and the possibilities of projection around who is listening to whom, or not.)

Carina: Maybe I shouldn't have said that bit about having had enough.

Coach: Of not being heard?

Carina: Mmmm.

Coach: Mmmm. I'm wondering what he did hear? I'm wondering what he thinks you've heard or not?

Carina: You know, I wasn't really listening after his first visit . . .

Notes

In this session some conflict had clearly arisen and the experience of it was quite novel to the coachee. She had certainly noticed what was happening around both her avenues of experiment and the second session allowed some debrief from that. Reflection on appropriate experiments is a part of gestalt coaching . . . the existential stance asks that the experiments are dealt with in a way that encourages awareness and responsibility and does not lead to further entrenchment of interruptions related to judging ourselves or others. When the coachee gave themselves a 'shouldn't', the coach could have chosen to see that as an introject cue, however the phenomenological information offered another avenue of enquiry that assisted a moment of contact and further discovery.

The session, in line with the original stated intention, had also included conversation to explore the meanings of 'strategy' and 'leadership', both for the coachee and as officially defined by the organisation. Mismatches, agreements and areas of curiosity were noted. The coach was of the view that the coachee's understanding and capability were not at issue in this regard but that her repertoire of useful behaviours was narrower than might be expected given her knowledge and comprehension of the organisational system.

Homework

Simply for the coachee to notice communications in which she felt heard or not heard, communications in which she felt seen or not seen, and communications when she felt she really listened and attended to the other person.

Session 3

Extract: more connections

Coach: So how did you get along with your experiments and what's . . .

Carina: It's been really interesting. Just all about when I didn't listen to people and why . . . I can't say I've made a big change about it but def-
initely I stop myself from dismissing them while they're still talking
. . . I can't believe I even used to do that. The other thing is realising
that the people I don't like – the 'them' we spoke about, do that.

Coach: That's great. And there's something I just feel the need to let you
know . . . you probably know what it is.

Carina: I started talking while you were still talking.
(Both laugh, then are quiet for a while.)

Carina: Well, you know, sometimes I'm just going to talk over folks if I'm
really enthusiastic and somehow I think that could be OK as long as
I'm not talking over them for the rest of the time . . .

Coach: You'd like to keep some spontaneity . . .?

Carina: That's right. I am a person, after all. And sometimes I need to
remember that so are they (pause).

Coach: So, you've been noticing all sorts of things about communication.
How's the leadership going? Are you more strategic yet?

Carina: I wanted to talk about that. I've noticed how much I close down
when I talk to some people, including board members. And I think
that what's going on is that my commitment is questioned because I
don't come across as 'in there' enough.

Coach: You think that's what's going on.

Carina: It's a fairly sound guess. Actually I've been doing more listening
as you know and it's a combination of things I've heard about how
I'm viewed and what the MD wants from people . . . and I think it
connects with thinking people just should notice when I'm being
strategic, I shouldn't have to spell it out . . . but somehow it's very
confusing.

Coach: Actually you're looking a bit upset. Are you feeling upset?

Carina: I am upset. It's like I'm not seen or something. But I can't see what I
can do about it.

Coach: So you've been busy listening, which gave you all sorts of helpful
information, and now there's something going on about seeing and
visibility. You don't feel like you're being seen and you don't know at
the moment what to do about it.

Carina: That's right.

Coach: Would you be willing to do something a bit different, just to see what
emerges around this? (Coachee looked interested but not enthusiastic.) What I had in mind was to spend a few minutes sketching
things out in some way – seeing what could become visible.

Carina: Oh, you did warn me of this at the start, didn't you. Well OK. I can't draw though.

Coach: Fortunately that doesn't matter in the least (crayons and A4 coloured paper were supplied). All you need to do is draw something – anything you like – about not being seen, or even about being seen if you like.

Ten minutes pass; the coachee produces four sheets of drawings, and the coach enquires into them. Questions are 'Tell me a little about this.' 'Are these people you know?' or otherwise descriptors such as 'The colour is really strong on that bit', 'I see quite a distance between X and Y' . . . etc.

Carina: That's my family and that's me. I'm always in the middle of five. I can't win.

Coach: You can't win?

Carina: It doesn't matter what I want to say or do – I either have to tag along with the older ones or keep an eye on the younger ones and if everyone's together the volume of noise means nobody hears anything anyway.

Coach: Maybe it's just me but that sounds relevant to your situation at the moment. What do you think?

Carina: I'm in the middle – between my direct reports and the board you mean, or maybe when I'm in meetings with the board . . .?

Coach: I don't know exactly. Maybe. What makes sense to you?

Carina: I just gave up. That's what I said, I can't win.

Coach: And you'd like to win now?

Carina: Well, I don't want to beat anybody else.

Coach: So how will you win in your current situation without feeling that it's at anybody else's expense?

Carina: That's so amazing. That's what I hate about these people who blow their own trumpets but actually haven't done anything. If I do good things, then those things are good for me and good for the organisation and other people . . . it would be OK to talk about those things, and if I have good ideas maybe I can get them listened to . . .

Coach: So you want to be explicit about some of the things you do and the ideas you have, and you want to be explicit with the board and with your senior managers, among others.

Carina: Yes.

Coach: And that will be winning?

Carina: Yes.

Coach: What sort of thing might you let them know about. Just a few things off the top of your head.

Carina: Quite a long list.

Coach: How many of them count as strategic leadership around here?

Carina: More than half. Quite a lot more than half. But it's about how I'm doing things, isn't it? I mean I knew that and they do go on about it being 'how' not just 'what' but I didn't get it. I've got it now. But nobody has ever said for me to focus on communication – why's that?

Coach: When we started talking about hearing and seeing things being an issue, it was a fair bet that there would be some glitches in the wider system that you're part of, but I couldn't know what they were, so we worked with what we both knew . . .

Notes

This session felt quite different from the perspective of the coach. The coachee has achieved contactful clarity in a number of areas and is showing fewer interruptions or boundary disturbances. The coachee reports some confusion and she does this in a kind of 'existential' way – the coach can gain from her body language, intonation and so forth that the coachee is not blaming herself or others for this and is interested to explore it. The coach reflects back the 'upset' possibility and picks up on the theme of vision, both of which are accepted by the coachee. An experiment is offered that could make things more visually explicit in some way – drawing/mapping. This enables talk about the actuality or metaphor of 'visibility' to be conducted around a matched 'artefact'. And this is useful for this client who has normally a good facility with words but who is somewhat lost for them at this moment in time – she can just register 'confusion'.

Later in the session, with the aim to help support the coachee should any retroflection creep back in to interfere with the full contact she seems much more able to achieve, there was a discussion about simple and effective means of support for spontaneity, and appropriate trumpet-blowing or clarity with her senior managers and the board.

The retention of spontaneity and some amount of playfulness is useful in ensuring that a coachee doesn't spend the rest of their days spectating on their own behaviour in ways that actually prevent them from 'just getting on with it'.

The coachee pulled strands together from the previous sessions, related to the stated coaching issues, and gained a full appreciation of her experience of being 'stuck in the middle'. She left the session very clear that she could carry out her leadership in a way suitable for supporting those below her and informing/supporting the board.

Homework

Capture her own new personal vision in some way and seek feedback from trusted others on how she is being seen. Notice her sense of commitment and whether this was being noticed.

Session 4

Extract: planning, closing a cycle and opening one

Arriving for this session the coach noticed a variety of environmental changes which, on exploration, had been instigated by the coachee for reasons to do with relationship building and holding the vision. Many good conversations had been had and the physical space was a reflection of a mental space that was very much more productive for the coachee in relation to her leadership or strategy goals. And she was being usefully noticed by the board. However, Carina had doubts about how sustainable her level of activity was, despite her high enthusiasm.

Coach: Well that's good to be clear about. So is it worthwhile just explor-
          ing for a while how you will continue to be successful, demonstrat-
          ing strategic leadership and being appreciated, in a way you can
          sustain?
Carina: I'm not sure it's possible.
Coach: Not possible to do it or not possible to explore it?

At similar points with other coachees the coach has often found two types of exploration helpful. In this case both were used, the first in quite a short form. The first is a 'two-chair' type of conversation. These can be used to allow the coachee to converse with an absent other person known to them. In therapy this might be a sibling or a parent, living or otherwise; here it was used to allow the 'for' and 'against' parts of the coachee to converse. This was followed by using the senses in a 'timeline' type experiment in which the coachee imagines a point, say a year hence, in which they are successful, step into that success and then plot their time back to the present day in quarterly steps. This engages the physical body and the senses and works through the required 'plan' for the achievement.

Coach: So let's just have a conversation between the 'can-do' you
             and the 'pit' you, as you have named them (refers to anxiety
             in the pit of the stomach). Who will speak first?
Carina: Pit.

Coach:	OK, so go and sit in the pit chair. Move to the can-do chair for the can-do to speak.
Carina (pit):	I'm very anxious about all this good stuff you've been doing, it's taken a lot of effort and you know it can't go on
Carina (can-do – has swapped seats):	Well I'm sorry you're anxious and it has been a lot of effort but I think it's been really worth it.
Carina (pit):	It might have been worth it but you can't keep it up.
Carina (can-do):	I can.
Carina (pit):	That's not true.
Carina (can-do):	You're right (turns to coach). Now what?
Coach:	I'm not taking sides. Come and sit back in the Carina chair. I notice you let pit have the first word and maybe not exactly the last word but it was heading that way.
Carina:	It's really difficult to ignore anxiety, isn't it?
Coach:	Can-do wasn't ignoring pit, as far as I noticed.
Carina:	You're right. OK, another go (goes to can-do chair).
Carina (can-do):	I'm not ignoring you. We have to work out how to keep being successful even when you're anxious.
Carina (pit):	OK. You know, I like being anxious, it's my job.
Carina (can-do):	It's your job to be anxious? Why?
Carina (pit):	So you don't get in a fix.
Carina (can-do):	You think I'll get in a fix if you stop being anxious?
Carina (pit):	Yes.
Carina (can-do):	Right. Erm. Well. OK, you can be a bit anxious so I don't get in a fix but only a bit because when you're a lot anxious I end up having to work much harder and in fact maybe too hard.
Carina (pit):	OK. I'm going to stay a little bit anxious and as long as you listen to me a bit then I won't shout. (Coachee comes back to her Carina chair.)
Carina:	Right, this is getting ridiculous now.
Coach:	Ridiculous?
Carina:	Well for heaven's sake, I'm talking to myself, agreeing with myself about how anxious I need to be and deciding a little bit is just fine and I don't need to work so hard at it.
Coach:	So can-do and pit have an agreement now?
Carina:	Yes. I'll be looking for hairs on the palms of my hands next.

Coach checks out that the coachee is actually OK about the two-chair experiment (she is), then revisits the agreement and suggests walking the time line back from the future. Coachee chooses a very particular focus with just a three-month timeline. For the sake of space, this isn't documented here; however, the approach was:

1 Specify the desired outcome.
2 Imagine self in that place and notice very fully, using all the senses in the imagination, what it is like being there. For example, in this place what do you see? Hear? Wear? Etc., etc.
3 Step back one month. Repeat the process and then decide what needs to be done at that time in order for the success to be in place a month hence.
4 Repeat for the number of steps chosen. In this case, one month before and then back to today.
5 Review and capture the steps.

Note

By the end of this session, the coachee had discovered the ways in which she might allow striving to actually increase anxiety and decrease success and had raised her awareness about being sustainably successful. She thought it was quite fun that the job of 'pit' was to be anxious and she started calling 'him' Brad pit as a kind of in-joke to remind herself that anxiety had its place and might be OK to hang out with occasionally.

Anxiety can come from the mobilisation stage. The sudden change in activity level of this coachee was a clue to this, along with the use of a well-known phrase which did turn out to have some bearing on Carina's belief system and behaviour. However the point was not to make this 'wrong' in any way but to explore what was useful and what might need to be changed. Anxiety did turn out to be a driver, and making friends with the right amount of anxiety allowed Carina to proceed in Brad's company – a much more realistic outcome than deciding anxiety was a bad thing that must be avoided or ignored.

Carina then engaged her considerable capabilities to experience and start to embody her own success as a leader. She created a self-fulfilling prophecy that was working in her favour.

There was discussion from time to time about how she preserved her own boundaries and she started to consider the possibility of being a board member AND being her own person. Confluence (group-think or acquiescence are organisational faces of this) is an interruption to achieving the satisfaction of a job well done.

Summary

This case study has been presented selectively to illustrate certain elements of gestalt coaching, including the practical application of the cycle of experience. Other and different cycles could have been drawn out since complex situations don't really reduce to the movement through one cycle on one topic. However, the principles still apply for multiple cycles and with multiple entry points – i.e. the work doesn't necessarily start with sensation because the first figural issue might be satisfaction, as was the case in the coaching of a very busy executive who was always rushing on to the next project and never attending to the completion of the preceding ones (of which there were very very many!).

References

Beisser, A. R. (1970) The paradoxical theory of change. In J. Fagan and I. L. Shepherd (eds) *Gestalt Therapy Now* (pp. 77–80). New York: Harper and Row.
Clarkson, P. (1999) *Gestalt Counselling in Action*, 2nd edition. London: Sage.
Houston, G. (2003) *Brief Gestalt Therapy*. London: Sage.
Isaacs, W. N. (1993) Taking flight: dialogue, collective thinking and organizational learning. *Organizational Dynamics* (special issue on the learning organisation). Autumn: 24–39.
Latner, J. (1986) *The Gestalt Therapy Book: A holistic guide to the theory, principles and techniques*. Gouldsboro, ME: Gestalt Journal Press.
Nin, A. (1973) *Seduction of the Minotaur*. Chicago, IL: Ohio University Press.
Parlett, M. (1991) Reflections on field theory. *British Gestalt Journal* 1: 68–91.
Perls, F. (1957) Finding self through Gestalt Therapy. *Gestalt Journal* 1(1).
Perls, F. (1969) *Gestalt Therapy Verbatim*. Moab, UT: Real People Press.
Resnick, R. W. (1984) Gestalt Therapy East and West: Bi-coastal dialogue, debate or debacle? *Gestalt Journal* 7(1): 13–32.
Smith, E. W. L. (1976) *Growing Edge of Gestalt Therapy*. Gouldsboro, ME: Gestalt Journal Press.
Smuts, J. C. (1936) *Holism and Evolution*. London: Macmillan.
Yontef, G. (1980) Gestalt therapy: a dialogic method. Unpublished manuscript.
Zinker, J. (1978) *Creative Process in Gestalt Therapy*. New York: Vintage.

Discussion points

- Applying the quote from Resnick to coaching practice, what are the implications of this for your own coaching practice and that of others?

    Every Gestalt therapist could stop doing any gestalt technique that had ever been done and go right on doing gestalt therapy. If they couldn't, then they weren't doing Gestalt therapy in the first place.

They were fooling around with a bag of tricks and a bunch of gimmicks.

(Resnick, 1984: 19)

- Thinking about your coaching process and the Gestalt approach, how do you usually create experiments with your coaching clients and how might you now work differently?
- Focusing on the contact boundary, and reflecting on your recent experiences, what blocks to full awareness might be evident in your coaching practice and how might you work with these? You might want to consider how you are standing in the way of full contact with your self as a practitioner; how you are standing in the way of full contact with your client or how your clients are experiencing blocks at different stages of the cycle. Table 8.1, detailing blocks to awareness, may be useful to you.
- When you consider the case of Carina that is presented in this chapter, what are the key points in it that, for you, express a gestalt approach to coaching psychology? What stands out for you in this case study that has challenged your current way of working as a coach?

Suggested reading

Clarkson, P. (2004) *Gestalt Counselling in Action*, 3rd edition. London: Sage.

Houston, G. (2003) *Brief Gestalt Therapy*. London: Sage.

Nevis, E. C. (1987) *Organizational Consulting: A Gestalt approach*. New York: Gestalt Institute of Cleveland Press and Gardner Press.

Perls, F. (1969) *Gestalt Therapy Verbatim*. Moab, UT: Real People Press.

Chapter 9

Motivational Interviewing

A specific approach for coaching psychologists

Jonathan Passmore and Alison Whybrow

Introduction

Motivational Interviewing (MI) is a person-centred, non-directive method of communication, which works collaboratively with the coachee supporting them to enhance their intrinsic motivation towards personal behavioural change, by helping them resolve their historical ambivalence to the change that they face (Miller and Rollnick, 2002; Resnicow et al., 2002). MI has its roots in the Rogerian, humanistic counselling style.

Unlike the behavioural approaches to coaching, which are based on the concept of behaviour being the result of external reinforcement or extrinsic motivators such as pay, praise, status (see chapter 5) MI focuses explicitly on enhancing intrinsic motivation. The underlying view of the MI approach is that lasting and meaningful change occurs when an individual is intrinsically motivated. Using MI techniques, the coach explores the values and goals of the coachee, how their current behaviour may be out of step with their ideal behaviours, and helps the coachee resolve this conflict. The aim is that it is the coachee who begins verbalising to the coach why change may be beneficial, while the coach offers an empathic, reflective environment, helping the coachee stay focused on 'change talk' (Miller and Rollnick, 2002).

A core belief within the process is the innate capacity of individuals to naturally evolve in a healthful direction under conditions of acceptance and support, where people use their own positive, creative energy and insight to discover the best solutions for themselves (Miller and Rollnick, 2002).

Development of MI

MI was developed by an American psychologist, William Miller, through his endeavour to answer the question 'Why do people change?' His work drew on his experiences of observing alcohol dependent clients in therapy. He found that change processes in therapy mirrored natural change outside therapy. A key predictive factor as to whether people would change or not was the way they spoke about change in therapy. He argued that substance abusing clients who make statements indicative of high motivation and commitment to change are those most likely to make change. Further, the therapist has a role to play in working with clients helping them to strengthen their commitment to change (Miller and Rollnick, 2002). Miller observed that the style of therapeutic interaction affects the frequency of change talk, with empathic styles facilitating change talk, and confrontational methods generating resistance, resulting in less active change.

Most of the evidence base for MI comes from the clinical psychology environment where MI has been referenced in the addiction literature, and there is strong data for its successful application in alcohol and substance abuse counselling (Miller and Moyers, 2002; Solomon and Fioritti, 2002; Burke et al., 2003). MI has also been applied to the field of chronic illness management, for example helping people with diabetes to achieve better control of blood glucose (Channon et al., 2003; Prochaska and Zinman, 2003). MI has also been shown to be effective in encouraging teenagers to change their behaviour, increasing their use of contraceptives (Cowley et al., 2002).

The specific use of MI in the coaching sphere appears to be limited to date, with little documented evidence. The approach has been used with cardiac coaching to produce better health, to enhance the patient's quality of life, and to produce savings to the healthcare system (Kazel, 1998). Our experience suggests there is an opportunity to use the MI approach within the broader context of coaching psychology, whether applied to work or life settings.

Theory and basic concepts

The MI approach draws together a number of concepts within the broader psychological and psychology of change literature which are weaved into this section. However, there are three underlying tenets to the approach, which we specifically discuss. First, the need for the coach's style to match the coachee's readiness to change. Second, the concept of motivation to change and how it develops. Here, we consider motivation to change as 'being ready, willing and able to change'. In the 'ready, willing and able' triumvirate, no amount of readiness will compensate for perceived inability (Rollnick, 1998), which leads to the third concept, that of self-efficacy. The coach needs to work with the coachee to develop the three strands in parallel.

First, then, is the need for the coach to continually assess the coachee's state of readiness to change towards the target behaviour. The transtheoretical model of change (initially developed by Prochaska and DiClemente, 1992) is a well-researched and influential model, describing how people prepare to change their behaviour, and how successful change is maintained. The model argues that individuals progress through certain stages, as part of a change cycle (see Table 9.1).

Movement through the stages is not always a straight path from precontemplation to maintenance, with relapse to an earlier stage, and spiralling

Table 9.1 Change cycle

Stage	Behaviour
Pre-contemplative	The possibility of change has not been considered by the coachee.
Contemplative	The coachee is considering the benefits and disadvantages of change, resulting in ambivalence.
Preparation	The coachee is making preparations for action.
Action	The coachee is making attempts to change.
Maintenance	Successful change in behaviour has occurred, and has been maintained for six months.

Source: adapted with permission from Prochaska, J. O., DiClemente, C. C. and Norcross, J. C. (1992) In search of how people change: applications to addictive behaviours. *American Psychologist* 47(9): 1102–1114. Published by the American Psychological Association.

through the stages typically occurring before long-term maintenance is achieved. The transtheoretical model argues that people experience different thought patterns at different stages of change, with consciousness raising, where a person learns new facts or ideas that support making change, occurring at the contemplation stage, and self-liberation, such as making a firm commitment to change, occurring at the action or maintenance stages (Perz et al., 1996). Likewise, the balance between the pros and cons of a particular behaviour varies with an individual's stage of change. For example, a coachee in the preparation stage is suggested to experience more negative cognitions and emotions towards their current behaviour, than a person in the contemplative stage of change (Prochaska and Zinman, 2003).

People vary in their motivation to change throughout the change cycle. Thus, the coach's interventions and style of helping need to be tailored to meet the coachee's stage of change. Motivational Interviewing is thought to be particularly useful to overcome ambivalence to change. Ambivalence keeps people stuck in their current suboptimal behaviour, and not able to make changes, even when they want to. From an MI perspective, ambivalence is seen as a natural part of the change process, indeed resistance is described as being at the heart of change. Identifying and exploring this barrier is a key challenge for the motivational coach. Exploration of resistance is managed using non-confrontational methods, such as collaboration and empathy, as opposed to more directive methods such as authority (Miller and Rollnick, 2002).

Ambivalence is particularly thought to occur in the pre-contemplative, contemplative or sometimes preparation stages. Ambivalence can be identified in coachee's dialogue and typically involves statements such as 'I want to work fewer hours, but if I stop, then I won't be able to . . .'. At this point, a directive response from the coach (for example, offering advice or options of action) is likely to increase resistance from the coachee. Resistance is likely to be expressed through behaviours such as arguing, interrupting, denying, ignoring and 'yes but' responses from the coachee (Miller and Rollnick, 2002). Resistance behaviours in part are seen to result from a mismatch between the coachee's stage of change, and the coach's approach, leading to frustration for both the coach and the coachee.

It has been found that the more a person argues against change, the less likely it is that change will occur (Miller et al., 1993), in part due to the human desire to be regarded as consistent (Hargie and Dickson, 2004).

In sum, if a person is ambivalent about change, a confrontational approach, such as increasing the negative consequences of a particular behaviour as a deterrent, is more likely to entrench rather than reduce the target behaviour, with an individual identifying and verbalising further the benefits of maintaining the status quo. Even what is perceived as gentle persuasion, perhaps where the coach highlights the urgency, or potential benefits of change, generally increases resistance and diminishes the probability of change (Miller and Rollnick, 1991).

As well as being mindful of the coachee's language, the coach can simply ask the coachee to rate their perceived readiness to change on a scale of 0–10 (0 = not at all interested in changing; 10 = they have already made the change).

A coachee's motivation to change is seen as stemming from the perceived discrepancy between the coachee's values and goals, and their current behaviours. For successful change to occur, the individual needs to be willing to believe that the target behaviour is important, i.e. in line with their values, and be ready to make the change a priority in her or his life. MI will not induce behaviour change unless the coachee believes that the change is in his or her own best interest (Miller and Rollnick, 2002). Similarly, change will not occur unless the individual feels that it is congruent with who they are (e.g. Hargie and Dickson, 2004).

From a humanistic perspective, MI facilitates coachees in defining their current and ideal selves, movement can then be pursued from the current towards the ideal. A coachee may become aware that their current, perhaps problematic behaviours, meet certain short-term needs, but do not fulfil more deeply held values or long-term satisfaction. Through general coaching techniques, such as open questions and active listening, the coachee will be describing to the coach, the discrepancy between current and ideal behaviours valued by themselves. Focusing on the coachee's values increases an individual's sense of importance of change, as well as helping a person to detect how their current behaviours may be incoherent with the ideal (Miller and Rollnick, 2002).

Coaches using the MI approach should not seek to develop discrepancy at the expense of other MI principles. The coach empathically and gradually focuses the coachee's attention on the discrepancy that they themselves have generated.

Focusing on the coachee's ideals can decrease defensiveness and increase desire for change, by shifting focus away from negative behaviours, towards a focus on a positive lifestyle, and potentially more deeply satisfying performance goals (Miller and Rollnick, 2002).

The third element of MI (referred to earlier) involves the concept of self-efficacy, i.e. a person's belief in their ability to carry out and succeed at a task (Bandura, 1977). Without this perception of ability to make the desired changes, change will not take place.

These three concepts of MI are related; for example, readiness relies on a perception of intrinsic importance and confidence to change. A coachee who does not see change as important is unlikely to be ready to change. Furthermore, a coachee who perceives change to be impossible is unlikely to rate their readiness to change as very high. Exploring coachee ambivalence through MI helps to clarify which of these three concepts is keeping a client stuck in ambivalence, in turn identifying to the coach which aspect of motivation needs to be the focus of change talk.

The MI approach is consistent with other psychological approaches to change in that there is no 'right way' to change, and if one given plan for change does not work, a coachee is limited only by their creativity as to the number of other approaches that may be tried (Miller and Rollnick, 2002).

Practice

Here we explore how Motivational Interviewing can be applied by coaching psychologists. For MI to be an effective approach, the coaching relationship needs to be collaborative with a good rapport. This basis is likely to facilitate coachees' trust more so than a relationship that is coercive or hierarchical (Miller and Rollnick, 2002). The approach advocates empathy and support, rather than criticism of the coachee's efforts. The relationship is compared to a partnership (Miller and Rollnick, 1991), with the coachee taking responsibility for their own progress.

The goals and methods of change need to come from the coachee to increase the likelihood of long-term success. Overall, the coaching interaction should feel more like 'dancing' and not like 'wrestling' with the coachee. Feedback and suggestions from the coach are seen as useful only once the coachee becomes ready to consider them, once the coachee has resolved ambivalence and is getting ready to take action.

MI has two distinct phases, the first of which can be likened to climbing a hill. This phase involves exploring ambivalence, and building intrinsic motivation and self-efficacy for change. Several useful elements that are particularly effective for this phase of exploration include:

- open questions
- reflective listening statements

- confidence to change assessment using the confidence ruler method
- offering affirmations.

Open questions facilitate information from the coachee and drive forward the coaching process. For example, 'I'd like to understand how you see things, what's brought you here?' The coachee, after all, should be doing most of the talking with the coach actively listening.

Reflective listening statements should constitute the majority of responses from the coach. The essence of reflective listening is that the coach checks, rather than assumes, the meaning of what the coachee has said. For example, a coachee may express 'I wish I had more time to spend on the project'. Possibilities of what the coachee means by this statement include: I wish I had more time to think about the project – to discuss the project – to plan the project – or it may be that the project is not very high on the priorities list. An example of reflective listening statements is given below:

Coachee: I've been referred by my boss for this coaching.
Coach: You've been asked by your manager to attend this discussion.
Coachee: I don't really feel that it's fair. In fact most of what he does is not fair.
Coach: And that doesn't seem right to you and you feel frustrated by your manager's actions.

Miller and Rollnick (2002) distinguish between questions, where voice tone goes up at the end, in comparison with a reflective statement, where voice tone goes down.

Reflective statements demonstrate active listening and empathy to the coachee, and encourage verbalisation of further change talk (Miller and Rollnick, 2002). Reflection is not a passive process, but it is the coach who decides what to reflect on and what to ignore. Skilful reflection moves forward, rather than just repeating, what the coachee has said, adding momentum to the exploration process – but not too far, to avoid potential resistance.

Where the need to change is high (the change is important), but the confidence to change is low, ambivalence may be expressed by the coachee (Miller and Rollnick, 2002). This situation can be easily assessed using a *confidence ruler*. Here the coachee is asked to rate their confidence to make the necessary changes on a scale of 0–10 (0 = low confidence to make change; 10 = high confidence to make change). To understand what is underpinning the coachee's confidence, or lack of it, two questions are used to explore the coachee's self-assessment on the confidence ruler:

- 'Why are you an X on the scale and not a zero?'
- 'What would it take for you to go from X to a higher number?'

Offering affirmations also has an important place in MI. Affirmations facilitate an atmosphere of acceptance, helping to build confidence to change in the coachee, and a belief that they can overcome their current situation.

During phase one, the techniques highlighted above help clarify and explore ambivalence; however, there is a danger of the coachee becoming stuck in ambivalence. Some of the techniques above can be used by the coach to move carefully towards change. However, when the coachee is stuck, to maintain or restart momentum the coach can use more directive techniques to elicit and encourage reflection on change talk.

The ability to recognise change talk is a key element of the MI coach's skills. Change talk can be differentiated along a dimension moving from a focus on the current situation towards stating a clear intention to change (Miller and Rollnick, 2002). A coachee may begin to discuss the disadvantages of the status quo e.g. 'I cannot do what they want', or recognising the advantages of change 'I would begin to enjoy work like I used to.' Change talk can involve expressing optimism or intention to change e.g. 'I could rearrange some of my daily tasks' or 'I can't keep going on like this indefinitely.'

Change talk can be provoked, or elicited through a conscious focus on the part of the coach. To elicit change talk, the ruler method described previously can be utilised. For example, it may be appropriate to clarify the coachee's rating of importance to address change and then to ask:

- 'Why are you at an X and not a zero?'
- 'What would it take for you to go from X to a higher number?'

It may be useful for a coachee to fill in a decisional balance sheet (see Table 9.2), to reflect and reinforce the resolution of ambivalence previously explored and discussed with them. A simple checklist of the pros and cons of the current state of affairs compared with the goal is a further technique that works well in the MI approach.

Whether a person will continue to explore change talk or veer away, depends on how the coach responds. However, the skilful handling of resistance will either increase or decrease change talk. When resistance occurs, it indicates that that there is a mismatch between the coach and coachee. The coach therefore regards resistance as an opportunity rather than a character flaw.

Table 9.2 Coaching for change balance sheet

Benefits of activity	Costs of activity	Benefits of change	Costs of change

Further, rather than relying on simple reflective statements, amplified reactions with an exaggerated emphasis on the outcome encourage the coachee to elicit the opposite argument to their ambivalence. For example:

Coachee: I couldn't go on a training course, what would my colleagues think if I failed?

Coach: You couldn't handle your colleagues' reactions?

It is important that amplified reflections must be made in a supportive, matter of fact tone, with no hint of impatience or sarcasm, which is likely to elicit resistance (Miller and Rollnick, 2002).

Finally, reframing is a technique which acknowledges the validity of the coachee's claim, but the information is reflected back in a new light, more supportive of change, for example:

Coachee: I've tried so many times to change and failed.

Coach: It sounds as though you are determined in the face of a challenge; this change must be important to you.

Emphasising personal choice and control, or shifting the focus away from the resistance are other useful strategies to help the coach roll with and not confront the coachee's expressed resistance.

Stage 2 of the Motivational Interviewing approach is likened to journeying down the other side of the hill. It involves strengthening the coachee's commitment to a collaborative change plan. The coach needs to look for signs of readiness within the coachee to discuss options for change. These signs include

- decreased resistance
- an increase in questions about change
- decreased discussion about the problem from the coachee's perspective.

The coach can then shift direction to strengthening commitment to change. To maximise motivation, this involves creating coachee driven goals, those that the coachee is eager to pursue. If a goal is inappropriate, this will soon become apparent to the coachee. The coach does not impose their own goals on the coachee. The goal also has to be realistic: too large a goal between ideal and current behaviour may decrease confidence to change (Miller and Rollnick, 2002).

Following goal clarification, the next step is to consider methods to achieve the goals. One route to achieve this would be to brainstorm a menu of options; the coachee's task is then to select a preferred option. This discussion leads towards devising a plan for change, including summarising issues such as: why change is important, how specific goals can be reached, predicting obstacles, and evaluating how change will be measured. Once the change plan is devised, the coach must obtain the coachee's commitment to the plan. The more the coachee verbalises the plan, from our experience, the more commitment is strengthened.

Motivational Interviewing is an interpersonal style, a balance of directive and client-centred components, aiming to resolve ambivalence. If it becomes a manipulative technique, the spirit of MI has been lost (Miller, 1994).

The key aspects of MI may be summarised as:

- empathising with the coachee's perspective through summaries
- keeping the coachee focused on change, through reflecting on change talk offered by the coachee
- continually monitoring readiness to change
- affirming and reinforcing the coachee's proposed methods of change.

Which clients benefit most?

The underpinning perspective of MI used as part of the psychological coaching and general coaching frameworks can enhance the dynamics of all coaching interactions, and facilitate seamless movement towards coaching goals. MI as an approach is also a valuable tool for specific coaching assignments that we have outlined below.

Motivational Interviewing focused on overcoming ambivalence, suits situations where the coachee may not be the client, but has been referred by others. This arises in two main ways within an organisational context. First, where the organisation as part of a wider programme has commissioned coaching for a group of managers, and an individual within the group expresses major concerns about their organisation or about their competence, but is reluctant to see the coaching as a potential resource to overcome the issue. The implication for the individual is that in the short to medium term the organisation will address the attitudinal or performance issues, through capability or disciplinary procedures.

We have encountered a number of coachees whose situation reflects this, and where more traditional behavioural and cognitive interventions did not, during the early sessions, enable the person to move forward. In these situations the coachee seemed highly resistant to change, yet they continued to attend coaching, as the organisation had mandated their attendance. Such situations can often arise in organisational mergers or restructures where new roles have been identified and to support the change a development or coaching programme has been commissioned.

A second circumstance is where the coachee is referred for coaching as a final step prior to the commencement of capability or disciplinary action. In this situation the threat of consequences is clear, but from our experience the coachee either rejects their manager's view that they need to change or believes that their manager is being unfair and will by some 'act of God' see the light and recognise their true worth. The coachee is thus apparently 'stuck' in ambivalence.

In these cases the organisational client is often seeking explicit behavioural change, but before behavioural based coaching can commence, the coach needs to explore and resolve the ambivalence to the situation, or threat faced by the coachee (willing), and develop within them intrinsic motivation to change (ready). Behavioural coaching can then be used to develop the new skills or attitudes for success.

Case study

Andy, a head of service for ICT, reports to a strategic director within a small unitary local authority. At the time of our first meeting he had recently taken up a new role with enhanced responsibility and new line management relationships.

The coach was invited to coach Andy as part of a wider coaching programme within the organisation, following the appointment of several new directors and heads of service as part of a restructure. A series of six coaching sessions had been agreed with no explicit objectives set for the team or individuals within it. Additionally, the client had agreed a confidentiality clause and there was no expectation to report back. The implicit objective was to support the team as it settled in to its new roles and to support the development of effective team working.

Andy, like the rest of the team, had been 'invited' to take up coaching, but as Andy made clear in the first session, the expectation was that everyone would attend but he did not see how coaching would be of any benefit. Andy had been in the organisation for more than ten years and was disappointed that he had not been selected for redundancy. Others in the organisation who had been made redundant had received significant severance pay.

In session one, having discussed ground rules and the essence of the coaching, Andy was invited to share information about his role and how he might like to use the coaching sessions. The initial aim was to draw upon a behavioural model, to help Andy to establish clear goals and identify and resolve issues of performance through problem-solving techniques.

It quickly became clear however, that while rapport had been established, Andy failed to see that he needed to adapt in the new environment. A constant theme during this first session was Andy's belief that he should have been made redundant, that the decision to retain him was unfair, that he wanted to leave and that he had no desire to change or adapt. His main wish was to leave the council with a financial settlement some time in the 18 months after his fiftieth birthday.

At the close of the session the coach asked whether coaching would be of benefit to Andy and whether he wished to continue with the sessions. He said he had found it of value, and as he was expected to attend, he would come to the second session.

The second session was six weeks after the first, and having reflected on a general failure to generate engagement, the coach focused on exploring Andy's mental blocks to engaging with coaching. Andy's values and beliefs about work, and the role it played for him, were also discussed. This approach provided further evidence that Andy did not want to be there, and that work was a source of funding to pay for holidays and other luxuries. During this session unrealistic assumptions were challenged, and reflections on alternative ways to view work were encouraged by the coach.

At the close of the session Andy had developed a clearer view about his values and beliefs. However, the coach felt that the cognitive approach was unlikely to facilitate further progress. Andy was ambiguous about his need to respond to the developing agenda in the council, and remained fixated that his current role was not for him and that he wanted to be made redundant when he was 50.

In the third session, while maintaining a cognitive approach, some of the MI techniques were introduced. Andy was asked to rate his perceived readiness to change on a scale of 0–10. Andy scored himself down at 1, and reiterated his reasons. The coach then explored what it would take for him to score 10. Andy initially resisted the question, but after several false starts, he suggested that if he really loved his job that would be an incentive. The session continued exploring these ideas utilising MI techniques, and towards the end of the session, Andy was talking actively about jobs he had enjoyed and why the current role was preventing him from becoming engaged, but also what it would look like in an ideal world if he had designed the structure.

During the fourth session Andy's confidence to change was reviewed. Using the confidence to change ruler, Andy rated his confidence on a scale of 0–10. Andy scored more highly here at 4. After some further discussion, the coach returned to the scale inviting Andy to consider why he rated himself at 4 on the scale and not a zero and what it would take for him to go from 4 to a higher number.

During the session the balance sheet was used to review the advantages and disadvantages of a 'wait for redundancy' approach, compared to the notion of making the best of the current job and trying to reshape it to better suit Andy's skills and interests. This exercise highlighted that dismissal could become a real possibility for Andy, as his employer saw his performance was disappointing and experienced Andy's poor attitude to work. Team members would also suffer from Andy's poor morale, as would his home life if he continued to express dissatisfaction to his partner about his work. Andy could not guarantee that redundancy would be on offer, indeed, it might be five or ten years before Andy could leave (this represented maybe 20–50 per cent of the rest of his life). On the positive side, Andy recognised that work had been fun in the past and began to believe that he did have the confidence and potentially the power to influence the organisation structure and make it fun again.

By the close of the fourth session the content of Andy's talk had shifted from a feeling of frustration that he had not been made redundant, a belief that work was a bad thing, and a lack of desire to move forward in the new environment, to consideration of alternative ways of seeing the world generated through MI and cognitive techniques, alongside a growing intrinsic motivation to do something positive about his situation.

During the fifth and final sessions, while maintaining an awareness of both MI and cognitive intentions, there was a return to a more strongly behavioural approach with a focus on what behaviours would make a success, and on establishing and working through key challenges.

References

Bandura, A. (1977) Self-efficacy: towards a unifying theory of behaviour change. *Psychological Review* 84: 191–215.

Burke, B. L., Arkowitz, I. I. and Menchola, M. (2003) The efficacy of motivational interviewing: a meta analysis of controlled clinical trials. *Journal of Consulting Clinical Psychology* 71: 843–861.

Channon, S., Smith, V. J. and Gregory, J. W. (2003) A pilot study of motivational interviewing in adolescents with diabetes. *Archives of Disease in Childhood* 88(8): 680–683.

Cowley, C. B., Farley, T. and Beamis, K. (2002) 'Well, maybe I'll try the pill for just a few months' . . . Brief motivational and narrative-based interventions to encourage contraceptive use among adolescents at high risk for early childbearing. *Families, Systems and Health* 20: 183.

Hargie, O. and Dickson, D. (2004) *Skilled Interpersonal Communication: Research, theory and practice*, 4th edition. London: Routledge.

Kazel, R. (1998) Cardiac coaching produces better health savings. *Business Insurance* 19 October.

Miller, J. H. and Moyers, T. (2002) Motivational interviewing in substance abuse: applications for occupational medicine. *Occupational Medicine* 17(1): 51–65.

Miller, W. R. (1994) Motivational interviewing, III. On the ethics of motivational intervention. *Behavioural and Cognitive Psychotherapy* 22: 111–123.

Miller, W. R. and Rollnick, S. (1991) *Motivational Interviewing: Preparing people to change addictive behaviour*. New York: Guilford Press.

Miller, W. R. and Rollnick, S. (2002) *Motivational Interviewing: Preparing people for change*, 2nd edition. New York: Guilford Press.

Miller, W. R., Benefield, R. G. and Tonigan, J. S. (1993) Enhancing motivation for change in problem drinking: a controlled comparison of two therapist styles. *Journal of Consulting and Clinical Psychology* 61(3): 455–461.

Perz, C. A., DiClemente, C. C. and Carbonari, J. P. (1996) Doing the right thing at the right time? The interaction of stages and processes of change in successful smoking cessation. *Health Psychology* 15: 462–468.

Prochaska, J. O. and DiClemente, C. C. (1992) Stages of change in the modification of problem behaviours. In M. Hersen, R. Eisler and P. Miller (eds) *Progress in Behaviour Modification*. Sycamore, IL: Sycamore Press.

Prochaska, J. O. and Zinman, B. (2003) Changes in diabetes self care behaviours make a difference in glycemic control: the Diabetes Stages of Change (DISC) study. *Diabetes Care* 26: 732–737.

Prochaska, J. O., DiClemente, C. C. and Norcross, J. C. (1992) In search of how people change: applications to addictive behaviours. *American Psychologist* 47(9): 1102–1114.

Resnicow, K., DiIorio, C., Soet, J. E., Borrelli, B., Hecht, J. and Ernst, D. (2002) Motivational interviewing in health promotion: it sounds like something is changing. *Health Psychology* 21(5): 444–451.

Rollnick, S. (1998) Readiness and confidence: critical conditions of change in treatment. In W. R. Miller and N. Heather (eds) *Treating Addictive Behaviours*, 2nd edition. New York: Plenum.

Solomon, J. and Fioritti, A. (2002) Motivational intervention as applied to systems change: the case of dual diagnosis. *Substance Use and Misuse* 37(14): 1833–1851.

Discussion points

- Referring to the Change Cycle outlined in this chapter, think back to the most recent example of a specific, challenging situation requiring you to personally change. Describe the situation and the change(s) that you made. What support did you particularly appreciate? What interventions did you find particularly unhelpful? Reflecting on your responses, where were you on the change cycle when each of these helpful or unhelpful interventions occurred?

- Thinking about your coaching practice, provide a specific example of a useful intervention made with a coachee in the pre-contemplative stage of change. How did the coachee respond? What evidence do you have that your intervention was useful?

- What activities can you engage in as a coach to ensure you remain mindful of the coachee throughout your coaching sessions and the broader coaching relationship?

- How does Motivational Interviewing complement or contrast with your existing coaching approach? What might you integrate into your practice from this chapter and how?

Suggested reading

DiClemente, C. C. and Prochaska, J. O. (1998) Toward a comprehensive, transtheoretical model of change: stages of change and addictive behaviours. In W. R. Miller and N. Heather (eds) *Treating Addictive Behaviours*, 2nd edition (pp. 3–24). New York: Plenum.

Miller, W. and Rollnick, S. (1998) *Motivational Interviewing: Professional Training DVD*.

Miller, W. and Rollnick, S. (2002) *Motivational Interviewing: Preparing people for change*, 2nd edition. New York: Guilford Press.

Passmore, J. (2006) Integrative coaching. In *Excellence in Coaching: The industry guide*. London: Kogan Page.

Chapter 10

Narrative coaching and psychology of learning from multicultural perspectives

Ho Law

Introduction

Narrative coaching is for enhancing well-being and performance of individuals or groups within organisational or community settings through storytelling. Narrative coaches help coachees to achieve their aspirations, hopes and dreams through active listening to their stories of lived experience, identifying the hidden meaning, values, skills and strengths and redeveloping new storylines towards a plan of action.

The narrative coaching is based on cultural anthropology in addition to the basic principle of psychology such as learning theories. We advocate in this chapter that the narrative approaches that underpin coaching, should be grounded in the psychology of learning.

While the definition is very similar to that adopted by the Special Group in Coaching Psychology within the mainstream (Palmer and Whybrow, 2006, adapted from Grant and Palmer, 2002), it is more in line with Philippe Rosinski's (2003) proposal that by integrating a cultural dimension into coaching, we can help our coachees unleash more of their potential to achieve meaningful objectives. The key difference is that the approach is sensitive to cultural aspects and thus is particularly applicable within different community settings.

Development of narrative coaching

The narrative approach was originally grounded in cultural anthropology, for example, the use of metaphors such as the 'rite of passage' and rituals that mark the transition through the 'liminal space' (van Gennep, 1960; Turner, 1967; Turner and Brunner, 1986). These metaphors were transported into applications of psychotherapy as they were found to be powerful vehicles to transform human perceptions, emotions, cognition and well-being. Narrative therapy is one of these examples. For example, the metaphor of life as a story or script in re-membering of significant 'actors' during storytelling and regarding 'life as the performance' of the story definitional ceremony (retelling of the story) were drawn from the work of Barbara Myerhoff (1982, 1986 respectively). A body of writings on the topic could be found during the 1980 and 1990s with applications in communities, groups, children and family therapy (Epston and White, 1992).

The narrative therapy has been systematically developed by Michael White at Dulwich Centre, Adelaide, Australia (White, 1995, 2006). Its adaptation as a narrative coaching technique was introduced into the UK by the author in one of the community coaching programmes (Law, 2006; Law et al., 2006; see also CIPD, 2006: 10).

In terms of the linkage between narrative approaches and psychology of learning, its linage can be traced back to Vygotsky's ([1926] 1962) proximal development (White, 2006). The author took the concept a step further by grounding the narrative coaching in the psychology of learning with Kolb's (1984) learning cycle and embedding it into a meta-model called Universal Integrated Framework (Law et al., 2007).

Theory and basic concepts

Both cultural anthropology and psychology of learning were concerned with non-clinical population with specific sensitivity of cross-cultural issues. It is therefore quite appropriate to relocate narrative applications within the mainstream arena of diversity coaching.

The major central concepts

As a starting point, learning is grounded in concrete coaching experience when coachees/learners and coaches interact (the point of engagement). The coaching process is effectively a learning process, called the learning wheel (Figure 10.1). It is modified from Kolb's (1984) learning cycle.

The learning wheel consists of four stages of learning:

1   Concrete experience – provides the coachees with real examples to understand how they experience the situation.
2   Reflection – think about the lessons learnt (how and what).
3   Abstract conception – translate the experience into a meaningful concept.
4   Action – taking a decision or action as a consequence from the previous three stages.

Note that in the coaching context, the term 'action' is defined quite broadly (in contrast to Kolb, who narrowly referred to the end stage of the learning cycle as an active experimentation). For instance, action may include decision, and thus the decision not to act could be an option.

The learning process described above embeds the coaching condition, which consists of two kinds of transformation:

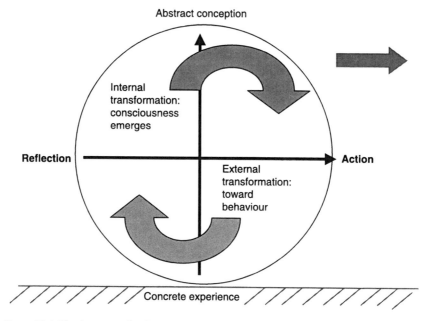

Figure 10.1 The learning wheel.

Source: Law et al., 2007, adapted from Kolb, 1984.

- internal/vertical transformation – from experience, consciousness emerges
- external/horizontal transformation – from reflection to action as reflect
  ive practitioners.

The above transformations are an active process. It is not an automatic process, and very often learners may 'get stuck', as a barrier or gap may exist between each stage of learning. Vygotsky (1962) referred to such a learning gap as the 'zone of proximal development'. The concept of proximal development in learning can be translated into the coaching practice. People consult coaches and mentors when they are facing barriers in improving their performance at work or raising aspiration in their lives. In these situations, people tend to reproduce the solutions to the problem (or behaviours) that are familiar to them (based on the past experience). Adopting Vygotsky's distancing tasks for scaffolding, this gap between the known and familiar and what is possible to know and do can be bridged. This method consists of the following steps:

1 *Description:* encourage coachees to characterise specific objects or events of their world (characterisation of initiative).
2 *Relation:* initiative in relationship – develop chains of association

through establishing relations between these objects and events (analyses/pattern matching).

3   *Evaluation:* reflect, draw realisation and learning about specific phenomena from the chains of association.
4   *Justification:* judge above evaluation – abstract the realisation and learning from their concrete and specific circumstances in formation of concepts about life and identity.
5   *Conclusion/recommendation:* formulate the planning for and initiation of actions – predict outcome of specific actions founded upon this concept development.

The basic assumptions

The basic assumptions are twofold. First, a meta-model for coaching psychology should consist of the following elements (Law et al., 2005):

*   learning cycle (for example, see Kolb, 1984) with supervision, and continuous professional development
*   appreciation of cultural environment
*   coach/coachee fluidity – coachees have skills and knowledge; coaches learn as much as coachees.

Second, to transport Michael White's narrative practice to our coaching context, we have the following assumptions about human nature and communities:

1   Meaning shapes our lives (see White, 2006; see Law et al. (2007) for detailed theoretical discussion).
2   Life consists of multi-stories, not a single story. However, some stories become more prominent in coachees' life while other stories may be neglected, which might be important for their development.
3   Primary meaning-making frame: storylines – narrative practitioners regard the storyline told by the storyteller as a primary meaning-making frame, which enables them to construe meaning from it. This in turn gives meaning that shapes our lives (as described in assumption 1).
4   Individuals and communities have strengths, knowledge and skills, but when they come to contact us, they may not be noticeable to themselves. This is particularly prevalent to those people who contact us in the coaching situation (a blind spot in the Johari window).

How do people block themselves from achieving their life, social, work and subsequent coaching goals?

Following on from the last point, those forgotten or hidden strengths that individuals have may appear as thin traces in their stories. The role of coach is therefore to redevelop those strengths, skills and knowledge. The tasks of the coach are therefore to locate the significant moment in the client's life journey and help clients take stock of their living experience that they tend to have neglected (thin traces). Viewed from the narrative perspective, coaches and coachees can be regarded as 'meaning makers'.

How does the approach help coachees to achieve their goals?

Narrative approaches in coaching enable clients (in particular those from different cultures) to become aware that they have more knowledge and skills to cope with the new situation than they previously realised. Through the coach–coachee engagements, the coachees redevelop the account from the story that they told, of what gives value to their lives. This account may embody concepts about their life and identity, hopes and dreams, etc. The new story, developed through the narrative practice, provides a foundation for people to proceed. The coaching task is to contribute to the scaffolding of the proximal zone of development. Michael White (2006) develops a systematic method of scaffolding the proximal zone of development through mapping the steps of distancing tasks on to the so-called 'landscape of action' and the 'landscape of consciousness'. In developing this scaffold, one takes a conceptual journey travelling through the 'landscape of action' and 'landscape of identity' (that links to one's consciousness via effective questioning to help coachees develop the stories of their life and of personal identity). As Michael White (2006) put it, 'It is through scaffolding questions that these alternative landscapes of the mind are richly described.'

Landscape of action

Landscapes of action are composed of events that are described by the storyteller. These events are likely to be interwoven or linked in sequence through time, which provide an autobiographical/historical journey of the storyteller's life. Like any story, the sequence of events told by the coachee is likely to develop a theme or plot, that reflects one's coping strategy, success or failure. In other words, the landscape of action consists of the following elements:

- time line – the time of the events in terms of recent, distant or remote history
- events – a number of singular events

- circumstance – under which the event takes place
- sequence – events are inter-related into clusters or sequence
- plot or theme – the events have consequence e.g. strategy, success, loss or failures.

Looking at the landscape of action through the lens of the Johari window (Figure 10.2), the stories that coachees choose to disclose during the coaching session represent the known and familiar knowledge to themselves, but some of the theme could have been hidden from the coach previously (quadrants I and III).

Landscape of consciousness

Landscapes of consciousness are composed of the storyteller's own identity, conclusions of their action and events that are shaped by their identity and contemporary culture. The landscape of consciousness represents the understanding that the listener has gained from the story. These understandings could either be intentional or internal:

- Intentional understandings – value, purpose, aspiration. Personal agency. Restoration.
- Internal understandings – Realisations (self-awareness). Learning.

In terms of the Johari window, the landscape of consciousness may show some blind spot of the storyteller, which usually appears as some thin traces in the plot, which the coach would need to understand and develop further.

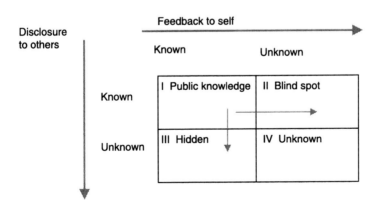

Figure 10.2 Giving feedback: the Johari window.

Practice

There are many techniques of the narrative approach. The combined narrative approach consists of the following techniques or stages:

- Externalising conversations (1: 1)
- Reauthoring/re-membering (1: 1)
- Outsider witness retelling (1: 1:n)
- Definitional ceremony (community) – retellings of retellings.

One may argue that any narrative techniques are a form of externalising conversation, where the coachees are speaking out about their inner experience in the form of a story. Certainly, externalising conversation is a starting point for any coach to learn whatever possible there is to know about the coachees' hidden identity and possibly identify some of their blind spots. Storytelling is a good way of externalising one's life experience during a conversation. However, there are subtle differences in ways of how the conversation is conducted as a story unfolds. Which technique is to be used depends on the content of the story that the coachee brings to the coaching session. Some may be about the story of a loved one in the distant past, for example one's great-grandmother etc., the coach may facilitate to develop the story using re-membering techniques. On other occasions, it may be a story about one's traumatic events, failures and loss of confidence and learned hopelessness. In this case reauthoring the story offers a possibility to develop an alternative story that may redevelop hopes and dreams. Outsider witness and definition ceremony are powerful tools in facilitating group discussion in sharing the stories of their experience and resonate the theme of the storyteller who takes the centre stage.

The goal of the narrative approach is to redevelop the coachee's skills and knowledge by reauthoring the stories of their life experience.

Externalising conversations

Vygotsky's distancing tasks for the proximal development, combined with Michael White's narrative inquiry constitute externalising conversations in our coach–coachee dialogues. These dialogues map onto the following steps in our scaffolding:

- *Step 1 Description:* coachees or storytellers describe their recent experience. In particular, coaches may like to guide coachees to talk about any unique outcome of their problem-solving skill, identify any barrier to their learning or achieving their goals.
- *Step 2 Relation mapping:* the coaches map the effects or influence of the barriers or problem identified through the various domains of the

coachee's life-story in which complications are identified. The domain may be about their home, school, workplace, peer contexts; or familiar relationships, including friendships and the relationship with themselves (self-identity), purposes, their life's horizons, including future possibilities, aspirations, values, hopes and dreams, etc. We do not encourage coaches to map the effects/influence of the problem through all domains of the coachee's life. The coach should just focus on those that seem most significant to the coachee's goal and aspiration.

- *Step 3 Evaluation:* toward the end of the conversation, coaches would evaluate the effects/influence of the themes/plots that emerge from the stories within the given domains.
- *Step 4 Justification:* judge or justify the above evaluation.
- *Step 5 Conclusion/recommendation:* although this step is not part of the narrative map, we added this step to complete our coaching session. In practice as a coach, we would recommend that coachees should formulate a plan of action for overcoming their performance barriers and achieving their objectives. For meta-methodology, an experienced coach could link it to other approaches such as cognitive behavioural techniques at this stage.

As a result of the coaches' explorations shaped by the above five stages of inquiry, coachees are guided and put into words valued conclusions about their lives and identities. These may be conclusions about their beliefs, values, commitments, desires, preferred purposes, longings, wishes, pledges, hopes, and dreams, etc.

Reauthoring

When coachees are telling coaches their stories, apart from listening empathetically, one of the skills of a narrative coach is to link the events of the story in sequences that unfold through time according to a theme or plot. As the story unfolds, coachees may refer to some significant figures who feature in the story, and share with coaches their conclusions about the identity of these figures. During reauthoring conversations, coaches assist coachees/ storytellers to identify the more neglected events of their lives and any unique outcomes or exceptions in those alternative storylines. These unique outcomes or exceptions provide a starting point for reauthoring conversations – a point of entry into the alternative storylines of coachees' lives. At the outset of these conversations, these unique outcomes or exceptions are visible only as thin traces. There are usually gaps between these storylines. Thus narrative coaches need to build a scaffold through questions that encourage coachees to fill these gaps. As Michael White (2006) put it, 'This is a scaffold that assists people to recruit their lived experience, that stretches and exercises their imagination and their meaning-making resources, and that is engaging of their fascination and curiosity.'

As a coaching outcome, narrative coaches need to help coachees develop these alternative storylines, and thicken the plot. Usually coaches would discover that in fact these storylines are more deeply rooted in the coachees' history.

In developing this scaffold, coaches conduct a series of narrative questions, like a journey, the coaches/coachees 'walk-the-talk' through 'landscapes of the mind' (following Jerome Bruner's (1964) metaphor). In narrative terms, we called them the 'landscape of action' and 'landscape of identity'. Through this kind of conversation with support of scaffolding questions from the coach, alternative landscapes of the mind become richly described.

Re-membering

Re-membering conversations are not about fragments of passive recollection of people that one remembers. The figures to be re-membered and retold in a story are significant figures of one's history or with the identities of one's present life. Using 're-membering' as a metaphor from the work of Barbara Myerhoff (1982), Michael White (2006) describes re-membering conversations as conversations that:

- Evoke 'life' as a 'membered' club, 'identity' as an 'association' of life.
- Contribute to a multi-voiced sense of identity, rather than the single-voiced sense of identity, which is a feature of the encapsulated self that is the vogue of contemporary western culture.
- Open possibilities for the revision of one's membership of life: for the upgrading of some memberships and the downgrading of others; for the honouring of some memberships and for the revoking of others; for the granting of authority to some voices in regard to matters of one's personal identity, and for the disqualification of other voices in regard to this matter.
- Describe rich accounts of preferred identity and knowledge of life and skills of living that have been co-generated in the significant memberships of people's lives.

In reviewing the memberships, the coach can further explore the accounts of the storytellers' own identities, their knowledge and skills. From the rich description, many significant outcomes, conclusions, learning, problem-solving practices may be discovered. They may have significant contributions to the storytellers' sense of identity, knowledge and skills. This awareness provides a foundation for coachees' personal development. As a result, it enables coaches/coachees to draw up specific proposals about how they might to go forward.

Outsider witness retelling

Externalised conversations described in the previous sections can be applied in group or team situations, where one or more members from the group are asked to act as witness to the story. Participants are provided with the option of telling the stories of their lives before an audience. The selected outsider witnesses can also act as assistants to the narrative coach as they can provide an extra support to the coachees beyond the tradition of acknowledgement. After they have listened to the story, the outsider witnesses are asked by the coach to retell the story. In particular, they are guided by the coach's questions on which aspects of the story resonate with their own experience. The retellings by the outsider witnesses do not necessarily constitute a complete account of the original story, but focus on the aspects that have most significantly engaged their fascination.

The outsider witnesses respond to the stories by retelling certain aspects of what they heard. Depending on the culture of the place the outsider witness retellings take place, these activities may be shaped by certain traditions of acknowledgement. According to Michael White (1995, 1997, 2000, 2006) there are four categories of reflective responses from outsider witnesses. Narrative practitioners could ask or guide the outsider witnesses to

- identify the expression of the storyteller
- describe the image that the story has evoked
- embody responses in their own life experiences
- Acknowledge any 'transport' of knowledge from the story to their own life.

Definitional ceremony (community) – retellings of retellings

Within the context of the narrative practice (and within the broader context of poststructuralism), a person's self-identity is not governed by a private and individual achievement, but by the following social, historical and cultural forces:

- one's own history
- one's own sense of authenticity
- public and social achievements
- acknowledgement of one's preferred claims about one's identity.

From the above reference, the definitional ceremony is a powerful way to provide social acknowledgment of the storyteller's self-identity, which might have been previously denied access from their social condition (in particular cross-cultural situation). In narrative terms, a definition ceremony thickens many alternative themes or counter-plots of the story and amplifies the empowerment that the storytellers received, that would not otherwise be available to them.

Definitional ceremony is multilayered and has the following structures:

1   Storytellings – undertaken by the storyteller who is at the centre of the ceremony.
2   Retellings of tellings (first retelling) – by the outsider witnesses.
3   Retellings of retellings (second retelling) – by the initial storyteller.
4   Retellings of retellings of retellings (third retelling) – by the outsider witnesses, or by a secondary group of outsider witnesses.

Theoretically speaking, the above process of retelling could continue indefinitely. In practice, the layers of retelling of the story depend on the physical and time constraints.

Definitional ceremony is 'moving' of all participants and therefore is ideal for group or community work in conference styles or community gatherings. It provides an opportunity for the storytellers to become who they want to be rather than who they were. Metaphorically speaking, the storyteller is being moved or transported, from one place to another in life (here and now) as a direct consequence of the participation.

In addition to the conversation between coaches and coachees, other forms of communication can be used in this approach, for example, via writing, emails, diary or letters, and issuing certificates to honour coachees' stories in a conference situation.

Which clients benefit most?

We have found that clients who travelled from one country to live and work in another country would find this approach most helpful. The typical type of problems for clients who suffered from a dislocation of place and hence culture include taking for granted their own signature strength, values and beliefs.

As the nature of narrative coaching relies heavily on the articulation of stories by the clients, the approach is limited to verbal communication. If the clients have a language problem or are poor in verbal communication skill, a different mode of communication such as drawing and dramatic performance may be used.

The approaches can easily be adapted for children and young people. In fact, most of the original practices by Michael White were based on his family therapy with children (for example, see White and Morgan, 2006). In doing so, coaches would need to be more creative to use metaphors that are suitable for children. For example, if a child has talked about a toy that s/he was fond of, instead of asking, 'What does the story tell me about your values and belief?' the coach could ask, 'Imagine, if you were the toy, what would you be thinking about?' or 'If the toy could hear you now, what would you say to the toy?'

Apart from observing the British Psychological Society's Code of Ethics and Conduct, coaches working with children and young people should also refer to the Children Act 2004 and its guidance on sharing information.

Case study

The method of the definitional ceremony metaphor was applied to a community coaching programme. Before that, a three days' coaching programme was led in Peterborough (UK) between February and March 2006. It was part of the Positive Image project funded by the Home Office. The project was led by Peterborough Racial Equality Council (PREC) and delivered by its partners. Empsy Ltd is one of the partners that delivered the coaching component of the project. It aimed to create sustainable communities through coaching. (The author was one of the role models.) As the Positive Image was a large project with diverse activities and partnership, in this case study, only the community coaching programme component was reported here. Snowy Aga, No Fear Ltd and the author were appointed to deliver that programme.

The client

Over 40 people from the diverse community of Peterborough attended a Community Network Conference. The conference celebrated the successful completion of the Positive Image project. There were multilayers of clients in the programme:

- Funding partners – PREC, the Positive Image Project manager.
- Positive Image Project partners and role models.
- Coachees – diverse communities including Black and Minority Ethnic sector, the women's group, travellers, and people of all ages.

The concerns/problems

Most problems the community groups brought to the definition ceremony included language and cultural barriers, how to seek social support and funding from the mainstream culture.

The coaching

As an introduction to facilitate the definitional ceremony, the author retold the story that he acquired from the International Narrative Therapy Festive Conference at Adelaide, Australia (Combrink et al., 2006):

In Karos and Kambro, drama, dance, stories, mime, creative writing and sharing of life stories around the campfire were all woven into an intricate pattern of hopes and dreams.

> Around the campfire,
> They sang and danced
> It's freedom from all things.
> Because children could talk freely
> About the good moments
> All the good things in life
> They're able to know . . .

This story had a particular resonance to the storyteller as a similar Chinese story was told through centuries using arrows instead of sticks. A chopstick was passed around the audience and they were asked to break it. The first participant broke the chopstick without any effort. A bundle of chopsticks was then shown.

The point was:

> To be alone, we are weak.
> Together we are strong.
> Social collaboration is our strength.

After the keynote addresses, the participants were naturally divided into six small groups according to the table that they gathered together. A facilitative workshop was then carried out to redevelop their skills and knowledge using narrative approach. This is based on the principle of reauthoring the stories of participants' life experience (as described in the earlier sections).

Each group was asked to have at least one participant to volunteer as a storyteller and one as an interviewer. The storytellers were asked to remember a recent skill or knowledge that they had learnt and talk to the interviewer. The other participants in the group acted as outsider witnesses. Each outsider witness group was asked to have a minimum of one volunteer to perform the retelling later at the plenary session after lunch.

The theme of the exercise focused the participants to produce the following outputs:

- a list of relevant skills and knowledge to the Community Network
- a list of values that is relevant to a social contract
- a list of actions to proceed to the next phase

- a list of volunteers (with contact points) to sign up to be champions of the Community Network and take the above actions forward.

The audience in the plenary session became the largest outsider witness group and acted as a community for witnessing and honouring the retelling and retelling of retelling the various stories. The outcome of the group discussion was both enlightening and empowering. It was most moving to see that an 8-year-old girl had the courage to speak as the storyteller. She told us about her experience of learning to speak English. She said when she and her family first arrived in England two years ago she could not speak a word in English. It was very encouraging to see and hear her now addressing the large audience in English. Interestingly, once she started, her younger brother also began to join in, speaking about his experience too. His resonance was transported into courage to speak.

The groups generated a number of concrete actions:

1　Join the Community Network.
2　Be part of the Community Network.
3　Be involved, don't just 'talk', but also take 'action'.
4　Share and participate at all levels.
5　Create and foster opportunities for involvement of others especially the diverse minority groups.
6　Discuss and take forward the ideas of 'camp fire' and storytelling in their organisations (e.g. Wildlife Trust and Nature Reserves etc.)
7　Ensure contact details and interests were shared.
8　Ask the question, 'What we can bring to the party?'
9　Get involved with networking opportunities.
10　Help the Community Network to regenerate deprived areas.

To summarise, the resonance of listening to the re-telling of participants' own stories generated the following emotions/values (landscape of consciousness) and actions (landscape of actions):

Landscape of consciousness

- A sense of pride.
- Respect.
- Reassurance.
- Realisation of self and new skills.
- A sense of self-achievement.
- Realisation of the past sacrifice.

- Self-awareness.
- Self-realisation.
- Moral considerations.
- Happy memories.
- A sense of trust.
- A sense of responsibility.
- Courage.
- Motivation.
- Commitment.

Landscape of action

- Communicate.
- Get involved with others.
- Break the barriers.
- Make decisions.
- Make stronger commitment.
- Overcome hostility.
- Overcome prejudices.
- Translate theory into action.
- Take positive action.

It was a pleasant surprise to see the idea of telling stories around the 'campfire' in Karos and Kambro had caught the community's imagination. A participant at the story retelling session asked, 'Where is the campfire in Peterborough?' Many other participants had a similar resonance to create their own campfire in their communities. As a part of the outcome, a new Community Network was set up. The campfire metaphor was implemented by the Community Network as part of the Black History Month Celebration in October 2006 and also by the Wildlife Trust in one of their community events in its nature reserve, which attracted over 200 participants (including adults and children).

Difficulties encountered

- The validity, reliability and representation of the primary authors who told the stories – as a narrative practitioner playing an ethnographer's role to retell, report and disseminate the stories of individuals and groups from the diverse communities, we felt an ethical dilemma whether we had done justice in honouring and respecting those people. Some of the stories were very personal and politically sensitive. Questions raised include: are the retold stories a fair representation of the intention of the storytellers? Are the retold stories valid, and reliably representing the meaning of the original stories?

- Acknowledgements to the stakeholders – in order to maintain confidentiality, the names and identities of the storytellers are kept anonymous. In doing so, acknowledgements to those individuals in honouring the source of the stories became difficult.
- Our responsibility as coaches, consultants and researchers in disseminating those stories – on the one hand, like academic researchers, we felt that we had a professional duty to publish those stories, to share those skills and knowledge among our colleagues. While on the other, this had to balance with the sensitivities and honouring those individuals who contributed to those stories and knowledge.
- Ownership of the stories – as some of the stories were highly idiosyncratic and personal, yet once they were told and retold at the conference, and published in the public domain, skills and knowledge were shared among communities. While some may be very happy with the dissemination of the stories, which embed and transport the knowledge, some may feel the stories were too private to share in a wider domain. This raises the questions of ownership and authorship of those stories. Do the writers who write and report the stories own the authorship, or should the storytellers own their own stories? Who has the power, responsibility and control for disseminating the stories and knowledge, for whose benefit?
- Rules and regulations – owing to the rules and regulations of the organisation, setting up the fire at a nature reserve was judged as highly undesirable by the management. So at the end, we had to use the metaphor: lighting up a candle and setting up a marquee instead of creating a real fire.
- English weather – setting up a campfire and telling stories outdoors in England turned out to be very challenging. Even though we chose the date of the follow-up event to be in the summer (it had been the hottest week of the year), it had to be cancelled at the last minute due to the rain and thunderstorm on the day!

References

Bruner, J. S. (1964) The course of cognitive growth. *American Psychologist* 19: 1–15.
CIPD (2006) News – Sort it with a story from down under. *Coaching at Work* 1(2): 10.
Combrink, A., Maree, J. and Mabolo, M. (2006) Breaking the silence: stories as tool for healing in marginalized communities. Presentation at International Narrative Therapy Festive Conference, Dulwich Centre, Adelaide, 1–3 March.

Epston, D. and White, M. (1992) *Experience, Contradiction, Narrative and Imagination: Selected papers of David Epston and Michael White.* Adelaide: Dulwich Centre.

Grant, A. M. and Palmer, S. (2002) Coaching psychology workshop. Annual Conference of the Division of Counselling Psychology, British Psychological Society, Torquay, UK, 18 May.

Kolb, D. A. (1984) *Experiential Learning: Experience as the source of learning and development.* Englewood Cliffs, NJ: Prentice Hall.

Law, H. C. (2006) Can coaches be good in any context? *Coaching at Work* 1(2): 14.

Law, H. C., Ireland, S. and Hussain, Z. (2005) Evaluation of coaching competence self review on-line tool within an NHS leadership development programme. Special Group in Coaching Psychology Annual National Conference, City University, London, December. Published (2006) in *International Coaching Psychology Review* 1(2).

Law, H. C., Aga, S. and Hill, J. (2006) 'Creating a "camp fire" at home'. Narrative coaching – community coaching and mentoring network conference report and reflection. In H. C. Law (ed.) *The Cutting Edge*, volume 7, no. 1. Peterborough, UK: Peterborough School of Arts Publication.

Law, H. C., Ireland, S. and Hussain, Z. (2007) *Psychology of Coaching, Mentoring and Learning.* Chichester: Wiley.

Myerhoff, B. (1982) Life history among the elderly: performance, visibility and re-membering. In J. Ruby (ed.) *A Crack in the Mirror: Reflexive perspectives in anthropology.* Philadelphia, PA: University of Pennsylvania Press.

Myerhoff, B. (1986) Life not death in Venice: its second life. In V. Turner and E. Brunner (eds) *The Anthology of Experience.* Chicago, IL: University of Illinois Press.

Palmer, S. and Whybrow, A. (2006) The coaching psychology movement and its development within the British Psychological Society. *International Coaching Psychology Review* 1(1): 5–11.

Rosinski, P. (2003) *Coaching across Cultures.* London: Nicholas Brealey.

Turner, V. (1967) *The Forest of Symbols: Aspects of Ndemby ritual.* Ithaca, NY: Cornel Paperbacks.

Turner, V. and Brunner, E. (1986) *The Anthology of Experience.* Chicago, IL: University of Illinois Press.

Van Gennep, A. (1960) *The Rite of Passage.* Chicago, IL: University of Chicago Press.

Vygotsky, L. S. (1962) *Thought and Language.* Cambridge, MA: MIT Press. (Originally published 1926.)

White, M. (1995) *Re-Authoring Lives: Interviews and essays.* Adelaide: Dulwich Centre.

White, M. (1997) Definitional ceremony. In M. White, *Narratives of Therapists' lives.* Adelaide: Dulwich Centre.

White, M. (2000) Reflecting team-work as definitional ceremony revisited. In M. White, *Reflections on Narrative Practice.* Adelaide: Dulwich Centre.

White, M. (2006) Presentation in Narrative Therapy Intensive Workshop, Dulwich Centre, Adelaide, 20–24 February.

White, M. and Morgan, A. (2006) *Narrative Therapy with Children and their Families.* Adelaide: Dulwich Centre.

Discussion points

- This chapter linked narrative coaching to psychology of learning within a cross-cultural context. In particular, Vygotsky's proximal development and Kolb's learning cycle were described. Could you identify any other learning theories that might be adapted in coaching applications? Would these learning theories be sensitive to the cultural dimensions as discussed in the case study?
- The goal of reauthoring conversation is to redevelop coachees' skills and knowledge by redescribing the stories of their life experience. Reauthoring conversations provide platforms for participants to step into the near future of their lives (the 'landscape of action'). As a coach, could you devise questions that encourage the storytellers to generate new proposals for action? What would these questions look like? What are the characteristics of these questions? Note that the narrative coach would need to first scaffold the rich story development in the landscape of consciousness before one could proceed with the reauthoring questions. Within what context should these questions best be applied?
- The initial responses from the coachees to landscapes of consciousness questions are likely to be about various categories of their self-identity such as attributes, characteristics, deficits, drive, motives, needs, resources, strengths, traits, etc. However according to the assumption of the narrative approach, these conclusions may provide an inadequate basis for the coachees to proceed (in other words, they 'get stuck'). What does a narrative coach need to do in order to guide the storytellers with alternative categories of identity? What in general should these categories look like i.e. their characteristics?
- Outsider witness retelling can be carried out when you have three or more participants in a group situation. In this situation, one or more participants from the group can act as outsider witnesses. What are the differences between the outsider witnesses in a narrative setting and observers in the context of say, performance assessment in terms of the process of listening, note taking and providing feedback? Can outsider witness retelling be modified and applied into group exercises such as an assessment centre in selection for organisations? If so, what particular value would that be?

Suggested reading

Law, H. C., Ireland, S. and Hussain, Z. (2007) *Psychology of Coaching, Mentoring and Learning*. Chichester: Wiley.

This book expands on the Universal Integrated Framework with theories and practices in detail, linking them to a lot more practical exercises and case studies. It also includes a chapter on evaluation of the framework.

Law, H. C., Ireland, S. and Hussain, Z (2006) Evaluation of the Coaching Competence Self Review on-line tool within an NHS leadership development programme. *International Coaching Psychology Review* 1(2).

The article succinctly explains the Universal Framework and demonstrates how it was implemented as an on-line tool for a leadership programme within the National Health Services. It reports on the evaluation of the tool and the quantitative results of the study.

Rosinski, P. (2003) *Coaching across Cultures*. London: Nicholas Brealey.

This book has been regarded as one of the pioneering stages of developing the emerging discipline of cross-cultural coaching. It is based on the works of socio-cultural anthropology. It provides a Cultural Orientations Framework in dealing with cultural differences and advocates an ethno-relative coaching. At the highest level, coaches should aim to leverage differences by making the most of differences and achieving unity through diversity.

White, M. (1995) *Re-Authoring Lives: Interviews and essays*. Adelaide: Dulwich Centre.

This book provides a collection of inspiring interviews and original essays of narrative therapy by Michael White that demonstrate the theory in practice.

Chapter 11

NLP coaching

Bruce Grimley

Introduction

Neuro-linguistic programming (NLP) coaching is an atheoretical, pragmatic approach which shares a philosophy with constructivist, behaviourist and experiential psychology. It is unashamedly eclectic in its orientation drawing on many psychological approaches. The founders of NLP unlike Kurt Lewin would not say 'there is nothing so useful as a good theory'. They made no commitment to theory, regarding such as being more complex and not as useful. Instead they described NLP as a meta-discipline. As they studied the structure of subjective experience, their prime concern was a *description* of how somebody worked without needing to understand why they worked that way.

With Gregory Bateson as the early mentor to the co-founders, John Grinder and Richard Bandler, it is understandable that one should also describe this 'art and science' as imbued with their respective influences – systems theory, transformational grammar and Gestalt. NLP has been described as an attitude with a methodology that leaves behind it a trail of techniques. When one works as an NLP coach one adopts an approach which emphasises usefulness for the client rather than truthfulness for the coach.

Development of neuro-linguistic programming

One important thing to realise about NLP is that its core activity is not coaching but modelling. Many of the coaching NLP books on the market would be properly described as NLP^{training}. In other words they are not about NLP but rather about training others in the application of models which have been built and are useful for facilitating change in others. The first model to be built was the Meta model in the mid-1970s. The Milton model, eye accessing cues and the six-step reframe followed on. They are all models and techniques, of which you will discover more as you read through this chapter.

The two co-founders of NLP parted company in the 1980s. There seems to have been some acrimony, with Richard Bandler eventually filing a legal action against John Grinder in 1996 alleging a number of things connected with the origins and practice of NLP. This was settled in February 2000, when both parties mutually agreed to refrain from disparaging each other's efforts concerning their respective involvements in the field of NLP. Judy De-Lozier, Robert Dilts, Leslie Cameron-Bandler, Frank Pucelik, Stephen Gilligan, David Gordon, Steve and Connirae Andreas, Lara Ewing, Christina Hall and Wyatt Woodsmall were all co-developers of NLP in the early days, building models according to their own areas of interest. One of the key paradoxes, of which there are many in NLP, is that it claims to produce models of excellence, which are essentially algorithms, however the discovery, coding and verification of patterns which describe the modelling process itself has no algorithm, being described by Grinder as 'artistry' (Bostic St. Clair and Grinder, 2001).

Theory and basic concepts

As mentioned above NLP is regarded by many of its practitioners as atheoretical. However, when psychologists look at, and use many of the techniques developed they notice striking similarities between NLP techniques and the techniques they use as coaching psychologists. When facilitating a workshop recently a gestalt psychologist commented, 'I could have done that demonstration just as well.' Gestalt psychology was one of the early modelling projects of NLP, so in the demonstration I was not doing NLP, rather I was applying the Meta model and perceptual positioning, which came from gestalt.

A theory that underpins the whole of NLP is constructivism. This is formally recognised by the United Kingdom Council of Psychotherapy (UKCP) in putting the Neuro-Linguistic Programming therapy and Counselling association (NLPtCA) in the experiential constructivist section of its umbrella organisation. Similar to Immanuel Kant, NLP does not suggest we have access to the objective world, only our phenomenological representation of it, called First Access or F^1. Our linguistic transformations of First Access (in NLP terms referred to as F^2) are immediate and create our conscious 'reality' which forms the basis of both our successes and problems. Paradoxically it is this 'reality' that both connects us to the world when we are successful, and alienates us from it when we are unsuccessful.

A number of other theoretical and philosophical roots have informed NLP practice. Some of the key ones are highlighted here.

Goal setting theory

Goal setting theory is essential to NLP coaching. If you do not know where you are going it does not matter which turning you take. Goal setting gives us direction and provides us with stability and the ability to make meaningful decisions. For the NLP coach goals need to be stated in the positive, based upon sensory evidence, measurable, within a timeframe, owned by the coachee, and they need to be something which really accords with the beliefs and values of the coachee. For NLP coaching the most important aspect of goal setting is to ascertain whether or not the coachee really wishes to obtain this goal, compared with them being obliged to do so because of societal, organisational or parental approval.

After parting with Richard Bandler, John Grinder developed 'new code' which puts a much greater emphasis on the unconscious in selecting which goals are appropriate for our personal and professional development. He points out that the conscious mind is not as equipped as the unconscious to make such momentous decisions (Bostic St. Clair and Grinder, 2001).

Gestalt

Gestalt therapy was NLP's first model. One of the results of this modelling project was the 'Meta model'. This is designed to assist the coachee, in true Fritz Perls fashion, to come to their senses. John Grinder describes the model as a collection of 13 syntactic patterns in human speech along with the appropriate challenges (Bostic St. Clair and Grinder, 2001). Essentially and simplistically they are the what, when, who, how, and where questions. Not only are these questioning skills useful for ensuring the coachee manages to ensure their goal is formed using sensory based language, but also, once that goal has been formed, it assists them to understand specifically what prevents them achieving the goal.

When a client complains they go to pieces when providing a presentation to the board of directors, a useful question to ask is 'precisely how many pieces?' This has the effect of preventing the coachee using abstract language, instead requiring a description of the experience in precise sensory-based language creating a connection with the real source of the problem. This enables the client to take full responsibility for their problem. The Meta model is often contrasted with the Milton model, which uses language in a deliberately vague way so as to bypass the conscious mind and communicate with the unconscious mind directly.

Another technique that came from gestalt was that of perceptual positioning. A useful technique to gather information for our client would be for them to put themselves in the position of one of the people receiving the presentation and see and hear through the eyes and ears of that person. What does that person see? What does that person hear? This provides the coachee with multiple descriptions as to what is going on. What the Meta model and perceptual positioning do for the coachee is allow them to engage more fully with their whole self and make adjustments there, rather than in a futile way only engaging in first order changes based upon the client's rationalised phenomenology, which tends to be a function of F^2 transformations.

To a great extent these aspects from gestalt psychology address the need for self-awareness which NLP calls for. Once one has such self-awareness the next stage, if one must talk in linear terms, is flexibility. Are my constructs or representations sufficiently loose to be amenable to alteration in particular contexts? For many clients the answer is no. Such clients are a bit like someone wishing to go on a journey from place A to place B by car and their map shows them only one way to get there. What happens if that route is closed one day? Such a client with an impoverished map is literally stuck. However, a client with a map which accurately represents the multitude of choices available simply chooses a different route and obtains their outcome.

The systems concept of requisite variety is one of NLP's presuppositions: 'the internal regulatory mechanisms of a system must be as diverse as the environment with which it is trying to deal' (Morgan, 1997: 41). The NLP coach assists the client to develop richer maps of the world so as to provide them with more choice. This emphasis on flexibility and the provision of choice is key to NLP coaching.

Transformational grammar

The Meta model was to a great extent brought into existence because of Grinder's understanding of transformational grammar (TG). Indeed he describes TG and its methodology as the 'single most pervasive influence in NLP' (Bostic St. Clair and Grinder, 2001: 66), and elsewhere as 'the cornerstone of modeling' (Bostic St. Clair and Grinder 2001: 77). The heart of TG is that our linguistic behaviour is rule governed. The appropriate object for description, analysis and explanation is not the actual language, as was previously thought, but the underlying set of rules, implicitly and unconsciously understood by the native speaker of that language. The NLP counterpart is that excellence in human behaviour is also rule governed. These underlying rules identify the behaviour that needs to be the centre of attention at a particular point in time.

These underlying rules are made explicit in NLP through each individual modelling project. For instance in modelling Erickson, Bandler and Grinder (1975) discovered that two types of verbal pacing were crucial to access an individual's governing rules. First, descriptions of clients' ongoing, observable experience, and second, descriptions of clients' ongoing non-observable experience. Thus, the synergy between the coachee's perception of themselves and the coach's ability to describe the coachee's perception is key.

For the NLP coach this model of the client provides a deep understanding of how the client systematically sabotages themselves through adherence to their particular underlying rules. This adherence for the coachee is largely unconscious. Part of the coaching process for the NLP coach is assisting the coachee to become aware of this patterning and then discover an alternative set of patterns that will generate more productive language and behaviour, moving the coachee towards their goal.

If our client says to us, 'When I see David look at me like that I know he thinks I've lost the plot', we are presented with a surface structure, the actual language. For the NLP coach the first step is to ask: is this surface structure a complete representation of the deep structure? The Meta model generates specific challenges when the coach notices that there are, in fact, pieces missing. These include: 'Like what?', 'How do you know?', 'How have you lost the plot?', 'Whose plot is it?', 'What exactly is the plot?' . . . and so forth. As the client fills in the different pieces, an enriched model of this particular situation is created and more choices presented.

Behaviourism

In accordance with self-perception theory, a development of behaviourism, we learn through association and labeling (Hampson, 1984). Johnny falls over and bangs his head, Mummy says, 'Oh dear, that must hurt', so it does. We learn the meanings of our feelings and experience through a socialisation process which relies largely on behaviourism. The reason the bang on the head *hurts* is that it is congruent with the 'map' of Mummy and becomes internalised in the child. In this way the child learns. However, it does not stop there: to become a 'fact' the hurt must be supported by society, so little Johnny finds that health care workers, social service providers, teachers, doctors and psychologists all say the same thing. Two of the distortions which create this map for NLP are *cause and effect* – 'Johnny hitting his head on the table *causes* a sensation in the temple region of his head' – and *complex equivalence* (a term from linguistics referring to how we create meanings through associations in an idiosyncratic way). 'This sensation *means* this hurts and is therefore painful.' It is this mixture of F^1 and F^2 transformations which produce Johnny's 'reality'.

In the film *A Man called Horse* (1970), starring Richard Harris, he goes through the rites of passage where he is hooked up by the nipples and raised from the ground. I imagine the Sioux culture of the nineteenth century had a very different complex equivalence (F^2 transformation) concerning somatic sensations and what they meant.

However, unlike behaviourism, NLP is very interested in what goes on in the 'black box' of the mind, and like social learning theory attends to memory, motivation, cognitive organisation and attention. The child also learns, as Albert Bandura suggested (Gross, 1987: 534), through imitation, noticing the rewarded behaviours from significant others. The child then models such a person, so as to use such behaviours in an appropriate context in the future. This is regarded as a largely unconscious process.

NLP uses many terms which have similar behaviourist psychology counterparts, for example, anchoring used in classical conditioning. A typical technique in NLP could use anchoring in the following way. Let us say giving a presentation is the context, and the trigger is a senior manager asking our coaching client to give a presentation. The NLP coach would help the coachee find a very positive experience which elicited the desired emotional state. An anchor would be agreed and would be the same as the conditioned stimulus in behaviourism, it could be a physical action, an internal picture, an internal word, etc.

In our example, the coach notices the coachee can genuinely recall the situation when she felt very confident being asked to captain the Under 16 hockey team for her school. The coach would then encourage the coachee to associate her emotional state of confidence with her chosen anchor. Often the association needs to be made a few times and on each time it is essential the timing is just at the peak of the experiential state of confidence and that the anchor is exactly the same each time.

Once the association has been made between the emotional state and the anchor, the client practises associating this new anchor with the problem trigger and within the problem context. This too is repeated till the new associations have been made. After future pacing and ensuring through calibration, that the client really does now feel confident each time she hears her manager's voice, the 20 minute exercise is over. The sound of the manager's voice automatically activates, via an anchor, the emotional resource of confidence (conditioned response). A further NLP presupposition is that 'You have all the resources you need to achieve your outcomes'. In this case, the client has always had this resource, but had never used the anchor in this particular context.

Test Operate Test Exit (TOTE)

By focusing on utility rather than theory NLP demonstrates its creativity by combining contradictory models. Not only does NLP import classical conditioning and social learning theory into its repertoire of techniques, but also central to NLP methodology is the Test Operate Test Exit (TOTE), which was designed by Miller, Pribram and Galanter (1960) to replace the stimulus–response paradigm as the basic unit of behaviour. TOTE is the mechanism used by an NLP coach to assist a coachee move from where they are to where they wish to be through a series of operations. It is operationalised by incongruence, and one finally exits after testing the operations, when one experiences congruence. The process is nicely summarised by the NLP mantra Outcome, Acuity, Flexibility.

To use our client as an example, the desired outcome is to behave in a very confident way when presenting to the board of directors. When thinking about presenting to the board initially, there is incongruence. Our client lacks confidence entirely in this situation. By focusing on the nature of that incongruence and with assistance from the NLP coach, the client will be able to identify what specifically needs to change. It may simply be posture; it may be a cluster of tasks such as positive self-speak, greater preparation, and more eye contact or some other activity. This is the operation aspect of TOTE where one elicits what needs to change and then tasks the coachee to make those changes.

When operationalising such changes it is important to be sensitive to feedback so as to understand the extent to which the feedback one actually receives is commensurate with the feedback a very confident person would get. When, after the task, we notice the feedback is just as we would like, we experience congruence and can exit the TOTE with a new set of proceduralised operations in the context of giving a presentation. In the case of feedback that does not accord with our desired outcome, a new set of operations is tested, or the existing ones are refined. The TOTE is cycled again and again till one achieves one's goal, and experiences congruence which is the signal to exit the TOTE.

Summary

It would be impossible in this short chapter to touch upon all the psychological theories which NLP draws from. These include general semantics, systems theory, reattribution theory, social comparison theory, cognitive dissonance, clinical hypnosis, family therapy, ego state theory, cognitive theory, and psychodynamic theory. I hope that the above has given you some idea of the way NLP in its development has been able to draw upon similar themes in the discipline of psychology.

Practice

A key presupposition of NLP is that there are no resistant clients, only inflexible coaches. What this means in practice is that the NLP coach needs to have a range of 'techniques' in their tool box, to know which ones to use and when. However, to pull this off the NLP coach needs to be sufficiently advanced to use such techniques seamlessly. This concurs with the thoughts of Carl Rogers, who said the best anything technical which is taught can achieve is some temporary improvement (Rogers, 1967). In practice to get to this level of unconscious competence one needs to train as an NLP coach with a reputable trainer, rather than read a book. What this means to the NLP coach is there is no fixed format to a session. In this section I will run through how a typical NLP coaching intervention might go, rather than unpack literally hundreds of NLP techniques. I will stick with our friend who goes to pieces every time they have to present to the board of directors.

Outcome

Before the NLP coach does anything with the client, rapport needs to be obtained. Rapport tells your client you understand their map of the world at a very deep level; only when they believe this will they give you 'permission' to lead them to their outcome. Rapport is obtained in a number of ways.

Representational system

For the NLP coach the client acts indirectly on the world through their representational system. We represent the world to ourselves first through our five senses. Dogs for instance have a great sense of smell, a hawk has a great visual sense, and bats use their auditory system to see. As humans we use all of our five senses, with perhaps a preference for one over another. The client provides clues to their preference, and in order to obtain rapport we need to match that preference in our communication. If the client talks quickly, looks upwards, breathes from the upper part of their chest, stands erect, wears bright colours, tells you the future often looks bright, and gesticulates a lot, the chances are the representational system preferred is visual. One will need to talk about seeing the client standing upright, colourful, and speaking with confidence in front of others. It is important to provide the client with tasks which are visual in nature, such as noticing how people look when they talk confidently and drawing pictures of what they notice. There are similar clues for the other representational systems, but it is important the NLP coach notices what these are and uses them in communicating back to the coachee.

Language

A client's words represent their feelings and thoughts. It is important when feeding back to the client (back tracking in NLP talk) that one uses the client's exact words to do this. Paraphrasing may get close, however the key point with paraphrasing is you are using *your* reality to interpret *the client's* reality. To gain rapport at an unconscious level your client needs to understand you understand totally what their reality is.

Body language

Another presupposition of NLP is that the mind and body are part of one system. You think something and as a result there is some movement in the body. An important way of gaining rapport is not only matching your client's body movements, but also being congruent so your body movements also match your own language. When you watch a video of people who are in rapport, you find one person will engage in a piece of body language, say crossing their legs, and a few seconds later the other will do the same.

Sometimes there may be what NLP calls cross over matching – the other may fold their arms rather than cross their legs – however the principle remains the same. This needs to be done in a congruent and subtle way; if it is not then it has the reverse effect and your client will find ways of disengaging.

Meta Programmes

Meta Programmes are unconscious ways in which we sort information. They are like templates for organising our lives. Often the term Meta Programme is used interchangeably with personality. You might know someone who is very good with detail and crosses every *t* and dots every *i*, working slowly and methodically as they do (small chunk rather than big chunk). You might know someone who is never motivated and slouches around all the time . . . until there is a disaster and they are then the most motivated person in the world (reactive rather than proactive). For a final example you might know someone who can exist only if they have a plan, they are really good time keepers, and enjoy organising not only themselves but others as well (procedure rather than options). The development of Meta Programmes is credited to Leslie Cameron-Bandler in NLP, who is claimed to have discovered around 60 different patterns (Rose-Charvet, 1997). To obtain rapport the NLP coach will notice which patterns the coachee characteristically adopts and will use these patterns in feedback to the coachee.

Perceptual positioning

To assist in obtaining rapport, adopting what NLP calls the second position is very useful and can often provide intuitive insights as to the map of your client. Literally the coach imagines they are the client. In the coach's mind, the client's physiology, pace and pitch of language is adopted during the coaching session.

Obtaining the well-formed outcome

Once one has obtained rapport with the client one can begin to assist them to clarify what their well-formed outcome is according to the principles outlined above. Often they will have difficulty doing this as they are so used to experiencing life through a map which has consistently prevented them from achieving their outcome. The use of perceptual positioning is useful here. The coach can invite the client to imagine someone who has achieved what they would like and ask them to second position them. Another technique is to use the *as if* frame and talk and behave *as if* they had already achieved their goal. What would that be like? The client will need to know what emotional state they wish to achieve when presenting, what response they wish to elicit from the board, and how they will do this behaviourally and linguistically in precise terms. What will the evidence be that the client has obtained their outcome? How will they measure that evidence? The client will also need to notice examples of when they are *not* engaging in such behaviour.

Acuity

Often in coaching after a client has gone through the above process they feel so great in clarifying the outcome there is no need for further coaching. Recognising that they themselves have all the resources to do what they wish to do is enough and they succeed.

However, in other cases there is the big BUT. After eliciting who they wish to be in a particular context, the map the client brings to coaching begins to formulate all the objections as to why they cannot be this person. In order to move forward the NLP coach needs to address these. Borrowing from psychodynamic theory NLP assumes there are often primary and secondary gain issues, even in well-functioning senior managers. These prevent people making the best use of their private resources (thoughts and emotions), and public resources (language and behaviour). Thus the client is prevented from congruently obtaining their well-formed outcome.

NLP maintains people can change the nature of their map to create a different phenomenology, and thus more productive thoughts, feelings and behaviour. At the heart of NLP are many *presuppositions*, a relevant one to mention here is *all behaviour has a positive intention* (Dilts and DeLozier, 2000: 1004). When our client complains they go to pieces when having to provide a presentation to the board of directors, the assumption is they are doing the best they can and there is a positive intention behind the trembling, lack of eye contact and memory loss. Hypothetically, the client may wish to impress the board. Another facet of this presupposition is the client has *learned* to behave in this way. Primary gain suggests keeping the symptom is easier than the client allowing the original learning episode into their conscious mind. Secondary gain suggests the client obtains some advantage from the symptoms. Maybe the client does not believe they could cope with promotion and so consistently sabotages themselves in this way when presenting to the board.

While NLP is solution orientated and does not suggest an archeological approach where the coach digs up the past, a set of techniques are needed to overcome the above complexities. Again the use of perceptual positioning is useful to obtain another description of what is really going on for the client. Cognitive dissonance prevents our true beliefs coming to consciousness, by inviting the coachee to see themselves trembling, avoiding eye contact and forgetting what they wish to say makes it easier to understand and admit, there is some fear. Without such an understanding one proceeds with a bogus foundation, for example, 'I don't prepare enough for my presentation'. There are many other NLP techniques to assist raise acuity; Robert Dilts (1998) mentions that psychometrics are even part of the NLP repertoire, though the NLP purist would scoff at such.

Flexibility

At this stage the coach has obtained rapport, elicited a well-formed outcome, assisted the coachee to accurately identify areas of difference between how they present to the board now and how they would like to present. By this time much movement towards presenting effectively will have already been achieved through the coaching to date. A powerful NLP technique to assist the coachee develop greater flexibility to accomplish their outcome is the six-step reframe (O'Connor and Seymour, 1995). The reframe takes the client through the following steps:

1   Identify the behaviour to be changed.
2   Establish communication with the *part* responsible for the behaviour.
3   Separate the positive intention of that *part* with the behaviour presently being produced.
4   Ask the creative *part* to generate a range of alternative behaviours that will produce the same positive intention.
5   Ask the *part* responsible for the problem behaviour if they are willing to accept and try on the alternative behaviours in the future over a set period of time.
6   Check there are no other *parts* who object to this new behaviour, and elicit total congruence in the task at step 5.

Metaphor is a second valuable NLP technique to promote flexibility. Milton Erickson was fond of metaphor: it is useful for bypassing conscious resistance in change. The NLP coach could in this instance tell a story of a young person who developed a limiting belief about the ability to perform in public, and how they successfully overcame it. This not only normalises the coachee's present experience but also matches the deeper structure of their journey and provides a solution for them without realising it consciously. The metaphor needs to be sufficiently disguised to work effectively.

Calibration is an NLP technique that enables the coach to see when the client is accessing their 'problem state' even when the client is not talking about it. By noticing eye movement and other cues when the client accesses their 'problem state', the NLP coach can then anchor such times with a resourceful state, so in the future whenever the client attempts to access the problem state they find themselves automatically laughing internally as they access a resourceful state as a result of persistent anchoring. The key in calibration is accuracy. There is an NLP saying: once is an event, twice is a coincidence, and three times is a pattern. It is important that the coach's association of eye accessing and other minimal behavioural movements with the internal state in question is accurate. When the coach is confident this is the case, then they can begin to anchor such minimal cues to positive, desired states and beliefs which have been agreed upon.

There are other tools the NLP coach can use to assist the coachee develop greater flexibility in moving from A to B (see Dilts and DeLozier, 2000). It is hoped that the above provides an understanding of the thinking behind the process and some examples of NLP techniques.

Which clients benefit most?

NLP being a process-oriented discipline believes it can assist everyone. Clients who have a willingness to explore and experiment are the ones who benefit most from an NLP approach. Clients who share NLP's interest in excellence rather than just above average tend to be those who warm to the approach. Finally, those clients who have the capacity to generate a positive response to ambiguity and enjoy the challenge of suspending the reality which has limited them for so long will benefit. Clients who recognise they have the capacity to create many selves and readily adopt the self most appropriate for their desired outcome are those who enjoy the benefits of NLP coaching the most.

As already mentioned, a presupposition of NLP is that the only bar on the effectiveness of the NLP coach is a lack of flexibility in their approach. Given the importance at the outset of obtaining rapport, coaches who coach clients who come from their own domain and area of expertise might find it easier to develop rapport and therefore move the process forward more quickly.

Case study

Beginning (outcome)

Matthew was educated at a top English public school and was until recently a well-paid sales executive (earning over £100,000) for an American company. Despite improving sales considerably, he had been laid off and was exceptionally angry about this.

The beginning for this client was for him to explain what he wished from coaching. It transpired he was 'in a rut' and he wished to get out of it. This was his outcome; he agreed if he could achieve this the coaching would be successful. In the first session it became clear a part of what was creating this 'rut' was multiple problems, and that the client wished for multiple outcomes for each of them. Because he clustered all of his 'problems' together in his mind his perception of them was that together they were insurmountable and he experienced anger and feelings of helplessness as a result.

The coach acknowledged his problems and started the process of sorting his problems into categories. The two categories identified were:

- urgent / not so urgent
- important / not so important.

The client felt that his anger at his previous employer was the underlying reason he was in such a rut and felt if he could manage his anger better he would be able to focus more effectively on the other problems and use his skills to address them. His other problems were concerning unsatisfactory personal relationships, new business ventures, weight problems, and development or selling of various properties.

The 'Meta model' was used to clarify, separate and articulate exactly what the real problems were, and to identify outcomes for each of these problems. This put the client in a position to do something about it, back in control.

The middle (acuity and flexibility)

In order to develop acuity the client worked with the model shown in Figure 11.1 (adapted from Turner, 2003). The model was shared with the client with the purpose of supporting his own insight at the beginning of the intervention (pacing in NLP terms). That was if he could manage his anger better, by freeing up, he would be able to focus more clearly on the other issues which were important to him. As a result of improved focus the client would then be able to organise himself to achieve his multiple outcomes.

This model also matches the TOTE approach quite closely. Once the client recognised his goals he needed to ascertain how he would achieve the goals and whether his strategies were enabling him to achieve his goals. If not he would need to alter or refine his strategies until he achieved the outcomes he wanted, experienced congruence and as a consequence exited the learning loop.

Perceptual positions were used to assist the client deal with his anger. The client was asked to adopt the first position which was his own angry perception of the past situation. He was then after 'shaking out' that perspective invited to pretend to be the various senior managers in the company and see, feel, and think from their perspective and their perspective alone. After this he was to go to the third perceptual position where he was like a fly on the wall and could see the connection and relationships between the two viewpoints. Finally a fourth position looked at how the connection and relationships between the client and his colleagues looked from an even wider perspective in the business world and their particular market and domain within that business world. In each perceptual position the client would stand in a different place in the coaching space.

At this point the client was invited to think of ways in which his present feelings were impacting upon other areas of his life like his personal relations,

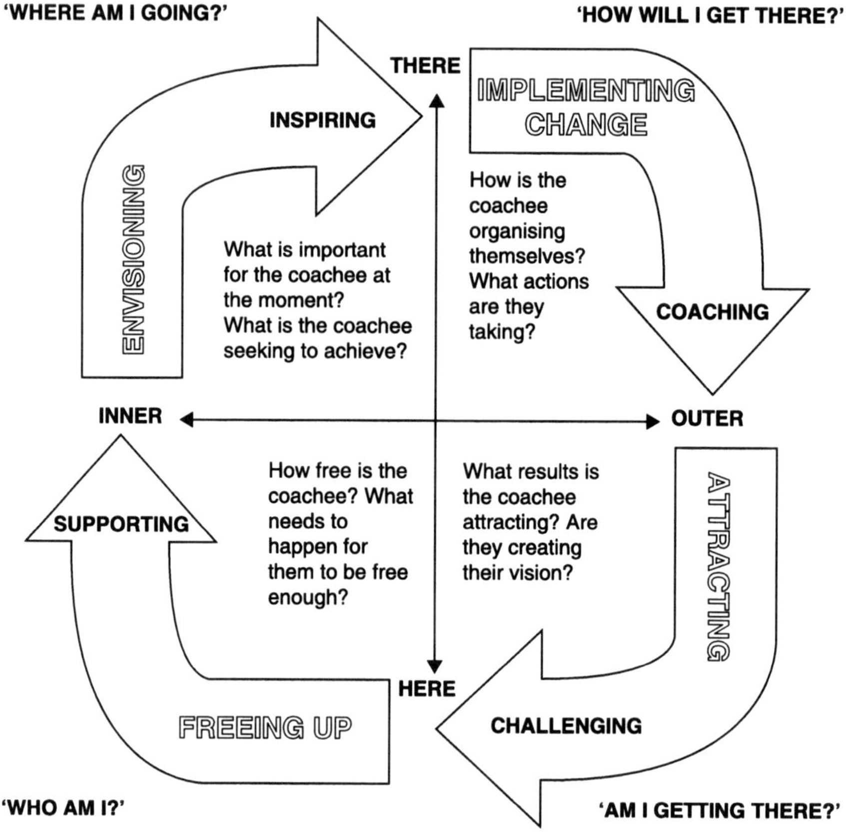

'WHERE AM I GOING?'   **'HOW WILL I GET THERE?'**

THERE

INSPIRING

IMPLEMENTING CHANGE

ENVISIONING

What is important for the coachee at the moment? What is the coachee seeking to achieve?

How is the coachee organising themselves? What actions are they taking?

COACHING

INNER ←→ **OUTER**

SUPPORTING

How free is the coachee? What needs to happen for them to be free enough?

What results is the coachee attracting? Are they creating their vision?

ATTRACTING

HERE

FREEING UP

CHALLENGING

'WHO AM I?'   **'AM I GETTING THERE?'**

Figure 11.1 Coaching framework.

Source: Four Quadrant model, www.mikethementor.co.uk, reproduced by permission of Dr Mike Munro Turner.

his wish to lose weight, his new business venture and the development and selling of properties. Spatial anchors were used to separate the different areas of his life, so he could appreciate the differential effects in each area. By the end of this session he felt much clearer about how he had been creating his own problems by being so angry about being laid off. When he looked at this from differing perspectives his anger was replaced by a desire to plan and take action. Indeed, during the next sessions the client was much more energised about the specific activities he could engage in to achieve his outcomes.

Rapport skills and future pacing were used to encourage the client and for the coach to act as his sponsor on these ventures. Context reframes (when would this behaviour be useful? . . .) and content framing (what else could this mean? . . .) as well as metaphor were used throughout this middle period to mobilise the inner resources of thought and emotion and to align them with his well formed outcome.

The Milton model was used throughout the coaching. For example the client used to display a pattern of getting really angry during coaching and using expletives. When he began to do that the coach interrupted the pattern and would say something like

> Being angry is really useful when you wish to scare people off and alienate them, however there are many other states you can access when some-one says that to you and you can surprise yourself with the ease with which you can just gently reply and notice how that provides you with a different response and puts *you* in charge . . .

The client was interested in personality and completed a personality profiling tool that assisted him obtain further clarity about one way of understanding his personality. Through this, he discovered how people are, in fact, system-atically quite different. This exercise was useful as it clarified for the client how he could use his preferences for providing structure, direction and clar-ity of focus in order to achieve his coaching outcomes. He also appreciated a possible blind spot was effectively dealing with emotional arousal. He found the structured process of looking at his situation from a variety of perceptual positions when he became emotionally aroused, a very useful technique he could use in future situations.

The client joined a gym and started to cycle, row and walk on a treadmill. He wrote up a 1,800 word document to clarify his objectives concerning his multiple outcomes and began to develop higher commitment to action concerning each of those outcomes. The client also kept a 'food diary'. The purpose was to stop 'automatic eating' by asking the client to record on a 1–10 scale how hungry he really was before he ate anything (1 = being very hungry; 10 = being not at all hungry). If he recorded a score of 4 or under it was suggested that eating something sensible would be OK. The task required him to record the exact quantities and qualities of food eaten. However, if he scored 5 or over it was suggested that rather than eat something, he should find some specific task to assist him to move towards one of his outcomes. An outcome sheet of specific activities was designed in one of our sessions for the purpose of allowing the client, without thinking, to go to the list of neces-sary activities to get on with. These activities would take him towards his multiple outcomes.

Another exercise at this point was to go into what NLP calls down time (internal focus), and clarify that, if he wasn't hungry (based upon the score of 5 or over), what precisely was it that encouraged him to wish to eat at that time and in that context? An inner feeling of frustration, an internal voice telling him he could not do it, an internal visual representation of him failing in one of his tasks? In this way he was encouraged to surface the previous internal representations which had maintained his eating habit. By doing this he could then exert control over them, changing them according to what was most useful for him.

The ending (flexibility, future pacing, consolidation)

The final two sessions of ten were spent in future pacing. This is an NLP concept which means the client is oriented towards the future so he can see specifically what he needs to do, but can equally surface any possible problems. Potential problems that were raised included moving too fast for other people, maintaining the weight loss and managing his emotional state if things did not go quite as he had planned. These were dealt with by reinforcing the work that had been done. Additionally, he worked to develop an understanding of other personality types, and role played how he could most effectively work with them.

By the end of the tenth session the client felt he was truly out of his rut and moving forward in his life. The quantifiable outcomes that confirmed his progress included ending his unsatisfactory personal relationship (on friendly terms), selling one of his properties, moving down to London, starting serious talks with potential business partners, and losing a stone in weight with which he was very pleased. He felt good because he believed he looked more presentable in a business suit.

Brief NLP glossary

'The map is not the territory'   The problem of clients is never in the world, it is in their representation of the world.

'And how does that assist you achieve your outcome?'   A useful question to surface the positive intention behind unwanted behaviour.

Analogue marking   Using your voice tone, body language, gestures, etc. to mark out key words in a sentence or a special piece of your presentation.

Calibrated loop   Pattern of communication in which behavioural cues of one person trigger specific unconscious responses from another person in an ongoing interaction.

Chunking   Organising or breaking some experience into bigger or smaller pieces. Chunking up involves moving to a larger, more abstract level of information. Chunking down involves moving to a more specific and concrete level of information.

References

Bandler, R. and Grinder, J. (1975) *Patterns of the Hypnotic Techniques of Milton Erickson, M.D.*, Volume 1. Cupertino, CA: Meta.

Bayne, R. (1997) *The Myers-Briggs Type Indicator*. Cheltenham: Stanley Thornes.

Bostic St. Clair, C. and Grinder, J. (2001) *Whispering in the Wind*. Scotts Valley, CA: J and C Enterprises.

Dilts, R. (1998) *Modeling with NLP*. Capitola, CA: Meta.

Dilts, R. and DeLozier, J. (2000). *Encyclopedia of Systemic Neuro-Linguistic Programming and NLP New Coding*. Scotts Valley, CA: NLP University Press.

Gross, R. D. (1987) *Psychology: The science of mind and behaviour*. London: Edward Arnold.

Hampson, S. (1984) Sources of information about the self. In P. Barnes et al. (eds) *Personality, Development, and Learning: A reader*. London: Hodder and Stoughton.

Miller, G. A., Galanter, E. and Pribram, K. H. (1960) *Plans and the Structure of Behavior*. New York: Holt, Rinehart and Winston.

Morgan, G. (1997) *Images of Organization*. London: Sage.

O'Connor, J. and Seymour, J. (1995) *Introducing NLP Neuro-Linguistic Programming*, revised edition. London: Thorsons.

Rogers, C. R. (1967) *On Becoming a Person*. London: Constable.

Rose-Charvet, S. (1997) *Words that Change Minds: Mastering the language of influence*, 2nd edition. Dubuque, IA: Kendall / Hunt.

Turner, M. (2003) Mike the mentor, http://www.mikethementor.co.uk/

Discussion points

- Type theory suggests we remain the type of person we are throughout our life, and that our preferences are possibly innate. Concerning the concept of preference Rowan Bayne tells us 'there is no formal definition in the MBTI literature and it is perhaps best defined by analogy. The analogy most used is handedness' (Bayne, 1997: 4). If we accept this, how, as an NLP coach, can we suggest to a client they have the capacity to suspend and unfreeze their internal architecture in certain contexts so as to become fundamentally, and authentically different?

- In talking about how psychology functions John Grinder suggests research is directed at finding independent variables which can raise *average* performance. He challenges the psychology community and asks why are we not more concerned with excellent performance and the study of that? To what extent does he have a point?

- The words 'cognitive behavioural' fundamentally marginalise the most leveraged aspect of information processing, that at the level of emotion. NLP, in presupposing the mind and body are one system, produces sustainable results so quickly, because in its model it fundamentally embraces this missing link. Discuss.

- NLP has been accused of lacking a research base. Go to your web browser and type in 'NLP research'. In the light of what you find, to what extent do you feel this accusation is justified? If you feel it is justified, how would you progress researching the claims NLP practitioners make concerning rapid, sustainable change in a coaching environment?

Suggested reading

Bandler, R. and Grinder, J. (1979) *Frogs into Princes: Neuro Linguistic Programming*. Moab, UT: Real People Press.

De Lozier, J. and Grinder, J. (1987) *Turtles All the Way Down: Prerequisites to personal genius*. Scotts Valley, CA: Grinder and Associates.

Dilts, R. and DeLozier, J. (2000) *Encylopedia of Systemic Neuro-Linguistic Programming and NLP New Coding*. Scotts Valley, CA: NLP University Press.

Dilts, R., Grinder, J., Bandler, R. and DeLozier, J. (1980) *Neuro-linguistic Programming*. Volume 1, *The Study of the Structure of Subjective Experience*. Capitola, CA: Meta.

Chapter 12

Person-centred coaching psychology

Stephen Joseph and Richard Bryant-Jefferies

Introduction

Person-centred coaching psychology is a way of working with people based on the meta-theoretical assumption that people have the potential to develop, and to grow, and that when this inner potential is released they are able to move toward becoming more autonomous, socially constructive, and optimally functioning. But this does not happen automatically. Without the right social environment, the intrinsic motivation toward optimal functioning is usurped leading instead to distress and dysfunction. Thus, the task of the person-centred coaching psychologist is to provide a social environment in which the client's intrinsic motivation is facilitated. The person-centred coaching psychologist holds that the client is their own best expert and that if they are able to offer the client an accepting and authentic relationship in which they do not feel judged or pushed, then the client will be self-determining and motivated towards optimal functioning. In this chapter, we will describe the development of the person-centred approach, and how it is applicable to coaching psychology.

Development of the person-centred approach

The person-centred approach was originally developed by the psychologist Carl Rogers (1951, 1961). The person-centred approach is well established in counselling and psychotherapy, but is also applicable to coaching. Unlike some other therapeutic approaches, person-centred practice is not concerned with 'repairing' or 'curing' dysfunctionality, and never adopted the 'diagnostic' stance of the medical model in which the therapist is the expert. The focus of the person-centred practitioner, no matter where the client lies on the spectrum of psychological functioning, is to facilitate the self-determination of the client so that they can move toward more optimal functioning (Joseph, 2003, 2006). The person-centred approach is a meta-theoretical approach to working with people, and applications of the person-centred approach have been not only to therapy, but also to education, parenting, group learning, conflict resolution, and peace processes (see Barrett-Lennard, 1998), all based on the same philosophical stance that people are their own best experts. These are ideas which will be easily recognisable to coaching psychologists (e.g. Kauffman and Scoular, 2004).

The person-centred meta-theoretical perspective is an established psychological tradition supported by over 50 years of research and theory (see Barrett-Lennard, 1998), as well as recent developments in positive psychology (e.g. Joseph and Linley, 2004, 2005, 2006; Linley and Joseph, 2004). This assumption that human beings have an inherent tendency toward growth, development and optimal functioning provides the theoretical foundation that it is the client and not the therapist or coach who knows best (Joseph, 2003; Levitt, 2005). This serves as the guiding principle for client-centred practice, which in essence is simply the principled stance of respecting the self-determination of others (B. Grant, 2004). Person-centred psychology is not a set of therapeutic techniques but an attitude based on the theoretical stance that people are their own best experts (Joseph, 2003; Levitt, 2005).

Theory and basic concepts

Carl Rogers proposed the meta-theoretical perspective that human beings have an inherent tendency toward growth, development, and optimal functioning, which he termed the *actualising tendency* (see Rogers, 1959, 1963). But these do not happen automatically. For people to *self-actualise* their inherent optimal nature they require the right social environment. The right social environment Rogers proposed was one in which the person feels understood, valued, and accepted for who they are. In such an environment, Rogers reasoned, people are inclined to self-actualise in a way that is *congruent* with their intrinsic actualising tendency, resulting in well-being and optimal functioning. But when people do not feel understood, valued or accepted for who they are, but rather feel valued only for being the person they perceive someone else wants them to be, then they self-actualise in a way that is *incongruent* with their intrinsic actualising tendency, resulting in distress and dysfunction.

Necessary and sufficient conditions

What the therapist or coach tries to do is to provide the right social environmental conditions. Rogers (1957) described six conditions that he held were necessary and sufficient for positive therapeutic change (see Box 12.1). Rogers believed these conditions to underlie *any* therapeutic personality change, and thus believed that they must be in operation in any successful helping relationship.

Box 12.1 The necessary and sufficient conditions of constructive person-ality change

1   Two persons are in psychological contact.
2   The first, whom we shall call the client, is in a state of incongru-ence, being vulnerable or anxious.
3   The second person, whom we shall call the therapist, is congruent or integrated in the relationship.
4   The therapist experiences unconditional positive regard for the client.
5   The therapist experiences an empathic understanding of the client's internal frame of reference and endeavours to communicate this experience to the client.
6   The communication to the client of the therapist's empathic under-standing and unconditional positive regard is to a minimal degree achieved.

Source: adapted with permission from Rogers, C. R. (1957) The necessary and sufficient conditions of therapeutic personality change. *Journal of Consulting Psychology* 21: 95–103. Published by the American Psychological Association.

Condition one is referring to a precondition that, if not met, would mean that the following five conditions were redundant. What Rogers means by psychological contact is whether or not the two people are aware of each other, and that the behaviour of one impacts on the other. So, for example, with someone who is in a catatonic state it would be difficult to judge whether there was psychological contact. In the second condition, incongruence is explained as consisting of an incompatibility between underlying feelings and awareness of those feelings, or an incompatibility between awareness of feelings and the expression of feelings. For example, someone who appears anxious to an observer but has no awareness themselves of feeling anxious would be said to be incongruent in terms of their underlying feelings and their awareness of those feelings. Someone who is aware of their anxiety but says that they are feeling relaxed would be said to be incongruent between awareness and expression. In the third condition, the therapist is congruent, that is to say, he or she is accurately aware of their inner experience, such as feelings of anger or sadness, and is able to express this openly and honestly if thought to be appropriate. In the fourth condition, the therapist is able to provide unconditional positive regard, that is to say, he or she is able to warmly accept the client without imposing conditions of worth on the client. In the fifth condition, the therapist has empathic understanding; that is to say, he or she is able to sense and have an appreciation of what the client's experience must be like. Finally, in the sixth condition, the client perceives the therapist's empathy and unconditional acceptance. Rogers believed that if these six conditions were in existence then constructive personality change would occur, but only if all six were present, and that the more they were present the more marked would be the constructive personality change of the client.

> the final condition ... is that the client perceives, to a minimal degree, the acceptance and empathy which the therapist experiences for him. Unless some communication of these attitudes has been achieved, then such attitudes do not exist in the relationship as far as the client is concerned, and the therapeutic process could not, by our hypothesis, be initiated.
>
> (Rogers, 1957)

> It is interesting that he uses the words 'minimal degree', suggesting that the client does not need to fully perceive the fullness of the empathy and unconditional positive regard present within, and communicated by, the counsellor. A glimpse accurately heard and empathically understood is enough to have positive, therapeutic effect although logically one might think that the more that is perceived, the greater the therapeutic impact. But if it is a matter of intensity and accuracy, then a client experiencing a vitally important fragment of their inner world being empathically understood may be more significant to them, and more therapeutically significant, than a great deal being heard less accurately and with a weaker sense of therapist understanding. The communication of the counsellor's empathy, congruence and unconditional positive regard, received by the client, creates the conditions for a process of constructive personality change.
>
> (Bryant-Jefferies, 2005a: 11)

The necessary and sufficient conditions outlined by Rogers (1957) describe the attitudinal qualities of the client-centred therapist or coach, and describe their practice in terms of their endeavour to be congruent and empathic, and to experience unconditional positive regard for their client. The fundamental idea of client-centred therapy is that these core attitudinal qualities are the social environment that facilitates the constructive expression of the actualising tendency. It is this aspect of theory that makes sense of the core conditions theoretically. In an environment where a person does not feel judged or evaluated, they no longer feel the need to defend themselves, and congruent self-actualisation can therefore begin to take place.

Positive psychology

The terminology of Rogers' (1957, 1959) theory will be familiar to psychologists, few of whom will not have heard the terms unconditional positive regard, empathy, and congruence. However, it is perhaps the case that these terms are so familiar that the depth of the theory is often overlooked, and is mistaken for a much more superficial approach than it truly is. Joseph and Linley (2004, 2006) have attempted to reframe the core conditions of client-centred therapy within current more mainstream terminology of emotional intelligence and self-determination.

Relating the 1957 statement of Rogers, describing the six necessary and sufficient conditions of personality change, to current terminology, Joseph and Linley (2004, 2006) describe client-centred therapy as a profound experiential approach founded on the *emotional intelligence* of the therapist. The basis of the client-centred therapeutic approach is condition 3, the therapist's congruence. Congruence refers to the person's awareness of their underlying thoughts and feelings, and their ability to express these thoughts and feelings appropriately in the context (Bozarth, 1998; Wyatt, 2001). That is to say, there is congruence between the internal cognitive and emotional states of the person, their conscious awareness of those states, and their ability to articulate the expression of those states. Congruence, when combined with condition 5, empathic understanding, would involve all four facets of emotional intelligence as discussed by Salovey, Mayer and Caruso (2002; Salovey et al., 2004). The congruent therapist who has an empathic understanding of the client's frame of reference is perceptive of how the client is feeling and of how they themselves are feeling, able to manage their own emotions and to use their own emotions creatively in the service of the therapeutic relationship, and they are able to understand emotions and to label them appropriately. What this means in practice is that the client-centred therapist is someone who has a deep understanding of themselves and is able to be present in an authentic way with the client. The therapist strives to understand the client's world from the client's perspective, and they are accepting of the client's directions in life without imposing their own agenda, that is to say, the self-determination of the client is paramount.

Non-directivity

Thus, the crux of client-centred therapy is not the provision of the core conditions per se, but the therapist's meta-theoretical assumption that people are intrinsically motivated towards constructive and optimal functioning and that under the right social environmental conditions this force is released.

> Client-centered therapists make no assumptions about what people need or how they should be free. They do not attempt to promote

self-acceptance, self-direction, positive growth, self-actualization, congruence between real or perceived selves, a particular vision of reality, or anything. . . . *Client-centered therapy is the practice of simply respecting the right to self-determination of others.*

(B. Grant, 2004: 158, original emphasis)

It is that respect for the self-determination of others that underpins the unconditional attitude of the therapist and the principled stance of non-directivity, which is the distinguishing feature of the approach (see Levitt, 2005). As Brodley (2005) wrote:

The non-directive attitude is psychologically profound; it is not a technique. Early in a therapist's development it may be superficial and prescriptive – 'Don't do this' or 'Don't do that'. But with time, self-examination and therapy experience, it becomes an aspect of the therapist's character. It represents a feeling of profound respect for the constructive potential in persons and great sensitivity to their vulnerability.

(Brodley, 2005: 3)

This latter point, being accepting of the client's directions without imposing one's own, is as we have seen already, the crux of client-centred therapy (i.e. condition 4) and is communicated through the therapist's congruence and empathy (see Bozarth, 1998). It is fundamental to the client-centred therapist, because of his or her trust in the actualising tendency as the one central source of human motivation, that they do not intervene, and have no intention of intervening. As Bozarth (1998) put it:

The therapist goes with the client, goes at the client's pace, goes with the client in his/her own ways of thinking, of experiencing, or processing. The therapist cannot be up to other things, have other intentions without violating the essence of person-centred therapy. To be up to other things – whatever they might be – is a 'yes, but' reaction to the essence of the approach. It must mean that when the therapist has intentions of treatment plans, of treatment goals, of interventive strategies to get the client somewhere or for the client to do a certain thing, the therapist violates the essence of person-centred therapy.

(Bozarth, 1998: 11–12)

Within an authentic and emotionally literate relationship, people are able to drop their defences and get to know themselves better, and feel free to make new choices in life.

Research support

A central question for any audience of psychologists is inevitably whether or not client-centred psychotherapy is an effective way of helping people. Early research throughout the 1960s and 1970s provided evidence consistent with Rogers' hypothesis of the necessary and sufficient conditions (see Barrett-Lennard, 1998). However, over the next two decades the research tradition in client-centred psychotherapy dwindled, in large part because the new generation of research active psychologists tended to be interested in the new cognitive approach to psychotherapy, and client-centred psychotherapy became increasingly a marginalised approach within mainstream psychology (Joseph, 2003). As a consequence, the question of whether the six conditions posited by Rogers are necessary and sufficient remains largely unanswered, with different researchers interpreting the available data very differently indeed. Researchers from traditions other than the client-centred one have tended to interpret the evidence to suggest that the conditions might be necessary, but that they are not sufficient. Consequently, there is seen to be a need by therapists from other traditions to further intervene in some way, for example, using various cognitive or behavioural techniques.

However, client-centred therapists have interpreted the same data to suggest that the conditions might not be necessary, but that they are sufficient. It is thought that personal development and growth can also come about through a variety of vehicles of change, from religious conversions to traumatic experiences, and so the conditions might not be necessary, but when they are present they are sufficient (see Bozarth, 1998 for a review). There is therefore no need for further intervention. In support of the client-centred view, there is now overwhelming evidence for the importance of the therapeutic relationship (see Duncan and Miller, 2000; Wampold, 2001; Hubble and Miller, 2004; Bozarth and Motomasa, 2005).

Practice

We will now describe the practice of person-centred coaching psychology in light of this discussion on the importance of the meta-theoretical perspective that the client is their own best expert, and how it is that this work is also applicable to coaching psychology. The person-centred way of working does not make a distinction between people in terms of their level of psychological functioning, because the process of alleviating distress and dysfunction is the same as that for facilitating well-being and optimal functioning (Joseph, 2006). Both ends of the spectrum of functioning are defined in relation to the extent to which self-actualisation is congruent with the actualising tendency. When there is greater congruence, greater well-being and more optimal functioning results. But when there is less congruence, greater distress and dysfunction results (see Ford, 1991; Wilkins, 2005).

Person-centred versus medical model

Thus, the person-centred approach offers a genuinely positive psychological perspective on mental health because of its unified and holistic focus on both the negative and the positive aspects of human functioning (Joseph and Worsley, 2005). Coaching psychology is the same activity requiring the same theoretical base, and the same practical skills, as required for working with people who are distressed and dysfunctional. Person-centred coaching psychology views understanding and enhancing optimal functioning and the alleviation of maladaptive functioning as a unitary task, as opposed to two separate tasks as is the case when viewed through the lens of the medical model (see Joseph, 2006). Person-centred coaching is not about the alleviation of distress and dysfunction *per se*, but is about the facilitation of well-being and optimal functioning. However, from the person-centred perspective these are in reality a unitary task rather than two separate tasks. Thus, within the person-centred perspective, there is no theoretical difference between counselling and coaching. It does not matter where the person starts. As John Shlien, one of the founders of person-centred psychology, said in a talk originally given in 1956:

> if the skills developed in psychological counselling can release the constructive capacities of malfunctioning people so that they become healthier, this same help should be available to healthy people who are less than *fully* functioning. If we ever turn towards positive goals of health, we will care less about where the person begins, and more about how to achieve the desired endpoint of the positive goals.
>
> (Shlien, 2003: 26)

Counselling versus coaching

Depth and duration of training are the only issues therefore in determining where on the spectrum of psychological functioning a person-centred coaching psychologist is able to work. In terms of person-centred coaching psychology practice, the task of the coach is to nurture a social relationship which is experienced as authentic by the coachee and in which they feel accepted and understood. But although the therapeutic process is the same as in counselling, the fact that we have developed these different professional arenas based on the medical model creates difference in content (see Joseph, 2006). Quite simply, what terms we use will determine what clients we work with. The public understanding is that counselling is about looking back in life at what has gone wrong, whereas coaching is about looking forward to what can go right. If we offer counselling we will get clients who want to look back, and if we offer coaching we will get clients who want to look forward. The task of the person-centred therapist or coach is the same in either case, to stay with the person and to facilitate the person's self determination. Thus, at a theoretical process level, the person-centred psychologist's task is always the same, be they employed as a coaching, counselling or clinical psychologist, but at the practical level of content the sessions would be different, simply because clients will generally bring different material to counselling compared to coaching.

> A therapeutic approach such as person-centred affirms that it is not what you do so much as *how you are* with your client that is therapeutically significant, and this 'how you are' has to be received by the client.
>
> (Bryant-Jefferies, 2005b: 114, original emphasis)

Case study[1]

Anne sat in the psychologist's room. It was her third session. The first two sessions she had spent reflecting on her recent life, the end of her marriage with Dennis, how he had left her, how she had been so miserable and depressed, unable to do anything except dwell on the past, on what she had lost, and on the loss of the future that she had anticipated that they would be having together. It had all been so sudden. There she was, at 46, and falling apart. Her friends, her daughter and her parents had all been supportive, but she had felt stuck. And it was only now, following the 12-month anniversary of his leaving, that she felt she needed to try and rebuild her life in some more sustainable way.

The previous sessions she had ended saying that she felt she needed to start to look forward. She had greatly appreciated how Michael had listened to her, given her the space she needed. She had felt heard in her struggle and her confusion. But she knew she did not want to dwell on it any more.

Michael sat looking across at Anne. 'So, last time you said you wanted to focus more on the way forward, is that still how it is?' He didn't want to make assumptions. As a person-centred coaching psychologist he wanted to work with his clients and not impose, or force, a process on them. At the heart of his approach lay an unwavering acceptance of the presence of the actualising tendency which he knew could be trusted to enable the person to move towards the most fulfilling and satisfying experiences that they needed or felt they could reach out to.

'I do. I have to. I can't keep on dwelling on the past. I can feel it there, though, part of me, and so many feelings, of anger and shame in particular. But I need to move on.'

---

1 The use of fictitious dialogue in this way has been developed by Richard Bryant-Jefferies in the *Living Therapy* series of books on person-centred counselling, published by Radcliffe Publishing.

'Mhmm, need to move on, move clear of those feelings.' Michael kept his empathic response focused.

'It's like I need to build a *new* life, you know?'

'A sense of needing to build a *new* life.' Michael slightly accented 'new', it was how he had heard Anne speak.

Anne nodded. She felt able to continue. 'I don't know what it will look like, and that's scary and a bit exciting, but mainly scary.'

'Yes, mainly scary, a little bit exciting. What will that future be like . . .?' (1)

Anne shrugged. She appreciated the way Michael spoke. He seemed unhurried, allowed her to hear her own words, hear herself somehow. It seemed to give her time to really be in touch with what was present for her.

She felt herself take a deep breath and her heart began to thump a little. She felt anxious, slightly on edge. She didn't like it. She tightened her lips and looked down.

Michael felt the silence, it was as though it was suddenly very present. And he noticed Anne's head movement. The suddenness of it.

'I don't want to disturb what is happening,' Michael spoke softly, 'but it feels like something has happened for you.'

Anne was very much within her own experiencing. Yet she wasn't sure what it was. Just that somehow, what had just been said had left her feelings so, so . . . well, anxious, that was the only word for it. But she wasn't sure why. She said nothing. In fact what was happening was material that was on the edge of her awareness was beginning to make its presence more clearly felt, material that perhaps contradicted her sense of self as a capable and confident woman in her own right. Her sense of self had taken a battering in recent months, but she had had good support and she had clung to the knowing that she was a good person and that she just had to find a way through it all. (2)

Michael respected the silence that had developed. For him, a silence required its own kind of special empathy that allowed the silence to be. He had acknowledged his sense as it had started, now he would leave Anne to be with what was present for her while maintaining his own warm acceptance of her as a person, his sensitivity to whatever she might say, and to his own inner experiencing as well.

Anne took a deep breath and sighed. She looked up and into Michael's eyes. He seemed to be so present in the room. But so did what was within her. She swallowed. The anxiety was shifting, it was taking on a fresh tone. It was the scariness. She'd mentioned it, but it had been more a case of just being words. It was now present in her experience and in her awareness. 'I'm scared.'

The words were spoken quietly and Michael had to be very focused in his listening to hear them. He responded in a similar tone. 'Scares you.'

Anne felt weak, her arms tingled and yet felt strangely heavy and numb. She felt hot. She swallowed and shook her head. 'I-I can't actually see myself sort of, I don't know, enjoying myself. I can't see how I'll enjoy it on my own. And I can't see myself with someone else. And . . .' Her voice trailed off.

'And . . .?' Michael did not attempt to empathise with what had been said, it would take Anne away from where her process had brought her. He waited for her to say more, if she felt able, or felt that she wanted to.

'And I have to, don't I? I have to. I have to find a way. But part of me wants to shrink away, and yet I know, I know I have to move on.'

'Mhmm, that tension with part of you wanting to shrink away and another part knowing you have to move on.'

'Like a battle inside myself. And I'm scared in the middle of it.'

'Scared in the middle of a battle within yourself.'

Anne felt words forming as she heard Michael respond. 'Scared in the middle of a battle that *is* myself.'

Michael nodded. 'That *is* yourself.' It felt an extremely important differentiation that Anne was making for herself. He trusted her process, he stayed with her, keeping his empathic responding simple and maintaining the warmth he felt for her, his acceptance of her as a person seeking to move through what was such a difficult process within herself, in the context of a difficult phase in her whole life.

Anne found herself nodding. 'That *is* myself. It feels like it's come out, like I'm more sharply aware of it, of the choice, the battle, and I know I have to move forward. I *know*.' She paused. 'And yet it feels so uncertain, so scary.'

'You know you have to but you feel it's so scary.'

'Like part of me wants to look forward but wants to shrink back, and another part wants to just, well, not look forward, but I've been there, been there for too long. I have to move on.'

'Feels like you've been in that place for too long, and that however scary it feels, you have to move on.'

Anne nodded, aware that the anxiety had eased and the scariness while still present, wasn't so intense. 'I need to make things happen. My daughter is really supportive. She wants me to go on holiday with her and, well, I've sort of been unsure, but, well, I know I need to, she's right, it will be good for me, won't it?' (3)

Michael did not want to say for sure, in truth he did not know. What mattered for him was that Anne made a decision based on her evaluation of her needs and not on what someone else thought was best for her. 'It seems like while you feel unsure you also sort of know that she's right. Is that how it is?'

Anne nodded, again taking a deep breath. 'Yes, yes, there's opportunity here for me, and it has to be a new me. I have to give myself a chance to grow into my future. And it won't always be easy, will it?'

Michael smiled. 'Not easy, but a chance to grow into your future.' It sort of stood out somehow in among what Anne had said. He smiled as he empathised with it. It enabled Anne, as she felt herself being heard – both the sense of it not being easy and the sense of growing – to feel more clearly a sense of hope and direction.

'So, what to do?'

'Mhmm, what do you want to do?' Michael was not going to offer suggestions and slip into a directive approach to coaching. The uniqueness of the person-centred approach to coaching was that it maintained a non-directive stance, trusting the individual to make the constructive choices they needed to make, for them. (4)

The question stayed with Anne. 'I've got to make the effort to get out more, with friends, not give excuses to stay in and mope around.'

'OK, so something about getting out more with friends.'

'And, I guess, making new friends as well. I mean, I've sort of wondered about an evening class. Haven't done anything like that in years, but it's been a thought though I've pulled back from it.'

'The idea has been around for you but you've pulled back.'

'Not sure how I'll cope, will I be OK, you know?'

'Mhmm, important questions, will I cope, will I be OK.'

'But I have to do it. And I'm going to take a more serious look at what's on offer. Do you think that's a good idea?'

'It sounds very positive.' It did sound positive and Michael was being genuine in his response. But he again was sure to not give Anne the impression that she should do something because he agreed with it. He wanted her to feel sure, in herself, that it was what she wanted to do. When her knowing and her wanting coincided her motivation would be so much stronger. (5)

Anne nodded. 'And I will plan that holiday with my daughter. And I guess just go out more with friends, but I don't want to do things on my own.'

'No, doing things on your own is too much at the moment, you want to be with friends or your daughter.'

Anne nodded, yes, she thought, yes, that feels sort of safer somehow. Well, not so much safer, more realistic, believable. 'I have to make it happen, don't I?'

'My thought in response to that is "in your own time and in a way that feels right for you".'

'Yes, people are good at telling you what you ought to do, but I don't like that, I don't want to feel pushed. People have been telling me, but it's too much. Now it feels like it's possible.' Anne paused, collecting her thoughts. 'Yes, I need to find my own way, my own pace. I've stayed on the sidelines for long enough.'

'Mhmm, that sounds very clear, that sense of having been on those sidelines for long enough.' (6)

Anne felt a renewed sense of motivation. Yes, she'd been there, done that, and it had played its part in her coming to terms with things, but now she had to move on and had some ideas as to how and where to begin.

Commentary

This case illustrates that the person-centred approach does not prescribe what the client should do, but is grounded in the meta-theoretical assumption that people have an inherent tendency toward growth, development and optimal functioning, and thus the coach is able to trust the coachee to find her own directions if he is able to provide the right social environment. In particular, it illustrates the role of the empathy and warm acceptance of the coach for their client, the importance of relationship building as prelude to coaching process, and the coach's ability to trust the client to find her own directions. Also, we chose this example because it illustrates the interface there is between counselling and coaching. Here, there is a shift in focus as the client moves from exploring issues in her past to making new decisions and setting goals for herself in the future.

Although the case study shows how the person-centred coaching psychology is not defined by the use of techniques, but by the relationship that develops, we would emphasise that there is no prohibition of the use of techniques *per se*. There has been much theoretical and practical development in the world of client-centred therapy over recent years, and the idea of the client as expert can be interpreted in various ways in practice. The coaching psychologist is able to draw ideas and ways of working (see Sanders, 2004), ranging from the classical client-centred approach to therapy (Merry, 2004), with its principled role of going with the client, at the client's pace, through to more process-directed approaches (Worsley, 2001, 2004). What is different about the person-centred way of working is that the techniques, when they are used, become an expression of the meta-theoretical assumptions of person-centred theory (see Joseph and Linley, 2004, 2006). It is not the fact that the coach uses a particular technique or assessment device that is the issue, but *how* they use it.

Process description

At (1) above the person-centred coach is capturing the dilemma that the client is facing, letting her hear what he has heard, being, if you like, a mirror not only to her words but also to her feelings, her future seems a bit scary, exciting, uncertain, he holds her on the wonder of what it will be like, allowing her to look ahead and to contemplate what it means for her. Being heard allows her to be more open to her own experiencing, anxiety emerges and at (2) we see material from the edge of the client's awareness begin to emerge. Though her awareness has not yet become open to the content, the presence of the anxiety is an indicator that what is emerging is in some way uncomfortable and perhaps challenging to her self-concept. Mearns and Thorne (2000) write of 'edge of awareness' material, of elements that are present within the organism's experience but are not present in the person's awareness.

As the content emerges and as it is grasped and understood by the client, the anxiety eases (3). This may not always be the case. Material that emerges can profoundly disrupt the person's concept of self. The person-centred coach will not be forcing this material to the surface, his or her role is to offer the therapeutic and relational conditions within which the client's own process will allow this to happen. The client is looking forward, seeking a positive direction, but is now becoming more fully open to her own experiencing, and therefore more fully present. From this place she can more realistically embrace her vision of the future and her motivation is likely to be more focused and certainly less fragmented by the internal contradictions within herself which in this case stem from that which is trying to hold her back.

The client is still left with a not knowing, a 'what to do?' (4) and the person-centred coaching psychologist allows this question to be. It is not for him to answer it. The non-directive stance of the person-centred approach is crucially important. The client is trusted to find their own direction (5), aligning with Rogers' assertion that 'individuals have within themselves vast resources for self-understanding, and for altering their self-concepts, basic attitudes, and self-directed behaviour; these resources can be tapped if a definable climate of facilitative psychological attitudes can be provided' (Rogers, 1980: 115).

The client begins to recognise what she needs to do, a strategy begins to emerge, driven by her knowing what is called for. And she wants this as well, although, as she acknowledges, another part of her wants to pull her back. Yet the person-centred coach knows the importance of allowing the client's wanting and knowing to become as one, but in a way that enables the client to recognise and experience those elements that are pulling her back. There needs to be a fullness, more of a completeness in her awareness so that she can find the energy and the clarity of direction that will enable her to take action. Again, though, when the time is right for her.

As the client affirms to herself her need to make changes, and her readiness to make changes, she is actually processing her experience of herself within her awareness within the session. At point 6 the client has journeyed and the coach powerfully responds not to all that has been said as might be encouraged in 'empathic reflection' but picks up on where the client's process has taken her. This is powerful. It holds the client in the place that she has reached for herself. It is affirmed and from this point she may then move on, or she may discover some other element within her nature blocking her progress. If so, space will be given for this to be acknowledged and explored. The person-centred coach knows that if something emerges then the timeliness of that emergence should be trusted.

Often people grow in spurts, sometimes in quite radical ways. It can seem as though what Mearns and Thorne (2000: 180) term as 'the restraint of social mediation' is broken through, the conditions of worth that hold a person back from realising potentialities are shattered. Of course, such spurts may not always be sustainable, and they highlight that perhaps what is needed is a healthy balance, a gradual movement which embraces an ongoing process of dialogue between the actualising tendency and the restraints of social mediation (Mearns and Thorne, 2000: 180). The person-centred coaching psychologist will offer scope for this within the sessions with their clients. Where the person-centred coaching psychologist's approach will probably be unique within the field of coaching will be their readiness to allow this dialogue to be fully present, and not to side with what would be perceived as the growth aspect and to try to force growth. Another way of viewing this process might be from the perspective of 'growthful' and 'not for growth' configurations within self (Mearns and Thorne, 2000: 114–16).

Conclusion

The person-centred approach has much to offer the field of coaching psychology. It provides a robust theoretical system for defining and understanding psychological process – including both those that limit and those that enhance the person. It contains, within its theory, a central notion of an actualising tendency, urging the individual to achieve a fuller and more satisfying life experience. It emphasises a well-researched set of relational principles which, when present, foster the fuller emergence of this tendency within and through the person, bringing with it the possibility of achieving greater human potential. Nothing is imposed. The client's psychological processes are trusted and encouraged in the experience of a person-enhancing, person-to-person coaching relationship.

References

Barrett-Lennard, G. T. (1998) *Carl Rogers' Helping System: Journey and substance.* London: Sage.

Bozarth, J. (1998) *Person-centred Therapy: A revolutionary paradigm.* Ross-on-Wye, UK: PCCS Books.

Bozarth, J. D. and Motomasa, N, (2005) Searching for the core: the interface of client-centered principles with other therapies. In S. Joseph and R. Worsley (eds),

Person-centred psychopathology: A positive psychology of mental health. Ross-on-Wye, UK: PCCS Books.

Brodley, B. T. (2005) About the non-directive attitude. In B. E. Levitt (ed.) *Embracing Non-directivity: Reassessing person-centered theory and practice in the 21st century* (pp. 1–4). Ross-on-Wye, UK: PCCS Books.

Bryant-Jefferies, R. (2005a) *Counselling for Problem Gambling*. Abingdon, UK: Radcliffe Publishing Ltd.

Bryant-Jefferies, R. (2005b) *Counselling for Eating Disorders in Men*. Abingdon, UK: Radcliffe Publishing Ltd.

Duncan, B. and Miller, S. (2000) *The Heroic Client: Doing client-directed, outcome informed therapy*. San Francisco, CA: Jossey-Bass.

Ford, J. G. (1991) Rogerian self-actualization: a clarification of meaning. *Journal of Humanistic Psychology* 31: 101–111.

Grant, B. (2004) The imperative of ethical justification in psychotherapy: the special case of client-centered therapy. *Person-Centered and Experiential Psychotherapies* 3: 152–165.

Hubble, M. A. and Miller, S. D. (2004) The client: psychotherapy's missing link for promoting a positive psychology. In P. A. Linley and S. Joseph (eds), *Positive Psychology in Practice* (pp. 335-353). Hoboken, NJ: Wiley.

Joseph, S. (2003) Client-centred psychotherapy: why the client knows best. *The Psychologist* 16: 304–307.

Joseph, S. (2006) Person-centred coaching psychology: a meta-theoretical perspective. *International Coaching Psychology Review* 1: 47–55.

Joseph, S. and Linley, P. A. (2004) Positive therapy: a positive psychological theory of therapeutic practice. In P. A. Linley and S. Joseph (eds), *Positive Psychology in Practice* (pp. 354-368). Hoboken, NJ: Wiley.

Joseph, S. and Linley, P. A. (2005) Positive psychological approaches to therapy. *Counselling and Psychotherapy Research* 5: 5–10.

Joseph, S. and Linley, P. A. (2006) *Positive Therapy: A meta-theory for positive psychological practice*. London: Routledge.

Joseph, S. and Worsley, R. (2005) A positive psychology of mental health: the person-centred perspective. In S. Joseph and R. Worsley (eds), *Person-centred Psychopathology: A positive psychology of mental health* (pp. 348-357). Ross-on-Wye, UK: PCCS Books.

Kauffman, C. and Scoular, A. (2004) Toward a positive psychology of executive coaching. In P. A. Linley and S. Joseph (eds), *Positive Psychology in Practice* (pp. 287-302). Hoboken, NJ: Wiley.

Levitt, B. E. (ed.) (2005) *Embracing Non-directivity: Reassessing person-centered theory and practice in the 21st century*. Ross-on-Wye, UK: PCCS Books.

Linley, P. A. and Joseph, S. (2004) *Toward a Theoretical Foundation for Positive Psychology in Practice*. In P. A. Linley and S. Joseph (eds), *Positive Psychology in Practice*. Hoboken, NJ: Wiley.

Mearns, D. and Thorne, B. (2000) *Person-Centred Therapy Today*. London: Sage.

Merry, T. (2004) Classical client-centred therapy. In P. Sanders (ed.) *The Tribes of the Person-centred Nation: An introduction to the schools of therapy related to the person-centred approach* (pp. 21–44). Ross-on-Wye, UK: PCCS Books.

Rogers, C. R. (1951) *Client-centred Therapy: Its current practice, implications and theory*. Boston, MA: Houghton Mifflin.

Rogers, C. R. (1957) The necessary and sufficient conditions of therapeutic personality change. *Journal of Consulting Psychology* 21: 95–103.

Rogers, C. R. (1959) A theory of therapy, personality, and interpersonal relationships as developed in the client-centered framework. In S. Koch (ed.) *Psychology: A study of a science*. Volume 3, *Formulations of the Person and the Social Context* (pp. 184–256). New York: McGraw-Hill.

Rogers, C. R. (1961) *On Becoming a Person*. Boston, MA: Houghton Mifflin.

Rogers, C. R. (1963) The actualizing tendency in relation to 'motives' and to consciousness. In M. R. Jones (ed.) *Nebraska Symposium on Motivation*, Volume 11 (pp. 1–24). Lincoln, NE: University of Nebraska Press.

Rogers, C. R. (1980) *A Way of Being*. Boston, MA: Houghton Mifflin.

Salovey, P., Mayer, J. D. and Caruso, D. (2002) The positive psychology of emotional intelligence. In C. R. Snyder and S. J. Lopez (eds), *Handbook of Positive Psychology* (pp. 159–171). New York: Oxford University Press.

Salovey, P., Caruso, D. and Mayer, J. D. (2004) Emotional intelligence in practice. In P. A. Linley and S. Joseph (eds), *Positive Psychology in Practice* (pp. 447–463). Hoboken, NJ: Wiley.

Sanders, P. (ed.) (2004) *The Tribes of the Person-centred Nation: An introduction to the schools of therapy related to the person-centred approach*. Ross-on-Wye, UK: PCCS Books.

Shlien, J. M. (2003) Creativity and psychological health. In P. Sanders (ed.) *To Lead an Honourable Life: Invitations to think about Client-Centered Therapy and the Person-Centered Approach* (pp. 19–29). Ross-on-Wye, UK: PCCS Books.

Wampold, B. E. (2001) *The Great Psychotherapy Debate: Models, methods, and findings*. Mahwah, NJ: Lawrence Erlbaum.

Wilkins, P. (2005) Person-centred theory and 'mental illness'. In S. Joseph and R. Worsley (eds), *Person-centred Psychopathology: A positive psychology of mental health* (pp. 43–59). Ross-on-Wye, UK: PCCS Books.

Worsley, R. (2001) *Process Work in Person-centred Therapy*. Basingstoke: Palgrave.

Worsley, R. (2004) Integrating with integrity. In P. Sanders (ed.) *The Tribes of the Person-centred Nation: An introduction to the schools of therapy related to the person-centred approach* (pp. 125–148). Ross-on-Wye, UK: PCCS Books.

Wyatt, G. (ed.) (2001) *Rogers' Therapeutic Conditions: Evolution, theory and practice*. Volume 1, *Congruence*. Ross-on-Wye, UK: PCCS Books.

Discussion points

- How can a non-directive approach be applied to coaching?
- What are the key relational factors that need to be present for effective coaching?
- How can the client be sure that they are developing in ways that are true to themselves, and not simply following the agenda of the coach?
- What is the difference between coaching and counselling as seen from the perspective of the person-centred approach.

Suggested reading

British Association for the Person-Centred Approach www.bapca.org.uk

Embleton Tudor, L., Keemar, K., Tudor, K., Valentine, J. and Worrall, M. (2004) *The Person-Centered Approach: A contemporary introduction.* Basingstoke: Palgrave Macmillan.

Merry, T. (2002) *Learning and Being in Person-Centred Counselling*, 2nd edition. Ross-on-Wye, UK: PCCS Books.

Rogers, C. R. (1980) *A Way of Being.* Boston, MA: Houghton-Mifflin.

Chapter 13

Conversational learning

Applying personal construct psychology in coaching

Kieran Duignan

Introduction

Personal construct psychology (PCP) interweaves themes of constructivist, humanistic and contextual psychology with techniques of psychological measurement, soft systems methodology and behavioural reinforcement.

'Conversational learning' epitomises the application of PCP in coaching and presents three faces. One expresses how both coach and client may learn through dialogue. Another gives voice to the contrasting models of human behaviour proposed in PCP, namely, a person acting as a scientist and a person acting as a playwright and actor in the story of his/her own life. A third points to how much the analysis of tasks can be used to fuel a client's commitment to raising the bar of accomplishment.

This chapter outlines the development of PCP and introduces five key themes of personal construct theory. Five methods of applying PCP in coaching practice are profiled and a case study illustrates their application. References indicate sources that can help with follow-up lines of enquiry which interest you.

Development of personal construct psychology

With the hindsight possible after more than half a century since the 'release' of personal construct psychology, we can distinguish two 'waves' in its evolution. The distinction between two 'waves' reveals differences in the key task goals of practitioners in therapeutic contexts *vis-à-vis* those in coaching situations.

'First wave' personal construct psychology

Enlarging personal choice by experimenting with behaviour has been the signature theme of PCP since it was developed by the American psychotherapist and psychologist, George Kelly (1991). Kelly practised as a clinical psychologist, engineering psychologist, psychotherapist, supervisor and teacher of clinical psychologists and psychotherapists. His work expressed a panoramic lifespan perspective yet he also explicitly stated that the primary task of PCP was to assist people to control their experiences of 'stress', a challenge that coaching psychologists can readily relate to more than half a century on. Kelly – whose primary degree was actually in engineering, a discipline which studies stress of materials – invented PCP with the explicit assumption that some stress or disequilibrium is actually normal and healthy: in humans, stress is not a condition to simply be avoided. This perspective remains remarkably fertile in coaching as a pragmatist springboard for squaring up to reality and for commitment to action based on personal values.

'First wave' applications of PCP were shaped not only by Kelly himself but also by two British clinical psychologists, Don Bannister and Fay Fransella. Bannister and Fransella (1990) gave particular emphasis to Kelly's observation how ordinary people can usefully apply scientific methods to day-to-day living. This cornerstone of personal construct theory is epitomised in the concept of 'man the scientist' – or in the less stereotypical currency of Shaw (1980) 'the personal scientist' – a concept which Kelly actually derived from the Polish epistemologist, Alfred Korzybski (1994). As the distinctive achievement of Kelly was to create a remarkable synthesis from diverse strands of intellectual life of his time not limited to conventional boundaries of the discipline of psychology, coaches should be aware how John Dewey (1991; see also Morganbesser, 1987), a philosopher in the American traditions of Pragmatism and of semiotics, also exercised considerable influence on his design of PCP.

As a framework for client-centred enquiry that is scientifically grounded yet engaging enquiry, over time PCP has been recognised across several professions dedicated to improving the health and rehabilitation of people categorised by society as 'psychologically unwell': clinical psychology, speech and language therapy, counselling, psychotherapy and psychiatry.

'Second wave' personal construct psychology

'Second wave' applications of PCP emerged from Kelly's original writing which presented a second model of the person, as an individual with a personal story which he/she can not only share but also enact and, what's more, recurrently invent. It is the PCP model of a person as a narrator-cum-actor in the drama of his/her own life that can be of tremendous use to coaching psychologists who wish to facilitate a client to make sense of the character and present state of his/her personal story.

Salmon (1985) may be viewed as the epitome of the 'personal story' stream within PCP. This stream gradually made progress with applications of PCP in education as indicated by Pope and Keen (1981) and Claxton (1984). And it surfaced intermittently in organisational psychology as indicated by Stewart and Stewart (1981), Kolb (1984), Brophy (2003) and Harri-Augstein and Thomas (1991), who applied the expression 'learning conversations'™ to PCP in coaching.

Theory and basic concepts

Figure 13.1 presents a picture of PCP theory that summarises it in five themes relevant to coaching. At a theoretical level, it was Kelly's *dovetailing* of these themes – the personal story of a client, strategic task analysis, 'dimensions of transition', alternative personal roles and making behaviour happen – that constituted a remarkable contribution to the discipline of psychology with wonderful potential for conversational learning.

Personal story of the client

The concept of 'the personal story of an individual' is an integral part of personal construct psychology. It is assumed in this psychology that everyone can make sense of their lives in terms of a personal story with degrees of continuity, of disruption or transformation; and that, at any point in one's life, he/she can choose to be the author of the emerging phase in his/her personal story of his/her life. Like a theme in a well-written musical drama, it is the interplay between the client's personal story and the four other theoretical 'chunks' that endows PCP with psychological richness.

The 'Constructive Alternative' (Kelly, 1991, vol. 1: 3-31) component of

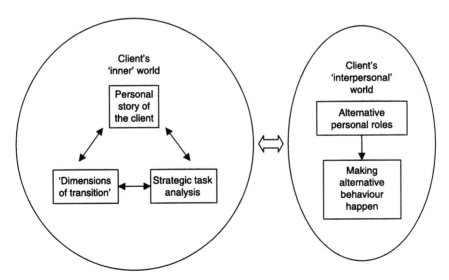

Figure 13.1 A personal construct theory representation of a coaching client's 'inner' and 'interpersonal' worlds of experience.

personal stories is that the story of a person's life remains open-ended right to the end. To facilitate clients to appreciate possibilities of re-creating a story through personal action, a coach may draw on several of the principles of the 'benign' disequilibrium and on the 'dimensions of transition' perspective to explore a client's personal story with him/her.

'Dimensions of transition'

The concept of 'dimensions of transition' is an integral part of the model of each person as a scientist; it facilitates systematic ways in which a practitioner, and a client themselves, may gather and explore data about a client. As personal scientists, we may use 'dimensions of transition' less as administrative labels than as hypotheses for testing to explore implications of alternative possible roles and forms of behaviour of the client, through 'experiments'. These experiments may be designed, conducted and evaluated within a process of helping, including coaching, or in 'the real world', or both. Sometimes the experimental results validate a hypothesis; when they don't, they can stimulate a reframing of the questions a client asks about him/herself.

While Kelly acknowledged how a dimension of transition may become a 'disorder', he made a clear distinction between the two, which allows a coach to recognise practical boundaries between coaching and therapeutic work in counselling and psychotherapy. He wrote (Kelly, 1991, vol. 2: 193): 'From the standpoint of the psychology of personal constructs we may define a disorder as any personal construction which is used repeatedly in spite of consistent invalidation'; a 'disorder' therefore involves refusal to face the facts of reality – a defining feature of only the 'hostility' dimension of transition. By contrast, he characterised 'dimensions of transition' as particular ways of being that a person experiences while living in disequilibrium, benign or otherwise. He grouped these dimensions of transition (Kelly, 1991, vol. 1: 259–392) in two classes of disequilibrium – 'construction' and 'dislodgement'. They are profiled in Table 13.1.

The inclusion of the 'dimensions of transition' perspective in conversational learning acknowledges an important reality which not only colours but also may complicate human behaviour: a person may experience more than one dimension of transition at any particular time so that he/she experiences a strong sense of 'double bind' confusion and tensions with the result that stagnation may appear to him/her to be the 'least worst' option. In this light, a critical challenge for the coach is to get alongside the client well enough to appreciate how he/she – or the real world organisational or educational context which has conditioned his/her thinking – may be contributing to such a 'double bind'; once the coach can appreciate this well enough, there are grounds for suggesting an alternative hypothesis to the client.

Whatever the problem or opportunity of interest to the client, a coach can use 'dimensions of transition' as a resource for generating hypotheses to

Table 13.1 'Dimensions of transition' in personal construct psychology

Broad class	Label used	Summary
'Construction'	The creativity cycle	A phase of expanded awareness – 'loosening' of patterns of thinking and feeling – followed by a phase of crystallisation of the implications of enlarged awareness – 'tightening' of patterns of thinking and feeling, often by using tools of psychological measurement.
	The decision-making cycle	Phases of circumspection, pre-emption and control leading to a choice which leads the person into a particular situation.
'Dislodgement'	Aggressiveness	The active expansion of a person's field of perception and attention through putting ideas to the test through action in the real world.
	Threat	Awareness of imminent comprehensive change in one's own psychological structures, allied with an overwhelming sense of dread.
	Fear	A new, incidental construct, the source is a particular event, people or things and the stress relatively modest.
	Anxiety	The recognition that the events taking place are outside the range of a person's construct system so that they are unable to make sense of them.
	Guilt	Awareness that the self is dislodged from a person's core role structure.
	Hostility	Self-centredness and bias that is so dominant and pathological that the person continues to ignore evidence despite feedback.

Source: Kelly, 1991, vol. 1: 259–392.

guide the process of conversational learning about the behaviour and experience of the client. As the case study indicates, a client concerned about starting effective relationships in an appealing job in an organisation that she is stepping into, is going through several dimensions of transition.

Strategic task analysis

If you imagine that personal construct psychology is a drama in which the 'personal story' stream is presented in Scene 1 and 'the personal scientist' comes on stage in Scene 2, you can appreciate how the plot of the drama then requires that the next scene, Scene 3, should introduce a social mechanism that facilitates a relationship between these two personae.

And so PCP theory postulates that a person relies on principles of 'disequilibrium' to throw light on the key tasks in the life of a person (or group or organisation); and that strategic task analysis is required to make some sense of how he/she may apply these principles to avoid intolerable, extreme stress of the degree known as 'burnout'.

Within the PCP framework, a person is never simply 'steady state'; rather, from birth to death he/she is assumed to be so 'dynamic' that he/she is recurrently in a form of healthy *dis*equilibrium which stimulates him or her to reconsider what is actually happening in both his/her 'inner' and 'social' world. Kelly (1991, vol. 1: 32–127) advanced a methodology for helping clients to manage strategic tasks and disequilibrium of living within cycles of change and continuity in their personal experience. Pragmatist philosophy is a cornerstone of this methodology based on the principle that a person can discover 'constructive alternative' perspectives by exploring contrasts in their experience. Kelly set this out in a format of twelve principles. The cardinal principle, from which the other eleven derive, he called the Fundamental Postulate which states 'A person's processes are psychologically channellised by the ways in which he anticipates events' (Kelly, 1991, vol. 1: 32). In other words, each individual's behaviour and experiences are shaped by what he or she finds meaningful. When faced with situations of change a client may attend to elements of events depending on the personal role he/she chooses within that situation, their chosen position is reinforced by the elements of the situation to which they then give attention. From this perspective, change can be seen as part of the gift of human participation in life's adventure.

It is curious how the fact that the methodology of strategic task analysis is deeply embedded in PCP yet has not been remarked on before. Yet this fact is not altogether surprising since Kelly served in an engineering psychology role – one now known as a human facters specialist – in the United States Air Force during the Second World War (Fransella, 1995) and task analysis is a lynchpin of ergonomics.

Alternative personal roles

Within Scene 3 of PCP-as-drama, Kelly (1991, vol. 1: 268–334) offers a framework for facilitating a client to exercise choice about psychological roles he/she may adopt in order to serve his/her own personal needs as well as task demands arising in work and other situations. Kelly as the playwright assumed that the elusive psychological and semantic spaces between personal experience and task demands offer a client sufficient scope to discover a strategic basis for alternative personal roles that will enable him/her to move on in a relevant dimension of transition with some peace of mind.

Mair (1976) accounts for this potential personal resourcefulness with the metaphor of a 'community of selves' that is more or less to the fore within each person – and which the person can use to regulate how he/she relates to social worlds he/she inhabits. In the case study, for example, the client eventually identifies how she may create a psychological role of diplomacy, not mentioned in her formal job description, as a vehicle for better managing tensions in an actuarial job with technical and commercial demands world-wide, on the one hand, and political demands arising from local ties to a national regulatory authority, on the other.

In the interplay between the client's personal story and alternative personal roles of a psychological kind, the coach may directly or indirectly propose possibilities related to the dimensions of transition the client is grappling with. In our case study, the phase in the client's personal story, touched on in coaching, concerns her ambition to broaden from a 'technie' role and her anxieties about her capabilities to go beyond her comfort zone in that role; during the coaching process, she figures out an alternative discretionary personal role according as the coach and the client discover how to illuminate the 'dislodgement' and 'constructive' dimensions of transition the client is going through.

Making alternative behaviour happen

Bearing in mind how the 'first wave' model of the person in PCP is of a 'personal scientist', the focus of Scene 2, language of science applies to coaching with PCP. Within that language, 'behaviour' is the dependent variable in the experiment of living of a person as a 'scientist' and the client's system of experiences and thoughts are independent variables that he/she may use to vary his/her behaviour. It was this understanding of scientific method by Kelly that underpins his application of strategic task analysis and his model of benign disequilibrium.

For a person to feel empowered and able to make action or behaviour happen, he/she needs to have some sense of the 'role' in which action or behaviour may be fruitful; otherwise, the action or behaviour would seem random or even 'mad', a condition which can be experienced as quite literally terrifying when your life appears to be disordered. For Kelly recognised the significance of 'action methods' of psychodrama and sociodrama, invented by the Romanian-American psychiatrist, Jacob Moreno (1988), acknowledged as the 'grandfather of humanistic psychology'. Although PCP literature overlooks the significance of these methods, Kelly himself (1991, vol. 1: 268–334; vol. 2: 408–429) appreciated how Moreno's methods can empathetically and robustly engage the emotions, imagination and commitment of a client often rather better than through talking about them.

In a coaching context, this is the tipping point of PCP-as-drama. Kelly, like Moreno, grasped the significance of the psychological roles a person may choose and how much of our behaviour has an unavoidable private-and-public character. For a person does more than conduct a purely personal experiment in presenting him/herself to society through his/her behaviour: he/she is not only a 'personal scientist' as a private act as if he/she were alone in a closet. He/she is also the playwright and actor of the drama that is her life, visible and audible to others as part of the stories of their lives. At any moment, a person's actions contribute to the unfolding personal story he/she creates in living; and by colouring his/her experiences, these actions not only provide feedback to him/her on a behavioural experiment but they also signal messages to others about goals that he/she strategically chooses.

Practice

The primary task goal of personal construct coaching is to facilitate a client's appreciation of tradeoffs between task goals he/she chooses and the behaviour to which he/she is willing to commit as a visible, measurable expression of meanings in his/her personal story at the time of coaching. Depending on the timescale for which coaching is funded, secondary task goals include, on the one hand, to help the client to appreciate the dimension or dimensions of transition salient for him/her at the time of coaching, and, on the other hand, to introduce him/her to methods that encourage reflexivity and mindfulness that are congruent with the principles of benign disequilibrium.

To the extent that PCP coaches behave congruently with the principles of benign disequilibrium, they can advance its goals through distance communications. A disciplined coach may provide the guidance, support and stimulation a client needs and values without always sharing the physical location of a client. The practical flexibility and relatively modest cost of telephone, fax, letter and email communications make distance communications as media of coaching a viable economic option. While PCP coaching encourages self-monitoring, even brief distance communications can add resonance, encourage updating and make adaptation that bit more manageable.

The systemic character of PCP is rather at odds with a 'set format' or 'rules' for applying it in coaching, with two exceptions. One that Kelly called 'a credulous approach' (1991, vol. 1: 241–244; vol. 2: 170, 284) – wholehearted attention to indicators of thoughts, emotions, sensations and values of a client – is required for the coach to appreciate just what the client means, however faltering, clumsy or apparently lacking in coherence it may be. The 'credulous approach' colours PCP coaching with any tools used.

The other applies the message from the research of Kouzes and Posner (2003) and Daniels and Daniels (2006) that feedback plus goals creates traction and encourages people to stay aligned to their strategic task goals when they flag. Whatever other tools a PCP coach may use, agreeing a Personal Accomplishment Scorecard (PAS) framework for feedback should be included in every coaching session. The precise design of the scorecard may vary yet its purpose, to lead the client to honestly review how he/she is managing relationships between his/her goals and behaviour he/she chooses, remains central to PCP coaching.

Figure 13.2 presents a visual summary of tools for a conversational learning as PCP coaching in practice. Underpinning this representation of applying

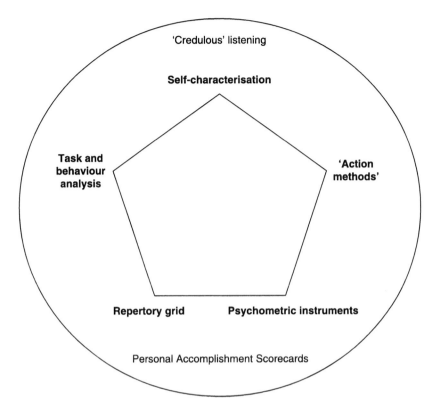

Figure 13.2 Conversational learning: PCP coaching in practice.

PCP in practice, the 'personal scientist' model of the 'first wave' supports congruent use of task and behaviour analysis, of repertory grids and psychometric instruments; and the 'personal story-narrator-cum-actor' model of the 'second wave' supports deft use of self-characterisation and 'action' methods of psychodrama or sociodrama. Because of the flexibility of use of methods in PCP coaching, a wise coach gives very careful thought in advance to how he/she will blend responsiveness to the client and firm compliance with data protection legislation.

Self-characterisation

The purpose of using self-characterisation in PCP coaching is to read or listen to the current phase of his/her personal story *in the language, contexts and timeframe of his/her choice.*

Kelly introduced his analysis of self-characterisation (Kelly, 1991, vol. 1: 239–267) with the simple aphorism: 'if you do not know what is wrong with a person, ask him; he [*sic*] may tell you'. This directness he called 'a guileless approach' (vol. 1: 139). Kelly's rider – 'The clinician who asks such a question will have to be prepared to do some careful listening for the answer will be couched in terms of the respondent's personal constructs, not only of himself but of the psychologist and of the situation' – highlights the reflexive nature of the coaching process. For the manner in which a client constructs his/her story unavoidably itself becomes part of the drama of conversational learning that the coach and client are conducting: it facilitates the client to enact dimensions of transition he/she currently experiences within the coaching relationship.

The coach and client can use a self-characterisation to construct hypotheses about the personal story of the client, drawing on the dimensions of transition and the principles of 'benign disequilibrium'. Unless the client is stuck in a 'hostility' dimension of transition, the coach's responses can quicken the reflexivity and mindfulness the client brings to his/her unfolding story. In the 'guileless' manner advocated by Kelly, the coach may, more or less explicitly, introduce a simple framework, such as 'Context(s) – Plot – Character(s) – Action – Outcome (CPCAO)', as a unobtrusive catalyst to this.

Self-characterisation may be designed in various formats including writing, videotape or audiotape. Whichever format is deployed, when self-characterisation is used with empathy, it usually yields rich indications of how a client perceives personal risks and opportunities in the present stage of the personal story.

If a coach works with a client over a period of months or longer, repeating the self-characterisation exercise is an opportunity for the client to uncover the contours of how he/she has reframed the dimensions of transition used to navigate through life by changes in behaviour. And an exchange of self-characterisations about their collaborative work may provide a congruent reflexive exercise for drawing coaching to a close.

Task and behaviour analysis

As noted in the above sketch of PCP theory, Kelly conceived of strategic task analysis to enable individuals to exercise responsibility and ingenuity about adapting their behaviour to variations in their economic and other environments. Kelly (1991, vol. 2: 292–369) explores techniques a practitioner may use to explore with a client the functioning of principles of strategic task analysis as well as benign disequilibrium in his/her life.

In coaching, a sufficient task analysis will disclose the 'rich picture', 'root definition' and systems thinking (Checkland, 1984; Duignan, 1996) that a client is using in his/her personal story, and in considering decisions about his area of interest. Soft systems methodology known as 'SSM' (Checkland and Scholes, 1999) enables the coach to reflect back these components of the client's patterns of thinking and feeling as data to colour his/her evolving personal story. This process serves as a device to enable the client to make qualitative shifts in thinking and feeling that empower the client to recognise ways in which he/she can now act, or behave in ways that he/she has simply not seriously considered as personal steps in living heretofore.

Although task analysis remains a rather neglected area of human resource management strategy and practice, it is proving its effectiveness in professional sports coaching and has become a standard process in that domain. There is, however, no need for the video analysis now commonly used in professional sport and coaches in other domains can conduct SSM-style task analysis with quite simple, 'low tech' pencils, preferably coloured ones, paper and 'credulous' listening.

According as the coach completes the best practicable task analysis, he/she may apply behavioural research on performance management (Daniels and Daniels, 2006) and on leadership (Kouzes and Posner, 2003) to assist a client to explore options for managing the private-and-public character of personal behaviour congruent with his/her strategic task goals. It sometimes helps when a coach sketches a decision tree to illustrate how a client may move from the present state in the his/her personal story through different levels of abstraction in thinking and feeling about personal dilemmas to the behavioural alternatives available in his/her world.

Repertory grids

The purpose of using a repertory grid within coaching with PCP is to dovetail qualitative methods of client assessment with quantitative methods within the 'personal scientist' model of the person. A structured format for gathering data from a client, it offers a coach an economical way of using available time to both deepen aspects of the personal story of the client and, during the feedback dialogue to explore hypotheses about the dimensions of transition he/she is negotiating. A coach familiar with the SSM method of task analysis can use a repertory grid as the engine which generates data on the 'rich picture' to make up the 'root definition' of the client's system of thinking and feeling about his/her presenting issue(s), as the case study illustrates.

Kelly goes into some detail to explain his rationale and procedures for a repertory grid (1991, vol. 1: 152–238) which he adapted from the Q sort methodology of another British psychologist, William Stephenson (1953). At the time of its invention, the repertory grid was regarded as controversial in its characterisation of a statistical population as a set of data within experiences of a single person, its mathematical robustness as a method of exploring the statistical structure of a person's patterns of thinking and feeling about his or her world has been well charted (Shaw, 1980).

A coach may administer a repertory grid with pencil and paper and conduct basic arithmetical calculations in his/her head or with a pocket calculator. Free or inexpensive software now permits speedy statistical and mathematical analysis of repertory grid data on the personal computer or laptop computer of a coach.

Pope and Keen (1981), Stewart and Stewart (1981), Thomas and Harri-Augstein (1985), Harri-Augstein and Thomas (1991), Jankowicz (2004) and Stewart and Mayes (2006) present stimulating illustrations of diverse ways in which repertory and other grids, congruent with the PCP models of the person, can be used as tools in coaching. As the case study illustrates, sometimes the main contribution of feedback with a grid lies in activating a creativity cycle, facilitating a client to loosen her patterns of thinking and feeling. Fransella et al. (2003) explain how the evolution of PCP has been marked by the growth of a diversity of grids congruent with the philosophy outlined in the principles of benign disequilibrium.

In situations where coaching functions within a tight timeframe, the repertory grid may serve as a powerful facilitation tool. Yet the strength of the grid techniques can also present a pitfall to be borne in mind. The precision afforded by the repertory grid may incline its users to become so reliant on it that they fail to appreciate the strength of the other techniques advocated by the inventor of personal construct psychology (see Kaplan, 1964).

Psychometric instruments

A coach may introduce psychometric tools based on conventional concepts of what is technically known as 'internal' validity to inform the evolving personal story of the client with objective data about aspects of his/her psychological make-up (e.g. personality traits, cognitive functioning, values and interests) in relation of other people using the same measures. When a client's first language is not English, psychometric tools available in his/her vernacular language may also facilitate his/her engagement in coaching.

Adroit use of psychological measures in PCP coaching requires attention not only to information in technical manuals and peer reviews but also to congruence with PCP theory (Kelly, 1991, vol. 1: 138–151) as well. Ensuring that feedback data relates to the client's personal story, and current dimensions of transition may contribute powerfully to little shifts in self-awareness and self-understanding that permit the movement in his/her creativity cycle and decision-making cycle that facilitate experimenting with alternative forms of behaviour. The research of Bazerman (2006) on controlling for bias is helpful in this regard.

As the case study illustrates, sometimes the contribution of feedback with a personality inventory or other psychometric tool lies in activating a creativity cycle, facilitating the client to loosen his/her patterns of thinking and feeling. Here, the specific payoff may lie in how it fuels conversational learning although additional forms of intervention may be needed to generate changes in psychological role and in behaviour that the client is seeking. At other times, a well-chosen psychometric instrument may directly further the work of the coach and client in pinpointing behavioural options through which the client can better pinpoint and manage dimensions of transition he/she is negotiating through coaching.

'Action methods'

Self-characterisation, task analysis and measurement tools contribute to a powerful framework around which a coach may work to appreciate a client's personal story and to channel his/her 'dislodgement' dimensions of transition, yet some clients experience difficulty in 'making behaviour happen', that is, in actually doing what is needed to change behavioural habits and to improve work performance, lose weight, control anger, stop shouting heedlessly at others and so on.

The purpose of introducing 'action methods' in conversational learning is to provide that vital little spur or catalyst that stimulates memories and imagination on the part of clients to enable them to experiment behaviourally with one or more alternative personal roles. In terms of a dimension of transition, they also enable the individual to try out a brief time exploring movement through a dimension of transition he/she finds difficult. They appear to have the effect of fine-tuning rapport and of animating communication so that it becomes just that bit less daunting for the client to risk emotional discomfort in new kinds of verbal behaviour, to express him/herself to the coach and with other people. When they are well handled, 'action methods' of psychodrama or sociodrama can also have a cathartic impact on clients' interactions: smiles, laughs and, on occasions, tears enter the room. The client's expression of passion facilitates his/her acknowledgement and assessment of core emotions along with negotiated boundaries for directing and controlling them, with moderated energy.

Conversational learning readily lends itself to spontaneous use of a form of psychodrama performed solo, 'monodrama', in which the coach briefly guides a client to enact different roles in the social situation he/she occupies in the real world, his/her 'social atom', the people with whom a client chooses to reach out towards or to reject, and who may reciprocate.

Simple artefacts – typically doors, chairs, tables, static and mobile phones – can serve as adequate 'props' for supporting and encouraging a diffident client (or indeed an extremely domineering one!) to test out principles of choice and of negotiating changes of behaviour in relationships with other people. Playback of the client's behavioural experiment in an alternative role enhances the quality of reflection. To manage it sensitively, a coach takes care to negotiate the basis for a recording on video, audio, CD or other media, and for using it later.

As coaching may well become the domain in which 'action methods' of psychodrama or sociodrama come to the fore in PCP practice, coaches can draw on the guidance of Blatner (1973), Wiener (1997) and Sternberg and

Garcia (2000) as well as some delightful illustrations of role enactment outside therapeutic contexts in a recent volume on PCP and the arts (Scheer and Sewell, 2006).

Case study

Marie, an actuary, approached Ciara, a chartered occupational psychologist, to ask for coaching to, in her own words, 'develop interpersonal skills' as a self-funded client. They negotiated a time-limited agreement to work together for some months and Ciara gave Marie instructions for writing a 'self-characterisation'.

Marie's self-characterisation included these observations:

> She has a great deal of tenacity. She is a fighter, and doesn't give up easily. When required, she acts decisively, and is loyal to those she trusts, likes and respects. She is not afraid to face up to her own shortcomings and seek help and advice in overcoming them, although she can be too self-critical. At work, she is happy to challenge the status quo and likes to find new ways of doing things and put her own stamp on existing processes . . .

> Marie's main worry is around her perceived interpersonal limitations. She can feel uncomfortable communicating in non-setpiece situations, such as chairing meetings or joining in the office banter, despite having had a significant amount of experience in these situations. She can clam up, become defensive or simply lose energy, and feels that these behaviours hold her back from fulfilling her potential. While she respects and relies on her technical abilities, she doesn't want to be pigeonholed as a 'technie' and would like the opportunity to make her skills count in a wider arena.

Marie's self-characterisation included this passage:

> She is unsure as to the extent to which it is within her gift to change some of her behaviours. She has recently read up about Asperger's syndrome, a condition that her cousin's son has been diagnosed with, and she identifies with many of the symptoms. She has a tendency to become stressed or angry and believes she has poor self-organisation skills, as evidenced by her untidy house.

When Ciara gently probed Marie's use of the clinical term 'Asperger's syndrome' to describe herself, Marie explained in a candid, matter-of-fact manner that what she wrote was based simply on an informal self-attribution intended to be honest about the extent of her worries and eagerness to improve. Marie added that her medical history did not include a referral for clinical assessment or an episode of psychosis or other severe form of disturbance. Ciara began to form a hypothesis that Marie's use of the clinical expression was an indication of a relatively normal anxiety, fear or even threat associated with demands of the career transition she was going through.

One way in which Ciara addressed Marie's anxieties about the adequacy of her interpersonal skills was simply giving her a copy of the description of Asperger's syndrome presented by the World Health Organization (1992). They discussed it briefly and Ciara assured Marie that, if there were evidence of a significant psychological disturbance, she would offer Marie an introduction to a psychiatrist with whom she had a referral arrangement. They agreed to proceed with the coaching arrangement on this basis.

Another way forward arose from listening credulously to Marie. She indicated how she was quite tolerant of her level of performance as a 'mere' player in an orchestra and in a triathlon club; she did not demand excellence of herself in these spheres and was content to enjoy them simply as intrinsic sources of satisfaction and as social scenarios. She also revealed how she had been elected chairman of her university's inter-collegiate orchestra, which actually involved considerable political resourcefulness when the orchestra began to seriously rebel against the conductor.

Discussing Marie's self-characterisation with her, Ciara learned that Marie viewed an impending career transition to a management post with a world-class firm, with a lot of trepidation and strong excitement. Marie's self-characterisation indicated that her recent experiences of what she perceived as harsh treatment by a line manager – whom she referred to as 'a lousy boss, J' – in the firm she was leaving had profoundly undermined her confidence in her interpersonal and political competence. Marie clarified this source of tension with the explanation that the manager was an accountant and Ciara inferred that J had felt at a loss about how to communicate about technical actuarial issues with extensive commercial and political strands. Ciara offered Marie the hypothesis that she (Marie) might be creating a 'guilt' dimension of transition for herself, perhaps under the shadow of her memories of frustration in response to the previous line manager, 'J', with the result that she was now applying standards of precision in areas of mental accomplishment that were accentuating in Marie's own mind her low self-evaluation in the social domain of her working life.

As a way forward, Ciara concentrated on the hypothesis that an appropriate creativity cycle for Marie would involve greater discernment on Marie's part about her emotions and those of others at work, and next about taking initiatives in working relationships. As Marie's work as an actuary made her comfortable with numerical data, Ciara proposed to explore this hypothesis with a well-researched personality inventory, as well as with a repertory grid designed to gather data from Marie about the mental frames she used to interpret the behaviour of herself, the managers to whom she was reporting in the matrix system of management which she had stepped into as well as her peer professionals at work.

Introducing Marie to the 'Context(s) – Plot – Character(s) – Action – Outcome (CPCAO)' framework for reviewing the self-characterisation, Ciara asked her to do some 'homework' using the labels from the personality inventory as one side of the scales or 'constructs' of a repertory grid to reflect on her self-image at different stages as well as on people Marie interacted with in her new job and her previous job. Table 13.2 presents a portion of data of the repertory grid completed by Marie.

To facilitate the convergent phase of Marie's creativity cycle, Ciara also used a computer program to provide feedback about some statistical and mathematical aspects of the grid data:

- a cluster analysis to indicate patterns of similarities in Marie's mind among the people she had considered
- a principal components analysis to pinpoint the principal frame (not shown here) that coloured Marie's acknowledged proneness towards anxiety and tension: 'self-conscious' as compared to 'blasé'.

In reviewing the grid data and the statistical feedback, Ciara responded to the questions Marie raised and also probed Marie about her perceptions of the contrast between herself and the 'pleasant colleague – X'; this uncovered Marie's belief that 'X' was 'much more decisive' than her. Ciara asked Marie a couple of questions to test the hypothesis that she might have a history of difficulties about managing the 'pre-emption' stage of the 'decision-making cycle' dimension of transition. As she was answering, Marie stopped short abruptly. After what seemed like a long silence, she sighed,

> Ye – es. That's it! O my heavens! I now think I realise how I've developed a bit of an addiction to information really. Instead of making up my mind about an important matter, for as long as I can remember I have always procrastinated in the sort of hope that more information will act like some kind of magic. You get away with it when you're at school and university as long as you play the game of writing essays and exams OK! I've known for some time it doesn't really work in the real world. My

Table 13.2 Repertory grid completed by Marie: perceptions of herself and other people in her working life

Max. 7	Me as I interact now at work	Former helpful boss 'S'	Pleasant colleague 'X'	Me as I interacted when I was 16	Former lousy boss 'J'	Current senior manager in New York: 'C'	Me as I want to interact at work	Sister	Friend	Min. 1
Excitable	6	2	3	5	3	3	3	4	4	Calm
Extravert	3	4	4	4	2	5	4	3	6	Intravert
Open to experience	4	4	4	6	2	3	4	3	5	Close-minded
Agreeable	2	4	4	3	2	4	4	3	4	Hardnosed
Conscientious	3	3	3	1	3	3	5	3	2	Disorganised
Psychologically healthy	4	7	6	3	2	4	7	4	5	Psychologically unwell

partner tries to help but even he now tends to lose patience with me. I can now see why, recently, he's begun to call this procrastination habit 'your bloody Aspergers game'. He says I prefer to just look on at life as a spectator and avoid actually living. I simply couldn't understand what he means till now. Oh, dear! It's awful, really!

Observing how Marie was on the tipping point to tears, Ciara wished to facilitate her to tighten her understanding about a personal role she might discover as an alternative to 'Aspergers-game-player'. She invited Marie to do a monodrama exercise designed to surface Marie's pattern of thinking when she saw herself 'procrastinating' at meetings at work. As Marie enacted the behaviour involved, as agreed earlier Ciara used an audiotape to record Marie's 'cognitive walkthrough' of what occurred. They then listened to it together so that Marie could recall her thoughts and feelings at those moments when she 'stalled'.

Marie and Ciara then negotiated two specific forms of 'homework' that she could test out in her life. One was to make a decision about a value that was really important to her when she felt inclined to procrastinate, choose at least one action that appeared to represent some progress and to just do it. The other was to gather data on patterns of her behaviour in interaction with her new managers – behaviour dwelling on technical actuarial issues with 'C', the company's worldwide Chief Actuary based in New York with whom she liaised by telephone, and her local manager, an accountant, with whom she liaised about politically sensitive matters to do with legal compliance – which they could then compare.

Shortly afterwards, Marie said that she realised she was moving beyond her habitual habit of 'self-conscious' preoccupation at work. She said she had crossed the threshold which a short time earlier had left her feeling tongue-tied, at a loss and frustrated.

> Specifically, I realised I was 'crossing the threshold' when I began to pre-pare different options for getting across my views at meetings, rather than just sitting like a dummy and feeling irritated by not being asked. Actually, when I circulated a single A4 page summarising key issues during a meeting, very much as you had recommended, I felt like I was playing a winning hand in a game!

Marie reported that she had come to the view that, given her actuarial knowledge, it was less risky for her to assert herself more strongly with London colleagues with whom she interacted continually than allow the perception to grow that she was inclined to allow slip-ups to simply pass. Marie gradually came to the view that gaining credibility in London would be the critical way to avoid becoming trapped and submerged by differences between 'C' and her London colleagues, which might in time prove to require bridge-building on her part.

Listening attentively, Ciara encouraged Marie to have particular regard for the quality of her own experiences on occasions when she felt able to communicate most effectively, even without the active support of those she found most helpful. To enable Marie to *reconfigure* personal roles so she might manage the perceived 'interpersonal limitations' sketched in the original self-characterisation, Ciara discussed the concept of 'empowering herself' by creating a personal, psychological role of 'active diplomat' (a 'root definition' that coordinated the 'rich picture' and systemic pattern within Marie's personal story); Marie expressed a mixture of excitement and relief that this role offered a challenging alternative to the role of an 'Aspergers-game-player'.

Ciara invited Marie to observe the difference between basic, 'threshold' competence and proficiency or excellence, drawing an analogy between Marie's proficiency 'playing' an oboe in an orchestra and her basic level of ability to 'play with' a violin. Marie recognised from her own experience how the spiral of learning to play a musical instrument well required patience as well as effort. She now realised how attitudinal adjustments involved in diplomacy were more likely to emerge from a 'tortoise-style' manner of reflection about dilemmas arising from behaviour she observed than from swift, sharp computer-aided analysis in a 'hare-brained' style.

Recalling her experiences in the orchestral society, Marie also appreciated how viewing herself in the personal role of a musician, rather than in the occupational role of an actuary, she was able to recall lots of instances of interpersonal behaviour she had performed which enabled her to bring a very different mindset to participating in political aspects of organisational behaviour. In this light, Marie gradually observed ways in which she might more proactively take diplomatic initiatives with those with whom she worked day-to-day in London than with 'C', very much senior in status and based in New York.

During their last meeting, Ciara and Marie exchanged self-characterisations about the phase of working together. In Marie's updated self-characterisation, she sketched the self-empowerment that the variable role of diplomacy was beginning to open up for her.

> Building trust in myself and in my abilities to observe and to conduct conversation across the Atlantic with 'C', as well as with my peers and

bosses here in London, is a more complex level of diplomacy. As I progress with exercising influence with them, I feel I'm gradually making headway at a tough kind of triathlon game in my career. I still keep that audiotape we did – to me, it now feels like when you blew a whistle that started me to swim in a more powerful style that I need when I'm in rough waters.

Which clients benefit most?

Coaching with PCP is relevant to clients with difficulties in dealing well with relentless change, or with actually getting things done, and who are prepared to learn from their experience as they adapt their behaviour.

While each of the practical techniques sketched above may be used with groups or organisations, care is required to tailor the technique to suit a specific need, for example, when a coach invites members of a group to share their personal stories, he/she should do so aware of how the social identity of the group emerges from the content and character of stories its members present to each other (Bruner, 2003), and be equipped to manage the emotional impact of this on behaviour of members of the group. Failure to tailor thoughtfully may block 'construction' dimensions or trigger 'dislodgement' dimensions of transition which benefit nobody.

When a client's first language is not English and a PCP coach has a reasonable standard of fluency in the client's preferred language, the blend of qualitative and quantitative techniques congruent with PCP can make for ease of rapport with the client.

Table 13.3 indicates the focus of coaching adults at an individual level as well as in groups and organisational contexts.

Provided the coach lightens up, many teenagers tend to express surprise and curiosity – after initial disbelief – about ways in which PCP can throw fresh perspectives on their options, with fidelity to their personal values. The coach can use 'dimensions of transition' to facilitate the creativity cycle in dialogue between teenagers and their parents, foster parents or step-parents or carers at times of tension and difficulty in strategic personal decision-making. The model of the personal story and techniques of self-characterisation, task and behaviour analysis can be very fruitful when handled well in coaching by teachers and personal advisers in areas of personal relationships; sex and gender; health and impairments; adulthood, freedom, discipline and personal responsibility; and career and course choices; writing CVs and 'personal statements'; presenting a portfolio and preparing for interviews for jobs or courses.

Coaching with PCP is *not* appropriate as the principal resource in some situations. Where a client wants a set format, PCP coaching is apt to swiftly trigger entry to a 'dislodgement' dimension of transition. Where a client, of any age, shows he/she is so attached to the 'hostility' dimension of transition

Table 13.3 Sets of individuals for whom PCP coaching is relevant

The client set	Focus of coaching
Individuals	• Sporting accomplishment through psychological fitness • From 'burnout' to healthy stress • Managing personal ill-health or a disability impairment • Challenges in 'third age', mid-life, career-launch stages of the lifespan • Controlling sales call aversion, reluctance and oppositional reflexes.
Groups and organisations	• Business risks and options for managing them • Leadership behaviour in relation to an underperforming function • Cost-effective implementation of support for diversity and fair discrimination • Cost-effective implementation of safe/healthy work behaviour and work environments • Leadership behaviour to cost-effectively adapt high, medium and low technology to needs of people using it • Coaching, refereeing, leading and managing professional and amateur sports performers • Solentrepreneurship in the theatre and music • Mentoring for business 'rainmaking' • Design, development, construction, adaptation and retrofitting of buildings and IT systems.

that it is evident that avoidance is his/her preferred behavioural strategy, coaching with PCP is not a good use of resources. For a client with reading difficulties or serious learning problems it may be suitable, provided appropriate psychometric or other assessment instruments are used.

Just as the challenge to live healthily that faces every human being presents an unavoidable paradox, so does the challenge of using PCP to create conversational learning. On the one hand, coaches can offer powerful interventions based on the rich intellectual heritage synthesised by Kelly in PCP, along with the development of tools like soft systems methodology and computer support for processing and feedback of repertory grids and psychometric instruments. On the other hand, this very combination generates the paradox which permits a coach to fail to the extent that he/she is inattentive to the core challenge of enabling clients to move on in their lives and is seduced by knowledge or technology.

References

Bannister, D. and Fransella, F. (1990) *Inquiring Man: Theory of personal constructs.* London: Routledge.

Bazerman, M. H. (2006) *Judgment in Managerial Decision-Making*, 6th edition. Hoboken, NJ: Wiley.

Blatner, H. A. (1973) *Acting-In: Practical applications of psychodramatic methods.* New York: Springer.

Brophy, S. (2003) Construing New Realities: an organisational case study. Unpublished diploma dissertation in counselling in occupational settings, The Centre for Personal Construct Psychology, London.

Bruner, J. (2003) *Making Stories: Law, literature, life.* Boston, MA: Harvard University Press.

Checkland, P. (1984) *Systems Thinking, Systems Practice.* Chicester: Wiley.

Checkland, P. and Scholes, J. (1999) *Soft Systems Methodology in Action.* Chicester: Wiley.

Claxton, G. (1984) *Live and Learn: An introduction to the psychology of growth and change in everyday life.* London: Harper and Row.

Daniels, A. C. and Daniels, J. E. (2006) *Performance Management: Changing behavior that drives organizational effectiveness,* 4th edition, revised. Atlanta, GA: Performance Management Publications.

Dewey, J. (1991) *How We Think.* New York: Prometheus. (Originally published 1909.)

Duignan, K. (1996) Using soft systems methodology to elicit user requirements for adapting a socio-technical system. Unpublished MSc in Ergonomics project report, University College London.

Duignan, K. (2005) Improving options for managing business and employee health. In P. Grant and S. Lewis (eds) *Business Psychology in Practice.* London: Whurr.

Fransella, F. (1995) *George Kelly (Key Figures in Counselling).* London: Sage.

Fransella, F., Bannister, D. and Bell, R. (2003) *A Manual for Repertory Grid Technique,* 2nd revised edition. Chichester: Wiley.

Harri-Augstein, S. and Thomas, L. (1991) *Learning Conversations.* London: Routledge.

Jankowicz, A. D. (2004) *The Easy Guide to Repertory Grids.* Chichester: Wiley.

Kaplan, A. (1964) *The Conduct of Enquiry: Methodology for behavioural science.* San Francisco, CA: Chandler.

Kelly, G. A. (1991) *The Psychology of Personal Constructs,* Volumes 1 and 2. London: Routledge (in association with the Centre for Personal Construct Psychology, London). (Originally published 1955.)

Kolb, D. (1984) *Experiential Learning: Experience as the source of learning and development.* Englewood Cliffs, NJ: Prentice Hall.

Korzybski, A. (1994) *Science and Sanity: An introduction to non-Aristotelian systems and general semantics.* New York: Institute of General Semantics. (Originally published 1933.)

Kouzes, J. and Posner, B. (2003) *Encouraging the Heart: A leader's guide to rewarding and recognising others.* San Francisco, CA: Jossey-Bass.

Mair, J. M. M. (1976) Metaphors for living. In A. Landfield (ed.) *Nebraska Symposium on Motivation: Personal Construct Psychology.* Lincoln, NE: University of Nebraska Press.

Moreno, J. L. (1988) *The Essential Moreno: Writings on psychodrama, group method and spontaneity.* New York: Springer.

Morganbesser, S. (1987) The American Pragmatists. In B. Magee (ed.) *The Great Philosophers: An introduction to Western philosophy.* Oxford: Oxford University Press.

Pope, M. and Keen, T. R. (1981) *Personal Construct Psychology and Education.* London: Academic Press.

Salmon, P. (1985) *Living in Time: A new look at personal development*. London: J. M. Dent.

Scheer, J. and Sewell, K. (eds) (2006) *Creative Construing: Personal constructions in the arts*. Giessen, Germany: Psychosozial-Verlag.

Shaw, M. (1980) *On Becoming a Personal Scientist: Interactive computer elicitation of personal models of the read world*. London: Academic Press.

Stephenson, W. (1953) *The Study of Behavior: Q-technique and its methodology*. Chicago, IL: University of Chicago Press.

Sternberg, P. and Garcia, A. (2000) *Sociodrama: Who's in your shoes?* London: Praeger.

Stewart, A. and Stewart, V. (1981) *Business Applications of Repertory Grid*. Maidenhead: McGraw-Hill.

Stewart, V. and Mayes, J. (2006) *Enquire Within*. Available www.enquirewithin.co.nz (2 August 2006).

Thomas, L. and Harri-Augstein, S. (1985) *Self-Organised Learning*. London: Routledge.

Wiener, R. (1997) *Creative Training: Sociodrama and team-building*. London: Jessica Kingsley.

World Health Organization (1992) *The ICD-10 Classification of Mental and Behavioural Disorders: Clinical descriptions and diagnostic guidelines*. Geneva: WHO.

Discussion points

- Write a self-characterisation of up to 500 words about yourself in relation to a dilemma in your life at present. Explore how two or more dimensions of transition may throw light on the dilemma.

- Identify three of the dimensions of transition profiled in Table 13.1 to which you are most inclined. In what ways, if any, might you behave that enable you to manage each dimension of transition with a firm sense of momentum and balance?

- Identify a relationship in some area of your life that is sufficiently important to you that you would very much like to improve its quality. Brainstorm a variety of things you could do to improve the relationship; exercise your imagination without conventional restraints and record your findings. Explore the possibilities of action during the coming fortnight. Then decide on, and rank, three specific forms of behaviour you will do, that you are not already doing; write down what you will do and the dates when you will start taking actions required to do them.

- To practise 'credulous' listening, enlist the cooperation of a colleague or friend. Negotiate a basis for 'coaching' him/her about a problem that really matters to him/her, for up to 60 minutes in which he/she plays the role of client who now experiences profound (95 per cent) loss of hearing.

Suggested reading

Kelly, G. A. (1991) *The Psychology of Personal Constructs*, Volumes 1 and 2. London: Routledge (in association with the Centre for Personal Construct Psychology, London). (Originally published 1955.)

For an exploration of applying personal construct psychology in coaching, use the citations in the chapter above to study the 'fount' of personal construct psychology. Although written in a dense style, like great classics this book can reveal unanticipated insights into human behaviour when you reread it over time.

Fransella, F., Bannister, D. and Bell, R. (2003) *A Manual for Repertory Grid Technique*, 2nd revised edition. Chichester: Wiley.

If you want to bolster your grasp of how to carry out statistical and mathematical analyses of grid, you will find this a sound reference book. with fidelity to the model of the person as a scientist.

Jankowicz, A. D. (2004) *The Easy Guide to Repertory Grids*. Chichester: Wiley.

If you need procedures for designing, administering and interpreting repertory and other grids, this is a nicely written guide with plenty of practical examples.

Salmon, P. (1985) *Living in Time: A new look at personal development*. London: J. M. Dent.

This is a lucidly written title, with charm. It illustrates the 'personal story' model of personal construct psychology and conveys a sense of the hope and optimism at the heart of its philosophy.

Wiener, R. (1997) *Creative Training: Sociodrama and team-building*. London: Jessica Kingsley.

Should exploring ways of applying 'Action Methods' of sociodrama with personal construct psychology in your coaching practice appeal to you, read relevant parts of Kelly's title referred to above along with Wiener.

Chapter 14

Psychodynamic and systems-psychodynamic coaching

Vega Zagier Roberts and Halina Brunning

Introduction

The term 'psychodynamic' links two ideas: 'psycho-' comes from the Greek word *psyche*, meaning soul or mind, and '-dynamic', from the Greek *dynamis*, meaning strength or power, used in physics and other fields to denote forces causing movement, action or change. Thus, psychodynamic coaching is based on a way of understanding how the mental forces operating in and between individuals and groups affect their thinking and behaviour.

Practitioners of psychodynamic approaches to coaching vary both in their theoretical orientation and in their practice. Many are therapists with a training grounded in one or other 'school' of psychoanalytic theory. Others practise from a systems-psychodynamics perspective. This brings together elements of psychoanalytic theory with its focus on the influence of unconscious mental life on individual and group behaviour, with elements of open systems theory with its focus on role, authority, and the design of work systems and processes. Because of the centrality of role in this coaching process, the approach is often referred to as role consultancy or role analysis.

Development of psychodynamic and systems-psychodynamic coaching

The history of psychodynamic and systems-psychodynamic coaching is given a useful contextual background by examining the typology of coaching proposed by Roberts and Jarrett (2006), who studied the key differences between the main approaches to coaching currently practised in the UK. The grid shown in Figure 14.1 is based on their interviews of leading practitioners of different kinds of coaching regarding the main aims and focus of their work. The primary *aim* of the coaching intervention is shown on the vertical axis, with insight at one end of the spectrum and outputs (e.g. higher sales) at the other. The horizontal axis indicates whether the primary *focus* of the coaching is on the individual or on the organisation and organisational role.

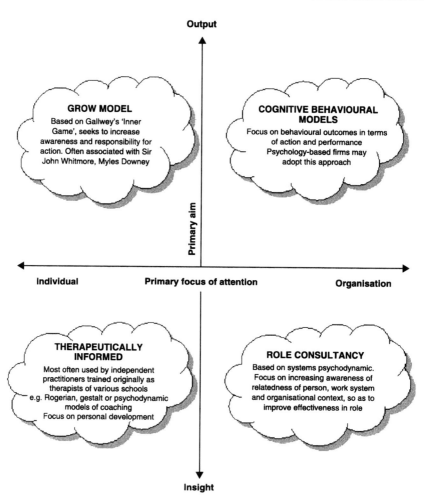

Figure 14.1 Four models of coaching.

© V. Z. Roberts and M. Jarrett, 2006.

The information is gathered in 'clouds' to show that these are not rigid categories but clusters of types of coaching interventions.

A striking finding was that whereas most of the leading approaches to coaching fell fairly clearly into one or other quadrant, psychodynamic coaching found a place in both lower quadrants: the more purely 'therapeutically informed' approaches on the left, and the systems-psychodynamics (role consultancy) approach on the right. In essence, the top two quadrants are based on goal attainment, whereas the bottom two quadrants are based on meaning-making. In the sections that follow, we will therefore consider both what these two main 'streams' of psychodynamic coaching share in common and how they are different.

The actual development of psychodynamic therapies can be traced back to the earliest years of the twentieth century when Freud developed his 'talking cure'. However, the development of psychodynamic coaching is relatively recent. We can trace the origins of psychodynamic coaching to two main sources, as follows.

From psychodynamically-informed work with organisations

During the Second World War, psychoanalysts from the Tavistock Clinic were involved in various ways in applying their clinical understanding to the war effort, notably to the selection of officers and to the rehabilitation of mentally traumatised soldiers. After the war, some of these psychoanalysts joined with social scientists, anthropologists and other disciplines at the newly established Tavistock Institute of Human Relations where they developed a body of theory and worked with a wide range of organisations including coal-mines, factories, children's nurseries, hospitals and many others (see Trist and Murray, 1990).

The first applications of systems-psychodynamics to addressing individuals' workplace issues (precursor of coaching) probably go back to the late 1950s when the Christian Teamwork Trust (later the Grubb Institute of Behavioural Studies) provided a variety of training events aimed at developing participants' understanding of organisational behaviour and dynamics. Organisational Role Analysis (ORA), a method to enable leaders and managers to take up their roles more effectively, emerged from this work (Reed, 1976; Reed and Bazalgette, 2003). ORA has been adapted by many practitioners of systems-psychodynamics who work with individual clients, often under the title 'organisational role consultancy' or more recently (for marketing purposes), executive coaching (Newton et al., 2006).

From psychodynamically-oriented therapy and counselling with individuals

Since the mid-1990s, there has been a growing trend for psychotherapists and counsellors of all persuasions, including psychodynamic, to extend their practice to the workplace in the form of coaching. In part, this may be driven by their need to find alternative ways of deploying their skills as long-term therapy wanes in popularity. As Peltier puts it, 'the talking cure . . . is too slow, too personal, it provides no guarantees, and it lacks the punch and focus demanded by those in the fast lane' (Peltier, 2001: xvi).

However, there is also an awareness within many organisations that something is missing which a psychodynamically-oriented coach might provide. At one level, there is some recognition of the need for 'space to think', away from the results-driven pressures of everyday life in most contemporary organisations, so as to develop deeper understanding of some of the less obvious or less conscious factors contributing to work difficulties.

Theory and basic concepts

Psychodynamic coaching works from an underpinning framework of theories and concepts primarily developed in a therapeutic environment that stem from the original work of Freud.

Concepts from psychoanalytic theory

Unconscious mental life

The cornerstone of psychodynamic thinking is the assumption that there is an unconscious – a part of our mental life which is hidden and affects us in ways we are not aware of. While it is easy to demonstrate that there are thoughts and memories lodged in our brain but out of conscious awareness – for example, when we suddenly remember a forgotten name or telephone number, or details of past experience are recalled when electrodes are planted in certain parts of the brain – psychoanalytic theory proposes that particular aspects of our experience become unconscious as a way of protecting us from anxiety and pain.

Unconscious anxieties and defences

Like 'unconscious', the word 'anxiety' is part of our everyday language, generally referring to a disturbing emotional state evoked by anticipating a threatening future event. The anticipation of the threat mobilises us to create a set of defences. In the workplace, for example, staff may have many conscious anxieties such as fear of redundancy, worries about accidents and dangerous mistakes, and so on. They are then likely to take certain actions in order to manage or reduce these anxieties, for example trade unions are formed, or elaborate protocols are set up to prevent errors.

Freud and subsequent psychoanalytic theorists put forward the notion that some anxieties are unconscious. For example, we may have impulses which we consider unacceptable – wanting to hurt someone we love, or sexual feelings towards a parent or child. If these feelings were to be fully conscious, they could pose a threat to our sense of ourselves as loving and generally decent people. Psychoanalytic theory suggests these feelings are pushed out of awareness into our unconscious, through the use of defence mechanisms. These include denial (the feelings do not exist), projection (the feelings belong to someone else), idealisation and denigration (seeing others as all-good or all-bad to avoid painful mixed feeling), and intellectualisation (explaining feelings away), among others (A. Freud 1966).

Psychonalytic theory suggests we all need defences to prevent our being flooded by unconscious anxieties. While some defences are helpful, others prevent our dealing adequately with reality, or prevent us using our full capabilities. For example, excessive use of projection can lead to blaming others rather than seeking ways of improving our own practice. It can also lead to feeling more helpless than we actually are, as when we locate all power and strength in our managers and feel 'prevented' from using our own initiative.

Containment

It is hypothesised that as infants and young children, we begin a lifelong process of learning to manage our anxieties, largely thanks to caretakers who are emotionally in touch with us and who, by attending age-appropriately to our needs, give us a sense of security (that the things we fear are manageable) and of being understood. The infant is thought to project their feelings into caretakers who 'absorb' the feelings in such a way that they are no longer so frightening. Transferring this idea to the workplace, it suggests good management can perform an analogous function, containing both our conscious and unconscious anxieties sufficiently that we can think and act effectively rather than needing to get rid of our feelings through counterproductive defence mechanisms. However, if our parents or managers are themselves overly anxious or preoccupied, they may not be able to assist us in managing our anxieties. At this point, we may become overwhelmed and resort to using unhelpful defence mechanisms. For example, faced with a takeover, we are likely to have anxieties about loss of identity. Regarding the other organisation as an evil empire-builder may temporarily serve to strengthen internal cohesion and identity, but in the longer term militates against engaging in appropriate pre-joining work.

Tranference

This concept is based on the idea that there is a universal tendency to bring our experience of early life figures into the present, i.e. to *transfer* them so that our perceptions of other people are coloured or even distorted. For example, someone whose 'internal' authority figures are benign ('my parents set limits which were helpful to me') is more likely to react to authority figures at work in a positive way, expecting a positive relationship with them. Someone who has experienced oppression, bullying or abuse in early life may have similar feelings at work, and perhaps be either overly compliant and dependent or overly aggressive and defensive with people in positions of authority in their organisation.

Counter-transference and unconscious communication

Counter-transference is a term from psychoanalysis referring to the feelings evoked in the analyst by the patient, for example feeling a strong urge to protect or rescue. Since the analyst was supposed to be emotionally neutral, listening and interpreting the patient's communications, counter-transference was initially regarded as a source of disturbance. However, gradually it came to be recognised that it could be understood as the analyst's response to unconscious communication from the patient, and hence as a crucial source of information about what was going on for the patient at an unconscious level. For example, the impulse to protect the patient might on the surface seem to have nothing to do with what the patient was actually saying, and the analyst might assume it came from some personal need in him- or herself. This might of course be the case, but another possibility is that the patient is unconsciously communicating his or her fears and also longings for protection from someone perceived as stronger (feelings about parents transferred to the analyst). It is this unconscious communication which might be stirring up the analyst's protective feelings.

Concepts from open systems theory

A living organism can survive only by exchanging materials with its environment, that is, by being an open system. This requires having an external boundary, a membrane or skin separating inside from outside. This boundary must be solid enough to prevent leakage and to protect the organism from disintegrating, but permeable enough for the necessary exchanges with the environment to take place. The simplest living system is a single cell; in more complex organisms, there will be a number of open systems operating simultaneously, each performing its own specialised functions but coordinated with the activities of other systems so as to serve the needs of the organism as a whole.

The work of Kurt Lewin (1947) in applying these ideas to human systems was extended and developed by Miller and Rice (1967) to provide a framework for studying the relationships between the parts and the whole in organisations, and also between organisations and their environment.

The primary task

This is the task the organisation must perform in order to survive (Rice, 1963). An organisation as an open system can be schematically represented as in Figure 14.2. The box in the centre represents the system of activities required to perform the task of converting inputs into outputs, for example turning leather (A) into shoes (B).

The primary task is defined by the main throughput. Inputs might be raw

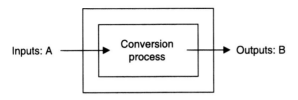

Figure 14.2 The primary task.

materials (e.g. leather), with outputs being finished products (e.g. shoes). In organisations working with people such as the NHS, inputs are people, in state A (e.g. people with an illness) and outputs are people in state B (e.g. people in better health).

Enterprises are far more complex than Figure 14.2 denotes, with many different kinds of inputs and outputs. A shoe-factory, for example, also takes in information from the environment and uses it to produce financial plans and marketing strategies. It is likely to have different departments such as production, sales, personnel and marketing, all of which need to be coordinated. However, how to allocate resources and how to prioritise among the organisation's various activities is determined by its *primary task*.

The concept of the primary task, despite its limitations in complex systems, remains extremely useful. Clarity about the purpose of one's work-system provides a kind of yardstick by which one can continually evaluate whether one is on course, and whether the design of the system and working practices remains appropriate. It also helps to identify and link the particular contribution of each subsystem to the primary task of the organisation as a whole.

Management at and of the boundary

Living organisms need a membrane which is neither too permeable nor too impermeable. Similarly, organisational systems need boundaries that regulate transactions with the environment. This regulation is a core function of management. For example, a manager needs to ensure that staffing levels and other resources match the production targets or the changing needs of consumers. For this reason, the open systems model locates the manager at the boundary of the system they manage (see Figure 14.3).

In Figure 14.3, m1, m2, etc. represent managers of subsystems such as teams or departments. *M* represents the line manager of all the *m*'s. Their position at the boundary of the system they manage enables them to be simultaneously in touch with inside and outside, and indicates their function as regulating transactions across the boundary.

This position *at* the boundary of the system enables the manager to be in contact both with the external environment and with the internal state of the system. This includes being in touch with the emotional state of the staff

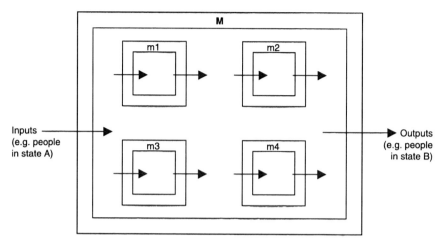

Figure 14.3 Management at the boundary.

he or she manages in order to provide the necessary *containment* of conscious and unconscious anxieties, as described above. The manager who loses this boundary position, either by being drawn too far into the system, or by being too cut off, can no longer manage effectively.

More senior managers or directors overseeing the work of multiple subsystems (shown as M in Figure 14.3) need also to coordinate the work of these subsystems. This requires vision and a broader grasp of how the specific purposes and activities of each link to each other and to the whole, and also the capacity to communicate this understanding to those he or she leads and manages.

Bringing the two theoretical strands together: systems-psychodynamics

Social defence systems

In his ground-breaking paper on 'The dynamics of social structure', Jacques (1953) proposed that 'one of the primary cohesive elements binding individuals into institutionalized human association is that of defence against anxiety' (Trist and Murray, 1990: 420–421). Within social structures, including organisations, individuals and groups take up unconscious as well as conscious roles. Jacques gives the example of the First Officer of a ship who 'is regarded by common consent as the source of trouble' for everything that goes wrong. This allows the ship's captain, on whom all lives depend, to be idealised as a reliable protector. Here, the whole 'social system' of the ship's crew is using the defences of splitting (into all-good and all-bad) and projection. Thus, all badness, weakness, etc. are projected into the First Officer, and all goodness, strength and knowledge are projected into the captain. These defences enable the crew to feel they are in safe hands, thus protecting them from the potentially terrifying reality that the captain is not omnipotent.

While this kind of splitting may be useful aboard ship or in an army in time of war, it is often dysfunctional in organisations, leading to blaming, scapegoating, and a reduction in realistic problem-solving capacities. Furthermore, the person who is the locus for projections may well experience these projections as intensely personal. The First Officer might actually start to feel inadequate and the captain could come to overestimate the value of his own judgement. Either or both could then be at risk of losing touch with reality as a result of the collective projective processes at work. Awareness of these kinds of systemic projections can reduce stress and conflict, and enable people to regain a more accurate perception of reality, which in turn enables them to take more effective action.

As already stated with regard to defences operating at the individual level, systemic defence systems are inevitable and necessary if we are not to be overwhelmed by anxiety. The question is whether existing defence systems in an organisation are working, and at what cost. We tend to take 'the way things are done around here' as a given. Insight into counterproductive systemic defences can provide an opportunity to do a kind of cost-benefit analysis, and if necessary to rethink how roles, systems and working practices are designed. An example of this might be to question whether existing bureaucracy and protocols are effective in preventing mistakes, or actually preventing the degree of flexibility required to meet constantly shifting demands.

The design of work systems

Boundaries around systems and subsystems within organisations serve an important function. They help to identify who is inside and who is outside the system, thus fostering a sense of group and also of individual identity: I am a member of team X, which has a task to which I contribute. Thus, they enable us to create mental maps of the system(s) of which we are a part. On the other hand, rigid boundaries can impede collaboration between teams, departments and organisations, or even fuel conflict. Again, a useful question is to ask whether the current boundaries are supporting task performance or inhibiting it.

Exercising authority and leadership

The exercise of authority can be understood using either psychodynamic or open systems theory or, ideally, both. From a psychoanalytic perspective, one's unconscious relationships with authority figures will affect how able we are to use our authority appropriately. Inappropriate exercise of authority includes being authoritarian (for example over-controlling or over-punitive) and also the opposite, abdicating authority (like the manager who joins his or her staff in feeling victimised by more senior management, rather than identifying actions which could be helpful).

However, the design of reporting relationships (systemic element) also has a significant impact on how authority is experienced and used in an organisation. For instance, nowadays many people have more than one line of accountability, perhaps one within their professional discipline and another in relation to their role in a multidisciplinary team. This may be a necessary and useful design, in which case people might need help in understanding how the different lines relate to each other. On the other hand, the design may have an unconscious defensive function, such as obscuring who is responsible for what, which can be both counterproductive and stressful.

Bringing the psychodynamic and systemic perspectives together helps us to see that authority is both *given* (by delegation, formal authority lines) and *taken* (interpreted by the role-holder) in light both of one's own psychological make-up and the culture of the system (Krantz and Maltz, 1997). Closely related to this is the question of how leadership is exercised. Is it entirely left with the most senior executives to provide leadership? Turquet (1974) proposes that in healthy creative teams, leadership can shift depending on who has what strengths to bring to bear on the situation in hand.

Role

All these concepts come together in the concept of role, where role is located at the intersection of person and organisation, as shown in Figure 14.4.

Role can be defined as 'the pattern of ideas in the mind by which one organizes one's behaviour in relation to a specific situation' (Grubb Institute, 1991: 8). Aspects of role are *given* by the employing organisation in the form of job descriptions, organisational charts, policies and so on. However, role (see the section on exercising authority and leadership above) is also *taken*: the person in role makes of it something personal, based on their skills, ideals, beliefs, unconscious relations with internalised past authority figures, and their understanding of what is required of them by the system in which they are located, and what is required of the system and themselves by the changing context.

As the pace of change has escalated since the mid-1980s, the capacity to read and interpret the wider context has become ever more essential. Figure 14.4 has therefore been expanded to include context, as shown in Figure 14.5 This version has been called the 'Transforming experience into action framework' because effective role-taking requires using and integrating

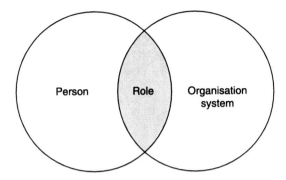

Figure 14.4 Role.

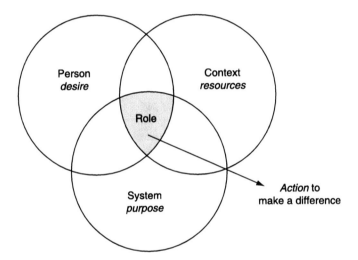

Figure 14.5 Transforming experience framework.

one's experience in all three areas – person, organisation/system, and context (Bazalgette et al., 2006). By adding this third element, the focus of taking action in a role shifts from outputs (what the organisation/system produces, as in Figures 14.2 and 14.3) to outcomes, defined as making a difference in the context.

Practice

It is easy to identify the goals of psychodynamic coaching by looking again at the typology of models of coaching (see Figure 14.1). Therapeutically-informed coaching will have as its core goal the development of personal insight by the client: to bring into conscious awareness what has previously been outside their awareness. They may for example develop insight into the drivers of repetitive patterns in their behaviour and interpersonal relations, and therefore be in a better position to choose to change these.

The primary goal of role consultancy is a better fit or alignment between the client's aspirations and abilities and the purposes of their organisational system. This includes the client having a deeper and broader understanding of their role: which system(s) or subsystem(s) they are in, which boundary or boundaries they are on, the sources of their authority and how they are using it, how well the organisational design of their role and system matches the requirements of the primary task, and so on. In addition, the client becomes more aware of systemic defensive processes of which they are a part, which makes for a greater level of choice about how they will act. They may of course also develop personal insights along the way, but these are not the primary goal of the coaching (see Figure 14.1).

Tools and techniques drawn from psychodynamic therapy

Bringing into view what is out of awareness

Psychodynamically informed therapies are based on bringing what has been unconscious into conscious awareness in order to bring about greater integration of the patient's self, or in Freud's terms, to enhance the capacity to love (to engage in meaningful and satisfying relationships) and to work (to be productive and creative). Techniques such as free association (the patient is encouraged to say whatever comes to mind without censoring) and analysing dreams make unconscious material available, and the therapist helps the patient to make integrating connections and gain insight through the use of interpretation. Core tools include working with transference and counter-transference (see earlier) as providing crucial information about the patient's inner world.

Psychodynamic coaching is clearly distinct from therapy. Clients are not patients, and coaches are not in the therapist role. On the whole, psycho-dynamic coaches do not deliberately attempt to surface deep unconscious material, nor do they directly interpret it. However, sessions are likely to be relatively unstructured compared to most other coaching techniques, in order to allow unforeseen connections to emerge. Less conscious material may also be surfaced through the use of drawings. (For an illustration of insight brought about through drawing, see Brunning (2001) and the second case study in this chapter.) The coach will not offer 'deep' interpretations of unconscious material, but is likely to offer hypotheses about what might be causing some of the client's difficulties. This may include the coach pointing out links of which the client was previously unaware, and encouraging the client to become curious about these – in other words, to enable them to become less rigidly defended.

What is transferred from therapeutic practice is not so much what psycho-dynamic coaches do but how they think and how they take up the coaching role. Key features include the following:

'Listening with the third ear'[1]

This is a particular kind of listening, not only to what is said but also to what is being communicated at other levels, in order to make new connections with the client. What is unsaid is not necessarily unconscious but may for some reason be unsayable. For example, a manager was talking angrily and defensively about a recent inspection of his service. He felt he could not say that he actually agreed with many of the criticisms in the inspection report. Subsequent exploration of why this felt too dangerous to say was very significant in changing a whole range of assumptions that had inhibited him from mobilising his full range of abilities at work.

Using one's own feelings as data

This is another kind of psychoanalytically informed listening, sometimes described as listening to 'the music behind the words' or 'parallel process'. It is based on the idea that the coach's feelings are not just their own, but may mirror the client's out-of-awareness emotional state, and therefore serve as essential information about what is going on under the surface. Some people listen to themselves in this way naturally, which may be the basis of intuition. However, it is also a skill that can be learned and practised, not only by coaches and therapists, but also by managers and others in the workplace, adding richly to the other sources of data on which they base their actions and decisions.

Providing containment and staying in role

In order for potentially disturbing unconscious thoughts and feelings to come to the surface, the client needs to feel safe. The therapeutic setting has a number of features to provide this safety, in particular the boundaries of fixed session times at a frequency that prevents the patient being excessively flooded by anxiety, boundaries around the relationship between patient and therapist, confidentiality, and the therapist's stance of total attention and careful non-judgemental listening with the sole object of assisting the patient to 'get better'. These together provide containment, that is, keep the client's anxieties at a tolerable level so that they are able to relax some habitual defences and thus become more available to learning something new.

---

1   This is Theodor Reik's term for describing a particular way of listening to patients' communications, again referring to listening for what is not necessarily put into words (Reik, 1948).

Psychodynamic coaching has different boundaries. The venue for meetings may change, sessions may take place at irregular intervals and so on. But the coach is attentive to the impact of these changes, and regardless of changes in the external environment, strives to stay in role throughout the work with the client. This includes remaining focused on understanding what is going on, even when the client is disengaged, denigrating or over-idealising the coach.

Clients' idealisation of their coach is potentially just as much of a threat to the coaching task as negativity: both can pull the coach out of role. When coaches are at the receiving end of negative projections, they may act out the feelings put into them rather than using them as information. When they have too glowing a rapport with their clients, they can become vulnerable to colluding unconsciously with the client in avoiding the difficult issues that need to be named and addressed.

The six domain model

As described above, systems-psychodynamics coaching takes account of the connections between person, role and organisation (P/R/O: see Figure 14.4). Brunning (2001, 2006) has developed a model of coaching practice called the 'six domain model', as illustrated in Figure 14.6.

In this version of the P/R/O model the three basic elements of person, role and organisation are opened up to also include more information about the client's personality, life story, set of skills, talents and competencies brought into the role. All six domains are considered to be contemporaneously present during the coaching sessions and any or all of them constitute a legitimate and appropriate focus of work. Figure 14.5 also identifies additional sources of expertise and knowledge that might inform or complement coaching; these feature in the diagram on the outside of each of the domains to which they relate.

The six domains are seen as being in continuous dynamic motion, as if they were a set of six interlinked cogwheels, each able to affect the movement of the neighbouring cogs. Thus, a disruption in the domain of 'current organisational role' is likely to affect the domain of 'life story' and vice versa. Each domain can influence others in ways that are either harmonious or disharmonious. For example, some personalities and some life stories might predispose a person-in-role to work more effectively or less effectively under different sets of external conditions and circumstances. This will be illustrated in the first case study in this chapter.

To practise within this model requires that the coach negotiate with the client relatively free access to relevant personal data and information so as to deepen the discourse that takes place within the coaching session. At the same time, it is crucial to be vigilant not to drift into providing psychotherapy instead of coaching and to ensure that the client is clear about this. It is not

Figure 14.6 The six domain model.

Sources: Brunning, 2001; Brunning, 2006.

uncommon for coaching clients to choose coaching as a less threatening option when at some level they 'know' they need psychotherapy and may be hoping the psychodynamic coach will provide this. In many such instances, referral for psychotherapy, either instead of, or in tandem with coaching may be the intervention of choice.

Tools and techniques used in role analysis

Thinking systemically

All of the tools described above are used in role consultancy. What is different is the assumption that whatever the presenting issue, it needs to be understood systemically. For example, psychodynamic coachees are often referred 'problem' individuals who are seen as the cause of difficulties in their organisation. As Obholzer (2003) puts it, it is absolutely essential to see individuals, or roles or subsets, as different but interconnected parts of the whole. Any 'individual' presentation thus always, and first and foremost, needs to be seen as a systemic symptom and addressed at that level.

(Obholzer, 2003: 156).

Organisation-in-the-mind

The essence of the practice of systems-psychodynamic coaching or role consultancy is to surface and articulate the client's internal model of the organisation: the client learns to become aware of and reflect on their emotional experience as crucial data. The coach is always alert to the organisationally determined dynamic in the client's material, whether the conversation is about a critical incident at work, a new strategy or project, or an anecdote apparently unrelated to the client's work preoccupations. The assumption is that whatever the client brings is at some level an echo or reflection of the organisation, and therefore relevant as a 'diagnostic' tool (Armstrong, 2005).

For example, if the coach invites the client to make a drawing of themselves (as a way of surfacing what is less conscious), they will see the drawing as representing something about the client's inner experience of themselves *in their organisational system*, and not just about the client's 'personal' internal world. The drawing is understood as providing data about 'organisation-in-the-mind', a term first used in organisational role analysis (ORA) at the Grubb Institute (as described earlier) and now widely used by practitioners of role consultancy and other systems-psychodynamics approaches to coaching.

Using experience as evidence

As organisation-in-the-mind comes ever more sharply into view, the client gains deeper understanding of their organisation as a system in a context, and an enhanced capacity for using the full range of their experience as a resource for understanding their own and others' behaviour. Coach and client together develop working hypotheses about what is going on, which the client then tests out in the workplace. There is thus an iterative process as the client moves back and forth between the organisation and the coaching sessions: the learning in each setting informs and feeds into learning in the other. Over several such cycles, the client also 'learns how to learn' in this new way: the process becomes internalised.

Which clients benefit most?

Peltier (2001) suggests that psychodynamic ideas can be extremely useful when the client wants to develop interpersonal skills, to enhance their self-understanding, to deal with 'difficult' subordinates, peers or bosses, and/or to overcome self-defeating behaviour. To this we would add that role consultancy, as a particular form of psychodynamic coaching, is particularly valuable in helping people discover what connections might exist under the surface between person/personality, the role and the organisational culture, so that they can both separate and link what is me and not-me, thus creating space for reflection and constructive action. Once this is achieved, there is a greater chance to enter into a conscious, rational and more determined pursuance of various professional options and to achieve congruence between self and role for the benefit of the organisational system.

For coaching from a systems-psychodynamic perspective to be delivered successfully, it is generally essential for there to be face-to-face interaction between coach and client. The work is likely at times to stir up difficult feelings as it taps into unconscious anxieties, and there is a risk with work at a distance (by telephone or email) that the coach may be unable to pick up vital clues about this, or to contain the client sufficiently. Distance coaching can also diminish the coach's ability to 'hear' unconscious communication. This said, email and telephone contact can provide essential continuity and containment under certain circumstances, as when the client's job requires frequent protracted travel.

Psychodynamic coaching has been used successfully in both the public and private sectors, for clients from all kinds of organisations from banking to hospitals, multinational corporations to schools and nurseries, and across all hierarchical levels from chief executives to front-line team leaders. It can help people with a wide variety of presenting issues, from 'difficult' colleagues to career progression, and is particularly relevant where there are issues around the exercise of authority and leadership.

It can also benefit young people, for example those having difficulty making the transition from school to work. However, role consultancy with its focus on role is relevant only in situations where the young person wishes or needs to explore and work on role issues. For most difficulties, children and adolescents are likely to get more appropriate help from coaching, counselling or therapy.

Regardless of age, the type of employing organisation, or the client's hierarchical position, psychodynamic coaching requires openness and a spirit of enquiry. The client who seeks a structured predictable approach to achieve pre-determined goals is likely to do better elsewhere. Indeed, both coach and client need to share the capacity to be curious and to tolerate 'not knowing' beforehand where the coaching journey will take them.

Case study 1: P/R/O in action

Karen was a senior manager in a public sector organisation. (The material described here comes from a real client. The client's permission has been obtained. Some details have been changed.) Karen referred herself for coaching in order to be able to take a critical look at her current role and to decide what she could do about her work in the immediate and longer term. The issue that bothered Karen in particular was a persistent lack of clarity about her current job description within her own organisation. Each time she attempted to address this with her line manager she ended up feeling more confused and nothing was ever resolved or clarified.

Given her under-defined role within the organisation and the autonomy usually expected of her profession, she had taken her own authority to redefine her own role to ensure that it was beneficial to her organisation, meeting the needs of the external customers, and based in her own areas of knowledge and expertise. As a result of this redefinition of her own role, she had begun to organise a number of training initiatives for external customers. These were appreciated and positively evaluated by all who attended, but were never formally acknowledged by her line manager.

During a hectic period of preparation for a training event for a hundred external participants, Karen felt yet again totally unsupported and isolated within her own organisation. As the deadline for the event approached, she worked excessively long hours on her own, without much administrative support. She felt overburdened and angry, but unable or unwilling to confront anybody within her own organisation. Despite the lack of support, the training event took place as planned and was a great success.

The second coaching session took place soon after this event. In listening to Karen's story, a seemingly small incident struck the coach as highly significant. On the surface, this was simply about a difference of opinion between Karen and her personal assistant (PA) concerning a crucial document that had apparently been lost on the computer. The PA protested that Karen must have deleted it herself; Karen on the other hand was convinced that she would never delete anything as vital as that particular document.

The word *deleted* suddenly became a metaphor for talking and thinking about a whole range of Karen's experiences and feelings. Karen realised that she felt 'deleted' within her organisation, just as her vital document had been deleted from the hard disk. Could it be that this tendency to 'delete' also existed in the third domain, namely *within Karen herself*, not just in her role or in the organisation? As the session progressed, Karen recognised that she had a tendency to 'delete' herself, ignoring her own needs and aspirations resulting in her not being sufficiently demanding of others in getting these met.

This presented a new perspective. There were now three overlapping domains in view in the coaching process – the person, the role and the organisation. In all three, the same imperative *to delete* was operating. Each domain was influencing and amplifying the other: Karen felt devalued, her talents were not being fully used, and her organisation seemed also to be using the 'delete' button by ignoring the successful training initiatives for which it was fast becoming well-known outside its own boundaries. At the same time, she could not value her own expertise and abilities enough either to renegotiate her role or to leave. Instead, she got stuck in an endless repetition of the dynamic as the interplay of person, structure and culture locked her into a position of being overworked and undervalued.

Discovering this overlap opened up a number of options for Karen, including:

- asking her line manager for specific feedback about the conference
- requesting a 360-degree appraisal as a way of gathering further evidence to support or disconfirm her new insight
- renegotiating her job description in such a way that her training work would be more clearly recognised and sanctioned
- or alternatively taking steps to find another job.

It is important to note that the coach deliberately chose not to explore in depth the reasons *why* Karen had developed a tendency to 'delete' her own needs and why she allowed others to do this to her: this is clearly the domain of personal therapy. For the purpose of coaching it was sufficient that the existence of this tendency was now within her conscious awareness, freeing her to address her current situation and longer-term career needs more effectively.

Of course, Karen had been to some extent aware of this tendency before she came for coaching, but she had not realised until now how significant this tendency was in maintaining her work-related difficulties, nor how profoundly it resonated with the prevailing organisational culture so that she felt deleted in her professional role.

Discussion

Whenever the same issue or dynamic is expressed simultaneously in all three P/R/O domains, there is a greater likelihood that the client will be unduly affected by their work role and will experience less freedom do anything constructive about their situation. This is due to the heavy unconscious fusion between the *me* (the person-in-role) and the *non-me* (the role-in-the-organisation) and the attendant difficulties of separating what belongs to the person and what belongs to the organisation. Once the personal element is recognised and owned, it becomes easier for the client to begin to separate the other two elements (the role and the organisation) from this heady fusion, to look at the inter-connections more dispassionately and to recover the capacity to act with authority on their own behalf and to the benefit of their organisation.

Case study 2: Role analysis

Gerald was a senior manager in a public sector organisation. He felt his successes were ignored by his line manager, Keith, who often stopped his initiatives from going forward. Gerald came to coaching partly to think about career development and about leaving his present job.

Over the previous 18 months, the culture of the organisation had changed radically from being mission-driven to being target-focused. Keith had been in post just over a year, and to Gerald and his team embodied everything they hated about the changes. Meetings with Keith focused almost entirely on how to achieve the government-imposed targets. In the first coaching session, Gerald remarked, 'I am more interested in making things happen than in targets', as if these two things were necessarily mutually exclusive. He saw Keith as repeatedly trying to 'kill off' his ideas. When the coach asked him to draw his work-system with himself in it, Gerald drew a picture of himself and his team at the hub of what looked like a wheel, the spokes being lines between the team and the external stake-holders. Neither Keith nor the rest of the directorate were in the picture. Might Gerald also be doing some 'killing off'? The lines in the picture looked like spears flying inward and outward: Gerald's organisation-in-the-mind seemed to be of an isolated group under siege.

In the second coaching meeting, Gerald talked about a 'crushing' email he had received from Keith, full of criticism of a recent decision he had made which he had thought was quite innovative. He contrasted this with his experience of his previous line manager who 'valued my delinquent creative bits'. It was as if creativity and delinquency (e.g. resisting being controlled by performance targets) were one and the same. As Gerald and the coach read the email together, it became apparent that the underlying complaint was that Keith had not been involved. The coach then invited Gerald to imagine he were Keith: what might Keith say about Gerald to a close colleague or friend? 'That man is a loose cannon, just does his own thing and ignores me. I never know what he's up to. And it's my head on the block if we don't meet these b****y targets.' The picture was shifting. Keith now emerged not simply as a force to squash Gerald, but also as frightened of him and the damage he might do. And for the first time, there was a hint that Keith was not happy about the targets either.

Gerald had arrived at the session very worried about a meeting with Keith scheduled for the next day, unsure whether or not to present his latest initiative. He could imagine only two scenarios: either he would share his ideas and Keith would crush them; or he would keep his ideas to himself and the initiative would 'get unravelled' later. In an attempt to find a third way, the coach wondered what might happen if he went into the meeting with a blank sheet of paper and did some brainstorming with Keith. Gerald was sceptical but agreed to try this. Afterwards, he described the meeting with amazement. Keith had covered the blank sheet with ideas in many colours. He had been full of an energy Gerald had never seen before. The final shape of the initiative was very little different from what Gerald had wanted to do in the first place, but Keith saw it as radically different and was backing it whole-heartedly. Not only did Gerald now have his manager's support, but also he had discovered a new side to him, a genuine passion for the 'real work' of the organisation.

Over the remaining coaching sessions, Gerald shifted his energy from resisting Keith to thinking about how his own passions and interpretation of the aims of his department contributed – *and could be seen to contribute* – to the aims of the directorate. Rather than putting his energy into keeping others out, Gerald started having conversations not only with Keith but also with other departmental managers about the vision and purposes of the work they were doing. Gradually a number of people began to recover a sense of meaning which had got drowned by the tide of recent government directives.

Gerald's thinking about his next career move also changed. Whereas before his primary objective had been to find a job under a boss who would support and value his delinquency and creativity, it now became important to find an organisation whose core purpose might give more scope for doing the kind of work that mattered most to him. Leaving his present job no longer felt urgent, but at the same time he realised that his deepest aspirations and desires required a different arena.

Discussion

In psychodynamic terms, one could understand the change as a shift in the projective system. The two tasks of the directorate – meeting targets and doing meaningful work that made a positive difference to clients – had been split. This split was a system-wide defence, acted out by Gerald and Keith, the one becoming more and more 'delinquent' as the other became more and more rigid and bureaucratic. This working hypothesis, developed during the coaching sessions, could then be tested in the workplace. Once a space opened for Keith to get back in touch with his own passion for the work – and for Gerald to share some responsibility for meeting targets – the whole system became more integrated and creative.

Although insight played a part, the shift was prompted largely by attention to systemic elements and to organisation-in-the-mind. Gerald's drawing indicated he had lost his boundary position: he was in touch with what was inside (the work of his team) and with the external world (the needs of clients and the community), but he had obliterated the rest of the organisation. As a result, he had restricted his role to fighting for the good of the clients and protecting his team's autonomy, ignoring the performance targets. This put the survival of the directorate at risk, and in the longer term therefore also threatened its capacity to continue to benefit clients. Bringing the missing bits of the organisation into view was a crucial first step. As Gerald worked at redefining the core purpose of his own subsystem and how it connected with that of other parts of the organisation, new conversations became possible at work. He was able to exercise leadership beyond his own team, by engaging with others to forge some essential connections which had been lost as a result of the anxieties stirred up by the rising level of government control.

Comment

As can be seen from these case studies, the outcomes of psychodynamic/ systems-psychodynamic coaching in terms of options opened up for the client are not always very different from those of other coaching methods. What is distinctive about psychodynamic coaching is that it focuses on helping the client to address, understand and harness some of the unconscious drivers of their situation. When the systems-psychodynamics perspective is added, the client is helped to make links between the organisational dynamic and structures, their personal dynamic and the wider context. This makes it possible for them to 're-imagine' their role. (For a discussion of reimagining one's role and organisation, with case studies illustrating the centrality of reflective thinking as an activity of management, see Hutton, 1997.)

Acknowledgements

This chapter draws extensively on two previously published chapters: V. Z. Roberts (2004) Psychodynamic approaches: organisational health and effectiveness. In E. Peck (ed.) *Organisational Development in Healthcare: Approaches, innovations, achievements.* Abingdon, UK: Radcliffe; and V. Z. Roberts and M. Jarrett (2006) What is the difference and what makes the difference: a comparative study of psychodynamic and non-psychodynamic approaches to executive coaching. In H. Brunning (ed.) *Executive Coaching: Systems-Psychodynamic Perspective.* London: Karnac. By express permission of the respective publishers to reprint in part the previously published work and associated diagrams.

References

Armstrong, D. (2005) *Organization-in-the-Mind*. London: Karnac.

Bazalgette, J., Irvine, B. and Quine, C. (2006) The absolute in the present. In A. Mathurd (ed.) *Dare to Think the Unthought Known?* Tampere, Finland: Aivoairut.

Brunning, H. (2001) The six domains of executive coaching. *Journal of Organizational and Social Dynamics* 1(2): 254–263.

Brunning, H. (ed.) (2006) *Executive Coaching: Systems-Psychodynamic Perspective*. London: Karnac.

Freud, A. (1966) *The Ego and the Mechanisms of Defence*. New York: International Universities Press.

Grubb Institute (1991) *Professional Management: Notes prepared by the Grubb Institute on concepts relating to professional management*. London: Grubb Institute.

Hutton, J. (1997) Re-imagining the organisation of an institution: management in human service institutions. In E. Smith (ed.) *Integrity and Change*. London: Routledge.

Jacques, E. (1953) The dynamics of social structure: a contribution to the psychoanalytical study of social phenomena deriving from the views of Melanie Klein. *Human Relations* 6: 3–24. Reprinted in E. Trist and H. Murray (eds) (1990) *The Social Engagement of Social Science*. Volume 1, *The Socio-psychological Perspective*. London: Free Association Books.

Krantz, J. and Maltz, M. (1997) A framework for consulting to organizational role. *Consulting Psychology Journal* 49(2): 137–151.

Lewin, K. (1947) Frontiers in group dynamics, Parts I and II. *Human Relations* 1: 5–41; 2: 143–153.

Miller, E. J. and Rice, A. K. (1967) *Systems of Organisation: The control of task and sentient boundaries*. London: Tavistock.

Newton, J., Long, S. and Sievers, B. (eds) (2006) *Coaching in Depth: The organisational role analysis approach*. London: Karnac.

Obholzer, A. (2003) Some reflections on concepts of relevance to consulting and also to the management of organisations. *Organisational and Social Dynamics Journal* 3(1): 153–164.

Peltier, B. (2001) *The Psychology of Executive Coaching: Theory and application*. London: Brunner-Routledge.

Reed, B. (1976) Organisational role analysis. In C. L. Cooper (ed.) *Developing Social Skills in Managers*. London: Macmillan.

Reed, B. and Bazalgette, J. (2003) Organizational role analysis at the Grubb Institute of Behavioural Studies: origins and development. In J. Newton, S. Long and B. Sievers (eds) *Coaching in Depth: The organisational role analysis approach*. London: Karnac.

Reik, T. (1948) *Listening with the Third Ear*. New York: Pyramid.

Rice, A. (1963) *The Enterprise and its Environment*. London: Tavistock.

Roberts, V. Z. (2004) Psychodynamic approaches: organisational health and effectiveness. In E. Peck (ed.) *Organisational Development in Healthcare: Approaches, innovations, achievements*. Abingdon, UK: Radcliffe.

Roberts, V. Z. and Jarrett, M. (2006) What is the difference and what makes the difference: a comparative study of psychodynamic and non-psychodynamic

approaches to executive coaching. In H. Br   *aching:*
Systems-Psychodynamic Perspective. London:

Trist, E. and Murray, H. (eds) (1990) *The Soc*   *Science,*
Volume 1. London: Free Association Books.

Turquet, P. (1974) Leadership: the individual   Colman
and M. H. Geller (eds) *Group Relations Lea*   K. Rice
Institute, 1985.

Discussion points

- How would you ensure that you practise systems-psychodynamic coaching instead of psychotherapy?
- How will you ensure that you pay attention to the person, the role and the organisational system instead of privileging just one of the domains while coaching?
- How can you understand and honour the origins of this approach without critiquing the entire psychoanalytic theory?

Suggested reading

Armstrong, D. (2005) *The Organisation-in-the-Mind.* London: Karnac. The Tavistock Clinic Series.

Further exploration of the concept of organisation-in-the-mind, illustrated with numerous case studies of coaching and other applications of the concept in work with individuals and organisations, developed by the author over 30 years, first at the Grubb Institute and later at the Tavistock Consultancy Service.

Brunning, H. (ed.) (2006) *Executive Coaching: Systems-Psychodynamic Perspective.* London: Karnac.

This book examines the ecology, anatomy and applications of the systems-psychodynamic approach to coaching.

Hutton, J., Bazalgette, J. and Reed, B. (1997) Organisation-in-the-mind. In J. E. Neumann, K. Kellner and A. Dawson-Shepperd (eds) *Developing Organizational Consultancy.* London: Routledge.

Clear exposition of the origins, development and use of organisation-in-the-mind in organisational role analysis (a form of systems-psychodynamic coaching) as developed by the Grubb Institute, with a case study and guidelines for coaches and consultants.

Newton, J., Long, S. and Sievers, B. (eds) (2006) *Coaching in Depth: The organisational role analysis approach.* London: Karnac.

This book provides an excellent overview of the history, theoretical developments, applications and practice of organisational role analysis internationally, illustrated with numerous case studies.

Obholzer, A. and Roberts V. Z. (eds) (1994) The *Unconscious at Work: Individual and organizational stress in the human services.* London: Routledge.

A good introduction to group and organisational dynamics and how these affect people. The first four chapters unpack the conceptual framework used in this chapter in accessible language; later chapters illustrate how theory from psychoanalysis, group relations and open systems can illuminate complex and painful dynamics at work. The book is illustrated with numerous vignettes.

Chapter 15

Solution-focused coaching

Bill O'Connell and Stephen Palmer

Introduction

Solution-focused coaching (SFC) is an outcome-oriented, competence-based approach. It helps clients to achieve their preferred outcomes by evoking and co-constructing solutions to their problems. SFC fits perfectly with the future-focused, goal-directed spirit of coaching. Rather than problem-solve, the solution-focused coach gives centre stage to the skills, strengths, knowledge and experience of the client. The coach's role is to stretch, clarify, support and empower clients to design and implement solutions which will work for them. It is a practical approach which enhances client cooperation by focusing clearly on their agendas. The relationship between coaches and clients is a transparent one as the coach explains the techniques to the client, in the hope that he or she will take them away and use them for themselves. It is a focused, respectful and progressive method which gains beneficial results in a short period of time. SFC has won an international following since the late 1990s.

Development of solution-focused coaching

It is difficult to identify a single founder of the solution-focused approach although its historical influences include Alfred Adler, Milton Erickson and John Weakland (O'Connell, 2003). The solution-focused approach originated in the field of family therapy. It was developed by a team of family therapists working at the Brief Therapy Centre in Milwaukee, USA in the 1980s. The leaders were Steve de Shazer and Insoo Kim Berg, both of whom became prolific writers on the approach, as well as expert practitioners. Other leaders include Bill O'Hanlon, a therapist in Nebraska. Families often presented with multiple and complex problems. Family members would argue among themselves about what exactly was the problem and who was to blame. This took up a lot of time. In such an atmosphere of conflict and hostility, family members understandably became defensive, and as a result, were typically unable or unwilling to make personal changes. Observing this unproductive stand-off led to the team changing tack. Instead of trying to create a consensus around the family's problems, the team tried instead to find agreement around what the solutions would look like. They asked each family member how they would know the situation had improved – what would they notice that was different? Taking this as a starting point, the team found that families spent less time arguing over their problems. The therapists discovered that when they encouraged family members to notice times when things went better, the family made more progress faster. As the family focused more on 'solutions,' they became less trapped in the problem vicious circle (see de Shazer et al., 1986).

Since those early days, solution-focused thinking and practice has won a vast international following among a wide range of practitioners who adapt its principles and techniques to their contexts and client groups (e.g. Berg and Miller, 1992; Lethem, 1994; LaFountain and Garner, 1996; Selekman, 1997; Triantafillou, 1997; Hoyt and Berg, 1998; George et al., 1999; Darmody, 2003; Devlin, 2003; Grant, 2003; Hawkes, 2003; Hoskisson, 2003; Norman, 2003; O'Connell and Palmer, 2003; Sharry, 2003; Bloor and Pearson, 2004; Berg and Szabo, 2005; Meier, 2005; Jackson and McKergow, 2007) including:

- education – tutoring, mentoring and teaching
- coaching, counselling, mediation, advice and guidance
- children
- mental health
- sexual trauma
- substance misuse
- social work
- psychology
- parent training
- support groups
- supervision
- reflecting teams
- business and management
- organisational change
- team coaching and development.

It is used extensively with groups, teams, couples and families, and young people and children (see O'Connell and Palmer, 2003). Many coaches have discovered the relevance of the solution-focused approach for themselves. Some use solution-focused techniques as one strand in their practice, others have integrated it with the cognitive behavioural approach (Green et al., 2006) while others use it as their core model (Berg and Szabo, 2005).

Theory and basic concepts

In its purest sense, the solution-focused approach is light on theory. It aims to be minimalist in its concepts and interventions following Occam's principle that 'it is vain to do with more what can be achieved with fewer' (see Russell, 1996: 462–463). This minimalism leads the coach to join with what is already working in the client's life, rather than feel it is necessary to start with a blank sheet. The client is already doing many things which are constructive and helpful: 'if it isn't broken, don't fix it.' It may be a case of simply doing more of what works. A strategy of building upon the client's customised set of problem-solving 'signature' strategies is likely to be more effective than importing a strategy that is foreign to the client. Cooperating with the client's goals and values ensures that solutions fit the person not the problem. SFC focuses on clients' resources, strengths and personal qualities. It assumes that:

- It is possible to help clients construct solutions with minimal, if any, analysis of their problems.
- Clients have many resources and competences, of many of which they, and others, are unaware. Most people do not use a fraction of their potential.
- Clients have many ideas about their preferred futures. 'Multi-problem' clients can be viewed as 'multi-goal' clients.
- Clients are already carrying out constructive and helpful actions (otherwise the situation would be worse!).
- Although we clearly carry our past with us and need to learn from our mistakes and successes, the principal focus in solution-focused work is on the client's present and preferred future. Our history can remind us of how far we have travelled and how we have overcome difficulties along the way. Learning the lessons of history can also warn us of the re-emergence of old problems.
- Sometimes it helps to try and understand the causes of problems, but it is not always essential or even helpful. Searching for causes can lead to a search for someone or something to blame. Arguing over the causes of a problem can lead to self-justifying behaviour and further escalation of the situation. Some forms of analysis make it more difficult to be hopeful about the future.

Solution-focused coaches do not put their own spin upon their clients' experiences. They do not presume to know how to fix something that has gone wrong. Instead they help their clients to become more aware of how they succeeded when they got it 'right'. Their question to their clients is, 'What was the difference that made the difference?'

The coach also asks the client, 'What difference will it make to you when you achieve your goal?' This is followed up with a further question, 'And what difference will that make for you?' This line of questioning can help clients to clarify their choices and priorities and identify steps towards achieving their goal.

The coach listens and acknowledges the client's problems while aiming to contain 'problem talk'. People often want and need to get things off their chest, particularly if they feel isolated and misunderstood. It is important that the coach acknowledges and validates people's concerns and feelings, while looking for an opportunity to move respectfully from 'problem talk' to 'solution talk'. At different times people will feel the need to explain their problem situation in more detail. If the coach is dismissive of 'negative' talk and pushes the client towards 'positive thinking', the client will resist and sabotage the coach's efforts. It is worth remembering, however, that clients often also have solutions to get off their chests. They will have their own ideas about improving the situation and need the opportunity to explore them with someone else. A wise coach will always listen carefully to the client's ideas and where possible cooperate with the client's preferences.

Just as people tend to repeat the 'same old' problems, they also tend to use a limited repertoire of well-tried strategies to solve them. Some of these will be failed solutions. The client adopts them even knowing they do not work, simply because he or she cannot think of anything else to try – in the words of Oscar Wilde, 'a triumph of hope over experience!' They will do this ignoring the fact that on the whole, 'If you always do what you've always done, you'll always get what you've got.' A solution-focused approach encourages the client to break out of such unhelpful patterns and 'do something different'. Working in a solution-focused way means that the coach and the client cooperate in searching for 'signature' solutions which are relevant and customised to the client.

To find solutions that fit the client the coach has to keep out of the client's way. By this we mean that the coach facilitates, but does not interfere with or take over, the client's unique solution-building processes. Providing solutions, especially formulaic ones, can feel like a helpful thing to do in the short term, but in the long run it undermines the client's confidence and increases dependency.

Solution-focused coaches encourage clients to switch the focus of their attention from 'seeing' mainly problems, to noticing when, and how, constructive and positive events happen in their lives. They can choose to see half-empty or half-full glasses for example. They can choose to dwell on a mistake they made or they can study how they were successful the rest of the time and how they might have acted differently when things went wrong. The more people become solution-sensitive, the more they become aware of solutions that are available to them.

Solution-focused coaches ask their clients to focus upon

- their hopes for the short and the long term
- how they manage to make exceptions to problems happen
- their skills, qualities and strengths – their resources
- the first steps they need to take
- the strategies they will use to achieve progress.

Solution-focused coaches see clients as the experts in their lives. They privilege clients' 'insider' knowledge above 'professional' expertise. The professionals cannot possibly know what the 'right' solutions for clients are. Solutions need to fit clients, not the problem. As Greene and Grant (2003) state:

> At its best, solution-focused coaching enables people to access and use the wealth of experience, skills, expertise and intuition that we all have. It allows people to find individual and creative solutions to the situation they find themselves in, both at work and in their personal lives.
>
> (Greene and Grant, 2003: 23)

Solution-focused coaches help clients to develop a language and an attitude which will motivate, empower and support them in achieving their goals. Solution-focused conversations stress the competence, skills and qualities that clients can use to achieve their preferred futures. Their tone is optimistic, hopeful and respectful. They heighten clients' awareness that change is always taking place and that they have the capacity to determine, at least to some extent, the direction of change.

Generally there is not a great emphasis on exploring psychological theory in the training of solution-focused practitioners. However, self-directed learning and self-regulation are usually considered as important aspects of the solution-focused approach as the theories explain how coaches are helped to attain their goals (Grant, 2006a). Grant (2006b: 158) states that, 'goal setting is the foundation of successful self-regulation and effective coaching'. This assertion can be supported by the research of Latham and Yukl (1975), Locke (1996) and Rawsthorne and Elliot (1999) which highlighted how important goal setting is to the coaching process when they examined published studies that reported on the relationship between goal setting and performance outcomes. However, more recently Scoular and Linley (2006) have challenged the 'sacred cows' of coaching and goal-setting. Their study used an experimental between-subjects design (N=117) with goal-setting and non-goal-setting conditions. They found that that there was no significant difference between the two conditions but personality difference was found to be statistically significant; when the coach and coachee differed on temperament the outcome scores were higher.

Practice

The relationship

The interventions described below take place within the context of a respectful, egalitarian, collaborative relationship, in which the client is regarded as the expert. The coach's role is not to offer solutions, give advice or provide pathology-laden insight (O'Connell, 2003; Grant, 2006b). The role is more of a facilitator who, through a process of supportive questioning and reflection, enables clients to tap into their own resources and realise that they have a reservoir of skills, strengths and strategies which are relevant to their current challenges.

Listening attentively, keeping the client on solution-track, reflecting back the client's competence, promoting the client's use of the imagination, summarising the client's unique set of strategies – these are the key contributions of the solution-focused coach. Technique does not make a coach solution-focused. It is the quality of the relationship underpinned by solution-focused values that makes someone truly solution-focused.

Skills and strategies

Pre-session change

When the client first requests a coaching session he or she will be asked to notice any changes that take place prior to the first appointment (O'Connell, 2003). In the first session many clients report that they have contained or even improved their situation. This gives the session a strong, positive opening in which the client's resources and strategies are centre stage. It gives the coach and the client a platform on which to build.

Problem-free talk

At the beginning of the first session coaches also give clients the opportunity to talk about themselves and their interests, without reference to their problems (O'Connell, 2003). These conversations often uncover information which is helpful to the coach in knowing

- how to work with the client
- which metaphors or examples will work for the client
- client strengths, qualities and values pertinent to solution construction.

Problem-free talk also highlights the fact that there is a lot more to the client than any difficulties he or she may be experiencing.

Competence seeking

While acknowledging the difficulties which clients face, solution-focused coaches pay particular attention to examples of their competence (O'Connell, 2003). The skilled coach senses the right time to draw to the awareness of the client the strengths and qualities they have and invite reflection on how they can be applied in the current situation. When done sensitively clients will own their skills and strengths, but when coaches oversell positive feedback clients are more likely to reject this rosy picture as one they do not recognise.

Building on exceptions

Instead of dwelling upon the times when clients experience problems, solution-focused coaches question them about times when they are managing the problems better. These episodes are described as 'exceptions'. Exceptions can always be found because everyone has highs and lows, ups and downs, good and bad times (O'Connell, 2001, 2003). Exceptions provide evidence of clients' constructive strategies. By highlighting and exploring these times, clients can find how to make these exceptions happen more often or for longer. The coach gently explores with the client the circumstances in which the exception took place. He or she may use questions such as, 'How did you do that? What was the first thing you did? How did you know that was going to be useful? What would need to happen for you to be able to do that again?' Exceptions follow the solution-focused principle of 'if it works keep doing it'.

The miracle question

The miracle question, devised by Steve de Shazer (1988) and his colleagues, is an intervention used by solution-focused coaches to help clients bypass 'problem talk'. It does this by encouraging clients to use their imagination to describe how their day-to-day lives would look if their problems did not dominate or define them. Its standard form is:

> Imagine one night when you are asleep, a miracle happens and the problems we've been discussing disappear. Since you are asleep, you do not know that a miracle has happened. When you wake up what will be the first signs for you that a miracle has happened?

The question is a powerful one, as it accesses imaginative material not usually unearthed by conventional questioning (O'Connell, 1998). A skilled coach follows up the miracle question by further questions closely linked to the client's answers. Each answer builds another part of the client's preferred scenario and helps to clarify strategies the client could use. As the coach explores the client's miracle answer he or she will be listening for any examples of exceptions – times when even a small part of the miracle has already happened. The coach will also listen for evidence of the client's strengths, qualities and competence. Questions will also include other significant people in the client's life, 'How will they know the miracle has happened? What will they notice that is different? How will they respond to that?'

Scaling

Coaches use a scale of zero to ten to help clients measure progress; to set small identifiable goals and to develop strategies (see O'Connell, 2001, 2003; Greene and Grant, 2003; Berg and Szabo, 2005; Grant, 2006a). Ten on the scale represents 'the best it could be' and zero the worst (Palmer et al., 2007). Coaches invite clients to think about their place on the scale by asking questions such as, 'Where would you say you were a day or two ago? What was happening when you were higher on the scale? Where do you hope to get to in the next few weeks? What needs to happen for that to happen?' Clients may also consider where other people would put them on the scale. Solution-focused coaches encourage clients to consider small steps they can take which will move them one point up the scale. This is consistent with the solution-focused principle that 'small changes can lead to big changes'. It is often the case that when clients commit to making small changes they build a momentum ('get on a roll') which takes them much further than they had originally planned. When things are difficult the best a client can do may be to work hard to stay on the same point on the scale. Scaling is a simple, practical technique which clients can use between sessions to measure their progress and to plan their next steps.

Between-session tasks

During the session solution-focused questions will usually have drawn out what the client is going to do next to improve matters. These tasks will more often than not follow the principles:

- If it works keep doing it.
- If it doesn't work stop doing it.
- Small steps can lead to big changes.
- Do something different.

Feedback

At the end of a session the coach gives brief feedback to the client. This follows a clear and simple structure:

- Appreciative feedback specifying helpful contributions made by the client in the session.
- A summary of the client's achievements as evidenced in the session.
- A link made between these and the client's stated goals.
- Agreement on what the client is going to do before the next meeting – the between-session task.

REFRAMING

By using the technique of reframing, coaches help coachees to find other ways of looking at a problem or issue (O'Connell, 2000). Other perspectives of the problem may enable the coachee to overcome the problem.

LETTER WRITING

Some solution-focused coaches write to their clients after each session summarising what was said in the closing feedback. They may also encourage clients to keep journals or diaries which capture those times when they overcame a problem or made positive changes. This record becomes a memory bank of solutions to be drawn upon in difficult times. Clients can continue to use solution-focused techniques on themselves by recording answers to scaling and miracle questions.

Which clients benefit most?

Generally most coachees in solution-focused coaching make progress. It is suitable for children, adults, couples, work teams, groups and older people. Individuals with clinical disorders may benefit from receiving solution-focused therapy or other forms of therapy such as cognitive behaviour therapy instead of coaching. Therapy can work in parallel with coaching if the therapist focuses on the clinical disorder such as anxiety whereas the coach focuses on a life or work-related issue. However, in these circumstances, the coach or coaching psychologist would benefit from having an understanding of clinical disorders. For example, depressed clients may feel overwhelmed and suicidal by the goals developed in the coaching session. This would be contra-indicated and considered iatrogenic.

Where solution-focused coaching does not work the reasons may include:

- poor skills-level of the coach
- inconsistent use of the approach by the coach
- coachees temporarily unable to tap into their resources
- coachees looking for a 'quick fix' and unwilling to put any effort into achieving the changes desired
- coachees with such poor levels of self-esteem unable to appreciate their strengths and qualities
- coachees wanting a deeper understanding of the roots of their problem
- coachees wanting the coach to be directive and a problem-solver.

If coachees are in the pre-contemplative stage of change (see Prochaska and DiClemente, 1992), then they may not be ready for coaching. This would become apparent during coaching when the client is ambivalent towards developing goals and undertaking any in-between session tasks. However, they may change during the first couple of coaching sessions or may benefit from returning to coaching sometime later.

Case study

Colin (35) was a team leader in a large company. When he came for coaching he presented as a genuine, warm, conscientious and intelligent person. Since his promotion six months previously, he had come to relish his new role – managing, supporting colleagues, troubleshooting, generating new ideas, chairing meetings and contributing to the development of policy.

However, one aspect of his new post caused him a great deal of anxiety – his performance at the monthly senior management meeting. He perceived the atmosphere as pushy and competitive and this intimidated him. For most of the time he kept quiet and hoped to avoid being put on the spot. When he did speak he felt that he was ignored. This experience of being marginalised was affecting his confidence. He felt bullied by some of the powerful members of the group and found it hard to stand his ground. He was beginning to see himself as a failure, letting his own team down by representing them ineffectually to management. When he reported to them that he had failed to raise their issues at the meeting, he felt he was losing credibility as a leader.

He dreaded the management meeting. He would toss and turn in his sleep the night before (often compounded by being disturbed by his 2-year-old child). On meeting mornings he felt sick and panicky on the journey to work. He described himself as, 'feeling like a nervous wreck' after these meetings.

When Colin came for coaching the coach acknowledged how difficult these management meetings were for him. Instead of asking for more details of his behaviour at the meetings Colin was surprised to be asked about his strengths as a team leader. In relation to his own team Colin felt that he came across as 'a hard worker, confident, supportive, enthusiastic'. When asked about how friends outside of work would describe him he said, 'loyal, caring, interested in others'. These opening exchanges began to put Colin's situation into context. It was only in the particular circumstances of the management meeting he found it difficult to be himself.

In fact he had many personal and social resources. He was able to describe non-work occasions when he showed that he could be assertive – for example in negotiating with the builders doing an extension in his house. When asked if he had ever had to deal with a similar situation to the one he currently faced at work, he remembered a time in another company when he had to challenge a senior member of staff who was making unreasonable demands of him. He had found that very difficult to do and had to 'psyche himself up' before doing it.

In relation to his resources the coach asked him, 'Which quality or strength do you have that would be really helpful if you could use it in the management meeting?' His answer was that he was normally a 'clear communicator'. This led into a discussion about what he does to make his communications clear. In relation to the meeting he thought that he would be communicating clearly when he

- offered his opinion on a subject early in the meeting
- asked a relevant question
- presented the team issue
- kept ownership of his ideas.

Rather than the coach give him tips on how he could do this, he asked him, 'Has there been a time in the meetings when you have done any of this?' The answer was hardly ever, but he did recall one occasion when he backed up a colleague who was under pressure. He had managed to say what he wanted and had kept to this point even when others disagreed. The coach also asked him 'Is there anything that you are doing in the meeting at the moment that you think it would be helpful to stop doing?' Colin said he could stop engaging in behaviours which put him in a subordinate position – 'I could stop sitting out of the Chairperson's line of vision and stop pouring out the coffee for everyone at the break.'

Using the solution-focused intervention known as the miracle question, the coach invited Colin to imagine that something amazing happened when he was asleep one night, a miracle if you like – and this miracle was that he was given the ability to perform well at the next management meeting. As he was asleep at the time he didn't know this had happened. So when he woke up on the day of the next management meeting, how would he begin to find out that something amazing had happened?'

In answering this and follow up questions the following picture emerged:

> I would be calmer when I woke up as I would have had a better night's sleep. I'd dress smartly. I would listen to my music on the way to work rather than think about how awful the meeting was going to be. I would have prepared what I was going to say about the team issue. I would remind myself that I am as good as anyone else at the meeting. I'd do some relaxed breathing before going into the meeting. In the meeting I would sit in a position where I can see and be seen. I would say something early on at the meeting- just to make my presence felt. I wouldn't look so worried, I'd be more relaxed.

Colin's answer to the miracle question led to the development of a plan. He decided to

- talk to his partner about not having any overnight baby duties the night before the management meeting
- make better preparation for the meeting – especially by thinking what he was going to say about the team issue
- take his iPod to work with him
- change where he sits in the meeting
- attempt to say something in the meeting early on, even if only to ask a question.

In the feedback at the end of the session the coach reminded Colin about his repertoire of skills as a team leader. He had proved to management that he was promotion material. He had lots of ideas for improving his performance in the management meeting. The coach expressed his confidence in Colin's ability to transfer his skills from one context to another.

When Colin returned for his second coaching session a fortnight later, the focus was on any changes which might have taken place since last they met. Colin reported that he had still felt anxious in the management meeting he had attended, but that he had succeeded in raising his team's issue. The coach was curious how Colin had managed to do this. Colin's view was that he had pushed himself to raise it because he kept thinking how disappointed his team would be if he had to tell them he had again failed to do so. He had also felt better going into the meeting because he had had a good night's sleep the previous night as the result of him having an undisturbed night. He had also carried out his plan to listen to music on the way to work and divert his mind from worrying about the day ahead.

In developing these solutions further the coach asked Colin a scaling question.

Coach: On a scale of 0 to 10, with ten being everything is fine and 0 really bad, where do you think you are now with the management meeting?
Colin: Three.
Coach: What makes you say three rather than two?
Colin: I think that I have begun to think about it differently. It's not a good meeting for me to think creatively in: it's too competitive. I need to adapt to this and find my own way of handling it.
Coach: So in your view what do you need to do to keep at three or even move to a four?
Colin: One thing I am going to do is to speak to my colleague Emma. She

feels the same about the meetings as I do but she seems to have found a way of handling it.

Coach: What else would need to happen for you to get to four?

Colin: Having seen the team's reaction when they heard I got a result for them at the management meeting; that will really keep me going forward.

Further discussion led to Colin formulating his plan for the next step that will move him up the scale. There may be setbacks along the way, but the coach will continue to encourage Colin to play to his strengths, to notice times when he achieves what he wants to achieve and to learn from his experiences. Many of the interventions the coach uses are those which he will encourage Colin to use himself:

- to notice times when he does something positive in the meeting and become aware how he did it
- to set small goals for himself which are achievable
- to use scaling to measure his progress and to identify the next step forward
- to train himself to use his resources and imagination to devise solutions which work for him.

Over a period of time Colin became more confident and assertive in the management meetings and his stock continued to rise as a team leader. Although attending management meetings continued to be the least liked part of his job, he felt that he was doing himself and his team justice.

References

Berg, I. K. and Miller, S. D. (1992) *Working with the Problem Drinker: A solution-focused approach.* New York: W. W. Norton.

Berg, I. K. and Szabo, P. (2005) *Brief Coaching for Lasting Solutions.* New York: W. W. Norton.

Bloor, R. and Pearson, D. (2004) Brief solution-focused organizational redesign: a model for international mental health consultancy. *International Journal of Mental Health* 33(2): 44–53.

Darmody, M. (2003) A solution-focused approach to sexual trauma. In B. O'Connell and S. Palmer (eds) *Handbook of Solution-Focused Therapy.* London: Sage.

De Shazer, S. (1988) *Clues: Investigating solutions in brief therapy.* New York: W. W. Norton.

De Shazer, S., Berg., I. K., Lipchik, E., Nunnaly, E., Molnar, A., Gingerich, W. and Weiner-Davis, M. (1986) Brief therapy: focused solution development. *Family Process* 25: 207–221.

Devlin, M. (2003) A solution-focused model for improving individual university teaching. *International Journal for Academic Development* 8(1/2): 77–90.

George, E., Iveson, C. and Ratner, H. (1999) *Problem to Solution: Brief therapy with individuals and families*, revised edition. London: BT Press.

Grant, A. M. (2003) The impact of life coaching on goal attainment, metacognition and mental health. *Social Behavior and Personality* 31(3): 253–264.

Grant, A. M. (2006a) Solution-focused coaching. In J. Passmore (ed.) *Excellence in Coaching: The industry guide*. London: Kogan Page.

Grant, A. M. (2006b) An integrative goal-focused approach to executive coaching. In D. R. Stober and A. M. Grant (eds) *Evidence Based Coaching Handbook: Putting best practices to work for your clients*. Hoboken, NJ: Wiley.

Green, L. S., Oades, L. G. and Grant, A. M. (2006) Cognitive-behavioural, soloution focused life coaching: enhancing goal striving, well-being and hope. *Journal of Positive Psychology* 1(3): 142–149.

Greene, J. and Grant, A. M (2003) *Solution-Focused Coaching*. Harlow, UK: Pearson Education.

Hawkes, D. (2003) A solution-focused approach to 'psychosis'. In B. O'Connell and S. Palmer (eds) *Handbook of Solution-Focused Therapy*. London: Sage.

Hoskisson, P. (2003) Solution-focused groupwork. In B. O'Connell and S. Palmer (eds) *Handbook of Solution-Focused Therapy*. London: Sage.

Hoyt, M. F. and Berg, I. K. (1998) Solution-focused couple therapy: helping clients construct self-fulfilling realities. In M. F. Hoyt (ed.) *The Handbook of Constructive Therapies*. San Francisco, CA: Jossey-Bass.

Jackson, P. Z. and McKergow, M. (2007) *The Solutions Focus: Making coaching and change simple*. London: Nicholas Brealey.

LaFountain, R. M. and Garner, N. E. (1996) Solution-focused counseling groups: the results are in. *Journal of Specialists In Group Work*, 21(2): 128–143.

Latham, G. P. and Yukl, G. A. (1975) A review of research on the application of goal-setting theory in organisations. *Academy of Management Journal* 18(4): 824–845.

Lethem, J. (1994) *Moved to Tears, Moved to Action: Solution focused brief therapy with women and children*. London: BT Press.

Locke, E. A. (1996) Motivation through conscious goal setting. *Applied and Preventive Psychology* 5(2): 117–124.

Meier, D. (2005) *Team Coaching with the Solution Circle: A practical guide to solutions focused team development*. Cheltenham: SolutionsBooks.

Norman, H. (2003) Solution-focused reflecting teams. In B. O'Connell and S. Palmer (eds) *Handbook of Solution-Focused Therapy*. London: Sage.

O'Connell, B. (1998) *Solution-focused Therapy*. London: Sage.

O'Connell, B. (2000) Solution focused therapy. In S. Palmer (ed.) *Introduction to Counselling and Psychotherapy: The essential guide*. London: Sage.

O'Connell, B. (2001) *Solution-focused stress counselling*. London: Continuum.

O'Connell, B. (2003) Introduction to the solution-focused approach. In B. O'Connell and S. Palmer (eds) *Handbook of Solution-Focused Therapy*. London: Sage.

O'Connell, B. and Palmer, S. (eds) (2003) *Handbook of Solution-Focused Therapy*. London: Sage.

Palmer, S., Grant, A. and O'Connell, B. (2007) Lost and Found: Special Report on Solution-Focused Coaching. *Coaching at Work*, 2(4): 22–30.

Prochaska, J. O. and DiClemente, C. C. (1992) *Stages of Change in the Modification of Problem Behaviors.* Newbury Park, CA: Sage.

Rawsthorne, L. J. and Elliot, A. J. (1999) Achievement goals and intrinsic motivations: a meta-analytic review. *Personality and Social Psychology Review* 3(4): 326–344.

Russell, B. (1996) *History of Western Philosophy and its Connection with Political and Social Circumstances from the Earliest Times to the Present Day.* London: Routledge.

Scoular, A. and Linley, P. A. (2006) Coaching, goal-setting and personality: what matters? *The Coaching Psychologist* 2(1): 9–11.

Selekman, M. D. (1997) *Solution-Focused Therapy with Children.* London: Guilford Press.

Sharry, J. (2003) Solution-focused parent training. In B. O'Connell and S. Palmer (eds) *Handbook of Solution-Focused Therapy.* London: Sage.

Triantafillou, N. (1997) A solution-focused approach to mental health supervision. *Journal of Systemic Therapies* 16(4): 305–328.

Discussion points

- Why does it make sense to spend more time focusing on the solution instead of spending time focusing on the problem?
- Is the miracle question an essential part of solution-focused coaching?
- Solution-focused coaching and therapy is light on theory. Is this really the case or are some solution-focused practitioners just unconcerned about the underpinning theories that could inform practice?
- Is goal-setting is a crucial aspect of solution-focused coaching?

Suggested reading

Greene, J. and Grant, A. M (2003) *Solution-Focused Coaching.* Harlow, UK: Pearson Education.

Jackson, P. Z. and McKergow, M. (2007) *The Solutions Focus: Making coaching and change simple.* London: Nicholas Brealey.

O'Connell, B. and Palmer, S. (eds) (2003) *Handbook of Solution-Focused Therapy.* London: Sage.

O'Connell, B. (2005) *Solution-Focused Therapy*, 2nd edition. London: Sage.

During the writing of this chapter Steve de Shazer and Insoo Kim Berg, the founders of solution-focused therapy, both died. This chapter is dedicated to them.

Understanding relationships, diversity and development in coaching and coaching psychology

Chapter 16

Reappraising the coach–client relationship

The unassuming change agent in coaching

Alanna O'Broin and Stephen Palmer

> Regardless of preferred theoretical perspective, the foundation of effective coaching is the successful formation of a collaborative relationship.
>
> (Stober and Grant, 2006: 360)

Introduction

The coach–client relationship is a fundamental factor in every coaching contract. In recent moves towards creating a conceptual Contextual Meta-model for Coaching, and in seeking to ask the question 'What are the common themes that are effective in coaching and within what context?' Stober and Grant (2006) propose seven thematic factors. Two of these themes directly relate to the coach–client relationship, attesting to its imputed critical importance within the coaching process:

- a meaningful relationship where the client believes that the coach will work in the client's best interest
- the coach's role within a collaborative working alliance is to enhance the client's development, performance or skill set, while appropriately pacing the intervention to both maintain challenge and facilitate change.

Surprisingly, despite its putative contribution to coaching outcome, little research literature exists specifically on the coach–client relationship at a detailed level of investigation (see O'Broin and Palmer, 2006a).

Conceptual coaching approaches construe the coach–client relationship differently, however few if any argue against the importance of a good working relationship between client and coach as an absolute minimum requirement.

A working definition of the coach–client relationship that reflects the approach taken within this chapter is as follows:

> a unique, co-created, evolving relationship comprising the coaching alliance plus additional client and coach contributions.

What the literature tells us

A tool for change

Within the largely executive coaching literature base the coach–client relationship is seen as an important tool for effecting growth (Stober et al., 2006) and change (Kilburg, 2000; O'Neill, 2000). The coach–client relationship is often compared and contrasted with the counselling and psychotherapy relationships, with which it logically has common ground. The coach–client relationship is seen as more collegial (Levinson, 1996) and more collaborative and egalitarian, rather than authoritarian (Grant and Cavanagh, 2004). There is an expectation of less dependency in the coach–client relationship (Hart et al., 2001) and the perception is that while the principles of counselling and therapy can enhance executive coaching, a major difference between their respective relationships is the depth to which issues are pursued (Kilburg, 2000).

There are also perceived to be a number of similarities between the coaching and therapeutic relationships, some of them very important in achieving a better understanding of the coach–client relationship. Perhaps one of the foremost similarities is that, much like the therapeutic relationship, the coach–client relationship involves the fostering and maintenance of a strong relationship of trust (Gyllensten and Palmer, 2007; Bluckert, 2005a).

Forging a strong coach–client relationship

In exploring the credentials for good coaches, the coaching literature attests repeatedly to the need for forging a strong coach–client relationship, both from the coach's viewpoint (Peterson, 1996) and from the client's (Wasylyshyn, 2003). Lowman (2005) develops this theme further, arguing the need for an empirical grounding for coaching research, identifying common themes derived from hypotheses from a special issue series on what works and what does not work in coaching and taking as his first theme that the ability to establish a trusting relationship may be critical to success (*Consulting Psychology Journal: Practice and Research*, 57, 1; see also Stober and Grant, 2006).

The need for a strong coach–client relationship is especially important given the consensus in the coaching literature that coaching seems to occur in stages (Diedrich, 1996; Witherspoon and White, 1996), the first of which, critically, is relationship building. Logically, the relative success in relationship-building is likely to impact on the later stages in the coaching process, such as feedback and evaluation.

The coaching literature also argues for compatible chemistry between coach and client (Banning, 1997) and for achieving a fine balance between support and challenge in the coach–client relationship (Bluckert, 2005b).

With the lack of research on the coach–client relationship, there is arguably an oversimplification in assumptions being made on the synergies and divergencies of the coach–client and therapist–client relationships, especially if, as has often been the case in the coaching literature, they are conceptualised as dichotomous opposites.

Evidence-based coaching

In the broader arena of the present-day professional and political climate, the term 'evidence-based practice' has come under close scrutiny by a number of professions, including psychology (Lane and Corrie, 2006). In attempting to address the tension between conceptual and practice-based knowledge, multiple narratives, methods and ways of being a 'scientist-practitioner' in differing contexts are proposed (see Haarbosch and Newey, 2006; Miller and Frederickson, 2006).

Coaching psychologists are contributing materially to this debate, positing a broader 'evidence-based approach to coaching' incorporating *best current knowledge*, often from allied fields, of psychology, adult learning and communication (Cavanagh and Grant, 2006; Stober and Grant, 2006) as well as integrating coaching-specific research, the coach's own expertise and taking into account client preferences (Stober et al., 2006).

With the background of a small coaching literature base on the coach–client relationship, this chapter adopts the principle of an 'evidence-based approach to coaching' (Cavanagh and Grant, 2006). Using examples from different sources of knowledge, this chapter seeks to open a dialogue on, and highlight areas for, discussion and potential research into the coach–client relationship as a critical and often underestimated change agent in the coaching process.

What allied professions and knowledge bases tell us

Stober and Grant propose that *best current knowledge*

> can often be found in the established literature in related fields of evidence, theory and practice. Informed-practitioner coaches need to be able to draw on such existing knowledge, adapt and apply this knowledge, and in the light of their own reflective practice, develop grounded frameworks that further inform their work with their client.
>
> (Stober and Grant, 2006: 6)

Embracing the tenets of an evidence-based approach to coaching psychology, examples are taken from the allied professions of counselling and psychotherapy outcome research, sports psychology, and from game theory, to illustrate how coaching psychology theory, research and practice and our understanding of the coach–client relationship can potentially be informed by such knowledge.

Counselling and psychotherapy outcomes

AVOIDING A REPEAT OF THE DODOVILLE EXPERIENCE

Kilburg (2004) draws a parallel between the emerging empirical coaching literature base and that of psychotherapy outcome literature. Citing the Dodoville conjecture of Saul Rosenzweig (1936: see Rosenzweig, 2002), with its metaphor 'Everybody has won, and all must have prizes', Kilburg (2004) concludes that the executive coaching studies conducted to date have demonstrated positive common effects, irrespective of the practitioners' conceptual approach, akin to those repeatedly found over 70 years in the psychotherapy outcome literature. This leads Kilburg to question the veracity of repeating such studies as the sole contributory path to understanding the processes and effects of coaching, and he concludes that 'the non-specific aspects of helping create most of the positive leverage for change in human lives' (Kilburg, 2004: 207). Following Kilburg's (2004) assertion, further exploration of the psychotherapy literature in this area is warranted.

COMMON PRINCIPLES OF CHANGE

Since the mid-1990s, two opposing camps, proponents of empirically based treatments (EST) and empirically supported therapy relationships (ESR) argued for their respective pre-eminence in therapy outcomes. These followed the direction of two Task Forces of the American Psychological Association's Division 12, Society for Clinical Psychology (Task Force, 1995) and Division 29, Division of Psychotherapy (Norcross, 2002) respectively. The Division 29 Task Force concluded that, first, the therapy relationship does make substantial and consistent contributions to psychotherapy outcome, regardless of the specific type of treatment, and second, adapting or tailoring the therapy relationship to specific patient needs and characteristics enhances treatment effectiveness. Among the general elements found to be demonstrably effective were

- the therapeutic or working alliance
- empathy
- goal consensus and collaboration
- degree of client resistance.

In an effort to optimise the effectiveness of therapy, a more recent joint Task Force of Division 12 and the North American Society for Psychotherapy Research (NASPR), took a more integrated approach (see Castonguay and Beutler, 2006a) focusing on answering these questions:

- What is known about the nature of the participants, relationships and procedures within treatment that induce positive effects across theoretical models and methods?

- How do these factors or variables work together to enhance change?

In seeking to find 'foundation principles that encompass a variety of therapeutic factors' (Beutler and Castonguay, 2006: 5), the Task Force described principles as being more specific than theoretical formulations and more general than techniques. Castonguay and Beutler (2006b) suggest that the principles of change delineated in the Task Force are termed 'empirically based' or 'empirically derived' to reflect their inferred determinants of change from correlational analyses. These common principles of effective change included those also identified by the earlier Division 29 Task Force, and include the therapist

- establishing and maintaining a strong working alliance
- attempting to facilitate a high degree of collaboration with clients
- conducting the relationship in an empathic way
- being caring, warm and accepting
- being congruent or authentic
- resolving alliance ruptures in an empathic way
- noting that the client's expectations are likely to play a role in outcome.

The Task Force also commented that each principle should be investigated within the context in which it takes place, emphasising the integrative process. As Castonguay and Beutler (2006b: 353) commented: 'since not all relationships are likely to bring change, one needs to be aware of interventions (including modes of relating) that should be encouraged or avoided'.

TRANSLATION TO COACHING

This concept of principles of change fits well within a contextual approach to coaching, and the findings from psychotherapy outcome research provide pointers for coaching psychology practitioners and researchers alike, as has also been suggested elsewhere (Linley, 2006; Stober et al., 2006). Research comparing and contrasting the coach–client relationship with that of the therapist–client relationship in a focused and empirically derived way would be useful.

Sport psychology

Many of the roots of the coaching concept are in sport and athletics (Whitmore, 2002). As Peltier (2001) notes, useful themes can be translated from the field of athletic coaching. The importance of the quality of the coach–athlete relationship as a critical determinant of the satisfaction (Bortoli et al., 1995), motivation (Amorose and Horn, 2001) and improved performance (Lyle, 1999; Gould et al., 2002; Jowett, 2005) of athletes is noted in the sport psychology literature. Studies also suggest that attending to the individual needs of athletes appears to be the best predictor of the coach–athlete relationship (Salminen and Liukkonen, 1996).

Paralleling developments in coaching psychology, more inclusive, evidence-informed approaches to the coach–athlete relationship in sport psychology theory, research and practice have begun to develop (Jowett and Cockerill, 2002; Poczwardowski et al., 2002; Mageau and Vallerand, 2003; Jowett, 2006).

One example of these developments is a motivational model of the coach–athlete relationship (Mageau and Vallerand, 2003), based on cognitive evaluation theory (Deci and Ryan, 1985) and the hierarchical model of intrinsic and extrinsic motivation (Vallerand, 2001), which takes up a number of themes synergistic to this discussion of the coach–client relationship. (See also Grant (2006) for a discussion of self-determination theory in the context of a goal-focused approach to executive coaching.)

Mageau and Vallerand's (2003) model proposes a sequence where three factors influence the coach's behaviours in the coaching process:

- the coach's personal orientation towards coaching
- the coaching context
- the coach's perceptions of the athlete's behaviour and motivation.

In the event of autonomy-supportive (rather than controlling) coach behaviours, the provision of structure and the coach's involvement, a beneficial impact on the athlete's psychological needs for autonomy, competence and relatedness is demonstrated. Having these needs met in turn determines the athlete's intrinsic and self-determined motivation.

IMPLICATIONS FOR COACHING

Mageau and Vallerand's (2003) model informs discussion of the coach–client relationship from three viewpoints:

- It highlights the importance of meeting the client's three psychological needs of autonomy, competence and relatedness for the client's intrinsic and self-determined extrinsic motivation.
- It identifies and unites determinants of the autonomy-supportive style (coach orientation, context, perception of athletes' behaviour and motivation) and suggests that the autonomy-supportive style can be taught (Reeve, 1998).
- It underscores how the coaching context may influence coaching behaviours. The model suggests that in the highly competitive nature of sports settings, coaches as well as athletes may feel highly pressured. The

potential high levels of stress created may tempt the coach to adopt controlling, rather than autonomy supportive behaviours.

Mageau and Vallerand's (2003) model provides one specific example of how contributions from the sport science literature resonate with the broader coaching literature and in the case of the model's third contribution, particularly the executive coaching context.

As part of a review comparing sport psychology and coaching psychology, O'Broin and Palmer (2006b) highlight parallels and differences between the coach–athlete and coach–client relationships argued to be potentially useful in progressing discussion, research and practice relevant to coaching outcome in both professions. Parallels cited are:

- increasing recognition of the importance of the relationship to the athlete/client's success and development
- the intentional nature of the relationship
- exploring 'effective' relationships
- the interpersonal context of the relationship.

The potential difference of emotional intensity and often longevity of the respective relationships is also noted, with the coach–athlete relationship often being very intense, having more frequent contact between coach and athlete, and taking place often within a highly pressured, competitive environment.

Using a specific and broader examples, evidence-informed approaches comparing and contrasting the coach–athlete and coach–client relationships are suggested to offer multiple opportunities for discussion, exchange of knowledge, and contributions to research and practice in both professions.

Game theory

Game theory (von Neumann and Morgenstern, 1944) is an interdisciplinary approach to the study of human behaviour, often in the areas of conflict and cooperation. Game theory has applications in the domains of management (Brandenburger and Nalebuff, 1996), sport (Palomino et al., 1999), social and behavioural sciences (Colman, 1995).

Using the analogy of a game, interactive situations between two or more 'players' can be modelled at various levels of detail. In *cooperative games* the strategies of the participants are coordinated in order to achieve the best outcome for the group or dyad, while in *non-cooperative games* each person maximises their own rewards regardless of others. *Zero-sum* games are those where the wins and losses (negatives) add up to zero, while in *non-constant sum* games, which more closely resemble 'natural' human interactions, wins and losses may add up differently depending on the strategies that participants choose. What is interesting here is that if two people can arrive at a cooperative solution, any *non-constant sum* game can be converted into a win-win game, and that there is no one generally accepted mathematical solution of the non-constant sum game, or put another way no clear answer to what is rational in such a game.

As a response to this latter point, game theorists and researchers have looked more broadly for explanations of what people and companies do in strategic situations, incorporating new factors to help explain strategies and experimental findings, and to make further predictions (Butler, 2005). *Psychological Game Theory* (PGT) (Geanokopolous et al., 1989) for instance introduces the dependence on player's beliefs (regarding the intentions of other players), not just on money. Another such approach is *Behavioral Game Theory* (Camerer, 1997, 2003) linking game theory to cognitive science, adding cognitive details about 'social utility functions' such as concerns about fairness, and the perceived intentions of other players.

TRANSLATION TO COACHING

Game theory sheds light on how some clients could approach coaching, particularly in the organisational context. Behavioural game theory in particular addresses areas such as moral obligation and how people bargain and trust one another. Simple bargaining games, used to bring out issues of social utility could prove informative here. As Camerer (1997) describes, Ultimatum games, the oft-quoted Prisoner's Dilemma game and the game of 'Chicken' (in this context a variant of the Prisoner's Dilemma game) could all be fruitful areas for exploration in helping explain strategic interactions.

For illustrative purposes, let's take the example of a manager, senior manager, director, or HR professional recommending that an employee attend executive, business or performance coaching. This may be an employee who sees the opportunity of coaching as a 'perk' and would be likely to be cooperative without any games being played. Or, the potential coachee could be a career-minded employee, who 'plays' the cooperative game to show willing – cooperating here could be said to be emotionally strategic in this approach, but the coachee in essence could feel coaching has been forced upon them rather than chosen by them. This transforms the Prisoner's Dilemma into a coordination game in terms of fairness equilibrium in Game Theory terms. As intentions matter, such a player who feels 'forced' to cooperate is predicted by fairness equilibrium not to be obliged to reciprocate, and will be more likely to defect than in the standard dilemma (Camerer, 1997: 171). When playing this particular game, looking to meet the perceived demands of a situation, an employee might state that they found the coaching effective regardless of the real impact. Findings of exceptionally high levels of coaching effectiveness are prevalent in the literature (e.g. Chartered Institute of Personnel and Development (CIPD), 2005; Gyllensten and Palmer, 2006) and could feasibly reflect in part this possible artefact.

Conceptual approaches

Each of the preceding chapters outlining their respective conceptual or theoretical approaches to coaching includes an exposition of the coach–client relationship. If we view the coach–client relationship from a contextual coaching viewpoint (Stober and Grant, 2006), we can also consider trans-theoretically factors that may be effective related to coaching outcome.

Working at a level of abstraction addressing principles of change rather than the level of conceptual approach alone, we can draw upon three models which can inform this discussion in the area of the coach's use of coach–client relationship.

The contextual coaching viewpoint argues for a coach–client relationship specifically tailored to the individual client's changing needs throughout the coaching contract, within the individual's context. Context can signify here the intra-personal sense of the individual's outlook, and, in the case of executive coaching, the interpersonal sense in terms of the client in relation to the organisational context.

Clarkson's (1995) *Five-Relationship Model of Counselling* connects modes of relationship from different theoretical orientations (see also Clarkson, 1994). The model suggests the possibility of overlaying the personal, developmental, transferential/counter-transferential, and transpersonal modes on that of the working alliance, as indicated by the needs of the client. This model has been used in adapted form in organisational consultancy to understand the impact of different relationships on work environments (Carroll, 1996).

The *Transtheoretical Model of Change* (TTM) (Prochaska and DiClemente, 1984) is a second model that can add to this discussion. As Prochaska and Norcross (2001) note, the stance adopted by the therapist at various stages of change can often resemble the *nurturing parent*, at the pre-contemplation stage; the *Socratic teacher* at the contemplation stage; the *experienced coach* at the preparation stage; and the *consultant* at the action and maintenance stages. The main point to note here is that the therapeutic relationship is matched to the client's needs at their respective stage of change.

The *Model of Relationship Stances* (Sullivan et al., 2005) is a more recent model that develops the notion of relationship 'stances' identified by Norcross (1993). Investigating 'master' therapists' construction and use of the therapy relationship to meet individual client need, these authors identified the *Safe Relationship Domain*, consisting of (1) Responding, (2) Collaborating and (3) Joining therapist actions, and the *Challenging Relationship Domain*, comprising (4) Using Self, (5) Engaging and (6) Therapist objectivity. Creating a secure and trusting relationship base within which the client feels able to express their feelings and try out new behaviours is the common theme of the *Safe Relationship Domain*. Sullivan et al. (2005: 64) stated that 'the relationship stances of the Safe Relationship Domain may contain the essential ingredients for the client to make necessary changes'.

In the more active *Challenging Relationship Domain*, use of the therapist's full range of abilities, energy and resources is required to elicit behaviours from their clients approaching the client's therapy goals. These stances of Using Self, Engaging and therapist Objectivity could involve therapist actions of intentionally using their personality and personal resources, taking responsibility for moving the therapy forward, and providing information, feedback and evaluation to the client to offer a more objective perspective on themselves, respectively.

Sullivan et al. (2005) note the premise in both their own and Clarkson's (1995) model that the therapy relationship may take different forms, intentionally constructed by the therapist, in response to different clients' needs.

TRANSLATION TO COACHING

The three models outlined above inform our discussion of the coach–client relationship by demonstrating three major elements that can translate from the therapist–client relationship into a coach–client relationship that is

- trans-theoretical
- intentionally constructed by the coach
- responsive to clients' changing needs throughout the coaching engagement.

The models of Clarkson (1995) and Sullivan et al. (2005) are relevant here in that they both emphasise the importance of the working alliance, without which it is difficult to work and achieve goals, a point argued to be particularly synergistic with the coaching alliance.

Collaborative contributions

Coaching alliance

As was discussed earlier in the section on common principles of change, the findings from the Division 12 and NASPR joint Task Force on the common principles of therapeutic change relating to the therapeutic relationship (Castonguay and Beutler, 2006b) suggest that:

- establishing and maintaining a strong working alliance during the therapeutic treatment is likely to lead to beneficial outcomes
- therapists should attempt to facilitate a high degree of collaboration or working alliance with clients during therapy.

Further evidence exists indicating that the therapist's skills and personal factors influence the development of a good alliance with the client (Horvath,

2001). Also Bedi et al. (2005) indicate that client and therapist perceptions of the nature and strength of the alliance differ. This is particularly the case early on in the formation of the alliance (Bedi, 2006).

As the importance of trans-theoretical therapeutic ingredients in psycho-therapy outcome research have been increasingly recognised (Wampold, 2001), a broader pan-theoretic reformulation of the working alliance (Bordin, 1975; Luborsky, 1976) was increasingly posited as an important ingredient in all helping relationships (Horvath, 2001). While used in a broader sense, the alliance is also frequently conceptualised as a term referring to the quality and strength of the collaborative relationship between client and therapist (Bordin, 1975, 1979, 1994; Horvath, 2001; Horvath and Bedi, 2002).

Bordin's (1975, 1979, 1989, 1994) theory of the working alliance is predicated on two assumptions. The first assumption is that the working alliance is a measure of the degree to which the dyad engages in purposive, collaborative work. The second assumption is that the alliance is manifested in an inter-changing, reciprocal relationship. Three features of the working alliance which Bordin associates with purposive, collaborative work are tasks, bonds and goals.

More recent literature on the working alliance (Hatcher and Barends, 2006; Horvath, 2006) revisits and develops Bordin's theory. Hatcher and Barends (2006) suggest further exploration of the degree, level and kind of collabor-ation and purposiveness of the work in the alliance, positing the existence of a more active negotiation of the alliance on the part of the client than was suggested by Bordin, and proposing investigation of different aspects of the bond and its link to purposive work. Horvath (2006) highlights the need to question the assumption that the alliance is uniform across time, arguing that beginning phases of therapies may demand different characteristics to later, more 'mature' phases of the alliance.

IMPLICATIONS FOR COACHING

Repeated findings on the importance of the working alliance in psycho-therapy outcome research are argued to be highly relevant to the coach–client relationship and the coaching process. A working definition of the coaching alliance deriving from the discussion in this chapter is as follows:

> The coaching alliance reflects the quality of the client and coach's engagement in collaborative, purposive work within the coaching rela-tionship, and is jointly negotiated, and renegotiated throughout the coaching process over time.
> (adapted from Bordin, 1975, 1979, 1994; Hatcher and Barends, 2006; Horvath, 2006)

Bordin's theory of the working alliance, with its emphasis on collaboration and purposive work, readily translates into the coaching context. His framework highlights three core features argued to be equally applicable in the coaching alliance as in the working alliance in therapy:

- *goals* – consensus about, and commitment to goals of coaching
- *tasks* – cognitive aspects relating to the work of coaching
- *bonds* – such as trust, liking, respect.

Bordin's framework also potentially enables the assessment of the degree, level and kind of collaborativeness and purposiveness of the work taking place that is optimal for the individual client.

Evidence-based coaching approaches to research and practice emphasise contextual models, focus on overarching commonalities and trans-theoretical areas for research and would in themselves suggest the working alliance as a prime candidate for research investigation in the coaching context. Broader and specific findings on the working alliance in the counselling and psychotherapy outcome research have further demonstrated the likely relevance of the working alliance to the coaching alliance and coaching outcome. This may be a noteworthy research area to enhance understanding of the coach–client relationship and its further exploration is considered to be a priority.

Combined participant contributions

Here we refer to combined client and coach contributions which exist outside the process of coaching itself, but nevertheless could influence the coach–client relationship, and hence coaching outcome. As psychotherapy outcome research has sought to answer the question 'What therapy, by whom, is most effective for this individual with that specific problem and under what circumstances?' (Paul, 1967: 111), multiple factors have increasingly been researched (Beutler and Castonguay, 2006). The study of therapist–client similarity has arisen out of this investigation.

Two diametrically opposed views have emerged, one arguing for the positive impact of therapist–client similarities and the other for the value of dissimilarities (see Fernandez-Alvarez et al., 2006). While these debates are ongoing to a certain extent in the counselling and psychotherapy outcome literatures, they are highly applicable in the coach–client relationship and hence potentially to coaching outcome.

The findings regarding the importance of coach–client matching

A number of coach–client issues could be related to a more effective coach–client relationship, and to improved coaching outcome. Those of gender, culture, modality similarity and broader personality are highlighted as potential candidates worthy of further investigation.

Gender

Peltier and Irueste-Montes (2001: 206) state, 'Gender is a central aspect of our identity.' However, there are differing views on how same or mixed gender coach–client relationships impact upon coaching and coaching outcomes (see Sparrow, 2006a). This difference in views mirrors mixed findings regarding the effect of gender matching on the therapeutic alliance in the psychotherapy outcome literature (Fernandez-Alvarez et al., 2006) as well as a lack of nuanced rather than broad generalisations on matching effects, including those of gender, on the relationship between therapist and client (Lebow et al., 2006).

Cross-cultural issues

Rosinski and Abbott (2006) highlight the large body of recent literature on the effects of national culture on business while making the important observation that groups of all kinds (e.g. profession, gender, geography, religion, social life, organization) have cultures. This means that the identities of any of us as individuals can be seen as a blend of the cultures of the multiple groups to which we may belong. Rosinski and Abbott (2006: 257) conclude that coaching from a cultural perspective: 'can raise awareness of identity and mobilize culture as a positive force in change processes'.

Rosinski and Abbott (2006: 263) continue, stating that taking a cultural perspective encourages both clients and coaches to be 'authentic', meaning that they act from a sense of who they really are, rather than from an expected or desired perspective. They also suggest that a strong, trusting client-coach relationship is paramount, describing true trust as *authentic trust*: 'a mature trust built up through routine, experiment and experience' (Rosinski and Abbott, 2006: 265), and argue that a successful coaching process is the ideal position from which to promote and develop such a relationship. This process can then be modelled and extended by the client into their broader work and social domains. Despite the interest in culture, little focused research has investigated the impact of culture on coaching outcomes.

Modality similarity

Multimodal therapy (Lazarus, 1989, 1993) identifies seven interactive modalities that alone or in combination, explain human functioning and experience at any one time. These seven modalities include Behavioural, Affective, Sensory, Imagery, Cognitive, Interpersonal and Drugs/Biological factors, easily remembered by the acronym BASIC ID.

Herman (1998) studied client–therapist pairs using Lazarus' Structural Profile Inventory (Lazarus, 1989), a self-report questionnaire assessing ratings of functioning in terms of the seven modalities in BASIC ID. Herman (1998) found that therapist–client modality similarity produced a positive impact on psychotherapy outcome, possibly through enhancement of rapport, and hence improved perception of the nature of their therapeutic relationship. He also hypothesised that modality similarity affected the psychotherapy process by enabling clearer communication and for techniques to be delivered more 'on target'. These findings build on Herman's (1992) earlier work where therapists' theoretical stances were found to be consistent with their profile of modality structures.

Further research suggests that cognitive similarity aids the formation and maintenance of rapport in the therapeutic relationship (Hunt et al., 1985). They argue the greater the similarity between client and therapist, the higher the likelihood for clear communication within the dyad.

Similarly, in a study of a 'virtual' mentoring programme in the higher education sector (Beddoes-Jones and Miller, 2006) matching of cognitive style of mentor and mentees was found to improve sustainability of the relationships over the year-long programme as well as achieving a quantifiable impact on organisational benefits. Such findings on cognitive similarity, if transferable to the coach–client relationship, would be valuable to ascertain.

IMPLICATIONS FOR COACHING

It is argued that these findings could have important implications for the advantageous use of the multimodal approach in coaching (Richard, 1999; Palmer et al., 2003). It has also been suggested that the multimodal approach can be useful for cross-cultural practice (Ponterotto, 1987; Jewel, 2002; Palmer, 2002a).

Personality

As Fernandez-Alvarez et al. (2006) note, some psychotherapy outcome research has suggested that broader 'personality' matching of client and therapist can positively impact on outcome. Matching the personality of client and coach may similarly have beneficial effects on coaching outcome, although certain personality differences between coach and client may well also prove to be beneficial to outcome, as was found in a recent coaching study on goal-setting and personality type, in which outcome scores were higher when coach and clients differed on temperament, as measured by the Myers-Briggs Type Indicator (MBTI: Scoular and Linley, 2006).

TRANSLATION TO COACHING

In the matching of client-therapist personality, as in other areas of client–therapist matching, such as gender, ethnicity, age, religion and spirituality, the psychotherapy outcome literature acknowledges limited research and mixed findings (Beutler et al., 2006; Lebow et al., 2006). This lack of clarity indicates the need for more nuanced research on these aspects of the therapeutic and coaching relationships connecting process to outcome.

Participants' individual contributions

What the client brings

Motivation

Client motivation is a factor that has been shown to impact on therapy outcome. Indeed, Castonguay and Beutler (2006b) found that the client's willingness and ability to engage in the process of therapy is likely to enhance outcome. If this is repeated in the coaching context, this contribution of client participation would be a valuable factor to evaluate and for coach and client to work with to optimise coaching outcome.

The Transtheoretical Model of Change (TTM: Prochaska and DiClemente, 1984; see chapter 9) is a six-stage cyclical model of change, unfolding over time. The stages include pre-contemplation, contemplation, preparation, action, maintenance and termination. Prochaska and Norcross (2001) suggest that at each stage of change, different change processes can optimise progress. Matching between the therapeutic relationship and the client's respective stage of change is necessary to enhance the therapeutic outcome over time.

Grant (2006) comments that the TTM has implications for guiding coaching practice and provides a number of stage-specific coaching strategies that coaches can use with clients within the cycle of change. In particular Grant (2006) points to the client's level of motivation or readiness for change as an important factor that the coach needs to mindfully assess rather than assuming the client is in the Action stage. Grant (2006) notes that the stages are overlapping, not necessarily consequential, and that relapse is possible, indeed probable, before permanent change is maintained.

A further motivational model that may be applicable in the coaching context is that of Holtforth and Castonguay (2005), where the therapist attunes their interventions to the client's motivational goals. They propose a CBT Motivational Attunement approach, based on *Consistency Theory* (Grawe, 2004). Motivational attunement is defined here as a 'meta-technique designed to individualize therapeutic interventions to foster and work with the therapeutic relationship' (Holtforth and Castonguay, 2005: 444). Motivational attunement can be used to tailor interventions to the motivations of the client and to attempt to provide clients with needs-satisfying experiences, and is useful in fostering the bond, goal and task components of the therapeutic alliance. Holtforth and Castonguay (2005) suggest:

- In addition to specific techniques, the therapeutic relationship deserves a central position in CBT research, training and practice.
- The therapeutic relationship is in continuous interaction with technique, either as a facilitator of the application of techniques, or as the object of techniques during fostering of the alliance or dealing with ruptures of the alliance.

From the discussion on sport psychology above, we have already seen the coach's influence on the client's individual extrinsic and intrinsic motivation has potentially important implications for the coach–client relationship and coaching outcome (Mageau and Vallerand, 2003). Grant (2006: 166) provides examples of the coach's potential impact on client motivation in a discussion of how to align the client's intrinsic needs and values with an externally perceived goal.

Personality

The client's personality may be a further factor impacting on the coach–client relationship, and coaching outcome. A common principle finding of the joint Division 12 and NASPR Task force (Castonguay and Beutler, 2006b) was that clients diagnosed with a personality disorder were less likely to benefit from therapy than those with no personality disorder. As Grant (2006) suggests, an understanding of key personality dimensions may be useful to the coach in aligning goals to clients' needs. Hogan and Hogan's (2001) dimensional model of personality traits, presenting a continuum from 'personality-disordered' to 'healthy expressions of personality style' can be useful in this regard, particularly when coaching the more challenging client. Grant (2006) presents some personality styles (adapted from Cavanagh, 2005) and summarises ways of framing goals likely to appeal to and to motivate these specific styles, for example the narcissistic personality style and motivational appeals of enhancement of public profile, opportunities for praise, potential to distinguish oneself, and emphasis on uniqueness.

Cavanagh and Grant (2006) note that the distinction between clinical and non-clinical issues is not always clear-cut, and that where the client falls along the continuum of any dimension will change over time and the issues considered. Client personality is another factor that impacts on client need in the coaching process, and needs to be considered in the dynamics of the coach–client relationship.

What the coach brings

Interpersonal variables

Therapists' individual differences have been found to account for a substantial part of the variance in both the alliance (Horvath and Bedi, 2002) and psychotherapy outcome (Wampold, 2001).

In relation to the therapeutic relationship, three factors associated with client-centred interpersonal skills of the therapist have been found to be common principles of change (Castonguay and Beutler, 2006b):

- relating to clients in an empathic way
- adopting an attitude of caring, warmth and acceptance
- adopting an attitude of congruence or authenticity.

Instinctively, these attitudes translate directly to the coaching context. These empathic responses could include empathic understanding, exploration, evocations and conjectures, with an overall task of understanding goals as well as moment-to-moment experiences and nuances. Similarly, as with other relationship factors, these interpersonal skills require tailoring to individual client's needs and the coaching context.

Indeed, what clients experience as empathic varies with different clients (Holtforth and Castonguay, 2005). Similarly, different kinds of empathic responses with different clients and in different contexts would be required, as psychotherapy outcome research studies suggest (Greenberg et al., 2001). The emphasis is again on the individual client's ongoing needs.

Style

The essential features of a therapist's communicative style, such as the patterned and consistent ways in which they use words, vocal qualities, facial expressions, postures, gestures, when listening and speaking, have been argued to be a factor impacting the benefit of therapeutic interventions (Geller, 2005). Geller argues that the optimal *style* in which to operate as a therapist needs to be recognised to truly individualise a programme of therapy. Geller focuses on discovering the kinds of stylistic choice that increase the possibility that therapeutic interventions will have their intended impact, suggesting that the decision-making process can be grounded in the question, 'What stylistic choices are required to individualise, as far as possible, the content of my communications?' (Geller, 2005: 476). Geller also posits that we can continue to identify and improve therapeutic interventions by strengthening the listening, looking, speaking and being-with capacities that lie at the heart of therapeutic competence. It is proposed that the same could be said in the coach–client relationship and coaching process.

Appropriate responsiveness

Research on common principles of change in the psychotherapy outcome literature has sought to identify how therapists might best work to optimise the effectiveness of interventions, resulting in a number of general principles or elements of effective change (Castonguay and Beutler, 2006b).

As part of this ongoing discussion Stiles and Wolfe (2006) note that the general principles of change identified by the Division 29 Task Force (Norcross, 2001, 2002) are qualities or goals to be optimised or sought by the therapist in working with their clients, rather than specified instructions. A substantial evaluative element, requiring the therapist's skill and judgement regarding their specific implementation is necessary.

Stiles and Wolfe (2006) describe *responsiveness* as behaviour being affected by context, remarking that psychotherapeutic (and indeed human) inter-action is responsive on vastly changing time scales in a dynamic process whose content and process emerge as the session proceeds.

Their analysis builds upon the evaluatively neutral notion of *responsiveness* with the principle of *appropriate responsiveness* (see also Newman et al., 2006). Appropriate responsiveness involves doing what is necessary to produce positive or beneficial change, dependent on the perspective of the treatment approach and the purposes of the participants. Appropriate responsiveness is therefore a fluid activity, highly dependent on the emerging needs of the client, client resources, the setting, the treatment approach, and goals.

Appropriate responsiveness can distinguish two types of elements – volitional actions and achievements.

- *Actions* are elements that can be classified and counted, which may be used responsively but may not necessarily be. Giving feedback to a client is an example of a volitional action, ie the therapist can choose arbitrar-ily to give feedback, and its classification as an action does not dictate that its use is appropriate, nor does it depend on evaluation from a specific perspective.
- *Achievements* are the goal of actions used with appropriate responsive-ness. They are elements defined partly by their positive evaluation from a specific perspective. It is not possible to view the contribution of a par-ticular action to an achievement when viewed out of context. In a differ-ent context with a different client, a particular action would contribute positively or negatively depending on whether it is appropriately respon-sive to the particular client's requirements, as well as other factors of circumstances such as timing and delivery.

All the demonstrably effective and five of the seven promising and probably effective elements identified by the Division 29 Task Force were achievements rather than volitional actions, and the Task Force acknowledged the importance of the role of appropriate responsiveness in its title (Steering Committee, 2002).

Translation to coaching

The notion of the coach shaping appropriately responsive actions readily transfers to, and is argued to be highly relevant to the coaching context. In this 'customised' approach to coaching, decisions on use of strategy or technique are dependent on client need, goals and context.

Cavanagh's (2006: 337) observation that 'effective coaches often do tell' could be an example of the use of appropriate responsiveness, which, as Stiles and Wolfe (2006) note, may, depending on the treatment approach, involve refusing to comply with a client's wishes. The work of Arnold Lazarus, and the concept of the 'authentic chameleon' (Lazarus, 1993), is another example of the concept of contributions to tailoring or customising the interpersonal relationship to the client's needs to maximise therapeutic outcome that appears to translate from the therapy to the coaching context.

Boundary issues

Brotman et al. (1998: 44) suggest that the most powerful tactic in coaching is the client-coach relationship, and that the working (or coaching) alliance is characterised by mutual trust and respect, and 'stabilised' by confidentiality. The importance of confidentiality as a key ingredient of a strong coaching alliance is also argued by Wasylyshyn (2003) and Kampa-Kokesch and Anderson (2001), while Hart et al. (2001) note a concern over ethical behaviour and issues of confidentiality in coaching.

In considering similarities and differences in the coach–client and therapeutic relationships, differing views on the issue of boundaries arise. Despite codes of ethics and conduct, there are extreme instances of therapists violating boundaries – by clients being exploited in therapy and counselling, and professional standards being breached with regard to client abuse, both sexual and psychological (Hetherington, 2000; Palmer, 2002b).

While generally viewed as unethical, associations outside the boundary of the therapy relationship have not universally been condemned. Lazarus and Zur (2002) explored the advantages and disadvantages of non-sexual dual or multiple relationships, concluding that certain boundaries and ethics can diminish therapeutic effectiveness. Their definition of associations outside the 'boundaries' of the standard client–therapist relationship included lunching and socialising. This rather challenging conclusion in the therapist–client relationship context enters the realms of possibility when translated into the context of the executive coach–client relationship. Examples of such activities exist in the coaching literature (Hart et al., 2001). Busy executives are usually happy to maximise time by having a working lunch in their office with their internal or external executive coach. If the executive coach raised this as a 'boundary issue' it would be seen as absurd by many executives and could unnecessarily later create a coaching alliance issue.

Noting multiple relationships do exist, particularly in large organisations, Gabriel (2005) notes that they can be beneficial. She asserts that the therapist is ultimately responsible and casts this as an issue firmly in the ethical problem-solving category.

Younggren and Gottlieb (2004) suggest that positions at both extremes of the argument, i.e. that all dual relationships are unethical and that dual relationships are not always harmful and may be beneficial, are oversimplifications of a complex area of professional practice. These authors present a three-component model incorporating ethically based, risk-managed, and decision-making factors that the professional can examine either when considering entering a dual relationship, or even when such a relationship inadvertently exists.

Implications for coaching

It is argued that Younggren and Gottlieb's (2004) approach could readily adapt to and help inform boundary issues in the coach–client relationship. The following are questions which the model suggests the professional asks. The first and perhaps most fundamental question is:

- Is entering into a relationship in addition to the professional one necessary, or should I avoid it?

If the answer is still yes, additional questions specifically relevant to this discussion are:

- Can the dual relationship potentially cause harm to the coaching client?
- How can I assess the risk of disruption to the coaching relationship of the dual relationship?
- Can I evaluate this matter objectively?

This topic has received limited coverage in the coaching and coaching psychology literature. While a professional coach's code of ethics and conduct can provide general guidelines, and supervision can assist in the provision of quality work by the coach (Carroll, 2006), a further requirement for investigation of the ethical, risk and decision-making factors relevant to the coach–client relationship and the coaching process is indicated.

Context

A major conclusion reached by the joint Division 12 and NASPR Task Force on principles of therapeutic change that work was that:

> each principle should be investigated within the context it takes place. Participants, relationship, and technique principles do not operate in isolation.
>
> (Castonguay and Beutler, 2006b: 367)

Recent coaching models and discussions within the evidence-informed approach to coaching and coaching psychology (Cavanagh, 2006; Stober and Grant, 2006) are consistent with this integrative approach, and share an emphasis on context.

Cavanagh's (2006) perspective on coaching argues from a complex adaptive systems viewpoint. A system comprises a group of interacting elements forming a complex whole over time, with the whole being greater than the sum of its parts. In complex adaptive systems, the parts making up whole systems are whole systems in their own right, making interaction and adaptation to each other a feature of the creation of the larger group system.

Cavanagh (2006) sees the coaching relationship itself as a complex adaptive system. In the complex interaction of the client and coach a conversation is co-created from which the coaching engagement emerges. Context is unique to the specific client in that the individual, as well as the organization is a complex adaptive system. As Cavanagh (2006: 326) states: 'working with the individual *is* working with the team/wider organization'.

While there is recognition that working at different levels of the system will impact at other levels, Cavanagh (2006) notes the importance of the coach being aware of, and intentional about, the level of the system being engaged at any one time (i.e. individual, team, organisation).

Stober and Grant's (2006) Contextual Model can be seen as a meta-model for coaching approaches, permitting an inclusive framework for evidence-informed practice. Rather than comparing the effectiveness of coaching models this approach instead seeks to understand the coaching process itself. The contextual model adopts seven themes and seven principles that provide a means of analysing *how* coaching is being conducted, and *what* is taking place in the coaching process respectively. They encourage the coach to ask themselves *why* they are acting in one way or another in the session with their client and to consider the consistency of their actions with the rationale and procedures within which they are operating. The common themes of this model include the concepts of the coach–client relationship, client and coach characteristics, and how these interact in the application of successful techniques to each individual client's context.

Stober and Grant (2006) advocate that the coach supports a context of positive potential growth by the client, highlighting the potentially negative impact of a forced or compulsory coaching context, commenting:

> Even if the coach is able to communicate an empathic, non-judgmental, and authentic stance, as in the humanistic approach, if the client is unable to trust that the context is set up for his or her success, the likelihood of success is threatened.
>
> (Stober and Grant, 2006: 359)

The impact of the organisational aspect of executive coaching on the coach–client relationship, as well as other contextual effects, and their interaction with other factors justify further theoretical and research exploration.

Email, webcam and telephone coaching

In a broad sense the term 'Online Therapy' includes health care services delivered via real-time and email communication media to connect across distances. Few studies, mostly with small sample sizes, and focusing on satisfaction with the technology rather than the effectiveness of the technology in delivering the services, exist (Foxhall, 2000), preventing a meaningful evaluation of its effectiveness. What the literature does highlight, however, is that future research should address the effect that online therapy has on therapeutic relationships (Griffiths and Cooper, 2003), particularly in a context where social changes in the role of client and caregiver are predicted to become more equal with the therapist being seen as 'more of a coach to a much more informed consumer'. Similarly, little research exists on email and telephone coaching in the coaching literature, specifically on the potential effect on the coach–client relationship.

Research by Marshall Goldsmith and others in eight organisations supported coaching by telephone, and Goldsmith suggests that phone coaching is a good way to coach (Rossett and Marino, 2005). Business articles suggest that online experiences and tools are a fundamental way of supporting the coach relationship. Benefits include the facility for 'matching' the client's needs, potentially with a coach who may not be geographically located nearby. Palmer (2004) notes in a case example, that a client who had experienced face-to-face, internet chat room and email sessions with the same practitioner found advantages with all three domains or settings. The client reflected: 'To conclude, from my point of view as a client, all that matters is a flexible method of communication. All methods we have used have proved to work effectively' (Palmer, 2004: 19). This suggests, as Rossett and Marino (2005) note, that the success of an e-coaching programme is based on those elements that make any coaching programme successful:

- Does the coach want to coach?
- Does the individual want to be coached?
- Is this the right match?
- The interpersonal dimension.

There are also a few elements unique to the technology.

Not all coaches believe that e-coaching works. Some doubt that trust and credibility can happen at a distance, consider that misperceptions can occur over this medium, hence emphasising the need for clear communication, or favour initial personal contact to establish trusting relationships (Feldman, 2002).

Similarly, telephone coaching has become more popular in the United States since the terrorist attacks on New York in 2001, and the UK could arguably be following the trend. In telephone coaching there is an emphasis on matching people rather than convenience (Sparrow, 2006b). As well as the need for preparation and focus, the need to establish a rapport before undertaking coaching by phone is also highlighted. While some coaches might view telephone coaching as an adjunct, there are those that as well as suggesting an increase in candour due to a greater sense of anonymity, would also conduct the whole coaching relationship by telephone (Faulkner, 2004).

Conclusion

This chapter has highlighted a surprising paradox: an implicit assumption of the importance of the coach–client relationship, with a lack of coaching research studies expressly addressing the relationship and its possible role as a change agent in coaching outcome (O'Broin and Palmer, 2006a).

An overarching theme of this discussion has been that common principles of effective change in other contexts are likely to translate to the coach–client relationship and are worthy of specific discussion, and research investigation. By linking specific examples from allied knowledge and research bases to existing coaching theory and practice, the chapter has adopted an evidence-informed coaching approach to discussion of several aspects of the coach–client relationship, providing a number of useful pointers for taking dialogue and future research on the topic forward.

Promising areas identified for future investigation include:

- the coaching alliance, devolved into sub-components of tasks, bonds and goals
- the coach's customisation or tailoring of the coach–client relationship to optimise outcome
- emphasis on appropriate responsiveness to the individual client's needs
- acknowledgement of the integrative roles of participants, relationship, technique and context to coaching outcome.

The many and varied contributions to the coach–client relationship considered during the course of this discussion illustrate Cavanagh's (2006: 337) point that 'the coaching relationship is a complex adaptive system'.

In such a complex adaptive system linking process to outcome we might expect multiple factors to be at work (see also Fillery-Travis and Lane, 2006), so further investigation at a rather more comprehensive level than whether there is a broad similarity of difference is required to unpack the various aspects of the relationship between client and coach, as is discussed elsewhere (O'Broin and Palmer, 2006b).

This chapter has argued the pressing need for discussion and research on the coach–client relationship and its imputed impact on coaching outcome. The potential benefit of an effective coach–client relationship, and possible coach contributions towards improving the relationship, have been neglected topics for investigation as potential agents for change in the coaching process. Such findings could have important implications for coaching outcome, coaching competencies, and coach training.

References

Amorose, A. J. and Horn, T. S. (2001) Pre-and post-season changes in intrinsic motivation of first year college athletes: relationships with coaching behavior and scholarship status. *Journal of Applied Sport Psychology* 13: 355–373.

Banning, K. L. (1997) Now coach? *Across the Board* 34: 28–32.

Beddoes-Jones, F. and Miller, J. (2006) 'Virtual' mentoring: can the principle of cognitive pairing increase its effectiveness? *International Journal of Evidence Based Coaching and Mentoring* 4(2): 54–60.

Bedi, R. P. (2006) Concept mapping the client's perspective on counselling alliance formation. *Psychotherapy: Theory, Research, Practice, Training* 53(1): 26–35.

Bedi, R. P., Davis, M. D. and Williams, M. (2005) Critical incidents in the formation of the therapeutic alliance from the client's perspective. *Psychotherapy: Theory, Research, Practice, Training* 42(3): 311–323.

Beutler, L. E. and Castonguay, L. G. (2006) The Task Force on empirically based principles of therapeutic change. In L. G. Castonguay and L. E. Beutler (eds) *Principles of Therapeutic Change that Work*. Oxford: Oxford University Press.

Beutler, L. E., Castonguay, L. G. and Follette, W. C. (2006) Integration of therapeutic factors in dysphoric disorders. In L. G. Castonguay and L. E. Beutler (eds) *Principles of Therapeutic Change that Work*. Oxford: Oxford University Press.

Bluckert, P. (2005a) The similarities and differences between coaching and therapy. *Industrial and Commercial Training* 37(2): 91–96.

Bluckert, P. (2005b) Critical factors in executive coaching – the coaching relationship. *Industrial and Commercial Training* 37(7): 336–340.

Bordin, E. S. (1975) The working alliance: basis for a general theory of psychotherapy. Paper presented at the Society for Psychotherapy Research, Washington, DC, September.

Bordin, E. S. (1979) The generalizability of the psychoanalytic concept of the working alliance. *Psychotherapy: Theory, Research and Practice* 16: 252–260.

Bordin, E. S. (1989) Building therapeutic alliances: the base for integration. Paper presented at the annual meeting of the Society for Exploration of Psychotherapy Integration, Berkeley, CA, April.

Bordin, E. S. (1994) Theory and research on the therapeutic working alliance: new directions. In A. O. Horvath and L. S. Greenberg (eds) *The Working Alliance: Theory, research and practice*. New York: Wiley.

Bortoli, L., Robazza, C. and Giabardo, S. (1995) Young athletes' perception of coaches' behavior. *Perceptual and Motor Skills* 81: 1217–1218.

Brandenburger, A. M. and Nalebuff, B. J. (1996) *Co-opetition*. New York: Doubleday.

Brotman, L. E., Liberi, W. P. and Wasylyshyn, K. M. (1998) Executive coaching: the need for standards of competence. *Consulting Psychology Journal: Practice and Research* 50(1): 40–46.

Butler, D. J. (2005) A reality check for game theory. *Journal of Economic Surveys* 19(1): 137–147.

Camerer, C. F. (1997) Progress in behavioral game theory. *Journal of Economic Perspectives* 11(4): 167–188.

Camerer, C. F. (2003) *Behavioral Game Theory*. New York: Russell Sage Foundation.

Carroll, M. (1996) *Workplace Counselling*. London: Sage.

Carroll, M. (2006) Key issues in coaching psychology supervision. *The Coaching Psychologist* 2(1): 4–8.

Castonguay, L. G. and Beutler, L. E. (2006a) Principles of therapeutic change: a task force on participants, relationships, and technique factors. *Journal of Clinical Psychology* 62(6): 631–638.

Castonguay, L. G. and Beutler, L. E. (2006b) Common and unique principles of therapeutic change: what do we know and what do we need to know? In L. G. Castonguay and L. E. Beutler (eds) *Principles of Therapeutic Change that Work*. Oxford: Oxford University Press.

Cavanagh, M. (2005) Mental-health issues and challenging clients in executive coaching. In M. Cavanagh, A. M. Grant and T. Kemp (eds) *Evidence Based Coaching. Volume 1, Theory, Research and Practice from the Behavioural Sciences* (pp. 21–36). Bowen Hills, Qld: Australian Academic Press.

Cavanagh, M. (2006) Coaching from a systemic perspective: a complex adaptive conversation. In D. R. Stober and A. M. Grant (eds) *Evidence Based Coaching Handbook: Putting best practices to work for your clients*. Hoboken, NJ: Wiley.

Cavanagh, M. and Grant, A. M. (2006) Coaching psychology and the scientist-practitioner model. In D. A. Lane and S. Corrie (eds) *The Modern Scientist-Practitioner: A guide to practice in psychology*. Hove: Routledge.

Chartered Institute of Personnel and Development (2005) *Training and Development 2005: Survey Report*. London: CIPD.

Clarkson, P. (1994) The psychotherapeutic relationship. In P. Clarkson and M. Pokorny (eds), *The Handbook of Psychotherapy*. London: Routledge.

Clarkson, P. (1995) *The Therapeutic Relationship*. London: Whurr.

Colman, A. M. (1995) *Game Theory and its Applications in the Social and Biological Sciences*. Oxford: Butterworth-Heinemann.

Deci, E. L. and Ryan, R. M. (1985) *Intrinsic Motivation and Self-Determination in Human Behavior*. New York: Plenum.

Diedrich, R. C. (1996) An iterative approach to executive coaching. *Counselling Psychology Journal: Practice and Research* 48: 61–66.

Faulkner, G. (2004) Listen and learn. *Contract Journal* 425(6497): 28–29.

Feldman, D. (2002) Distance coaching. *Training and Development* 56(9): 54–56.

Fernandez-Alvarez, H., Clarkin, J. F., Salgueiro, M. del C. and Critchfield, K. L. (2006) Participant factors in treating personality disorders. In L. G. Castonguay and L. E. Beutler (eds) *Principles of Therapeutic Change that Work*. Oxford: Oxford University Press.

Fillery-Travis, A. and Lane, D. (2006) Does coaching work or are we asking the wrong question? *International Coaching Psychology Review* 1(1): 23–35.

Foxhall, K. (2000) How will the rules on telehealth be written? *APA Monitor on Psychology* 31(4): 38.

Gabriel, L. (2005) *Speaking the Unspeakable: The ethics of dual relationships in counselling and psychotherapy*. London: Routledge.

Geanakopolous, J., Pearce, D. and Stachetti, E. (1989) Psychological games and sequential rationality. *Games and Economic Behavior* 1: 60–79.

Geller, J. D. (2005) Style and its contribution to a patient-specific model of therapeutic technique. *Psychotherapy: Theory, Research, Practice, Training* 42(4): 469–482.

Gould, D., Greenleaf, C., Chung, Y. and Guinan, D. (2002) A survey of US Atlanta and Nagano Olympians: variables perceived to influence performance. *Research Quarterly for Exercise and Sport* 73: 175–186.

Grant, A. M. (2006) An integrative goal-focused approach to executive coaching. In D. R. Stober and A. M. Grant (eds) *Evidence Based Coaching Handbook: Putting best practices to work for your clients*. Hoboken, NJ: Wiley.

Grant, A. M. and Cavanagh, M. J. (2004) Toward a profession of coaching: sixty-five years of progress and challenges for the future. *International Journal of Evidence Based Coaching and Mentoring* 2(1): 1–16.

Grawe, K. (2004) *Psychological Therapy*. Seattle, WA: Hogrefe-Huber.

Greenberg, L. S., Elliott, R., Watson, J. C. and Bohart, A. C. (2001) Empathy. *Psychotherapy: Theory, Research, Practice, Training* 38(4): 380–384.

Griffiths, M. and Cooper, G. (2003) Online therapy: implications for problem gamblers and clinicians. *British Journal for Guidance and Counselling* 31(1): 128–135.

Gyllensten, K. and Palmer, S. (2006) Workplace stress: can it be reduced by coaching? *The Coaching Psychologist* 2(1): 17–21.

Gyllensten, K. and Palmer, S. (2007) The coaching relationship: An interpretive phenomenological analysis. *International Coaching Psychology Review* 2(2): 168–177.

Haarbosch, V. and Newey, I. (2006) Feeling one's way in the dark: applying the scientist-practitioner model with young people who sexually offend. In D. A. Lane and S. Corrie (eds) *The Modern Scientist-Practitioner: A guide to practice in psychology*. Hove: Routledge.

Hart, V., Blattner, J. and Leipsic, S. (2001) Coaching versus therapy. *Consulting Psychology Journal: Practice and Research* 53(4): 229–237.

Hatcher, R. L. and Barends, A. W. (2006) How a return to theory could help alliance research. *Psychotherapy: Theory, Research, Practice, Training* 43(3): 292–299.

Herman, S. M. (1992) Predicting psychotherapists' treatment theories by multimodal structural profile inventory responses: an exploratory study. *Psychotherapy in Private Practice* 11(2): 85–100.

Herman, S. M. (1998) The relationship between therapist-client modality similarity and psychotherapy outcome. *Journal of Psychotherapy Practice and Research* 7: 56–64.

Hetherington, A. (2000) Exploitation in therapy and counselling: a breach of professional standards. *British Journal of Guidance and Counselling* 28(1): 11–22.

Hogan, R. and Hogan, J. (2001) Assessing leadership: a view from the dark side. *International Journal of Selection and Assessment* 9(1–2): 40–51.

Holtforth, M. G. and Castonguay, L. G. (2005) Relationship and techniques in cognitive-behavioral therapy: a motivational approach. *Psychotherapy* 42(4): 443–455.

Horvath, A. O. (2001) The alliance. *Psychotherapy: Theory, Research, Practice, Training* 38(4): 365–372.

Horvath, A. O. (2006) The alliance in context: accomplishments, challenges and future directions. *Psychotherapy: Theory, Research, Practice, Training* 43(3): 258–263.

Horvath, A. O. and Bedi, R. P. (2002) The alliance. In J. C. Norcross (ed.) *Psychotherapy Relationships that Work: Therapist contributions and responsiveness to patient needs*. London: Oxford.

Hunt, D. D., Carr, J. E., Dagodakis, C. S. and Walker, E. A. (1985) Cognitive match as a predictor of psychotherapy outcome. *Psychotherapy* 22: 718–721.

Jewel, P. (2002) Multicultural counselling research: an evaluation with proposals for future research. In S. Palmer (ed.) *Multicultural Counselling: A reader*. London: Sage.

Jowett, S. (2005) The coach-athlete partnership. *The Psychologist* 18(7): 412–415.

Jowett, S. (2006) Interpersonal and structural features of Greek coach-athlete dyads performing in individual sports. *Journal of Applied Sport Psychology* 18(1): 69–81.

Jowett, S. and Cockerill, I. (2002) Incompatibility in the coach-athlete relationship. In I. M. Cockerill (ed.) *Solutions in Sport Psychology*. London: Thomson Learning.

Kampa-Kokesch, S. and Anderson, M. Z. (2001) Executive coaching: a comprehensive review of the literature. *Consulting Psychology Journal: Practice and Research* 53(4): 205–228.

Kilburg, R. R. (2000) *Executive Coaching: Developing a managerial wisdom in a world of chaos*. Washington, DC: American Psychological Society.

Kilburg, R. R. (2004) Trudging toward Dodoville: conceptual approaches and case studies in executive coaching. *Consulting Psychology Journal: Practice and Research* 56(4): 203–213.

Lane, D. A. and Corrie, S. (2006) *The Modern Scientist-Practitioner: A guide to practice in psychology*. Hove: Routledge.

Lazarus, A. A. (1989) *The Practice of Multimodal Therapy*. Baltimore, MD: Johns Hopkins University Press.

Lazarus, A. A. (1993) Tailoring the therapeutic relationship or being an authentic chameleon, *Psychotherapy* 3: 404–407.

Lazarus, A. A. and Zur, O. (2002) *Dual Relationships and Psychotherapy*. New York: Springer.

Lebow, J., Kelly, J., Knobloch-Fedders, L. M. and Moos, R. (2006) Relationship factors in treating substance use disorders. In L. G. Castonguay and L. E. Beutler (eds) *Principles of Therapeutic Change that Work*. Oxford: Oxford University Press.

Levinson, H. (1996) Executive coaching. *Consulting Psychology Journal: Practice and Research* 48: 115–123.

Linley, P. A. (2006) Coaching research: Who? What? Where? When? Why? *International Journal of Evidence Based Coaching and Mentoring* 4(2): 1–7.

Lowman, R. L. (2005) Executive coaching: the road to Dodoville needs paving with more than good intentions. *Consulting Psychology Journal: Practice and Research* 57(1): 90–96.

Luborsky, L. (1976) Helping alliances in psychotherapy. In J. L. Cleghorn (ed.) *Successful Psychotherapy*. New York: Brunner/Mazel.

Lyle, J. (1999) Coaching philosophy and coaching behaviour. In N. Cross and J. Lyle (eds) *The Coaching Process: Principles and practice for sport*. Oxford: Butterworth.

Mageau, G. A. and Vallerand, R. J. (2003) The coach-athlete relationship: a motivational model. *Journal of Sports Sciences* 21: 883–904.

Miller, A. and Frederickson, N. (2006) Generalizable findings and idiographic problems: struggles and successes for educational psychologists as scientist-practitioners. In D. A. Lane and S. Corrie (eds) *The Modern Scientist-Practitioner: A guide to practice in psychology*. Hove: Routledge.

Newman, M. G., Stiles, W. B., Janeck, A. and Woody, S. R. (2006) Integration of therapeutic factors in anxiety disorders. In L. G. Castonguay and L. E. Beutler (eds) *Principles of Therapeutic Change that Work*. Oxford: Oxford University Press.

Norcross, J. (1993) Tailoring relationship stances to client needs: an introduction. *Psychotherapy: Theory, Research, and Practice* 30: 402–403.

Norcross, J. C. (2001) Purposes, processes, and products of the Task Force on empirically supported therapy relationships. *Psychotherapy: Theory, Research, Practice, Training* 38(4): 345–356.

Norcross, J. C. (ed.) (2002) *Psychotherapy Relationships that Work*. New York: Oxford University Press.

O'Broin, A. and Palmer, S. (2006a) The coach–client relationship and contributions made by the coach in improving coaching outcome. *The Coaching Psychologist* 2(2): 16–20.

O'Broin, A. and Palmer, S. (2006b) Win-win situation? Learning from parallels and differences between coaching psychology and sport psychology. *The Coaching Psychologist* 2(3): 17–23.

O'Neill, M. B. (2000) *Executive Coaching with Backbone and Heart: A systems approach to emerging leaders with their challenges*. San Francisco, CA: Jossey-Bass.

Palmer, S. (2002a) Counselling idiographically: the multimodal approach. In S. Palmer (ed.) *Multicultural Counselling: A reader*. London: Sage.

Palmer, S. (2002b) Boundaries, journals and counselling psychology: Stephen Palmer interviews Kasia Szymanska. *Counselling Psychology Quarterly* 15(4): 399–404.

Palmer, S. (2004) A rational emotive behavioural approach to face-to-face, telephone and internet therapy and coaching: a case study. *Rational Emotive Behaviour Therapist* 11(1): 12–22.

Palmer, S., Cooper, C. and Thomas, K. (2003). *Creating a Balance: Managing stress*. London: British Library.

Palomino, F., Rustichini, A. and Rigotti, L. (1999) The invisible foot. *The Economist* 351(8113): 62–63.

Paul, G. L. (1967) Strategy of outcome research in psychotherapy. *Journal of Consulting Psychology* 331: 109–118.

Peltier, B. (2001) *The Psychology of Executive Coaching: Theory and application*. New York: Brunner-Routledge.

Peltier, B. and Irueste-Montes, A. M. (2001) Coaching women in business. In *The Psychology of Executive Coaching: Theory and application*. New York: Brunner-Routledge.

Peterson, D. B. (1996) Executive coaching at work. *Consulting Psychology Journal: Practice and Research* 48(2): 78–86.

Poczwardowski, A., Barott, J. E. and Peregoy, J. J. (2002) The athlete and the coach: their relationship and its meaning – methodological concerns and research process. *International Journal of Sport Psychology* 33: 98–115.

Ponterotto, J. G. (1987) Counseling Mexican Americans: a multimodal approach. *Journal of Counseling and Development* 65: 308–312.

Prochaska, J. O. and DiClemente, C. C. (1984) Toward a comprehensive model of change. In J. O. Prochaska and C. C. DiClemente (eds) *The Transtheoretical Approach: Crossing the traditional boundaries of therapy*. Homewood, IL: Dow-Jones.

Prochaska, J. O. and Norcross, J. C. (2001) Stages of change. *Psychotherapy* 38(4): 443–448.

Reeve, J. (1998) Autonomy support as an interpersonal motivating style: is it teachable? *Contemporary Educational Psychology* 23: 312–330.

Richard, J. T. (1999) Multimodal therapy: a useful model for the executive coach. *Consulting Psychology Journal: Practice and Research* 51(1): 24–30.

Rosenzweig, S. (1936) Some implicit common factors in diverse methods of psychotherapy. *American Journal of Orthopsychiatry* 6: 412–415.

Rosenzweig, S. (2002) Some implicit common factors in diverse methods of psychotherapy. *Journal of Psychotherapy Integration* 12(1): 5–9.

Rosinski, P. and Abbott, G. N. (2006) Coaching from a cultural perspective. In D. R. Stober and A. M. Grant (eds) *Evidence Based Coaching Handbook: Putting best practices to work for your clients*. Hoboken, NJ: Wiley.

Rossett, A. and Marino, G. (2005) If coaching is good, then e-coaching is . . . *Training and Development* 59(11): 46–49.

Salminen, S. and Liukkonen, J. (1996) Coach-athlete relationship and coaching realized in training sessions. *International Journal of Sport Psychology* 27: 59–67.

Scoular, A. and Linley, P. A. (2006) Coaching, goal-setting and personality type: what matters? *The Coaching Psychologist* 2(1): 9–11.

Sparrow, S. (2006a) The gender gap. *Training and Coaching Today* April: 22–23.

Sparrow, S. (2006b) Hello, how are you? It's your coach calling. *Training Magazine* 24.

Steering Committee (2002) Conclusions and recommendations for the Task Force on empirically supported therapy relationships. In J. C. Norcross (ed.) *Psychotherapy Relationships that Work: Therapist contributions and responsiveness to patient needs*. New York: Oxford University Press.

Stiles, W. B. and Wolfe, B. E. (2006) Relationship factors in treating anxiety disorders. In L. G. Castonguay and L. E. Beutler (eds) *Principles of Therapeutic Change that Work*. Oxford: Oxford University Press.

Stober, D. R. (2006) Coaching from the humanistic perspective. In D. R. Stober and A. M. Grant (eds) *Evidence Based Coaching Handbook: Putting best practices to work for your clients*. Hoboken, NJ: Wiley.

Stober, D. R. and Grant, A. M. (2006) Toward a contextual approach to coaching models. In D. R. Stober and A. M. Grant (eds) *Evidence Based Coaching Handbook: Putting best practices to work for your clients*. Hoboken, NJ: Wiley.

Stober, D. R., Wildflower, L. and Drake, D. (2006) Evidence-based practice: a potential approach for effective coaching. *International Journal of Evidence Based Coaching and Mentoring* 4(1): 1–8.

Sullivan, M. F., Skovholt, T. M. and Jennings, L. (2005) Master therapists' construction of the therapy relationship. *Journal of Mental Health Counseling* 27(1): 48–70.

Task Force on Promotion and Dissemination of Psychological Procedures (1995) Training in and dissemination of empirically validated psychological treatments: report and recommendations. *The Clinical Psychologist* 48(1): 3–23.

Vallerand, R. J. (2001) A hierarchical model of intrinsic and extrinsic motivation in sport and exercise. In G. C. Roberts (ed.) *Advances in Motivation in Sport and Exercise*. Champaign, IL: Human Kinetics.

Von Neumann, J. and Morgenstern, O. (1944) *The Theory of Games and Economic Behavior*. Princeton, NJ: Princeton University Press.

Wampold, B. E. (2001) *The Great Psychotherapy Debate: Models, methods, and findings*. Mahwah, NJ: Lawrence Erlbaum.

Wasylyshyn, K. M. (2003) Executive coaching: an outcome study. *Consulting Psychology Journal: Practice and Research* 55(2): 94–106.

Whitmore, J. (2002) *Coaching for Performance: Growing people, performance and purpose*. London: Nicholas Brealey.

Witherspoon, R. and White, R. P. (1996) Executive coaching: a continuum of roles. *Consulting Psychology Journal: Practice and Research* 48: 124–133.

Younggren, J. N. and Gottlieb, M. C. (2004) Managing risk when contemplating multiple relationships. *Professional Psychology: Research and Practice* 35(2): 255–260.

Discussion points

- Is client and coach collaboration on the 'tasks, bonds and goals' of the coaching alliance necessary and sufficient for an effective relationship? For an effective outcome?
- In which ways might you need to tailor the coach–client relationship to your individual client? How would you do this?
- How would you foster and maintain a strong coaching relationship with your client in the event of an alliance rupture?
- How can the context, particularly the organisational context, impact on the coaching relationship? How can you work with these factors?

Suggested reading

Bluckert, P. (2006) *Psychological Dimensions of Executive Coaching*. Maidenhead: McGraw-Hill.

Hart, V., Blattner, J. and Leipsic, S. (2001) Coaching versus therapy. *Consulting Psychology Journal: Practice and Research* 53(4): 229–237.

Lane, D. A. and Corrie, S. (2006) *The Modern Scientist-Practitioner: A guide to practice in psychology*. Hove: Routledge.

Stober, D. R. and Grant, A. M. (2006) *Evidence Based Coaching Handbook: Putting best practices to work for your clients*. Hoboken, NJ: Wiley.

Chapter 17

A cognitive-developmental approach for coach development

Tatiana Bachkirova and Elaine Cox

Introduction

Coach training courses and postgraduate development courses for coaches and coaching psychologists have grown in number very considerably since 2000. However, at present, apart from Laske's (2006a) work, there are few theoretically based models of coach development. The emphasis on individual development is critically important for coaching and coaching psychology as a field of knowledge, but this has not been the subject of any significant research or analysis in relation to coaches or coaching psychologists and their development. In this chapter, we want to redress some of that balance and consider existing theories of individual development together with some specific areas where these have been adapted for a coaching context.

Our definition of development incorporates the view that adults are not unchanging, but are continually learning, developing and growing. In terms of the fundamental understanding of development as such we agree with Werner (1948: 126) that 'whenever development occurs, it proceeds from a state of relative globality and lack of differentiation to a state of increasing differentiation, articulation, and hierarchic integration'. In this context 'differentiation' refers the degree to which a system (e.g. an individual, a family, an organisation or humanity as a whole) is composed of parts that differ in structure or function from one another, while 'integration' refers to the extent to which the different parts communicate and enhance the other's goals. A system that is more differentiated and integrated than another could be said to be more 'complex' (Csikszentmihalyi, 1994). The cognitive-developmental tradition as applied to adult development postulates significant changes in the level of complexity as far as individuals, as systems, are concerned.

Therefore the purpose of this chapter is to present a description of developmental tasks for coaches, based on a synthesis of models of cognitive development and ego development. The chapter is divided into sections. First, we outline the theoretical background that underpins a number of models of adult development. We then explore relevant cognitive-reflective models, and include those by Kohlberg (1969), Perry (1970) and King and

Kitchener (1994) in this section. We then move on to consider the theories and models of development proposed particularly by Loevinger (1976), Kegan (1982, 1994) and Cook-Greuter (2004), which we title the 'ego-development strand'.

Following this, there is a brief discussion of three recent applications of these theories to coach, coaching psychologist or mentor development. The first of these is developed by Berger (2006) and draws on Kegan's (1982) work, the second is Chandler and Kram's (2005) application of adult development perspectives, mainly drawing on Kegan's theories, to what they term developmental networks. The third is the attempt by Laske (2006a, 2006b) to develop a framework focusing on changes in adult cognition and social-emotional capability, which can be applied to coach training.

Following these reviews, the chapter provides a model developed by us that could be appropriate for use in development programmes for coaches or coaching psychologists, or could provide a reference point during coaching supervision. A case study is also presented in order to provide a flavour of how the theories and the model might inform a supervision process and relationship.

Background

Cognitive-developmentalism (also called structuralism or constructivism) in psychology, although relatively young, already has a distinct place and role in explaining behaviour. It also brings an important and clearly defined dimension to understanding the development of individuals. The *cognitive* component of this tradition stems from the contribution of Piaget to understanding the role of cognitive structures in the development of a child. He was an advocate of the structuralist position where basic components or structures accommodate qualitative shifts in development. The shifts in development that are studied in this approach are manifested in the way individuals make sense of the world and themselves in it. Constructions become more differentiated, integrated and complex as development occurs.

The *developmental* element of this tradition has a distinct place and role in psychology and applied fields and could be seen as central for coaching psychology. There is a significant difference between this tradition and some others in psychology in terms of the main philosophical assumption about human nature. For example, the cognitive-developmental tradition does not share a pessimistic account of the human potential for development held in traditional psychoanalysis. However, it does differ from humanistic psychology because the positive view of human nature by cognitive developmentalists refers to the potential of humankind as a whole and not to each individual case. Each individual may or may not function during his or her lifetime across the whole spectrum of development or may even regress.

For all cognitive-developmental theories thought and meaning-making are fundamentally structured. The structures themselves – e.g. schema (Piaget), subject–object relation (Kegan) – are permanent or changing very slowly. Each person constructs his/her own frameworks according to his/her specific combination of external circumstances and internal factors. Where other traditions and schools of psychology are looking for common features of change in development of individuals and for specific conditions for facilitating this change, cognitive developmentalists identify patterns indicating qualitative shifts in the potential process of development itself and suggest ways of applying this knowledge to each individual.

Developmentalists do not deny that the process of change in individuals occurs in different ways, dimensions and at different rates, and not only through changes in the structures. People learn new skills, acquire new knowledge and change their personal qualities throughout their life in different ways and by very different means. However, the changes that are addressed in this tradition are much rarer. They signify significant shifts in the way an individual sees the world and interprets his/her experiences. They influence the depth and complexity of what he/she can notice and therefore represent a level of change that could be seen as vertical rather than horizontal (Cook-Greuter, 2004).

Fully developed cognitive-developmental theories see human potential as changing from simple, static and ego-centric to complex, dynamic and world-centric. The qualities of each stage of development, when transcended to the next level, remain as properties of the new stage. The person can utilise any skill that he/she learned before and with each stage is becoming more flexible, integrated and therefore more capable of functioning in the world that is also changing and becoming more complex.

What is particularly important in relation to development of coaches is that each stage enriches individual capacity for reflection and effective interaction with others. Their ability to notice nuances and details of situations is increasing. The resultant self-awareness gives them a better opportunity to articulate, influence and potentially change these situations. Their capacity to understand others at earlier stages is increasing with each new stage they reach. However, there is always scope and potential for further development at whatever stage the individual operates. The development process is an outcome of a combination of internal and external factors for each individual, but can also be further stimulated and facilitated by appropriate support and challenge within the coaching process.

We believe that the cognitive-developmental perspective is very important for understanding factors influencing changes in coaching process. It is also particularly useful for understanding development of the coach and growth of their capacity for helping others to develop. In this chapter we shall explore cognitive-developmental theories from two perspectives, which we believe are most significant for development of coaches and coaching psychologists. We call the first perspective the *cognitive-reflective* strand, which has its origins in Piaget's work and emphasises reasoning and learning capacities (specific examples include Kohlberg, 1969; Perry, 1970; King and Kitchener, 1994). The second perspective is the *ego-development* strand, with its origins in Loevinger (1976), which focuses on the development of self-identity and maturity of interpersonal relationships (specifically Kegan, 1982, 1994; Cook-Greuter, 2004).

Cognitive-reflective strand

In Piaget's (1976) model of cognitive development there are a number of ordered stages through which children develop, each suggesting a different way of understanding and constructing knowledge about the world. Piaget reasons that development occurs when the child's current cognitive structures can no longer reconcile conflicts between existing understanding and current experience. At this point some cognitive restructuring is necessary, resulting in progression towards the next, more sophisticated, level of development. The development culminates in a 'formal operations' stage some time in early adolescence.

Commons and Richards (2002) describe how the most common method of extending stage theory beyond the Piagetian 'formal' arena is to identify limitations in formal operations, then to describe a kind of thinking that enables the individual to transcend these limitations into 'postformal' stages. Often these attempts involve drawing on other disciplines. For example, Koplowitz (1984) draws on General Systems Theory (Checkland, 1981) and Buddhism. His theory incorporates Piaget's concrete operations and formal operations stages, but goes beyond this to posit a post-logical or system thinking stage followed by a fourth stage of unitary operational thought.

Perry's (1970) model of intellectual and moral development also goes beyond Piaget's framework in that it adds an element of responsibility. Perry suggested that there are structural changes in a person's assumptions about the origins of knowledge and value. Perry describes three overlapping phases of development that encompass nine cognitive positions. The research undertaken with college students in the USA during the 1950s and 1960s identifies three phases of development that move from basic duality in thinking at position 1, through a growing awareness of multiplicity and relational knowing at position 5, through contextual relativism towards the development of commitment and resolution at the more developed positions, 8 and 9. In the middle lies the complex dualism phase where progress towards a more diffuse acceptance of ambiguity begins to be realised. This, Perry points out, is possibly the most difficult transition: the shift from simple dualism to complex dualism.

Perry's findings also inspired Belenky et al. (1986: 104) to explore women's ways of knowing. In their categorisation, the dualist phase of Perry is termed 'subjectivist', while the move towards relativism is referred to as 'separate knowing': 'subjectivists assume that everyone is right; separate knowers, on the other hand, are especially suspicious of ideas that feel right.'

Also drawing on an initial study of Perry's (1970) work, King and Kitchener (1994: 31) developed their model of reflective judgement. They describe how educators need to engage students meaningfully in addressing ill-structured problems, i.e. problems where the solution cannot be described with any degree of certainty or completeness (King and Kitchener, 1994: 11–12) and suggest that development spans seven stages:

1   Knowing is limited to single concrete observations.
2   There are two categories for knowing: right answers and wrong answers.
3   In some areas, knowledge is certain, while in others knowledge is temporarily uncertain.
4   Since knowledge is unknown in some specific cases, all knowledge is uncertain.
5   Knowledge is uncertain and so must be understood within a context.
6   Because it is contextual, knowledge is constructed by comparing evidence and opinion.
7   Knowledge is the outcome of a process of reasonable enquiry towards a general principle that is consistent across domains.

King and Kitchener (1994: 22) acknowledge that the assumptions underpinning their reflective judgement model are based on Paiget's work with children and adolescents. They go on to highlight two main differences between their model and other contemporary models of critical thinking. The first is that epistemic assumptions are important to the reasoning process. The second difference endorses Dewey's (1991) assertion that true reflective thinking is uncalled for unless real uncertainty exists about the possible solution to the problem. Dewey had argued that over-analysis is to be avoided, unless there is a problem, when comparing presuppositions enables misunderstandings to be removed, reminding us that all learning comes through experience, but not all experience leads to learning. He is careful to emphasise that problems do need to be reflected upon, stating that 'where the shoe pinches, analytic examination is indicated' (Dewey, 1991: 216).

Dewey (1991: 215) also argues that it is necessary at some points 'to turn upon some unconscious assumption and make it explicit'. It is this emphasis on critical reflection and examination of assumptions that is at the heart of Mezirow's (1990) theory of transformative learning. Mezirow (1990: 1) describes reflection as enabling us to 'correct distortions in our beliefs and errors in problem-solving'.

Some authors have argued that critical reflection that enables people to examine rationally the assumptions and values by which they justify their beliefs, takes place only in late adolescence or adulthood (Brookfield, 1987;

Mezirow, 1990; Garrison, 1991). They argue that the ability to reflect critically happens not just as a function of physical maturity but because as people
get older their reasoning and reflective capacities develop due to the challenging experiences and encounters that occur over time. Mezirow (1990), in
particular, argues that it is only through transformative learning that changes
in psycho-social development can occur and that it is the role of the adult
educator to help to facilitate such learning:

> The adult educator actively precipitates transformative learning when, in
> the process of helping learners address their expressed needs, he or she
> seeks to move the learners' interest beyond their articulated needs to
> *understanding the reasons for them* and the way that psycho-cultural
> forces have shaped the learners' interpretation of the worlds of others,
> and of themselves.
>
> (Mezirow, 1990: 365, our emphasis)

A further model that has relevance for our discussion of cognitive development is that of Kohlberg (1969), who used stories about moral dilemmas
to explore how respondents explained their actions. The emphasis in this
model, therefore, is on moral justification. Kohlberg's responses were classified into three levels (pre-conventional, conventional and post-conventional)
and within each level there were two stages.

Kohlberg further stressed that the men he studied were not able to understand moral reasoning more than one stage ahead of their own: a person in
Stage 1 could understand Stage 2 reasoning but nothing beyond that. This
suggests that in learning situations only moral arguments that are one stage
ahead of the person's present level of reasoning should be introduced in
order to maximise movement to higher stages. Gowan (1974: 187) also cau-
tions against 'developmental abuse', suggesting that this occurs when the use
of characteristics of a higher stage are encouraged while the individual is
coping with the tasks of an earlier stage.

Gowan's work moved away from delineating stages of cognitive development and focused on the developmental process as a continuum that includes
but transcends the dimensions of cognition, affect, rational and emotional
development. In the next section we explore this notion of ego transcendence
in further detail.

Ego-development strand

The term 'ego-development' was introduced to the field of cognitive-
developmental psychology by Loevinger (1976) as the result of identifying a
new variable in her well-known and highly respected research. The variable
was confirmed to be developmental. It was closely associated with a factor
earlier studied by Sullivan et al. (1957), which they called interpersonal

maturity or the capacity for interpersonal integration. Loevinger (1987) writes that, although she was hesitant about using this term because of its specific association with the psychoanalytic concept restricted to the first years of a child's life, no other terms were inclusive enough to describe the phenomena that she identified. Her method was psychometric and geared to accentuate individual differences. At the same time she assumed a basic stage structure that was consistently identified. Each person in her study was progressing from one stage to the next as the result of his or her own pattern of interests and social circumstances. Specific stages in the development of self-identity with a corresponding interpersonal mode are identified in Loevinger's (1987: 226) study as follows:

Impulsive	Egocentric, dependent
Self-protective	Manipulative, wary
Conformist	Cooperative, loyal
Conscientious-conformist	Helpful, self-aware
Conscientious	Intense, responsible
Individualistic	Mutual
Autonomous	Interdependent
Integrated	Cherishing individuality

The next theory that well represents this strand is Kegan's (1982) orders of consciousness. We believe that this theory includes the most comprehensive description of underlying structures that give rise to the natural emergence of the self in relation to others. Kegan's theory is also very important for coaching psychology as it distinguishes between informational learning and transformational learning which changes the very form of the mind, making it more spacious, more complex, and more able to deal with multiple demands and with uncertainty. Transformative learning can take place during coaching, affecting not only the behaviour of the clients, nor just the way they feel, but also their actual way of knowing.

The theory addresses the two most fundamental and related processes that human beings are involved with: integration as movement towards relatedness and inclusion and differentiation as movement towards separation and autonomy. Meaning-making activity for Kegan revolves around what one takes to be self and what one takes to be other and what the relationship is between them. This psychological framework, subject–object relations, illustrates how individuals grow, like the dynamics of a balancing act, maintaining and then breaking out from the equilibrium between self and other.

Things that are Subject in this theory are by definition experienced as unquestioned, simply a part of the self. Things that are Subject cannot be observed because they are a part of the individual, they cannot be reflected upon – that would require the ability to stand back and take a look at them. While things that are Subject *have* us, we *have* things that are Object.

Things that are Object in our lives are 'those elements of our knowing or organizing that we can reflect on, handle, look at, be responsible for, relate to each other, take control of, internalise, assimilate, or otherwise operate upon' (Kegan, 1994: 32). The more individuals can take as Object, the more complex their worldview becomes, because they can examine and act upon more things.

The idea of development in Kegan's theory is best understood through the following analogy: to be subject is to 'see with' rather than to 'see through'. Drath (1990) describing this theory gives a good example of 'cultural blindness':

> We see with our culture-bound norms and expectations, accept them as given, and cannot examine them for what they are – that is, we cannot see through them. Our cultural heritage is something we are, not something we have. The culture holds us; we are embedded in it and cannot rise above it.
>
> (Drath, 1990: 486)

In some circumstances, however, and with further growth we may become aware of differences that are culturally determined and become aware of the distance from others in a way that we never did before.

This important element of the theory offered by Kegan has already an incredible value for the coaching process. Understanding of subject–object underlying structures can help coaches to see the dynamics of this process and to facilitate their clients' shifts from subject to object by recognising and providing support. They could watch for the re-absorption of the insight in the client helping to build *psychological muscle* in order to hold something out from a person as an Object. As Fitzgerald and Berger (2002: 31) say: 'one of the most powerful interventions coaches can provide is simply help to keep critical insights alive for their clients'.

Kegan (1982) describes six stages (orders of mind) through which people evolve:

1   At the *Incorporative stage* no object exists for a baby. Everything is subject.
2   At the *Impulsive stage* objects are recognised as separate, but each person is subject to his/her perception. If perception changes, the world also changes so the world is magic. Children at this stage have to be reminded about the rules and need to learn about the world.
3   At the *Imperial stage* the young person gains control over perceptions and impulses, which imparts the sense of freedom, power and independence. They develop the self as an agent but cannot separate themselves from their needs and wishes. They are aware of other people's feelings, but empathy is not possible yet. They are self-centred and see others as

helpers or barriers to getting what they want. They follow rules only to avoid punishment and need to be supervised.

4 At the *Interpersonal stage* the person *has* needs, not *is* her/his needs, so others are understood as also having needs. They are no longer a means to his/her ends. But people at this stage still *are* their relationship. They are self-reflective and can subordinate their needs to something greater, but they have no sense of what they want outside the expectations of others. They feel torn apart by the conflict between important others. This causes both difficulties in making decisions and issues of self-esteem, because people at this stage need other people to like them. They can do anything as long as they have someone whom they respect and who can help them make decisions.

5 The *Institutional stage* suggests that the person is someone who now *has* the relationship. This creates a self that exists even outside relationship to others, and has a sense of autonomy and identity. People at this stage are able to examine various rules and opinions and mediate between them. Unlike those at the Imperial stage they feel empathy for others and take their views into consideration. Unlike those who are at the Inter-personal stage they are not torn apart by others' views – they have their own system with which to make decisions. They are self-motivated, self-evaluative and can make good leaders. They can create their own rules and fight for them but may not be the best diplomats, because they are too invested in their own way of doing things.

6 At the *Interindividual stage* a person becomes someone who *has* identity, so becomes individual. They have achieved everything available to the previous stage, but in addition have learned not only the limitations of their own inner system but also the limitation of *having* an inner system. They can look across their inner systems and see similarities in what look like differences. They are less prone to black-and-white thinking and apply fewer dichotomies and polarities in their evalu-ations of the world. They could act as wise advisers and help individ-uals and groups to understand that everyone is a member of a larger community.

It is important to note here that according to this theory it is impossible to measure a person's worth by looking at his or her order of mind. What is more important is the *fit* between the order of mind and the task each person is required to do. Kegan (1982) also reminds us about the value of what he calls a natural therapy or natural psychological support whenever the indi-vidual is facing a transition or a new developmental task. The quality of this support very much depends on the presence of those 'who can see, recognise, and understand who the person is and who he or she is becoming. . . . Support is not alone an affective matter, but a matter of "knowing"; a matter of shape, as well as intensity' (Kegan, 1982: 260).

We are also in debt for the model we present in this chapter to the work of Susanne Cook-Greuter (1999, 2004) who developed further the developmental framework that emerged in Loevinger's (1987) research. Cook-Greuter presents the Ego Development Theory (EDT) in relation to adult development which describes a system with three interrelated components: behavioural, affective and cognitive. Her later approach to adult development is informed by Wilber's (2000, 2006) integral theory and addresses preconventional, conventional, postconventional and earlier post-postconventional ways of meaning-making in Wilber's model of consciousness.

Cook-Greuter (1999) gives a rich description of ego-development stages, listed here in parallel with corresponding action logics that are described by Torbert (1991, 2004) in the context of organisational leadership:

Ego-development stages **Cook-Greuter (1999)**	Action logics **Torbert (2004)**
Impulsive	Impulsive
Self-defensive	Opportunist
Conformist	Diplomat
Self-conscious	Expert/technician
Conscientious	Achiever
Individualist	Individualist
Autonomous	Strategist
Construct-aware	Alchemist

Three attempted applications of the cognitive-developmental theories to coaching

Cognitive-developmental theories are already successfully applied to various areas of practice. The levels of existence initially researched by Graves (1970), for example, were further developed and applied to organisational leadership by Beck and Cowan (1996). Beck and Cowan were arguing that the search for the means of motivating people should be secondary to the enquiry about natural motivational flows and the ways of relating to these. They describe several worldviews that represented different way of thinking and learning, different sets of means values and end values and existential problems specific to these worldviews. This approach suggests that managing people according to their worldview and developing them at the same time can be rewarding not only for individuals involved, but for businesses, societies and the entire world.

Rooke and Torbert (2005) in collaboration with Cook-Greuter created a survey tool, the Leadership Development Profile, that allows identification of what they call leaders' internal 'action logic'. Seven different action logics were identified that illustrate the ways individual leaders interpret their situation, respond to challenges and tend to influence others. Rooke and Torbert

(2005) argue for the importance for leaders to know their action logic, to evaluate their strengths and limitations in relation to current circumstances and to identify potential for further development.

Closer to the topic of this chapter there are currently several authors who write about the application of cognitive-developmental approaches in relation to coaching and mentoring and offer their perspectives and models. Chandler and Kram (2005) and Fitzgerald and Berger (2002), also Berger (2006), base their work on Kegan's (1982, 1994) developmental theory. Laske's (2006a, 2006b) work not only is based on the theories of adult development, primarily the work of Kegan, but also incorporates the notion of dialectical thinking developed by Basseches (1984) and the idea of human capability as developed by Jaques (1994).

Berger (2006), for instance, concentrating only on adult development, offers her description of four modes of meaning-making that differ in ways of making sense of the world in adulthood. Each mode results in different ways of perspective taking, orientations to authority and rules, key needs in relationship with others, etc. Berger's modes correspond to four levels of development, Prince/Princess, Journeyman, CEO and Elder, which are described in the context of organisational life. One of the most valuable contributions of Fitzgerald and Berger (2002) and Berger (2006) is that they not only identify key strengths, blind spots and areas of growth for each of these groups but also suggest potentially useful interventions for coaching and consider pitfalls that coaches may face when working with each group. We also find ourselves very much in congruence with these authors' perspectives on development, assessment of clients' stages and particularly their considerations of ethical issues for coaches when engaged with the cognitive-developmental approach. For example we would join Berger (2006: 95) in terms of warning about the illusion of simplicity of the approach and too hasty judgements of developmental stages particularly in organisational contexts.

Chandler and Kram (2005: 549) relate adult development perspectives to other developmental networks and relationships, such as mentoring. Their contention is that 'protégés at different stages will maximally benefit from developers at higher stages, given that they will have transcended the limitations that the protégé faces'. To support this argument, Chandler and Kram examine Kegan's stages in relation to the tasks of the protégé and the mentor.

Protégés who are at Kegan's Interpersonal stage, they argue, may be seen as 'indecisive and overly reliant upon [the mentor] for assistance' (Chandler and Kram, 2005: 553), and mentors at this level may not have the 'self-awareness and insight to offer different types of career and psychosocial support'. The Interpersonal mentor would be hindered by the lack of ability to transcend his/her dependence on relationships and to differentiate among different perspectives, and so, as a result, may unwittingly confirm and reinforce their protégé's values and decisions, rather than help to confront or challenge these.

In the next of Kegan's stages, the Institutional stage, the individual is more self-directed. At this stage, Chandler and Kram (2005: 557–558) maintain, individuals are better able to cultivate the relationships that facilitate learning and growth, and are likely to have 'a rich peer network', but their weakness is that they strongly identify with their occupation, their positions and their other affiliations. These 'institutions' then define who they are, despite their being self-directed and independent in relation to personal needs and other goals. Chandler and Kram (2005) suggest that such an individual may feel 'stifled, threatened, or controlled by efforts from a supervisor or formally assigned mentor to guide him.'

At the Interindividual stage, individuals are better able to adjust to new information and new situations. They have a strong sense of identity, yet they are reflexive and can see the potential in a wide range of relationships. Chandler and Kram (2005: 560) argue that a protégé at this stage may, if they have a mentor at a lower developmental stage, feel uninspired or under-mined. The mentor may not be able to provide support that resonates with the interindividual person. However, this may not be a significant problem because this protégé is not dependent upon one relationship for his/her development.

Chandler and Kram (2005) also identify how a variety of instruments and methods have been devised to assess developmental stages. Lahey et al. (1988) developed the subject–object interview, while the Washington University Sentence Completion Test is used to measure Loevinger's (1976) stages. Torbet (2004) has built on Loevinger's work and that of Cook-Greuter in order to create the Leadership Development Profile.

This emphasis on measurement leads us to pay particular attention to Laske's work in this area. Laske (2006a, 2006b) is interested in the develop-ment of coaches and describes a model of research-based coach education. He holds a strong position on the role of coaches in the development of clients and places great emphasis on the coach's ability to 'mediate' between clients and the 'ways in which they internally construct their thinking and emotions' (Laske, 2006a: 46). Following Kohlberg (1969), Laske suggests that coaches cannot, or should not, support clients who are at a higher level of development than their own.

A similarly strong position is declared in relation to education of coaches: 'I propose that coach education that does not engage coaches' own increas-ingly more complex sense of language and ability to listen, is missing the opportunity to make a major contribution to client growth' (Laske, 2006a: 46). In his model of coach development, assessment is made of trainees' cog-nitive and behavioural development. The subject–object interview, developed by Lahey et al. (1988), is used to explore socio-emotional development, as part of what Laske terms the 'developmental process consultation', aimed at arriving at a picture of the coach's developmental level. The assessed devel-opmental level could be an indicator of the progress made by the coach and a conglomerate of assessments in relation to groups of students on the programme can be used 'to compare programmes to each other in terms of their developmental efficacy' (Laske, 2006a: 54).

Although we support some of Laske's underlying assumptions and propositions, we have also explicit reservations against some of the others. We agree, for instance, that 'coaching competences are used by practitioners according to their present level of capability' (Laske, 2006a: 47) and share his concerns about current lack of research that transcends behaviourist frameworks and theories of change in the individual.

At the same time our relationship with a view on development that higher is better, is more complex than that presented by Laske. Although developmental approaches, by the very fact of creating hierarchies, make judgements, we believe that they do not transfer this judgement of the way of meaning-making to the individual's ability to function in his/her specific circumstances. What matters most is the fit between the environment and the individual's capacity for dealing with it. The tasks that are faced in the coaching process vary immensely, and so too does the potential contribution of those who facilitate this process.

We believe that imposing the necessity of development has potential ethical implications that are underestimated in this approach. We agree with Kegan who argues that 'among the many things from which a practitioner's clients need protection is the practitioner's hopes for the client's future, however benign and sympathetic these hopes may be' (Kegan, 1982: 295). Professional development of coaches has a number of important dimensions that could be and are addressed in training and education, but coaching programmes that declare their ambition to be the movement of the coach to another level of development would take too much on themselves to say the least. In the next section we will present a different philosophical and ethical position in relation to the focused development of individuals.

In terms of the practical consideration in applying Laske's approach to assessment of developmental levels, Derry (2006) has questioned whether this model of developmental process consultation can be applied to coach–client relationships because of the length of time such an assessment would take. We would add to this a point made by Berger (2006: 96) who suggests that 'simply understanding developmental trajectories leaves coaches far better equipped to understand the diverse needs of their clients; actually going as far as measuring clients' particular developmental space is less necessary.' Derry (2006) also suggests that there may be a role for the full assessment of the stage of development of coaches in 'continuing accreditation and supervision'. Although we have some reservations in relation to this as well and address this issue in the next section, where our own model and current position to coach development is presented, we do believe that Laske's method has much to contribute to research in the field of coaching and mentoring.

Our model of coaches' cognitive and ego development

In this section we introduce our position in relation to development of individuals, particularly in the coaching process. We discuss the implications of this position for the development of coaches and coaching psychologists. We also describe our model of coach development informed by the earlier discussed theories particularly ones developed by Kegan (1982), Loevinger (1987), Cook-Greuter (1985) and comprehensive overviews of the whole approach by Wilber (2000).

As presented in earlier sections, this approach postulates that various dimensions of development (also called lines, streams, spiral) (Wilber, 2000, 2006), such as cognitive, interpersonal, affective and moral, have a similar tendency to grow in complexity and unfold in progressive stages. The development of different lines is not necessarily synchronic. Different researchers pay attention to different dimensions, depending on their specific interests and consequent focus of investigation. Our focus of interest is the personal and professional development of coaches, which prompted us to observe closely how some lines and stages of individual development are manifested in various groups of coaches that we had an opportunity to know and work with. As the result we identified two specific developmental dimensions, a combination of which in our view affects the qualitative changes in coaches' personal style and expertise that can signify a stage in their overall development:

- The cognitive-reflective dimension describes the degree of the complexity of thought and reflective judgement as described by Kohlberg (1969), Perry (1970), King and Kitchener (1994).
- The ego-development dimension describes intrapersonal and interpersonal lines of developmental indicating ego-development, degree of openness, authenticity and inclusiveness of others as described by Kegan (1982), Loevinger (1987) and Cook-Greuter (1985).

We consider the cognitive-reflective dimension and ego-development dimension as most influential in terms of indicating coach's level of development. A combination of these two dimensions results in an identification of different aspects of coaches' philosophies of relationship and individual development, reflexivity, role of ego in motivation and actions, style of working with clients and attitude to problems and challenges. At present we believe that these two dimensions are equally important for the overall stage of development as described here and therefore they are presented jointly in the following six-level model of coach development (Table 17.1).

As described in all developmental models these stages are not clear cut. They indicate only what is called a centre of gravity: where the individual

Table 17.1 Stages and developmental tasks for coaching

Stage of development	Cognitive-reflective dimension + ego-development dimensions	Coach's typical pattern of working with coaching clients	Developmental tasks that coach could be effective in facilitating
The Teller	Polar thinking; concrete data; prescribed models; received knowing Self-protective; win-lose oriented relationships with others; manipulative	Take sides; give lots of advice on the basis of their own experience and preferences	Development of self-image and reputation; support in a competitive environment
The Helper	Abstract thought; careful comparisons; reliance on internalised systems and intuition; subjective knowing Self-conscious; group-oriented but realising their specialness; strong internalised super-ego; high moral standards and sense of duty; critical of others, but able to build good relationship	Give emotional support; help to investigate situation in order to 'figure it out'; heavy reliance on psychometric tools; offer own interpretations of situations; generate various solutions to problems	Developing confidence; learning new skills; dealing with concrete problems; adjustment to difficult situations
The Questioner	Multiplicity and patterns; clear separation of knower and the known; critical evaluation; rational and analytical; going beyond subjectivism; introspective; intellectually sceptical towards things that are not yet proven Strong ego; high self-esteem; genuine interest in self-understanding and understanding others; becoming aware of the potential for self-deception; can build intense and meaningful relationship	Effective listening and paraphrasing without unnecessary interpretations; in-depth questioning; identifying root causes and reasons of issues; developing rational arguments; examination of evidence; identifying contradictions; use of appropriate contracting	Identifying motives; making choices; attaining goals and ideals; focusing on action, achievements and effectiveness; taking calculated risks; future-oriented tasks; working with self as it should be

Continued overleaf

Table 17.1 Continued

Stage of development	Cognitive-reflective dimension + ego-development dimensions	Coach's typical pattern of working with coaching clients	Developmental tasks that coach could be effective in facilitating
The Acceptor	Relativism; awareness of the 'observer's' interpretation and cultural conditioning; turn to systems view and meaning making; move from purely rational analysis to more holistic approach Set to redefine oneself; awareness of many sub-personalities; explore internal conflicts; scrutinise own beliefs; focused on individuality and mutuality in relationship; enjoy diversity; high level of empathy	Minimal structures to the process: letting things unfold; exploring things: they are rarely what they seem; working with paradoxes; understanding 'now' rather than focusing on future; spontaneous interventions; accepting any expression of individuality	Developing unique individuality and authenticity; exploring role-personality match; discovering the meaning of critical situations or specific stages in life
The Cultivator	General systems view of reality; perceive systemic patterns and long-term trends; articulation of own models and strategies; contextualisation of problems; articulate ambiguity; insightful; overarching principles; truth can be approximated Strong autonomous self; integrate all elements of the self in a new meaning; the shadow is accepted; aware of mutual interdependency and its role in individual development; responsibility for relationship and helping others grow	Linking idealist vision with pragmatic and principled actions; exploring the self; coming to terms with conflicting needs; identifying qualitative differences; may be impatient with slowness of the others' growth	Creating a meaningful life; identifying strategic concerns and principles; working towards self-fulfilment; identifying psychological causation and processes; nourishing creativity

| The Playwright | Meta-cognition beyond culture and own life-time; cross-paradigmatic; reality is understood as undivided unity; truth is ever illusive because all thoughts are constructed and language is inevitably used for mapping of reality

The ego becomes more transparent to itself and not the main operator; self-critical about their own ego-attachments; understanding others in developmental terms; genuine compassion and adjustment to the individual's ways of meaning-making | Empathetic listening; timely challenging; transformational non-distorted feedback; drawing from unconventional, non-rational sources of information; help in reframing clients' experience in terms of their stage of development | Working with conflict around existential paradoxes; problems of language and meaning making; working beyond contradictions and paradoxes; facing together the need for theories and explanation; creating a new story of one's life |

draws his/her resources from. For example, a coach who is mainly 'The Questioner' may face a situation where her critical views are suspended while she gives emotional support to a client or when she relies on her intuition explicitly. Of course, a Questioner could, at times, move either way, reverting to Helper strategies (the stage she is just leaving) or adopting new, less familiar Acceptor strategies. As Kegan (1994: 326) noted, individuals 'gradually navigate' their evolution from one order or level to another.

The nature of the work of practitioners such as coaches and coaching psychologists involves facilitating development of their clients by engaging in the processes of making meaning of personal experience, critical reflection, problem-solving, exploring important existential issues, etc. The actual participation in these processes is in itself creating extensive opportunities for these practitioners in terms of enhancement of their own pace of development. Coaches are also required to have and be known for their dedication to continuing personal and professional development. These factors seem to contribute to their evolving cognitive capacities and influence shifts in ego-development. The exposure to the relevant knowledge of cognitive-developmental models and, as suggested here, potential landmarks of their development as coaches may further enrich this process.

We also want to expand here on how this model or other developmental models could inform coaching practice and contribute to further studies within coaching psychology. Although this may contradict to some extent the traditional view that coaching is about change, we do not believe that the agenda of development through stages or even a change in the Self should be explicit in the coaching process. There are a number of psychological traps and pitfalls that warrant attention in cases when a client sets up a task of consciously transforming him/herself to the next stage of development. Among the obvious consequences, we could first mention the fact that the pursuit of an abstract ideal implies a diversion of energy from the real life situation that clients may need to deal with. Second, continuous comparison with a higher level of development may undermine clients' belief in themselves and their current abilities, so diminishing their self-efficacy. Third, this pursuit may also create an illusion that qualitative developmental shifts can happen with sufficient motivation and effort. There is no need to reiterate that development of the nature of transformations discussed here is a much more complex process that involves a combination of known and unknown internal and environmental factors. This process happens through subtle shifts and this may take years even to be noticed and recognised. Therefore, we would argue that setting up an explicit task of moving through developmental levels or stages contributes to creating an illusion of easiness of this process and detracts from the tasks that may have to be understood fully and from the actions that may have to be taken immediately.

The more complex array of issues that might relate to conscious pursuit of higher developmental stages is indicated by various studies of the Self and by the wisdom of some spiritual traditions. Lind (2000), for example, describes the 'modern self' which constructs fictional goals that are the products of wishful thinking and cultural conditioning. They are assumed to be real and the self is believed to be capable of achieving them. Hillman (1983: 105) calls this: the self's compulsive tendency to striving. Lind (2000: 9) summarises the consequences of this seeking radical self-improvement, perfection or transcendence as the most common cause of chronic suffering that also 'ensnares the self in egoism, a false, heroic sense of unity and efficacy, and chronic internal conflict'. At the same time there are a number of traditions in psychology and philosophy, e.g. Gestalt, which claim that transformation of the Self is possible only when a person is fully oneself as he/she is now. It is argued that the intention of becoming someone that you are not can lead to creating an abstract ideal that because of its attractiveness may justify lack of full engagement in the process of understanding the self as it is. Krishnamurti (1991: 160), for example, calls pursuing an ideal 'an accepted and respected postponement'. It is very interesting that his related statement 'you can understand what *is* but you cannot understand what *should be*' (Krishnamurti, 1994: 127, original emphasis) is certainly in congruence with the main tenets of the cognitive-developmental tradition.

In relation to the above we want to emphasise one further ethical consideration for coaching that should be taken into account when coaches get engaged with this approach. They would need to ask themselves if establishing their own developmental level, and potentially having insights into the developmental levels of their clients, would lead them, consciously or unconsciously, to adopt an agenda for their clients above and beyond that brought to the coaching by the client. It would be easy for the coaching psychologist to assume that the client would want to be developed to a higher level and to hold that unspoken plan for the coaching.

We believe, however, that the coaching process provides an important condition for change and potential developmental shifts in individuals to occur. The important feature of coaching is that by definition it has a task that clients need to be engaged with. This engagement with a task leads to identifying relevant abilities and efforts to enhance them. If the task presents such a challenge to the client that his/her current stage, order of mind or action logic is not sufficient to deal with it, this could create an opportunity for transformation and individual development. The client is supported in this process but a desired level of change may not necessarily happen and the task could be successfully dealt with on an instrumental level or through horizontal development (Cook-Greuter, 2005). The coaching could still be considered in this case as effective.

At the same time a complex of attitudes and skills of developmentally minded coaches, coaching psychologists and coaching supervisors could be of significance in the development of their clients. They can recognise a stage or more precisely – a way of meaning-making that their client manifests even if they have to make a judgement 'on behalf of one stage over another' (Kegan, 1982: 292). They do not need to voice this judgement, not because it might be unjustified, but because this is not the point of the identification. The point is in the practitioner's awareness and sufficient attention to whether the client is presented with an opportunity to be heard with his/her new voice and generally to move from a less evolved state to a more evolved state. It also adds to the recognition that the client, as much as the coach, needs to be seen as a process rather than a stage.

Case study

In this case study we describe an example of coaching supervision, where both the coaching psychologist and the supervisor are aware of the developmental stages described above and have thought about how these impact on their work with coaching clients. The role of the supervisor in coaching is in supporting the coach through an adaptation and development process. The case study shows that when working with coaches in supervision an awareness of the cognitive-reflective and ego-development dimensions could be very useful.

The coach

We follow the supervision process of a hypothetical coach, Sonia, who is familiar with the model we have outlined above and perceives herself to be at the Helper level. Sonia is happy that, in most of her coaching work, her Helper strategies serve her well; however, she has one client, Alastair, where she believes that her approach is not working.

At the outset, Sonia worked with Alastair on a specific issue involving resolution of a conflict with a member of his team. Alastair now wants to continue the coaching with Sonia, but it appears to her that he has no clear idea of what he wants to work on. Sonia has managed to develop considerable trust with Alastair and now he is beginning to share his deep uncertainties, his resistance and his doubts in relation to his working life. However, he cannot seem to make links between what he says he values and specific actions. Sonia cannot find a way of helping him to move forward and begins to feel out of her depth. She suspects that her intuitive approach is not enough to meet the needs of her client and this particular development of the coaching process. This makes her uncomfortable and so she brings the issue to supervision. She feels she needs to understand if the next level of The Questioner would be necessary to meet the needs of this client and what would she need to do if this was the case.

The coaching-supervision process

The supervisor, Pat, is also familiar with the stages of development. She judges that Sonia has given appropriate support for her client in relation to the specific conflict issue. However, the problems she is presenting now seem to reflect the limitations of her current stage in relation to the client, who presents an increasingly complex array of problems in relation to his work life.

Pat considers that Sonia's interest in the next level and intention to understand more about it is natural in relation to this particular case. Pat has noticed that Sonia is already capable of abstract thinking, making perceptive comparisons and also making use of her intuition. Therefore the Questioner stage seems like a natural progression for her. Indeed she seems ready to embrace the deep learning that further development of this stage will entail. Sonia has faced the limitations of her work and has already suggested that she is ready for the challenge that will inevitably need to occur to her current conceptualisation and thinking.

However, Pat is also aware of the conflict in her own role, as a supervisor, between supporting the coach in using the opportunity for further development and ensuring that the client has the best possible support. She knows that in some cases this dilemma would be extended to the issue of protecting the client. Pat has already asked herself if Sonia is the best choice of coach for Alastair at this time. However, because Sonia did so well in coaching him in relation to the initial issue, Pat believes that Sonia's concurrent further development will enhance her work with Alastair.

Pat therefore encourages Sonia to pay more detailed attention to evaluation of her own coaching practice and invites the sharing of examples from work with clients that promotes comparison. In the safety of supervision, Sonia compares and contrasts her thoughts with those of her supervisor and relevant theorists, if appropriate, in order to strengthen her critical capacity. Pat asks Sonia to identify patterns in her coaching work by cross-relating incidents. When she is encouraged to reflect in this way, Sonia reveals that she has had another client who did not seem committed to his goals, and no matter how she tried to help him, he did not seem to be able to, or want to, focus on achievement of those goals. Through exploration of the current 'unmotivated' client and reflecting back to other times when clients behaved similarly, Sonia is able to recognise a pattern, both in the two clients and in her own response to the problem. Recognition of the pattern reveals a need for Sonia to understand 'fuzzy' goals and, rather than rely solely on her own intuition, to compare her approaches with those of relevant theorists. Such critical appraisal is indicative of the Questioner level.

In addition, Pat helps Sonia to look at issues from a number of other perspectives. She asks questions such as: 'If you were supervising your own practice, what would you ask?' or 'What might your client have been thinking at this moment?' or 'How would this intervention be looked at from a different theoretical perspective?' This emphasis on perspective-taking enables Pat to help Sonia make the move from subjective knowing with its resulting emphasis on helping at this stage, towards a more diverse, challenging, object-oriented, questioning approach.

Pat is aware that finding opportunities to refer to and question authorities is very important in Sonia's development and so she suggests that Sonia compare different theories, explore a number of new strategies, and analyse models which develop critical understanding of coaching. She recommends to Sonia relevant material and theories of resistance that help develop her understanding in order to work with Alastair.

Pat also works to provide Sonia with confidence in her own powers of rational judgement, her ability to really critique ideas and to develop healthy scepticism in relation to the quality of evidence presented, and ultimately to develop powers of critical analysis. Pat is aware, that at the Helper level, Sonia's identity is bound up with wanting to serve others and help them and so she is careful to provide feedback in a form that compliments Sonia's current 'Helper' frame of reference, emphasising the needs of the client.

Pat notices some behaviour in Sonia that she considers as signs of progress. She notices for instance that Sonia is much more willing to question herself. She is still making decisions intuitively, but now asks herself why she is doing it and compares and evaluates the effectiveness of her intuitive decision. In describing a recent intervention, Sonia said 'I think it worked well, but perhaps I am deceiving myself.'

Sonia is also paying more attention to Alastair's motives. She is not looking at what he has achieved or not achieved, but is exploring the clarity of thinking about the meaning of particular situations for him. She asks 'what does it mean to the client?' Recalling how Alastair's initial conflict was resolved satisfactorily, Sonia is making links between that event and his current dilemmas; she asks 'What does having good, solid relationships with his team mean for him?' and 'What compromises does he seem to be able to make without losing his integrity?'

As time goes on, her relationship with Alastair has in itself become more meaningful. She has become more open and is able to acknowledge that she does not have solutions for him. She recognises that the level of issues that he is dealing with may suggest that no perfect answers can be found. He appreciated her openness about her limitations and felt more encouraged to explore his issues in depth without fear of losing face.

In addition, Pat is encouraged because Sonia has asked her to discuss whether the relationship with Alastair needs recontracting, because of the different nature of the engagement. This indicates Sonia's heightened awareness of the nature of the coaching process, its boundaries and consequences for the sponsoring organisation.

There are also some signs that indicate that the development to the Questioner is far from being complete. Pat sees that the nature of Alastair's problems, which included some bigger organisational issues, his plans for future choices and the importance of the decision he needed to make at this point in his life, need to involve him in working with his own values. However, when reflecting on some meetings with her client, Sonia is still inadvertently imposing her own interpretation on the issues. She still occasionally makes assumptions and interpretations for the client, saying things like: 'In those circumstances a better course of action would be . . .' or 'If only I could help him see this'.

Outcomes of the case study

The experiences of adults are always in flux and are related to finding the right way to 'be' in the world. This was particularly evident in the issues that Alastair presented and Sonia has struggled initially to allow Alastair the reflective space to explore those issues freely. Pat, however, continued supporting Sonia's reflection on this particular case. The coaching came to a natural conclusion with Alastair, when the contract with the organisation ended, and both thought that some useful outcomes had been achieved. Alastair's feedback to Sonia was that she facilitated his thinking about the team and ultimately had promoted thinking about bigger issues, which was helpful.

In relation to Sonia's supervision, Pat carried on working with her. Sonia realised that she needed to have more theoretical knowledge and undertook some continuing professional development. Her choices in terms of reading about coaching became more evidence-based and critical. She had experienced how important contracting is, and had designed her own contract, realising the importance of responding to changes in the coaching process.

Conclusion

This chapter has focused on theories of adult development. We have drawn on existing theories of cognitive development and ego development in order to present a model of levels of adult development that has particular application to coaching.

We argued, along with other authors of cognitive-developmental perspectives, that this dimension is crucial for understanding individual differences in coaching clients and in the education and development of coaches. Therefore the awareness of this approach is important for individual coaches, coaching psychologists, trainers and educators in this field, and particularly for supervisors of coaches or coaching psychologists. We believe that the role of educators, supervisors and coaches is to understand and nurture natural progression of individual capacities along the cognitive-developmental and ego-development dimensions.

This approach does not imply specific tools and techniques. It implies careful consideration of the appropriateness of all tools and techniques that other approaches might offer to each level of development of clients as well as coaches. It is an artful balance of support and challenge appropriate for each stage of development that makes a difference in the work of a developmentally minded practitioner. We also believe that the best way of supporting this process of natural development is an active engagement of all skills and abilities of the coach in the process of addressing the work and life tasks of their clients. Finally this approach, in terms of its application, emphasises the importance of the personal growth of practitioners themselves. It is the development of the coach as a person, rather than the application of particular techniques or methods, that makes a difference in coaching practice.

Application to other contexts

The cognitive-developmental approach has the same, if not higher, relevance when considered in relation to adolescence and even younger children when coached. Our model, however, presents the development of adult coaches and coaching psychologists only. In relation to group processes, it is very clear why group work is sometimes incredibly difficult: when individuals with different levels of development are intensely involved in the same process, the chances of serious misunderstandings are numerous. However, opportunities for expected and unexpected growth are also present and possible. This is an area for further discussion and research.

References

Basseches, M. (1984) *Dialectical Thinking and Adult Development*. Norwood, NJ: Ablex.

Beck, D. and Cowan, C. (1996) *Spiral Dynamics*. Oxford: Blackwell.

Belenky, M. F., Clinchy, B. M., Golderberger, N. R. and Tarule, J. M. (1986) *Women's Ways of Knowing*. New York: Basic Books.

Berger, J. (2006) Adult development theory and executive coaching practice. In D. Stober and A. Grant (eds) *Evidence Based Coaching Handbook: Putting best practices to work for your clients*. Chichester: Wiley.

Brookfield, S. D. (1987) *Developing Critical Thinkers: Challenging adults to explore alternative ways of thinking and acting*. San Francisco, CA: Jossey-Bass.

Chandler, D. E. and Kram, K. E. (2005) Applying an adult development perspective to developmental networks. *Career Development International* (special edition on mentoring) 10(6–7): 548–566.

Checkland, P. (1981) *Systems Thinking, Systems Practice*. New York: Wiley.

Commons, M. L. and Richards, F. A. (2002) Four postformal stages. In J. Demick and C. Andreoletti (eds) *Handbook of Adult Development* (pp. 199–219). New York: Kluwer Academic/Plenum.

Cook-Greuter, S. (1985) A detailed description of the successive stages in ego development theory. Paper presented at the second annual meeting of the Society for Research in Adult Development, Cambridge, MA.

Cook-Greuter, S. (1999) Postautonomous ego development: its nature and measurement. Doctoral dissertation. Harvard Graduate School of Education, Cambridge, MA.

Cook-Greuter, S. (2004) Making the case for developmental perspective. *Industrial and Commercial Training* 36(7): 275–281.

Cook-Greuter, S. (2005) Ego development: nine levels of increasing embrace. Available www.cook-greuter.com/ (accessed 14 April 2007).

Csikszentmihalyi, M. (1994) *The Evolving Self: A psychology for the third millennium.* New York: Harper Perennial.

Derry, J. (2006) What relevance does adult development theory have for coaching? *The Bulletin of the Association for Coaching* Autumn (9). Available www.interdevelopmentals.org/pdf/Derry-Article.pdf (accessed 19 March 2007).

Dewey, J. (1991) *How We Think.* New York: Prometheus. (Originally published 1909.)

Drath, W. (1990) Managerial strengths and weaknesses as functions of the development of personal meaning. *Journal of Applied Behavioural Science* 26(4): 483–499.

Fitzgerald, C. and Berger, J. (2002) Leadership and complexity of mind: the role of executive coaching. In C. Fitzgerald and J. Berger (eds) *Executive Coaching: Practices and perspectives.* Palo Alto, CA: Davies-Black.

Garrison, D. R. (1991) Critical thinking and adult education: a conceptual model for developing critical thinking in adult learners. *International Journal of Lifelong Education* 10(4): 287–303.

Gowan, J. C. (1974) *Development of the Psychedelic Individual* (Chapter 6). Available www.csun.edu/edpsy/Gowan/contentp.html (accessed 19 March 2007).

Graves, C. (1970) Levels of existence: an open system theory of values. *Journal of Humanistic Psychology* 10(2): 131–144.

Hillman, J. (1983) *Healing Fiction.* Barrytown, NY: Station Hill Press.

Jaques, E. (1994) *Human Capability.* Falls Church, VA: Cason Hall.

Kegan, R. (1982) *The Evolving Self: Problem and process in human development.* London: Harvard University Press.

Kegan, R. (1994) *In Over our Heads.* London: Harvard University Press.

King, P. M. and Kitchener, K. S. (1994) *Developing Reflective Judgment: Understanding and promoting intellectual growth and critical thinking in adolescents and adults.* San Francisco, CA: Jossey-Bass.

Kohlberg, L. (1969) *Stages in the Development of Moral Thought and Action.* New York: Holt, Rinehart and Winston.

Koplowitz, H. (1984) A projection beyond Piaget's formal-operations stage: a general system stage and a unitary stage. In M. Commons, F. Richards and C. Armon (eds) *Beyond Formal Operations: Late adolescent and adult cognitive development.* New York: Praeger.

Krishnamurti, J. (1991) *Commentaries on Living, Third Series.* London: Victor Gollancz.

Krishnamurti, J. (1994) *Commentaries on Living, First Series*, 9th edition. London: Theosophical Publishing House.

Lahey, L., Souvaine, E., Kegan, R., Goodman, R. and Felix, S. (1988) *A Guide to the Subject–Object Interview: Its administration and interpretation.* Cambridge, MA: Harvard University, Graduate School of Education, Laboratory of Human Development.

Laske, O. (2006a) From coach training to coach education. *International Journal of Evidence Based Coaching and Mentoring* 4(1): 45–57.

Laske, O. (2006b) *Measuring Hidden Dimensions: The art and science of fully engaging adults.* Medford, MA: IDM Press.

Lind, R. (2000) *The Seeking Self: The quest for self improvement and the creation of personal suffering.* Grand Rapids, MI: Phanes Press.

Loevinger, J. (1976) *Ego Development: Conceptions and theories.* San Francisco, CA: Jossey-Bass.

Loevinger, J. (1987) *Paradigms of Personality*. New York: M. H. Freeman.

Mezirow, J. (1990) *Fostering Critical Reflection in Adulthood*. San Francisco, CA: Jossey-Bass.

Perry, W. G. (1970) *Forms of Intellectual and Ethical Development in the College Years*. New York: Holt, Rinehart and Winston.

Piaget, J. (1976) *The Psychology of Intelligence*. Totowa, NJ: Littlefield, Adams.

Rooke, D. and Torbert, W. (2005) Seven transformations of leadership. *Harvard Business Review* April: 66–76.

Sullivan, C., Grant, M. and Grant, J. (1957) The development of interpersonal maturity: application to delinquency. *Psychiatry* 20: 373–385.

Torbert, W. (1991) *The Power of Balance*. Newbury Park, CA: Sage.

Torbert, W. with associates (2004) *Action Inquiry: The secret of timely and transforming leadership*. San Francisco, CA: Berret-Koehler.

Werner, H. (1948) *Comparative Psychology of Mental Development*. New York: International Universities Press.

Wilber, K. (2000) *Integral Psychology*. London: Shambhala.

Wilber, K. (2006) *Integral Spirituality*. Boston, MA: Integral Books.

Discussion points

- If the client is developmentally more advanced than the coach, what could be seen as the negative consequences of their work together apart from the potential lack of progress and mutual frustration?
- The cognitive-developmental approach implies the need to make a judgement about the level of development that a client or coach represents in their behaviour. This is often related to the values that individuals hold. How does it fit with an implicit characteristic of coaching as non-judgemental?
- A number of the developmental theories quite explicitly state that the higher stages of development indicate the 'mastery of wisdom and spirituality' (Csikszentmihalyi, 1994). How compatible is this view of individual development with your vision of what coaching is about?
- What do you see as the main obstacles for the cognitive-developmental approach becoming more influential in coaching psychology than it is now?

Suggested reading

Cook-Greuter, S. (2004) Making the case for a developmental perspective. *Industrial and Commercial Training* 36(7): 275–281.

Fitzgerald, C. and Berger, J. (2002) Leadership and complexity of mind: the role of executive coaching. In C. Fitzgerald and J. Berger (eds) *Executive Coaching: Practices and perspectives*. Palo Alto, CA: Davies-Black.

Kegan, R. (1994) *In Over our Heads*. London: Harvard University Press.

Wade, J. (1996) *Changes of Mind: A holonomic theory of the evolution of consciousness*. Albany, NY: State University of New York Press.

Chapter 18

Role of coaching psychology in defining boundaries between counselling and coaching

Tatiana Bachkirova

Introduction

The fields of coaching and coaching psychology are rapidly changing. Issues that used to be prominent some time ago and indicating pressing needs for practitioners and clients alike are now projects in progress. For example the established professional coaching bodies are raising awareness of important issues in coaching practice and creating guidelines for practice and supervision of coaching practitioners. There are other more noticeable and successful efforts for collaboration between these professional bodies. The growing body of research indicates that the focus of attention is shifting from the efforts of individual practitioners to prove that coaching 'works' to careful and in-depth investigation of the nature and complexity of coaching processes. These include the nuances and dynamics of the coaching relationship, the interaction of specific influencing factors in clients, coaches and coaching contexts and the wider consideration of the role of coaching for organisations and societies (Whitney, 2001; Palmer and Whybrow, 2006).

It appears that coaching as a way of developing people does not now need to fight for a niche in the market and to establish itself in contrast to counselling and psychotherapy. Some time ago coaches tried to differentiate themselves from any association with in-depth psychological work. Now there seems to be a U-turn in the attitudes to the mention of psychology in relation to coaching: the need for psychological underpinning of coaching interventions is better acknowledged among professional coaches. More and more coaching courses include psychology-based subjects in their programmes and coaching psychology as a subject area is becoming known and more influential (Cavanagh and Palmer, 2006).

However, a need for a clearer differentiation between therapy/counselling and coaching remains important, not for the marketing purposes of coaching programmes but for other reasons that include for example, increasing use of psychological models and tools in coaching interventions. This distinction is needed for quality assurance in the coaching process, clearer orientation in the education and training of coaches and, therefore, for the further development of coaching as a profession. This distinction is particularly important for newcomers to the field of coaching, counselling and coaching psychology, for potential clients and sponsors and also for those who are qualified and experienced as coaches and counsellors.

Review of the existing attempts to clarify the boundaries

The attempts to clarify the boundaries between coaching and counselling or psychotherapy have been undertaken by individual practitioners who tried to explain the nature of their expertise. In the literature these attempts to clarify the boundary appear among the very first publications in this field. However, judging by the continuous misunderstandings between professionals, dissatisfaction at the lack of clarity for those who are new to the profession and definitions such as 'coaching is therapy for the people who don't need therapy' it appears that initial attempts at clarifying the boundary have not been particularly successful. The task is therefore not as simple as it may seem. The conceptualisation of coaching as a process and what is believed to be the underpinning knowledge for this developmental service needs to be addressed. Some specific reasons contributing to the difficulty of this task are discussed here.

One typical difficulty in drawing this distinction stems from the attempts to clarify the boundaries between two fields of practice by choosing to describe a unified type of coaching as well as a unified type of counselling/ psychotherapy. These uniformed types of practice are then attributed with some assumed features. The difficulty described is often exacerbated when attempts to differentiate coaching from counselling or psychotherapy are made by practitioners of coaching or practitioners of counselling in isolation, when neither is qualified to make an informed judgement about the other area of practice.

Indeed, simple distinctions are unlikely to satisfy either set of practitioners. For example, Parsloe and Wray (2000) describe the purpose of therapy as problem or crisis oriented with the emphasis on diagnosis, analysis or healing which 'might include testing, prescribed drugs, a focus on early life experiences, involvement of other family members' (Parsloe and Wray, 2000: 12). They describe how this practice relies on extensive theories. It could be argued that not many counselling practitioners would agree with this definition of their practice. On the other hand Parsloe and Wray describe coaching as typically result or performance oriented with the emphasis on taking action and sustaining changes over time. They state that coaching is used to improve performance in a specific area, is more practice driven and relies strongly on interpersonal skills. This definition of coaching would not satisfy many coaching practitioners either.

Another example of these uniform descriptions can be found in Peltier

(2001). Tables 1.1 and 1.2 (pp. xxvii and xxx) reflect a very narrow view on psychotherapy and counselling. For example, in one of the sections of the Introduction that is named 'Positive and Negative Themes from Therapy (What to Keep and What to Throw Out)' Peltier suggests that coaches should not borrow from therapy 'passive approach, data from client only, slow movement, reliance on the coach and meeting only in office at a regular time, for a regular period of time (50 min)' (Peltier, 2001: xxx). It is not surprising then why coaches would not want to be associated with therapy that is described in this way.

Similar attempts are made to define specific features of coaching without elaborating on counselling or psychotherapy but in contrast to them, e.g. 'Coaching assumes the presence of emotional reactions to life events and that clients are capable of expressing and handling their emotions. Coaching is not psychotherapy' (International Coaching Federation (ICF), 2002). This statement is full of assumptions about both practices and does not bring much clarity to the understanding of coaching process and the role of the coach in addressing clients' emotions.

Grant (2000) tries to draw a clearer boundary between coaching and counselling/psychotherapy by proposing that the population served by these practices could be divided into clinical, non-clinical and a mixed one (see also Grant and Cavanagh, 2004). This argument is also difficult to sustain, as the definition of mental health is still an area of academic debate. There is also a serious ethical issue bound up with identifying people as belonging to a clinical population only on the basis that they have decided to improve the quality of their emotional life with the help of a professional counsellor. On the contrary, it could be argued that it is a sign of mental health that a person recognises the critical periods in life and decides to engage actively in the process of exploring them through counselling.

To illustrate this point further, let us compare examples involving the different behaviours and decisions made by two executives whose situation and stage in life were otherwise very similar. One of them is blindly pursuing his career taking up more and more coaching to improve his performance. At the same time he is completely unaware that he is making choices to avoid facing the unbearable situation the pursuit of his career has created for him and his family. Another executive realises one day that he is in the 'rat race', and realises how damaging his current direction is for himself and his family. He has the courage to ask for professional help in order to explore the meaning of this stage in his life. The examples of these two cases do not need further discussion: it is very clear which of these two behaviours could be legitimately discussed as a 'clinical' case (Bachkirova and Cox, 2004). Practice shows that people who suffer from some mental health issues benefit from coaching as long as their mental health needs are addressed at the same time within an appropriate therapeutic context. The proposition of dividing the population into 'clinical' and 'normal' is continuously disputed and rejected for various reasons and on different levels. However, the idea of there being a divide between 'clinical' and 'normal' still significantly influences novices in the coaching field.

In sum, the attempts to distinguish coaching from counselling are prone to misrepresent the immense variety of approaches within the fields of counselling and psychotherapy and in a similar way are prone to misrepresent coaching. Categorisation of service users has also been unhelpful and misleading. It could be argued therefore that in relation to coaching, by keeping attention on the allegedly contrasting areas of practice instead of on coaching itself, these attempts at distinction have been delaying the process of deeper understanding of coaching and defining it on the basis of this understanding.

The need for clearer boundaries

There is a practical requirement to clarify the boundaries between coaching and counselling, it is not merely an issue of theoretical concern. According to practitioners, they have to make the judgement on a regular basis whether the process of development they are engaged in is within a coaching or a counselling realm. There seems to be a current agreement among practitioners in relation to the issue of combining psychotherapy/counselling and coaching in that:

- Psychotherapy/counselling can include elements of coaching if necessary (if this is consistent with the therapeutic approach and a practitioner has the additional skills and sufficient knowledge about the client's context).
- It is not appropriate to do psychotherapy within coaching.

Whereas the first view is relatively straightforward and well accepted, the second one, however obvious at first glance, does not have a clear rationale, particularly for those who are qualified to do both. One possible explanation of this view could be that the coaching process normally starts from the explicit contract to provide coaching and it is inappropriate to change the nature of the process, particularly without the client's consent. This explanation would be sufficient if it was clear for all parties involved where coaching finishes and counselling begins.

In this case we revert back to the same questions. Does coaching imply a specific set of skills? How specific are these skills in principle? Are the current definitions of coaching too narrow? In practice we know that it is impossible to work only with the future and the positive spectrum of clients' lives. Coaches are dealing with difficulties, blocks to development and dissatisfactions. Which of these are in the realm of coaching and most importantly, why?

There are explicit voices in the profession that argue for abandoning the view that it is inappropriate to provide counselling within coaching. Simons (2006), for example, concludes his research by suggesting that because a high degree of self-knowledge is essential for successful leadership, external coaching should comprise elements of counselling in order to address the influences of the client's past and consequent attitudes, feelings and beliefs that underpin behaviour. He suggests, 'successful leaders need to have faced up to, and dealt with any issues arising from their own self-concept' (Simons, 2006: 24). He advocates the need for professional coaches to undertake a counselling or psychotherapeutic training and ideally a qualification.

It appears that the problem of boundaries remains unresolved due to the real difficulties in defining coaching as a process. Although more and more new attempts are being made it seems that 'there is a lack of clarity as to what professional coaching really is and what makes for an effective or reputable coach' (Sherman and Freas, 2004: 84).

With this in mind, it is perhaps important to explore how the task of defining coaching is currently approached and how the outcomes of the efforts to date have assisted (or not) in differentiating coaching from counselling. Two approaches can be currently identified. The first approach has been to identify an ultimate end result or purpose of coaching on the higher level of generalisation. This is often expressed as individual development or enhancing well-being and performance (Grant and Palmer, 2002). These types of definitions are difficult to dispute as they truly reflect the ultimate intention of coaching. The problem, however, with these types of definitions is that they cannot differentiate coaching from counselling because counselling also ultimately implies giving clients 'opportunity to explore, discover and clarify ways of living more resourcefully and toward greater well-being' (Cross and Watts, 2002: 295)

The second approach is to give a more detailed description of how this end result is achieved. Grant (2006: 13), for example, describes coaching as 'collaborative, individualised, solution-focused, results oriented, systematic, stretching, fosters self-directed learning, and should be evidence-based, and incorporate ethical professional practice'. The problem with these types of definitions is twofold. First, they include some characteristics that cannot distinguish them from particular approaches in counselling as was already discussed in relation to the first approach. Second, they also include some characteristics that are so specific or just desirable, that they cannot be attributed to all the various forms of coaching.

A different way to distinguish coaching from counselling

In this section yet another attempt to compare coaching and counselling is outlined. The intention is to avoid some of the pitfalls already identified and take into consideration some other complexities. For instance, when coaching is contrasted with counselling, applying at the same time the notion that the client is resourceful (Berg and Szabo, 2005) or willing to engage in finding solutions (Hudson, 1999), it wrongly implies that counselling is not. Therefore the intention of the following attempt is to identify the differences and similarities between coaching and counselling that would be difficult to explain, for example, by the individual style of practitioners, by their theoretical background, or by the specific approaches that they take. In addition, those aspects of coaching that may lead to comparing it unfavourably to counselling due to a particular stage in the development of coaching as a profession (e.g. presence of an elaborated code of practice, ethics, supervision, theoretical underpinning of interventions) will be also avoided because the progress of the profession in relation to these aspects of professional development is apparent and seems inevitable.

A number of aspects that appear to be important for comparison between coaching and counselling processes have been considered and summarised in Table 18.1. This includes aspects that perhaps need to be and also could be differentiated. The list in Table 18.1 is not conclusive. There are other aspects that are not included here such as for example, length of relationship or focus on the past. They are seen, however, as too varied in both processes and so not consistently distinguishing one process from another.

The similarities between both practices as described in Table 18.1 are particularly noticeable in relation to the importance of factors contributing to the effectiveness of coaching and counselling alike. These are the importance of relationship between the client and the practitioner, the role of the practitioner's self and commitment of the client. Basic skills in both practices are very similar with the exception of specific counselling skills developed within specific counselling schools and approaches, e.g. use of techniques in Gestalt therapy, interpretation of dreams in psychoanalysis, etc. Not all counselling approaches on the other hand use explicitly the skills of setting goals and action planning as practised in coaching.

In terms of noticeable differences Table 18.1 shows that the initial motivation of clients to undertake counselling and psychotherapy is often different from coaching and mentoring. It varies from the wish of the individuals to eliminate psychological problems and dysfunctions to just a desire to explore some patterns or critical periods in life in order to improve their well-being. Motivation for coaching and mentoring, on the other hand, comes most often from the determination of the individual, supported or even stimulated by the organisation to improve performance. It could also be just personal and professional development, particularly in cases when the individual pays for this service and organisations are not involved. It could be argued that in this particular case the differences between coaching and counselling are not significant because whatever the initial motivation may be, the ultimate goal of the process is the same.

If organisations or other stakeholders are involved the differences become more significant in relation to a number of aspects. The focus of counselling is defined by the individual only and potentially there are no limitations as to

Table 18.1 Differences and similarities between coaching and counselling

Aspects	Counselling/therapy	Coaching/mentoring
Ultimate purpose and benefit	Development and well-being of individual	Development and well-being of individual (if sponsored – also benefit for the sponsoring organisation)
Initial motivation	Eliminating psychological problem and dysfunctions	Enhancing life, improving performance
Context of interventions	Open to any and potentially to all areas of client's life	Specified by the contract according to the client's goals, the coach's area of expertise and the assignment of a sponsor if involved
Client's expectations for change	From high dissatisfaction to reasonable satisfaction	From relative satisfaction to much higher satisfaction
Possible outcome	Increased well-being, unexpected positive changes in various areas of life	Attainment of goals, increased well-being and productivity
Theoretical foundation	Psychology and philosophy	May include psychology, education, sociology, philosophy, management, health and social care, etc.
Main professional skills	Listening, questioning, feedback, use of tools and methods specific to particular approaches	Listening, questioning, feedback, explicit goal setting and action planning
Importance of relationship in the process	High	High
Importance of the client's commitment	High	High
Role of the practitioner's self in the process	Very important	Very important

where the process may lead in terms of the contexts of the client's life, because counselling is potentially concerned with all aspects of the client's life. The focus of coaching may also be defined by the client, but if coaching is sponsored by the organisation, usually the goals are aligned in the direction that is considered useful for the organisation. The contract with an individual coaching client is arranged in such a way that the process remains within the boundaries of usefulness for the organisation with an expectation for specific outcomes. This often defines the timescale of coaching assignments and the involvement of different parties in evaluation of the outcomes. This may also create specific issues in terms of ethics and confidentiality in coaching, that counselling, being overtly individually oriented, can avoid.

It is possible that the individual needs of the client may dictate spending more time on developing qualities that could help him or her to move forward in more fundamental ways, or to overcome old blocks to development. If these are not within the spectrum of the immediate needs of the organisation or sometimes in contradiction to its interests, the scope of coaching would be limited. The counsellor, in contrast, is not restricted in terms of the context of the support he/she can provide for the client. Therefore, from the perspective of individual development the end goals of counselling can be more strategic than those of most types of coaching. They can extrapolate from dealing with specific problems, including psychological, to the process of becoming a 'fully functioning person' (Rogers, 1961). The goals of coaching, on the other hand, whether in organisations or not, are usually focused only on some specific areas of a client's life.

The next aspect of comparison is the context of interventions, which again is different for coaching and counselling. In counselling according to the wider strategic aims, that could be relevant to any area of a client's life, the contexts of interventions are not limited. The issues and developmental intentions could be explored in relation to any or all areas of a client's personal life, whether it is family, work, past or future. Even if a counselling practitioner is not familiar with the context of the situation that the client needs to work with the success of their work is rarely determined by this knowledge. In contrast, the context for coaching interventions is usually specified by the contract according to the specific request of the client, coach's area of expertise and assignment of the organisation if involved. The coach normally declares the area of their expertise as a coach, e.g. skills coaching, performance coaching or developmental coaching and – often by the request of the client – the fields where this expertise was developed, e.g. private or public sector or even more specific, such as e.g. NHS, business, sales, etc. The main focus of coaching is usually identified very early on in the coaching relationship; this also determines the context of interventions. If an organisation is a sponsor, the context is even more specific. It would be inappropriate to change the context of interventions without reconsidering the contract.

Another important difference of the coaching process from counselling is the degree of expectation for the outcomes. The expectations of coaching clients seem much higher than expectations of counselling clients. It could be argued that this degree is a consequence of the initial motivation to start the process. Eliminating psychological problems may lead to a reasonable contentment and balance in life, whereas if a particular goal is identified for coaching, clients seem to rightfully expect the successful achievement of that goal and full satisfaction. This does not imply that counselling clients may not enjoy some unexpected benefits of this process extrapolating onto different areas of their life, which can also happen in coaching. However, these effects in counselling would probably be considered as an extra bonus for the hard work involved.

Implications of differences and similarities between coaching and counselling for coaching and coaching psychology

It appears that the most significant differences between coaching and counselling apart from the initial motivation seem to be in the context of interventions and the degree of expectation for the outcomes. These differences are relevant to life coaching or coaching in organisations. General implications of these differences for coaches are as follows:

- Coaches need to engage only in contexts that match their expertise.
- Coaches need to work within the area that is specified by a client (if the area needs to be extended a different contract needs to be negotiated).
- The degree of expectation for successful change leads to the responsibility of the coach to align his/her ability and his/her assessment of client's readiness for coaching with the outcomes expected by the client.

Even if coaches are qualified as counsellors they are expected to work within the area that is specified by a coaching client. If this area needs to be extended because of the emerged needs, the contract needs to be renegotiated. The emerging issues and goals may require unrestricted exploration of various contexts in the client's life, making it impossible to predict the direct impact of such exploration on the specific coaching goals initially set by the client, particularly within a limited timescale. In these situations it is important for coaches to be clear about what type of coaching they provide (for example, performance coaching or developmental coaching) and how well they are qualified to provide the type of coaching that seems to be needed at this point of the process. The developmental coaching, for instance, in contrast to performance coaching, is less focused on the specific performance-related behaviours. It is more open to the long-term and emerging needs and aspirations of the client and so may justify interventions that in performance coaching would be considered too open-ended and/or unnecessarily psychologically deep. It could be noted here that coaching psychologists even without counselling qualifications at these points of decision-making may have an advantage of being able to identify psychological issues involved and the psychological implication of these changes.

Where the coaching may become developmental rather than performance-oriented, the expectations of the client for specific and significant changes dictate that the coach is responsible for informing the client about the scale of issues involved in the process of change and for the degree of unpredictability in terms of reaching the specific outcomes that the client may expect. Clients certainly have to be involved in the decision-making process about the changes in the nature of the coaching process that could affect the outcome. This is dictated by the assumption of equal responsibility of a coach and a client in relation to the outcomes of the coaching process.

An important implication of this comparison is that the more developmentally focused the coaching is the closer it becomes to counselling in terms of the context of interventions, transcending the contextual boundaries. Thus coaches who work developmentally need to be more knowledgeable of the nature of the self, psychology of individual development and the nature of processes involved in facilitating individual development, including blocks to development and the dynamics of helping relationships. This is why the role of coaching psychology as a subject area that focuses on the theories of individual development and understanding of the psychological implication of practical interventions in development, is becoming increasingly important for all those who coach.

It is useful to reflect on the issue of boundaries between coaching and counselling which have different areas of focus and therefore different implications for various groups of practitioners who coach, such as:

- non-psychologists and all novices to the profession
- psychologists who are specialists in one or two areas of psychology other than counselling/psychotherapy
- non-psychologists but highly experienced as counsellors/psychotherapists
- psychologists who are also qualified in counselling.

For the first and the second groups the main implication of the differences between the two practices is to recognise appropriately and in good time the limits of their interventions in relation to the psychological issues that they may be facing in their practice. These practitioners would benefit from considering the model outlined in Figure 18.1 that indicates the need for identifying underlying psychological issues and making a decision about the appropriate referral of the client. The model also highlights the importance of knowledge and awareness of such issues.

The initial point of the coaching process according to this model is assessment. This is not an assessment of the client only (needs, values, priorities, personality, etc.), but also understanding of the context of coaching or the client's system as a whole with its values and cultures, and of the situation in which the client wishes to succeed. All of these are also assessed while considering the degree of freedom and constraints that might be associated with the position that the coach is facing in this situation, his or her preferred framework of coaching and the details of the negotiated contract. Next, the results of the assessment are related to the targets set by the individual client (and the client organisation if involved) in order to evaluate how realistic the

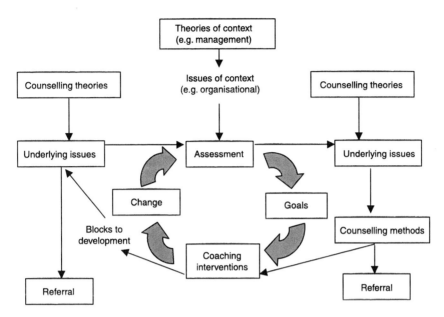

Figure 18.1 Role of theories in coaching process.

assessment is. Appropriate strategies are developed; methods are selected and this is followed by the chosen interventions and actions. If the desired change is happening and is seen as sufficient in relation to the targets and the situation, then the cycle is complete or targets are moved to a different level and the cycle repeats itself as long as necessary and possible, contract permitting.

However, this ideal scenario perhaps happens only theoretically. In reality coaches often have to work with clients who have underlying issues that might prevent their progress. These could be discovered even as early as during the first assessment. For example, a coach can find that a client who wishes to develop the skills of delegation finds it very difficult to trust anyone. This is an underlying issue that could constitute a serious block to achievement of the client's goals. This issue may need detailed exploration and possible intervention depending on the therapeutic approach applied. It is at this point that the coach needs to evaluate his/her ability to address this issue in the context as defined by the contract with this particular client (and the organisation, if involved) and discuss this with the client (and the organisation). The coach may consider referral to a counsellor who may be able to deal specifically with the underlying issue. Alternatively, if a decision is made to proceed, this underlying issue is evaluated via the knowledge of appropriate psychological theories, the coaching interventions are enriched by specifically selected counselling methods and the following reassessment is conducted in a context wider than performance improvement alone. For example, any progress in delegating would be assessed in this case with the consideration of the initial predicaments (e.g. lack of ability to trust anyone) as well as the established target goal (e.g. developing the skills of delegation).

In some cases the underlying issues may be discovered at the intermediate stage of the coaching process when it becomes apparent that significant blocks to development of psychological nature impede the progress of the client. The same process of decision-making based on the understanding of the nature of psychological predicaments is needed as described above.

The context of coaching may also dictate the need for applying specific, relevant background knowledge of a theoretical and practical nature. If, for example, coaching is offered in an organisational context, at the stage of initial or intermediate assessment, extra knowledge of management theories and organisational development will be an invaluable asset for the practising coach. The particular culture(s) and values of the organisation may dictate, for instance, a specific view on the leadership style of the client, which would obviously influence the targets and the process of coaching.

This model implies that a good understanding of major psychological theories is necessary in order to be able to notice and interpret developmental phenomena and blocks to development. For the first two groups of practitioners the main challenge of the decision-making process would be the initial identification of the underlying issues. It would be particularly useful if the coach were sufficiently knowledgeable with regard to at least one of the counselling approaches. It could help to enrich the repertoire of his/her skills when dealing with underlying issues and blocks to a client's development.

For coaching practitioners in the third and fourth groups, the main implication suggested by this model seems to be the necessity of contextual knowledge of the coach in relation to the client's system and particular sensitivity to the nature of the contract. As these two groups are qualified in both modes of practice the main challenge in the decision-making process is to consider all implications of deviating from the focused context-bound process of coaching and to respect the nature of contracting by involving the client in this process.

For all groups of practitioners, supervision seems to be an activity that in addition to a number of invaluable benefits for the client and for the coach also is designed to ensure the effectiveness of decision-making process in terms of the boundaries between coaching and counselling. It does indicate at the same time that supervisors who would be ideally (but not exclusively) suited to this job are those psychologists who constitute group 4: qualified as both coaches and counsellors and those who are especially trained as supervisors.

Role of coaching psychology in creating a clearer understanding of the boundaries

Coaching psychology as a rapidly developing subject area has a significant role to play in the process of creating a clearer understanding and practical appreciation of the boundaries between coaching and counselling. There are several areas where the contribution of coaching psychology would be invaluable to the development of coaching as a profession. One of these areas is a competent adaptation of existing counselling theories, methods, and ideas for the practice of coaching. This handbook and several others provide an important step towards this purpose (e.g. Peltier, 2001; Stober and Grant, 2005; Bluckert, 2006; Passmore, 2006).

There is an obvious need for new theories of individual development particularly in the organisational context. These theories need to be much more elaborate than simple models of abbreviated steps prescribing some coaching interventions. On the whole these theories may describe the phenomenon of developmental change in individuals by elaborating on the following essential elements:

- main concepts and assumption about human nature
- conditions for development
- obstacles to development
- tasks and goals of development
- methods and techniques of enabling change
- relationship between the coach and the client
- essential processes and dynamics
- pitfalls and limitations.

The theory that consists of these elements usually represents a big picture of the world including the nature of human beings and development of individuals. It should help coaches to recognise developmental patterns and plan their action in a coherent way. The use of such theories by coaches could give an opportunity to communicate with colleagues in their own fields of work and in the counselling field about developmental phenomena and so would enrich both practices by providing the framework for shared understanding and mutually beneficial research.

Coaching psychology is also an ideal field of knowledge that could alert coaches to the dangers of working with issues that require a specialist's attention. It could illuminate a murky area – that of identifying signs of extreme distress and/or personality disorders, possibly with the use of different means other than psychometric testing (Berglas, 2002; Cavanagh, 2005). For example, in Cavanagh (2005) practitioners already can find some very useful ideas when they have to make a decision about the mode of work that is needed for each individual client. These are questions that should be carefully considered in any situation that causes doubts in the coach about suitability of the client for coaching alone. They would alert the coach to the need of assessing his/her own limitations in terms of ability to address effectively the client's special issue:

- How long has the client been experiencing this distress or dysfunction?
- How extreme are the behaviours or responses of the client?
- How pervasive are the distresses and patterns of dysfunctional behaviour?
- How defensive is the client?
- How resistant to change are the dysfunctional patterns of behaviour, thinking and emotions?

(Cavanagh, 2005: 23)

There is another area where the contribution of coaching psychology would be extremely valuable. Supervision for coaches and coaching psychologists has dimensions that go beyond the traditional models used in counselling or in supervision for chartership status. Although some very good work in describing and utilising these dimensions has been carried out already by Carroll and Gilbert (1999), Hawkins (2006a, 2006b), and other experts, there is a need to continue an exploration of these dimensions and evaluation of the efforts already made.

As previous analysis suggests, clarifying the difference and boundaries between coaching and counselling is a task that should become easier with further conceptual and practical work in the field of coaching psychology. However this task is unlikely to become a straightforward one for individual practitioners in each case. The implications of this for practising coaches are not only in their professional expertise. The role of the self of the coach in being able to observe and interpret the nuances and complexities of the one-to-one process of engaging with a client's development and in making decisions on the basis of these, is impossible to overestimate. This in turn implies an important role for coaching psychology in enhancing training, further education and personal development of coaches and coaching psychologists in terms of their psychological literacy, skills and personal maturity. The role of coaching psychology will also remain prominent in the development of the concept and practice of supervision for coaches and in developing supervisors who could provide case-by-case support for coaches in balancing on the tight rope between coaching and counselling.

References

Bachkirova, T. and Cox, E. (2004) A bridge over troubled water: bringing together coaching and counselling. *International Journal of Coaching and Mentoring* 2(2).

Berg, I. K. and Szabo, P. (2005) *Brief Coaching for Lasting Solutions*. New York: W. W. Norton.

Berglas, S. (2002) The very real dangers of executive coaching. *Harvard Business Review* 80(6): 87.

Bluckert, P. (2006) *Psychological Dimensions to Executive Coaching*. Maidenhead: Open University Press.

Carroll, M. and Gilbert, M. (1999) *On Being a Supervisee: Creating learning partnerships*. Self-made manual.

Cavanagh, M. (2005) Mental-health issues and challenging clients in executive coaching. In M. Cavanagh, A. M. Grant and T. Kemp (eds) *Evidence Based Coaching. Volume 1, Theory, Research and Practice from the Behavioural Sciences* (pp. 21–36). Bowen Hills, Qld: Australian Academic Press.

Cavanagh, M. and Palmer, S. (2006) Editorial – The theory, practice and research base of Coaching Psychology is developing at a fast pace. *International Coaching Psychology Review* 1(1): 5–7.

Cross, M. and Watts, M. (2002) Trainee perspective on Counselling Psychology: articulating a representation of the discipline. *Counselling Psychology Quarterly* 15(4): 293–305.

Grant, A. M. (2000) Coaching psychology comes of age. *PsychNews* 4(4): 12–14.

Grant, A. M. (2006) A personal perspective on professional coaching and development of coaching psychology. *International Coaching Psychology Review* 1(1): 12–22.

Grant, A. M. and Cavanagh, M. J. (2004) Toward a profession of coaching: sixty-five years of progress and challenges for the future. *International Journal of Evidence Based Coaching and Mentoring* 2(1): 1–16.

Grant, A. M. and Palmer, S. (2002) Coaching psychology workshop. Annual Conference of the Division of Counselling Psychology, British Psychological Society, Torquay, UK, 18 May.

Hawkins, P. (2006a) Coaching supervision. In J. Passmore (ed.) *Excellence in Coaching*. London: Kogan Page.

Hawkins, P. (2006b) *Supervision of Coaches, Mentors and Consultants: Polishing the professional mirror*. Maidenhead: Open University Press.

Hudson, F. M. (1999) *The Handbook of Coaching*. San Francisco, CA: Jossey-Bass.

International Coaching Federation (ICF) (2002) *The Nature and Scope of Coaching*. Available www.coachfederation.org/ICF/For+Coaching+Clients/Selecting+a +Coach/Nature+and+Scope+of+Coaching/ (accessed 3 April 2006).

Palmer, S. and Whybrow, A. (2006) The coaching psychology movement and its development within the British Psychological Society. *International Coaching Psychology Review* 1(1): 5–11.

Parsloe, E. and Wray, M. (2000) *Coaching and Mentoring: Practical methods to improve learning*. London: Kogan Page.

Passmore, J. (2006) *Excellence in Coaching: The industry guide*. London: Kogan Page.

Peltier, B. (2001) *The Psychology of Executive Coaching*. Hove: Brunner-Routledge.

Rogers, C. (1961) *On Becoming a Person*. Boston, MA: Houghton Mifflin.

Sherman, S. and Freas, A. (2004) The Wild West of executive coaching. *Harvard Business Review* 82(11): 82–90.

Simons, C. (2006) Should there be a counselling element within coaching? *The Coaching Psychologist* 2(2): 22–25.

Stober, D. and Grant, A. (2005) *Evidence Based Coaching Handbook: Putting best practices to work for your clients*. Chichester: Wiley.

Whitney, G. (2001) Evaluating development coaching. In L. West and M. Milan (eds) *The Reflecting Glass: Professional coaching for leadership development*. Basingstoke: Palgrave.

Discussion points

- This chapter implies that the term 'psychological coaching' does not make sense. All coaching is seen as psychological because it consists of psychological processes. What is your view on this?
- Some people argue that 'psychologically minded' coaches could be as good as psychologically knowledgeable coaches. On which assumptions is this claim based?
- Can a coaching supervisor without counselling experience be useful for coaches and coaching psychologists?
- There are interesting and well-argued attempts to create services that do not emphasise the boundaries between counselling and coaching, e.g. 'personal consultancy' www.practicalpsychology.org/index.html. What needs to be considered when introducing and implementing these ideas?

Suggested reading

Berglas, S. (2002) The very real dangers of executive coaching. *Harvard Business Review* 80(6): 87.

Buckley, A. and Buckley, C. (2006) *A Guide to Coaching and Mental Health*. London: Routledge.

Cavanagh, M. (2005) Mental-health issues and challenging clients in executive coaching. In M. Cavanagh, A. M. Grant and T. Kemp (eds) *Evidence Based Coaching*. Volume 1, *Theory, Research and Practice from the Behavioural sciences* (pp. 21–36). Bowen Hills, Qld: Australian Academic Press.

Simons, C. (2006) Should there be a counselling element within coaching? *The Coaching Psychologist* 2(2): 22–25.

Chapter 19

Coaching and diversity

Helen Baron and Hannah Azizollah

Introduction

Diversity is integral to coaching. To be a good coach it is necessary to work from a diversity perspective – even if the 'd' word is not mentioned. Any two people are different from each other in some way; this affects the way they perceive and respond to the world and how they feel about it. Diversity considers these differences, and how they impact on the way people are and how they interact. In organisations, according to Kandola and Fullerton (1998), diversity work focuses on maximising the potential of each person.

We cover some of the basics of prejudice, equal opportunity and diversity in this chapter and consider how these are integral to coaching practice. This is followed by a discussion of the competencies required in working with diversity as a coach. We then present a number of case studies that illustrate some scenarios with a strong diversity element.

Rather than simply meet the need for political correctness by ensuring that a chapter on diversity is included in the handbook, we will invite you to consider how you would approach diversity issues through the chapter. We have included vignettes illustrating how diversity issues arise in coaching for you to review and reflect on. These should help demonstrate the practical implications of the more theoretical discussions and provide you with an opportunity to develop your own thinking around diversity in your coaching practice.

Prejudice, discrimination and stereotypes

It is naive to assume that sexist or racist attitudes are now a thing of the past. Research shows that prejudice is still alive both in overt offensive behaviour such as name calling or exclusion but more often in subtle forms embedded in people's attitudes and expectations of others. Signs of this may be different interpretations of the same behaviour depending on the identity of the person concerned (she retaliated, he responded), so-called office 'banter' that can in reality be quite offensive or a lack of social integration of people who are considered 'other' (e.g. Sheridan and O'Sullivan, 2003). Women in an organisation will often be aware of subtle or not so subtle sexism that men have overlooked (Wahl and Holgersson, 2003).

A well-meaning white manager may fail to develop a good relationship with a black employee reporting to her and avoid addressing his performance issues because she is worried about accidentally saying something offensive in his presence. The black employee may experience this lack of support, both personally and in terms of his professional development, as racism and his coach would be wrong to feel that he had a 'chip on his shoulder' or was oversensitive. The coach must not only avoid the manager's defective approach but also help the black employee gain insight into what is happening and develop effective strategies to cope with the situation and avoid any negative impact on his relationships with others or his career aims. A transsexual might be considering whether to 'come out' at work. His coach must be comfortable enough with gender reassignment and perhaps his own sexual identity to be able to discuss this issue and help resolve the dilemma.

Overtly prejudicial attitudes and discriminatory behaviour may be restricted to a few individuals, but often reflect a common consensus regarding what behaviour is appropriate. If they commonly occur, are tolerated by the majority and never openly challenged or are even encouraged by some influential individuals, the situation is not just one of individual prejudice but of organisational discrimination. It does not require that the organisation or many individuals within it have a desire or intention to discriminate for organisational discrimination to occur. People may be unaware of the detriment suffered by others as a result of their behaviour. Organisations often do not realise how their 'normal' practices may disadvantage some people. For instance, if allocation to favoured projects tends to happen in after-work informal discussions in the pub, those who do not take part in such sessions may be disadvantaged. This may include a woman who has caring responsibilities or someone who prefers not to for social or religious reasons. A good coach needs to be aware of the danger of these kinds of norms and processes when working with someone who is subject to this type of discrimination or someone who is perpetrating it.

Vignette

Jennifer's Jewish coach considers the organisation Jennifer works for to be quite anti-Semitic but that observation has not been discussed as it seems irrelevant to the coaching. After some months Jennifer tells the coach she is Jewish but has always kept this a secret. Now she wants to 'come out' to her team – but not to her bosses – as being Jewish.

- What relevance does the coach being Jewish have in this scenario?
- What would you do to facilitate Jennifer's aim?

Equal opportunities

Equality of opportunity is one aspect of diversity. It puts a focus on overcoming barriers and inequalities that members of some groups may face. It is particularly associated with dealing with the impact of unfair discrimination and the outcomes of negative attitudes such as racism or sexism. While gender and race are central to equal opportunity thinking, there are many other areas of potential inequality that a coach must be aware of. UK equal opportunity legislation is focused on eliminating discrimination and covers disability, sexual orientation, religion and age as well as race and gender. These are all areas that a coach should have some understanding of. Any number of other differences between individuals and groups in organisations (for example, social class, educational background, regional origin) can be the source of barriers which reduce individuals' ability to work together and form cohesive relationships, leading to inequality of opportunity.

Equal opportunity models view fairness as an absence of barriers for members of different groups. This is the approach embedded in the legislation. Equal opportunity with respect to coaching services requires coaches to ensure that their services are accessible by people from different groups and that the services they offer are equally effective for members of different groups. A male coach who feels uncomfortable working with a young woman is unlikely to develop a good coaching relationship with her, particularly if he views her male colleagues' jokes and double entendres as typical office 'banter'. He will have little insight into how this constant stream of sexist remarks makes her feel or what the real barriers are to her becoming an effective member of an otherwise male team. He might leave her feeling that she was the source of the problem rather than validating her experiences and the difficulties of being a woman in a sexist environment.

Vignette

Corrine wants to return to work after a five-year gap. Previously she was a very successful IT consultant and had worked for a number of consultancies. She has approached a coach as she is having difficulty getting a job. She has hearing difficulties and her speech is affected but this has had no adverse impact on her work in the past – she feels this can't be the cause of her problem now.

- How might the coach approach this?
- Is the difficulty to do with Corrine's gender, disability, time out, or the way she is marketing herself?

Diversity

In contrast to an equal opportunity approach, diversity has a greater focus on inclusivity and individuality (Kandola and Fullerton, 1998). Rather than addressing the issues around childcare that women often face, diversity looks at providing for the needs of every individual. Thus flexible working hours may be helpful to women with young children, but a man with children may have similar needs, as would someone with an elderly parent to care for. Flexible hours might also help someone wishing to attend religious services or writing a novel. Diversity also considers how people from diverse backgrounds work together. How do the dynamics in a heterogeneous group differ from those where everyone shares a similar background and assumptions about the world? Diversity values everyone's contribution and tries to provide increased opportunity for all to maximise their involvement to the benefit of each individual and the group or organisation as a whole.

The increasing heterogeneity of society today means individuals and organisations can not ignore the impact of diversity. It is in the customer base of a commercial company, in the student body of a university and in the clients of a public sector organisation. Organisations that do not make a real attempt to manage diversity are likely to suffer as a result – but those that do may reap the benefit. Research into organisational performance demonstrates a diverse workforce can improve creativity and innovation, but a diverse workforce also requires better management to prevent negative outcomes such as conflict or exclusion (Simons et al., 1999; Ely and Thomas, 2001).

Coaching and diversity

Sometimes a coaching programme is initiated in an organisation in order to address diversity issues. This may be explicit such as encouraging women in leadership but may often be implicit. The stated reason may not relate to diversity at all (e.g. a programme to improve communication among managers) but the underlying problem may still be a diversity one – people from different groups not working well together.

It is not uncommon for an individual who is different to be identified as 'the problem' and in need of coaching – when actually it is the response of others to the individual that is problematic. Introducing someone who is different from a team who are happy with their ways may upset the equilibrium. It is the new person who is blamed rather than the group's inability to show any flexibility or work with someone who is not like them. Identifying the locus of the problem is always important in coaching and it is critical to realise that there may be a diversity element more often than would appear at first glance.

The coach must be sensitive to both the situational factors that are contributing to the client's issues as well as the potential for changes in behaviour, attitude and approach. It is important to appreciate how difficult it might be to deal with prejudice in the environment. Coaching can be about helping clients to come to terms with their own identity and find solutions that work for them, rather than trying to make clients conform to mainstream conventions and ways of doing things.

Consider a company where there is a glass ceiling preventing black women managers from achieving the most senior positions. A coaching programme might be suggested to help more black women reach their potential. On the one hand this could help the women develop the skills they need to succeed as managers and gain promotion. On the other hand there is an underlying assumption that the women are not currently performing well enough to succeed – that they are the problem – and changing them is the solution to the problem. However, it may be the organisation which needs to change to appreciate their competencies and contribution or just to remove the barriers to performance they face. Perhaps they have not been assigned to the type of challenging projects which have helped other managers to demonstrate and develop their skills.

Coaches should beware of the impact of colluding with an unfairly discriminating organisation in undertaking such a programme. Of course it is possible for a coaching programme targeted at a particular group to be helpful. The formal coaching programme may be replacing the informal support networks ('old boys' network') that help members of other groups perform better. Clutterbuck (2003) describes the use of mentoring programmes in this context and Spear (2001) discusses executive coaching. Both stress the need to understand and work with difference issues and be aware of hidden prejudice within the organisation as well as having a generally well-structured and well-implemented programme.

Competencies for coaching in a diverse context

Coaching requires a range of knowledge and skills, indeed, the previous sections highlighted the breadth and depth of knowledge and skill that can be relevant to the coaching context. Here we highlight those competencies which are particularly relevant and necessary to work with heterogeneous clients, where the coachee has a different background to the coach. Most research in this area is from a counselling perspective but the competencies that are highlighted are equally or perhaps more, relevant to a coaching relationship because they are important in being able to understand and work effectively with the client. Counselling often involves more in-depth work on the individual through which issues may be revealed which could be missed in a more action-focused coaching process.

Pederson and Levy (1993) present a case for additional skills for working in multicultural contexts and Enns (2000) describes a related set of skills for dealing with gender issues in a counselling relationship. The work of Sue and

Sue (1990) has been particularly influential. They discuss a number of different competencies for cross-cultural counselling which they list under three main headings: self-awareness, knowledge and skills. We will discuss each of these three areas in turn.

Self-awareness

Self-awareness is crucial in any relationship aimed at change. In this context it is about being aware, as a coach, of one's own cultural assumptions, biases and stereotypes. All cultures make assumptions and have common values and attitudes that differentiate them from other cultures. Being a member of the majority culture it is easy to assume that one's own cultural assumptions and attitudes are more universal than is actually the case. It is easy to be unaware of making a cultural assumption at all. For instance coaches typically espouse the western value of the self as an autonomous unit. The coach works to enhance the way the individual operates as an independent actor within the organisational context. However this bias towards individual autonomy is not shared by all cultures. An individual from a more collectivist culture in which identity is more strongly defined by group membership (e.g. family, work group) is likely to find a coach emphasising an egocentric approach dissonant.

Being 'colour-blind', 'gender-blind' or 'disability-blind' is not an option. First, it is patently impossible to have a proper coaching relationship and not be aware of such basic facts about the client. Second, by ignoring a central facet of the client the coach is denying an essential part of the person's identity. Third, by denying that these and other facts about the client affect the relationship, the coach is certain to fail in understanding the world from the client's perspective – a necessary stage in working with the person for change. If the coach is not aware of making cultural assumptions, it is unlikely that a coachee with a different set of assumptions will develop the degree of trust required to really engage with the coach and in the coaching process. Burkhard and Knox (2004) and Gushue (2004) suggest that those who have a 'colour-blind' view of race differences may be less effective at evaluating clients' issues and developing empathy.

To be effective in a coaching relationship, coaches must continuously reflect on their own cultural assumptions and biases and how these may distort their perspective and the way they work with clients.

Vignette

A male coach develops a very close coaching relationship with his client, likes him a lot and is impressed by his insight and sensitivity. The client later reveals that he is homosexual and wants to explore the impact that his secret is having on his work. The coach is shocked and discomfited by the unexpected revelation. He had been unaware of some of his prejudices and needed to work with a supervisor on the issue before he felt able to continue working effectively with the client.

- How might the coach use his response to the client's homosexuality constructively in the coaching process?
- What impact will this have on the client? On the coach?

Knowledge

In order to successfully work with someone who is different it is important to have insight into others' experience of the world, and to understand how to ensure your behaviour does not contravene others' cultural 'norms'. This might mean an understanding of different cultural or religious groups, how people of the opposite gender experience the world or the needs of a person with a disability. For instance, it would be important to understand why joining the rest of the team for a drink after work might be difficult for a Muslim whose religious beliefs did not allow the consumption of alcohol.

While developing trust and empathy depends on adopting an appropriate style of behaviour, communication and interaction, a client may not have much confidence in a coach who does not have insight into even basic facts about their background. Consider how much confidence you would have in a coach whose behaviour clearly indicated a different religious or cultural background from your own.

Of course while knowledge of different cultures and groups is important, the coach must also be aware of the dangers of stereotyping. Just because an attitude or behaviour is typical of a particular group, it does not mean that it is so for the person from that group you are coaching. It would be wrong to assume a woman will be less competitive and more relationship focused, that an older person will be less career focused, or that someone from an economically disadvantaged background will be lacking in confidence.

Beyond the basic knowledge needed to have a good chance of initiating a positive coaching relationship, coaches should continually challenge their understanding of themselves, the client and the coaching relationship. There is an almost endless list of things it could be important to explore.

- Are there certain behaviours or language uses that the person might find offensive?
- Are you correctly interpreting the body language of someone from a different cultural group?
- Is the communication difficulty with someone who is hard of hearing leading you to oversimplify your responses?
- Is competitive striving differentially valued in men and women?

A good way to increase your insight into cultural difference is through meeting and talking to people from different groups about their experiences, as well as through study. Additionally, biographies, literary fiction, films and TV about people from different backgrounds are also good sources for broadening your knowledge and perspective. Being aware of where there may be gaps in your knowledge and how to deal with this is as important as adding specific information to your store. A coach needs to continuously check that there is good mutual understanding in the discussion or whether the coach or client has misunderstood what the other is trying to say.

There are several academic presentations of aspects of difference. For example the work of Hofstede and Hofstede (2004) and Trompenaars and Hampden-Turner (1997) provide an accessible introduction to cultural difference. They discuss dimensions of difference such as the degree of hierarchy in relationships (power distance) or attitudes to time. Locke (1992) has developed a model which he uses to review cultural groups in a multicultural counselling context. As well as understanding the specifics of individual cultures, an understanding of the dimensions along which cultures can differ is enlightening. It helps the coach to identify when an issue in the coaching content or relationship is likely to relate to cultural differences in perspective.

With all this work it is important to remember that even within a particular group everyone's experiences and attitudes will be different. People brought up in the UK but from another cultural background might espouse either set of cultural assumptions or their own personal integration of the two, or they might experience conflict between their 'British' self and their home self (see the discussion of cultural identity below). A disability may be central to a person's identity or peripheral to it.

As well as knowledge of the group to which the client belongs, the coach should understand how prejudice – subtle and overt, individual and organisational – can impact on the individual and on his or her ability to operate effectively. It is important not to underestimate either the frequency or the effect of discrimination, both the intended acts of racist and sexist individuals and the more insidious results of social and institutional factors. It is often the feeling of alienation from mainstream society that has the biggest impact. Being stared at or excluded or having to hide some basic fact about themselves takes its toll on how people feel about themselves and see the world. Power is typically vested in the representatives of the majority or mainstream groups and those outside can feel powerless and helpless in the face of organisational structures or behaviours they do not understand or which exclude them. These kinds of processes can undermine an individual's self-esteem, self-confidence and resilience to the stresses and strains of daily life.

Without this type of insight the coach would be unable to differentiate between an individual who was engaging in effective strategies for dealing with a hostile environment or someone whose inappropriate behaviour was generating hostile reactions in others. Taking supervision from a coach with experience in the area of diversity or networking with other coaches working in the domain can be helpful in developing awareness of these types of processes.

The coach should have some insight into how cultural identity develops and the different ways people come to terms with their differences from others. Some may be proud of being different and wear their cultural identity as a banner (e.g. Black is Beautiful, Gay Pride). Others may experience it as a source of shame or as something to be hidden or compensated for through greater efforts. A number of theorists have suggested models of how these factors affect personal identity and some have suggested that people may pass through a number of stages from aspiring to be like the majority through idealisation of one's own group to an integrated approach to both one's own group and the dominant culture. See Ponterotto et al. (2000) for a discussion of some of these models and their impact on counselling processes. For some individuals, working through the conflicts in their identity may be important to a successful coaching outcome.

A final point – no one can ever really understand or know things from another's perspective. The coach does not assume that they know what it feels like to be their client, insights are all that the coach can hope for. These can be more or less appropriate depending on the knowledge that the coach has as described above. A good knowledge base can help a coach to more frequent and more accurate insight.

Vignette

Andrew left school with few qualifications and started a small and very successful niche software company. It has grown to a company employing about 60 people and over the years Andrew has recruited a board of directors to support him and the growth of the company. He has chosen able and qualified people in Sales, Marketing, Operations, Finance and HR. He has now engaged a coach to help him manage his team of directors. He feels stuck. He values the directors' qualifications and education but does not trust them and is intimidated by them because of how different they are.

- How can he relinquish power to people he does not trust, but how can he benefit from their skills if he does not empower them to act?
- How can Andrew gain insight into his feelings of intimidation?
- What strategies would you devise with Andrew to assist him?

Skills

An effective coach in a diverse environment will have a broad range of strategies and approaches which will be differentially appropriate with different people. It is unlikely that a single approach will work with all clients and the approach used should be matched to the individual and to his or her cultural perspective. An individual who values understanding emotional responses is likely to benefit from a more introspective approach whereas someone who comes from a culture which views such activity as self-indulgent would likely progress better with an active problem-solving approach.

Diversity issues bring into focus the need for the coach to manage the boundaries between one, two or three other players in the work-based coaching scenario that are outside the one-to-one coaching relationship between coach and client.

An action-oriented approach may be necessary to overcome prejudice in the client's environment. If the person being coached is doing everything right and those around cannot see this or do not respond – coaching may not help without a more active intervention. The coach might help the individual develop strategies for challenging and dealing with the prejudice and provide support for their implementation. In extreme situations, where this is not effective despite the client's efforts, the coach should consider confronting the appropriate representatives of the organisation with the discrimination the client is facing and help them to address the issues appropriately.

While this may seem antithetical to the coaching relationship, to try to address the situation within the coaching dyad suggests that the coach believes that the client is responsible for the situation and both the feelings of blame and the difficulty of dealing with an objectively antagonistic environment are likely to undermine the trust between client and coach. In the first instance the issue should be raised and addressed within the coaching. The client's agreement should be sought before undertaking any action. Equally if the coach becomes aware that the client is behaving in a discriminatory manner towards others, then this should be raised as an issue, even if the client is perfectly comfortable with this aspect of his or her behaviour and wants to focus the coaching on other matters.

The coach also needs well-developed communication skills and needs to be comfortable using diverse styles. Being able to match the communication style of the person being coached – e.g. body language, emotional expressivity – will generally improve the effectiveness of communication. Some cultures value a more emotionally committed style of communication, others a more dispassionate approach. One person could view an emotion free western presentation of ideas as boring and lacking in conviction whereas another could confuse an emotionally laden style with being irrational and paying scant attention to the facts of the case. Both verbal and non-verbal communication can differ across cultures. For instance different conventions regarding when to make and avoid eye contact can lead to misattribution of aggression or diffidence to a client.

Referring a client

One coach can work with people from a broad range of backgrounds. However, where the coaching goals are very much centred on issues of identity, discrimination and group membership, coaches should be ready to refer the client to someone who can more readily relate to the client, where they feel they cannot do so adequately. Coaching is predicated on a good relationship between the coach and client, and if there is a problem with this relationship, the possibility of referring to another coach should always be considered. Where there is an additional diversity dimension which needs to be addressed this may be strongly indicated. In some cases there are benefits of working with a coach from a similar group although this is not necessarily a requirement. As discussed above, where someone is from a minority or underrepresented group, identity can be a central theme in the coaching process – whether this is tied in with gender, race, sexuality, regional origin, social class, educational background or any other area. In these cases consideration should be given to finding an appropriate coach from a similar group who may more easily gain insight into the worldview and problems faced by the individual and with whom the client may more easily develop a trusting relationship.

Case studies

The following case studies illustrate how diversity issues can be critical to the coaching process. They are based on real coaching experiences but details have been changed and amalgamated for the sake of illustration so they do not refer to real people. Each is followed by an analysis of the coaching issues from a diversity perspective. Consider what aspects of diversity are raised in each study, what the dynamics of the situation are and how you might address this as a coach, before reading our analysis of the case.

Case study 1: Just one of the boys

Sandra has a middle management position in a very technical communications engineering company. She is a high flier – and very different from the other managers. She is extremely able and she is unusually young for her position; she is the only woman in a very male environment, yet she gets on very well with her colleagues. She is being coached to prepare her for promotion, which shows just how well she is regarded by the organisation. The focus of the coaching is how to influence more effectively.

After a few sessions she reveals to the coach that she is pregnant but wishes to keep this secret until after the promotion decision has been made. Some months later, when she has already been offered the promotion, she admits to the coach that she has not yet told her manager that she is pregnant. Despite the fact that her pregnancy is now quite evident, she believes that no one is aware of it – 'They would not notice as they see me as a bloke.' It seemed shocking to the coach that Sandra could be so obviously pregnant and her colleagues not notice.

Up till now Sandra had exerted influence in subtle ways and the focus of the coaching was how to influence in clearer and more direct ways. She wanted her colleagues to value her intelligence, insight and different point of view, and she wanted the organisation to promote her and make better use of her skills.

Sandra was different in so many ways from her colleagues (age, gender, ability, insight) that one might expect her to have difficulties with other members of the team. However, she had managed her relationships in the organisation so that they saw her as a 'bloke'. This suited both them and her. It was as if they could not cope with her differences and her level of ability which they would expect to find in an older man. So they almost saw her as an older man. This was not an issue she wanted or needed to challenge. It made it easier for her that they accepted her in this light, although she did have to ignore some sexist language and behaviour and hide the feminine parts of herself.

Sandra did not seem particularly concerned about having kept the pregnancy secret, and yet she had been putting off revealing it for some time and now it was hard to believe that no one suspected anything. Her colleagues' inability to see her pregnancy was perhaps a result of this perception of her as 'one of the boys'. How could she be pregnant if she wasn't really a woman? And once she made them face the fact that she was pregnant – would she still be able to maintain the male persona that had worked so well for her? This was an important dilemma that needed to be discussed in the coaching sessions. Sandra needed to become aware of the way she was managing her relationships. It would not be appropriate for the coach to impose her own feminist response to the situation on Sandra, but it would be useful to Sandra to understand the dynamics of her relationships with others in the organisation.

From the perspective of the organisation, Sandra was a real asset, patently more competent than the other managers. Yet she had to disguise her difference in order to fit in. Would she be willing or able to maintain this subterfuge once the baby was born? Was it possible for her to work effectively as a young woman, rather than behaving as one of the men? In order for this to happen, the organisation would have to change and learn about working with people who are different. Up till now, Sandra had been making all the accommodations. However it would not be possible for the coach to broach this with the organisation, and in particular with Sandra's manager, without her consent, and she did not agree to this.

In the event the coaching was concluded before this issue had been resolved when Sandra went on maternity leave. Although originally intending to, and despite her new promotion, she did not return after the baby was born and the organisation lost one of its best managers. Perhaps Sandra could not face developing a new relationship with the team as a woman and a mother, or perhaps being outside the organisation gave her the perspective to see how much she had had to sacrifice to work in such a sexist atmosphere.

Case study 2: Doesn't fit in

Julian manages a team of sales managers in a large IT organisation. He brings in a consultant to help him in a number of areas:

- developing the team
- improving his own leadership skills
- as an individual coach for some of the team members

He is particularly concerned about Warren, whom he feels is one of the weakest members of the team. He is concerned that Warren does not have the skills for the job. Julian describes him as weak, not fitting in, and not delivering the right relationships with customers. He is beginning to feel that Warren should be dropped from the team although when pressed for hard performance data none is forthcoming. While the other sales managers are all graduates with a very middle-class background, Warren left school at 16 and comes from a poor council estate. Julian puts Warren forward for individual coaching although he has little hope that he is capable of improving his performance.

During the coaching it becomes clear that Warren is unaware of Julian's low rating of his skills. He feels very loyal to Julian for promoting him to a manager's job and tells the coach that he (Warren) has been offered another job but is so grateful to Julian for having faith in him that he will stay where he is for the experience and for Julian's sake.

During a team development day the consultant-coach observes some hints that Warren may be being scapegoated by two other team members. The consultant-coach also develops a strong dislike for Julian and his manipulative style which is becoming evident both during the team development day and in some individual work with him. The individual work with Julian is terminated but Warren's coaching continues.

The diversity issue in this case study is the extent to which the difference in background between Warren and the rest of the team, particularly Julian, is underlying the stated performance issues. While Warren is a white male in a predominantly white male environment, he is still seen as different and as not fitting in. As with most diversity issues, power is vested in the majority group, both in Julian as team manager and in the other team members who make life difficult for Warren.

Unusually the coach has some objective evidence regarding how Julian and the rest of the team respond to Warren since she is engaged with the team outside the coaching relationship. She has particular insight into Julian's feelings, both as the commissioning manager for the coaching, but also in her individual work with him and her work with the team as a whole. Intuitively her sympathies lie with Warren who she feels is being unfairly treated. She is concerned about the unhealthy power relationships and worries that she is being used as a pawn by Julian to manage Warren out of the organisation. At the same time she sees the coaching as an opportunity to help Warren gain some awareness of what is going on and how he can manage power relationships differently in the future.

For the coach there are a number of ethical dilemmas here. To what extent can she use the insight she has from private sessions with Julian in her work with Warren? How can she avoid being part of a collusive power relationship with Julian? Is she being influenced in her view of the situation by her dislike of Julian and her liking for Warren? If she encourages Warren to leave would she be breaching her duty to the organisation which is employing her as Warren's coach?

She decides to raise the issue of how Warren perceives his relationships with the rest of the team and with Julian within the coaching sessions. She avoids reference to information gained from her private conversations with Julian, but is open about her personal feelings towards him. Although Warren had appeared totally unaware of Julian's attitude to him previously, he shows a great deal of relief on hearing the coach's views. Clearly maintaining the denial of the discrimination he was facing had required a significant amount of energy, and admitting the truth releases him from this. It also allows him to consider his position and the new job offer more objectively. Although he did decide to stay on rather than taking the new job, he did so with a greater awareness of his position.

Case study 3: Is it because I am Black?

Paul is a training manager in a large utility. He is Black of African Caribbean origin and this is his first management position. Coaching has been initiated because of concerns about his performance. If it does not improve he is likely to be demoted. The evidence of his poor performance is quite vague with some complaints about his style of communication (that he focuses on broader issues and lacks attention to detail). There is also some concern over whether projects he is managing will deliver the expected results. On the other hand he is relatively new to the role and has, so far, few concrete outcomes (whether good or bad) to show for his efforts.

In the initial coaching meetings Paul is optimistic and feels that he is capable and things will work out. He is not overly concerned about his performance or the issues that have been raised. The coach (a white man) finds Paul's way of communicating positive and free flowing but sometimes imprecise and vague – there is some difficulty pinning him down.

In this case there is very little objective evidence of whether Paul is performing well or not. He considers that he is doing fine but his manager is worried that he is not. The differences in culture between this organisation and Paul's African Caribbean background may be one source of this difference. Cultural differences are often reflected in communication style and this is an area where Paul is seen to be deficient. Might this be because Paul's cultural assumptions about the communication process differ somewhat from those of the majority of [white] managers in the organisation?

British culture avoids expression of emotion in functional communication. In the workplace it is considered important to convey ideas, and emotion is seen as interfering with rational thought. African Caribbean cultures (and many others) value the expression of emotion more highly, and indeed rationality without emotion suggests detachment and a lack of interest or commitment to the subject under discussion. This difference in approach can lead to misunderstandings.

Paul's perceived tendency to take on more than he can cope with may be a result of miscommunication. If asked to do something, perhaps he agrees to it because he is emotionally ready to take on what the organisation wants of him and expects to be asked to do things within his capability. When the response is a rational but unemotional suggestion that he is not up to the task, he feels his commitment is being challenged and reasserts his readiness to take it on. In the face of this reiteration of his wish for the task, it is given to him. Paul may perceive the lukewarm response and grudging assignment of the task as a sign of others' lack of acceptance of him. It would not be surprising if he saw this as racism.

The coach seems to be responding to Paul in a similar manner as his colleagues do. On the one hand it is often helpful to use the coaching relationship as evidence of how the client relates to others, but on the other the coach needs to consider whether he has sufficient understanding of African Caribbean culture to work effectively on a potential communication issue stemming from different cultural styles. There is a danger that the coach will be seen as just as racist as the organisation if he is unable to understand the underlying dynamics which may be leading to the way Paul is perceived. Perhaps Paul should be referred to someone with greater experience of these issues and there may be a benefit for him to work with someone from the same background.

All of this is independent of any consideration of whether Paul is, or is not, capable of fulfilling the requirements of the role effectively, and how he could improve his performance, which will certainly need to be addressed in the coaching process. But prior to that it is important for Paul to understand how he and the other managers may be misunderstanding each other.

Summary

Coaching is a one-to-one activity. It is about working with individuals so they can be more effective at work or in their personal life. The coaching work has a structure and helps the client to explore in an organised way what needs attention and then to make appropriate changes in those areas. Almost by definition the process involves looking at the self in relation to difference – how does the individual differ from others or from an ideal self? Is the client pleased with those differences? Do they value them? Do they make the most of them? If we weren't diverse as individuals we would all do and see things in the same way.

A coach tries to do two things in relation to diversity:

- Help the individual value her or his difference and make effective use of it – this entails identifying and making use of positive diversity attributes. For example, a woman in a team of men may be more sensitive to the emotions in the team and could be labelled as emotional and difficult. She may be able to develop that sensitivity and turn it into an advantage by spotting issues that she can influence at an early stage.
- Identify and work with negative diversity issues – in the client's mind and in the environment. This requires finding a balance between helping the person to operate within a flawed system – get the best out of the way things are, perhaps changing the way they respond to the environment – and encouraging the client to challenge the status quo and change the environment.

References

Burkhard, A. W. and Knox, S. (2004) Effect of therapist color-blindness on empathy and attributions in cross-cultural counselling. *Journal of Counseling Psychology* 51: 387–397.

Clutterbuck, D. (2003) Diversity issues in the mentoring relationship. In M. J. Davidson and S. L. Fielden (eds) *Individual Diversity and Psychology in Organizations*. Chichester: Wiley.

Ely, R. J. and Thomas, D. A. (2001) Cultural diversity at work: the effects of diversity perspectives on work group processes and outcomes. *Administrative Science Quarterly* 46: 229–273.

Enns, C. Z. (2000) Gender issues in counselling. In S. D. Brown and R. W. Lent (eds) *Handbook of Counselling Psychology*, 3rd edition. New York: Wiley.

Gushue, G. V. (2004) Race, color-blind racial attitudes and judgements about mental health: a shifting standards perspective. *Journal of Counseling Psychology* 51: 398–407.

Hofstede, G. and Hofstede, G. J. (2004) *Culture and Organisations: Software of the Mind. Intercultural cooperation and its importance for survival* (2nd edition). New York: McGraw Hill.

Kandola, R. and Fullerton, J. (1998) *Diversity in Action: Managing the mosaic*, 2nd edition. London: CIPD.

Locke, D. C. (1992) *Increasing Multicultural Understanding: A comprehensive model.* Newbury Park, CA: Sage.

Pedersen, P. R. and Levy, A. (1993) *Culture Centred Counseling and Interview Skills: A practical guide.* Westport, CT: Praeger.

Ponterotto, J. G., Fuertes, J. N. and Chen, E. C. (2000) Models of multicultural counselling. In S. D. Brown and R. W. Lent (eds) *Handbook of Counselling Psychology*, 3rd edition. New York: Wiley.

Sheridan, A. and O'Sullivan, J. (2003) What you see is what you get: popular culture, gender and workplace diversity. In M. J. Davidson and S. L. Fielden (eds) *Individual Diversity and Psychology in Organizations*. Chichester: Wiley.

Simons, T., Pelled, L. H. and Smith, K. A. (1999) Making use of differences: diversity, debate and decisions comprehensiveness in top management teams. *Academy of Management Journal* 47: 662–673.

Spear, K. (2001) *Executive Coaching for Women and Minorities: Special challenges.* The White Paper Series. Durango, CO: Lore International Institute.

Sue, D. W. and Sue, D. (1990) *Counselling the Culturally Diverse: Theory and practice*, 2nd edition. New York: Wiley.

Trompenaars, F. and Hampden-Turner, C. (1997) *Riding the Waves of Culture: Cultural diversity in business*, 2nd edition. London: Nicholas Brealey.

Wahl, A. and Holgersson, C. (2003) Male manager's reactions to gender diversity activities in organizations. In M. J. Davidson and S. L. Fielden (eds) *Individual Diversity and Psychology in Organizations*. Chichester: Wiley.

Discussion points

- Have you ever worked with someone who was very different from you? How did this affect the relationship, for good and ill? What did you learn from the interaction?
- How does your own background (religious, cultural, social, gender affiliation, sexual orientation, etc.) affect the way you interact with others and work as a coach?
- What would you do if you saw someone behaving in a discriminatory manner to another person?
- Have you ever been in a situation where you were different in some way

from the other people you were working with? How did this affect your relationship with the group? How did it make you feel?

- What aspects of diversity are you comfortable dealing with and which less so?

Suggested reading

Benokraitis, N. V. (ed.) (1997) *Subtle Sexism: Current practices and prospects for change*. London: Sage.

Clutterbuck, D. (2003) Diversity issues in the mentoring relationship. In M. J. Davidson and S. L. Fielden (eds) *Individual Diversity and Psychology in Organizations*. Chichester: Wiley.

Kandola, R. and Fullerton, J. (1998) *Diversity in Action: Managing the mosaic*, 2nd edition. London: CIPD

Pedersen, P. R. and Levy, A. (1993) *Culture Centred Counseling and Interview Skills: A practical guide*. Westport, CT: Praeger.

Trompenaars, F. and Hampden-Turner, C. (1997) *Riding the Waves of Culture: Cultural diversity in business*, 2nd edition. London: Nicholas Brealey.

Chapter 20

Using psychometrics in coaching

Alan Bourne

Introduction

Psychometric measurement relates to the assessment of psychological attributes, such as personality, abilities, values or interests. This typically involves using a measure such as a questionnaire or test and the generation of quantifiable results in terms of a numerical scale or categories. The underpinning logic behind using psychometric assessment in a coaching context is to provide an accurate and valid measure of relevant psychological characteristics and, through this, provide objective information to help the development of greater self-insight. This may, for instance, help the client gain insight into their own behaviour to help them resolve issues such as overcoming difficulties communicating with others, managing their work more effectively or coping with pressure.

Typically psychometric assessments may be used to help address a particular issue and as such may be deployed as a technique within a broader coaching relationship. For psychometrics to be useful in coaching, it is essential that measures provide accurate insights into the particular issue at hand, that feedback is delivered in such a way that it is accepted by the client, and that the insights drawn help lead to positive behavioural changes in line with the client's goals.

This chapter explores the role that psychometric measures can play within the coaching process, including the theory behind types of psychometric assessment and, importantly, how to select an appropriate measure to use and how to feed back results to a client.

The development of psychometrics

Since the late 1960s, psychometric assessment has become widely accepted as a useful method for both assessing and developing people. Many assessment tools were originally designed for clinical use. However, there has been an increasing demand for tools which are tailored to the needs of the workplace and broader application in non-clinical settings. These have focused on the underlying psychological qualities of individuals that contribute to successful performance and preferences, including personality, cognitive abilities, values, motivation and interests.

Unlike theories such as psychoanalytic approaches which are based on clinical interpretation, the psychometric approach is based on statistical analysis and emphasises scientific rigour. Psychometric research has explored the nature of a range of psychological attributes which can be useful to understand in a coaching context such as aptitude and intelligence (Guilford, 1967; Sternberg, 1985), personality (Cattell, 1965; Costa and McCrae, 1992), values (Schein, 1990) and interests (Holland, 1973).

Throughout, the emphasis within a psychometric approach is on the use of measurement tools which are rigorous because they assess a clear theoretical model and have undergone considerable trialling and development using statistical measures to ensure they are standardised, accurate and valid.

Using psychometrics: key concepts

At a high level, psychometric assessment is focused on measuring the extent to which individuals possess particular psychological attributes and quantifying this in relation to a wider population. In this section, the different applications of psychometrics within coaching are outlined and the key issues to be considered when identifying and choosing an appropriate assessment are discussed. In a coaching context, it is important to consider how psychometric assessment might help the individual better understand themselves in relation to others and through this insight, overcome barriers to achieving their goals.

Within the field of psychometrics there are a number of underlying assumptions which underpin the approach. The most fundamental assumption, borne out by early work in psychometrics (e.g. Spearman, 1904), is that people show clear variability in terms of psychological characteristics (typically these are normally distributed). Psychometrics is based in understanding individual differences and from this identifying the implications for individuals in relation to 'the norm' for most people.

Second, it is important to understand the relative stability of the attribute being measured. For instance, although personality preferences do change over time, they are nevertheless fairly stable over long periods (Costa and McCrae, 2006). Because of this, these characteristics have an enduring impact on behaviour and are particularly useful for an individual to understand in order to help identify strengths they can utilise and understand areas they may wish to develop or change.

The main areas where psychometric instruments have been developed and their applications in a coaching context are described below.

Personality

Personality is concerned with an individual's preferred ways of behaving, thinking and feeling, which predict how people will behave in everyday situations (Cattell, 1965). There are relatively stable differences in terms of generally how they prefer to relate to other people and situations, carry out tasks and manage their own thoughts and emotions (Costa and McCrae, 2006). Because personality characteristics are fairly stable and have a significant influence on what people enjoy doing and as a consequence their development of skills, they are particularly useful to understand within coaching contexts. They can be useful to understand the individual's own preferred ways of behaving and better understand issues relating to communication, problem-solving and conflict with others.

Motivation

This is concerned with what drives people to behave in certain ways, in terms of their needs, aspirations and goals (Maslow, 1943; McClelland, 1961). Motivation relates to how people direct their energies and sustain effort. While motivation may be either short term and transient or sustained over a significant period, the underlying drivers of motivation are closely linked to understanding what an individual values (see below) and how this guides behaviour (Latham, 2007).

Values

The values held by individuals relate to the internal guidelines or rules which people use when deciding the best way to behave in a specific situation. Values may be both personal to the individual and at the group level, such as cultural values or the values of a particular organisation or profession. Values are largely developed through socialisation, the sharing of norms of behaviour within a particular group. Values tend to be well developed in an individual and closely linked to their sense of identity. As such they can be a source of considerable insight in helping clients understand their own behaviour, decisions and career choices (Schein, 1990)

Beliefs

Closely related, beliefs concern the basic assumptions individuals consider to be true or untrue. Beliefs are fundamental in determining behaviour and like values they influence how people interpret situations and relationships with others. For instance, if you believe that all people should be treated with equal respect and fairness, this is likely to guide your behaviour in relation to others.

While closely linked to values, they are not typically assessed via psychometric approaches.

While closely linked to values, they are not typically assessed via psychometric approaches.

Attitudes

The thoughts and feelings held by individuals about a particular aspect of their environment are the basis of attitudes. For example, commitment to an organisation (Meyer and Allen, 1991) or satisfaction with a particular job (Locke, 1976) may have a significant impact on how an individual feels about their work and how they focus their efforts.

Interests

Often used in relation to career guidance, interests relate to what people would most like to do, be that in terms of career or the kind of task they find stimulating, such as Holland's (1973) model of occupational interests. For instance, people may be more or less interested in helping people recover from an illness, playing a musical instrument, or designing a new building – with clear implications for the kind of roles they may wish to undertake.

Abilities and skills

Abilities and skills are concerned with understanding someone's potential or performance for a particular task, for instance numerical reasoning using facts and figures or verbal reasoning which is closely related to interpreting and working with written information (Guilford, 1967). These attributes are sometimes useful to understand or to clarify where an individual's cognitive strengths lie, for instance in helping a client make choices between different career paths.

Choosing which instrument to use

When using psychometric instruments within a coaching context, the key to effectiveness is ensuring the right combination of theoretical rigour and practicality. There are a large number of different scenarios where psychometric assessments may be helpful to a client who is engaged in coaching, almost as broad as the diversity of goals which clients may have. For example, for someone who wishes to understand more fully how they could develop their people skills and how they work with others, assessments of personality or values may be particularly appropriate. Similarly, someone who is exploring new career paths may benefit from reviewing their skills, abilities and interests.

Before deciding to use a test at all, you need to be clear about why you want to use the test and what benefits you think this will give you over and above any other method of assessment. Sources such as the Psychological Testing Centre of the British Psychological Society regularly review different instruments and provide some guidance as to tools available, additionally all good quality psychometric test publishers provide information on their tests and the evidence supporting their accuracy and validity.

Each of the areas covered below should be borne in mind when deciding what psychometric approaches and instruments may be useful to support coaching.

Accreditation requirements

It is clearly laid down in British Psychological Society (2006) guidelines that those who use psychometric tests should be trained to the appropriate standard so they have the necessary knowledge and practical skills in administration, interpretation and feedback to use assessments responsibly and ethically. Typically this involves foundation (Level A) training in using psychometric assessments of abilities, followed by specialised training (Level B) in a particular measure such as a personality questionnaire.

Given the necessary training investment, as a coach it may at times be more economically viable to call on an associate with specific accreditation in a tool you wish to use with a client. Some of the practicalities and nuances you might need to consider when looking at introducing a third party to conduct the psychometric assessment are discussed in more detail in the section on 'Introducing a third party to conduct the psychometric assessment'.

Scope

Assessment methods can be very broad or very specific in their focus. For instance, a personality questionnaire may take a broad view of personality characteristics or focus on a specific issue, such as potential 'derailers' within a leadership context. When choosing an appropriate measure, it is essential to consider whether the instrument addresses the particular client need and is likely to generate useful insights to help the client move forward.

Standardisation

The norm groups which a test publisher provides will give you the basis upon which you will assess individuals. For most psychometric measures to have value, it is usually important to be able to understand an individual's results compared to people like them. For instance, how does the client compare to other managers and professionals in terms of the values which drive their behaviour at work? As a user, you should be checking what norms the test has been based upon. Test publishers should provide you with information on request to help answer these questions.

Reliability

How accurately does an instrument measure what it says it measures? Sadly, there are many tools that can be found through a quick web search that sound appealing but with further investigation there has been no work done to demonstrate whether they are in fact accurate and reliable. Psychometricians measure reliability on a scale from 0 to 1, where the higher the number the better the reliability. Typically a psychometric instrument should have a reliability of around 0.7 or higher for it to be acceptable. In practice, having a reliable measure means that if you were to assess an individual twice, perhaps with a week in between the assessments, the results would be largely consistent on each occasion.

If an instrument is unreliable, it may be very inaccurate and lead to spurious results which could be misleading and even damaging for the client's interests. If there is no evidence of reliability provided by the test publisher, then the simple answer is not to use the assessment.

Validity

Validity relates to whether an assessment tool actually measures what it says it measures. Is what the instrument measures relevant to what we are trying to assess? Lastly, you will want to know whether the instrument has any data to show that a relationship between the results and actual behaviour or performance actually exists. This is usually expressed in terms of evidence to show there are significant correlations in studies linking the measure with relevant outcome variables.

When choosing which tool to use, you should give consideration to all these factors. Does the content covered fit the need you are addressing? Is there scientific evidence from the test publishers indicating that results are linked to key variables of interest, such as better performance? Is the assessment tool based on a clearly articulated theory that has scientific support?

Creating insight

When used in coaching, the purpose of using psychometric instruments is to help generate insights that the client wouldn't otherwise have access to, or would take a long time to develop. Through gaining these insights, the client may better understand what barriers may need to be overcome to achieve their goals. Because of its relative objectivity, underlying validity, reliability and comparison to relevant norm groups, a psychometric measure can help introduce new trusted information to help unblock a client's current thinking and provide new perspectives on difficult issues.

This is perhaps the most important factor to consider when choosing a psychometric approach and instrument. Will the assessment tool employed create unique insights for the client and help them move forward?

Acceptability

Is the nature of the assessment process and methods you are using acceptable to the client? Generally speaking, the closer the alignment between the assessment method and the goals in question, the more acceptable the method is likely to be to the client. The greater the client's acceptance of the assessment process, the more likely they will learn from the experience and take ownership of the assessment outcomes.

Freedom from bias

All assessment methods are susceptible to bias, which may be reflective of real differences between different groups (e.g. in terms of gender or age). It is important when using any instrument to understand what differences have been observed between groups in previous research to help inform your interpretation and ensure this is appropriate for the particular client.

Practicality

In reality, this is probably the second most important factor to consider when choosing a suitable psychometric instrument:

* How much administration is involved?
* How long will it take the client?
* What equipment will be needed?
* How much does it cost?
* What are the training requirements?
* How user-friendly are the outputs?

Many assessments are available online and will automatically score themselves and provide reports, reducing the workload involved and making their use notably easier than paper-based approaches. However, access to the internet is typically required.

In summary, it is important that you understand all of the above issues when adopting a psychometric approach to ensure that you provide the best possible service to your clients and comply with accreditation requirements around the use of different instruments. Each of the issues discussed are core to all BPS-accredited training courses.

Using psychometrics in practice

Having discussed the different types of psychometric assessment available, where these may be useful and how to choose an appropriate instrument, this section outlines best practice in terms of their administration, interpretation and feedback. Finally, guidelines for how to run a successful feedback session are outlined.

Administration

With all psychometric instruments, it is important to ensure administration is delivered in a structured and clear way, ensuring the client understands the purpose of the assessment, what will be expected of them and how their results will be used. Assurances about confidentiality of data should be given prior to using a psychometric instrument, including how data will be used and stored. It is your responsibility as the user to ensure that assessment results are not used for purposes other than those to which the client has given their consent. Whether administration of the assessment is communicated via email, or the session is conducted face-to-face, it is important to establish positive rapport with the client to encourage the adoption of an honest, open response and ensure the results are valid.

Interpretation

As with administering psychometric instruments, it is important to have been trained and accredited by test publishers to the relevant standards (e.g. Level A and Level B accreditation) to ensure you are equipped to make accurate inferences from results.

First, it is vital that you have a good understanding of the underlying model and scales for the instrument you have chosen to use (e.g. the different personality attributes measured). Beyond this, it is important to be clear as to the comparison or norm groups used to evaluate results. For instance, have the client's results been compared to an appropriate benchmark? When assessing a senior level executive or board member, can you compare their performance to that of other senior executives in similar organisations?

When considering specific development needs, for instance how to develop more effective leadership skills, the results of any assessment need to be viewed in relation to the demands of this particular task. For instance, if the individual has a preference for influencing others and taking the lead, but indicates they are significantly less willing than others to consult openly before taking action, particular insights can be drawn to help the client focus their development efforts. For example, they may develop strategies for improving their ability to influence and lead others by exploring new ways to involve colleagues in their decision-making to achieve desired results.

Feedback

The quality of the feedback process is also paramount in order to gain ownership and facilitate meaningful change. Good feedback should meet the following standards:

- *Accuracy:* feedback must be technically accurate and be delivered in a clear, jargon-free manner as far as possible to ensure understanding, taking account of the fact that no measure is 100 per cent accurate. To effect meaningful change, it is essential that the client has the benefit of accurate and valid information they can understand.
- *Rapport:* it is important that feedback is given in a non-judgemental, objective style and good rapport is developed with the client to ensure the process is seen as objective and helpful. The feedback process is about helping the client develop useful insights and, as with all coaching, this is aided by an atmosphere of trust and openness.
- *Ownership:* clients should have the opportunity to discuss their results and take ownership of them in order to accept the implications for their development.
- *Utility:* to achieve the goals of greater self-insight and successful behavioural change, it is essential for results from psychometric assessments to be put into the practical, real world context for the client. Structured feedback should enable discussion of the practical implications, what the client has learned from the feedback and what actions they might consider subsequently.

One of the biggest dangers in feeding back any psychometric assessment is what is known as the 'Barnum effect' named after P. T. Barnum, the entertainer whose catchphrase was 'There's a sucker born every minute!' When feeding back information about personality preferences it is particularly important to be aware of, and strive to avoid giving, ambiguous or misleading feedback. For example:

- 'You generally enjoy working with other people, although sometimes you prefer to work alone.'
- 'At least some of the time you are more positive than those around you.'

The above are ambiguous and say little concrete about how the client compares to others. However, the ease with which people can accept ambiguous feedback has been demonstrated through empirical research. Stagner (1958) administered a personality questionnaire to a sample of personnel managers but then gave them all identical feedback. Around half believed the report was highly accurate and the large proportion of the remainder also thought it wasn't far off the mark! In order for clients to understand themselves better through psychometric assessment, it is essential when giving feedback to always be specific when describing their results to avoid this problem.

Introducing a third party to conduct the psychometric assessment

It is clearly not ethical to use a tool without having been appropriately trained and accredited in its use. The British Psychological Society (2006) requires that users of psychometric assessments should always have received the necessary training to ensure they are used competently, reflecting the international guidelines developed by the International Test Commission (2001) guidelines on test use.

> A competent test user will use tests appropriately, professionally, and in an ethical manner, paying due regard to the needs and rights of those involved in the testing process, the reasons for testing, and the broader context in which the testing takes place.
> This outcome will be achieved by ensuring that the test user has the necessary competencies to carry out the testing process, and the knowledge and understanding of tests and test use that inform and underpin this process.

One of the most significant practical issues from a coach's perspective can be the time and cost of acquiring training. In order to use psychometric instruments it is necessary to have attained Level A, which qualifies the user in assessments of ability, and the relevant Level B training for specific instruments which assess attributes such as personality. If it is likely that training in the use of an instrument will benefit a range of clients, then this may well be an appropriate investment and enable a coach to integrate psychometric assessment into their approach without involving third parties.

However, if there appears to be a clear benefit from using psychometric tools within the coaching process but the relevant training has not been undertaken, it may be appropriate to involve a suitably trained third party with expertise in a particular tool to support the coaching process. Any such individual should hold the appropriate BPS or equivalent accreditation and ideally have significant experience in the use of the tool.

Introducing a third party can introduce some additional complexity into the coaching relationship. When doing so, it is essential that such involvement is clearly contracted with the client and the third party in relation to the parameters of the assessment feedback process. For instance, the coach may set the scene for the use of the psychometric assessment and agree goals with the client from the feedback session. The feedback session may then be delivered by the trained third party, following which the coach can discuss with the client what they learnt from the experience and integrate this into their broader coaching. Use of a third party may also have the benefit of helping a coach maintain independence from the assessment and feedback process.

How to conduct an effective feedback session

This section outlines how to provide effective feedback on a psychometric assessment. The example used is that of a personality questionnaire, given these are the most widely used psychometrics within a coaching context, but the guidelines apply to all psychometric measures.

First, in terms of structure, a feedback session should always cover the following steps:

- Give a clear introduction.
- Clarify practicalities (e.g. time available, confidentiality).
- Clarify the context for the feedback session from the client's perspective.
- Introduce the questionnaire and what it measures.
- Establish an open feedback style using active listening.
- Explain the questionnaire structure.
- Explain each scale and score, exploring the implications given the context.
- Give the client opportunity to question and understand each result that is fed back.
- Make links across scales to understand the depth of the profile.
- Summarise and clarify understanding and implications for action.

Below are outlined guidelines and tips to ensure each of these steps is done as effectively as possible, to set the context for helping the client draw useful insights from the feedback and providing an appropriate environment for this learning.

Introduction

When introducing the feedback session it is important to clarify the purpose of the session as you understand it, and check how the client found completing the assessment to gain an understanding of their impressions of the tool, their response style and any other external issues that may have influenced the results.

Confidentiality

Feedback should always be delivered in a private, controlled environment, whether that is face-to-face or remotely. Always clarify who has access to results; for instance, if coaching is sponsored by the client's employer, will the data be available to the client's HR department or kept private between you and the client?

Context

It is essential to understand the context from the perspective of the client. Areas you should cover to ensure you understand the background may include the client's current role or issues they are addressing, aspirations, career so far and specific objectives and expectations from the session. Often this will be part of an ongoing coaching relationship and much of this information may have already been discussed, nevertheless it is good practice to clarify these points during a feedback session.

Describing the psychometric assessment

This should cover the following:

- what the instrument is and what it measures (e.g. personality, values, etc.)
- that the results are not infallible and only as good as the answers provided by the client
- the basic structure of the model (e.g. key domains and scales)
- the comparison group used and why it is important to compare to a norm
- the importance of relating feedback to the client's objectives.

Feedback style

When feeding back results from a psychometric assessment, it is vital to ensure the discussion is very much a two-way process and a safe environment is created for the client to explore their thoughts and feelings. To this end, there are a number of elements in ensuring an effective feedback style:

- *Rapport and active listening:* in the first instance it is important to put the client at ease and develop an open and professional rapport. It is important not only to listen to what the client has to say about their results, but also to actively communicate this, through acknowledgement, paraphrasing and reflecting back what they have said to ensure you have understood and otherwise indicate you are listening actively. Non-verbal body language should be congruent with listening actively, for instance being open, acknowledging you have understood the client.
- *Open questioning and probing:* use open questions (e.g. What do you think the implications are for you? How do you feel about the results?) when exploring the meaning of the client's results, rather than closed yes/no questions which don't help develop discussion.
- *Non-judgemental style:* it is important in feedback to avoid making value judgements; rather you should be objective in feeding back results and invite the client to comment on them.

- *Challenge appropriately:* this should not be confrontational, but you should be prepared to probe clients further to explore any areas where they disagree with feedback.

Discussing and exploring the model, scales and scores

It is important when feeding back results to look for examples relating to the results, either confirmatory or otherwise, and probe for situational consistency (in what situations is the client's behaviour different and why?). This process enables a client to understand the implications of their scores in relation to their own challenges and needs.

Making links

One of the most powerful elements of any feedback discussion is making links across scales and between the examples given. This is vital for helping the client understand the practical implications of their results. The key types of linkage and how to make them are outlined below:

- *Making links across scales:* identify possible implications of combinations of scores, e.g. a high preference for being supportive but relatively low preference for listening to and consulting others. As you progress through an instrument, you will be able to increasingly link back to scales already covered.
- *Making links between scores and background:* the background information provided by the client may give insights into the nature of their personality profile, particularly their experiences, values and learned behaviours which may have shaped their development.
- *Making links between scores and examples of behaviour:* as you progress through the feedback session and the different examples provided by the client unfold, there may be consistent themes to be highlighted and discussed, or sometimes inconsistency in behaviour across different situations. These should be raised and discussed to help develop insight into consistent patterns of behaviour and where these may be either strengths to build on or potentially self-limiting.

Summarising and reflecting back

Throughout the feedback process, it is helpful to regularly summarise and reflect back to the client what has been established thus far. This will typically focus on the client's thoughts on key development actions to work on or give further consideration. The end of the session should always conclude with a summary of the key points, as agreed by both parties in the discussion.

Assuming the psychometric instrument being used meets the base criteria such as being reliable, valid and appropriate for the need, the power of psychometric assessments in coaching all comes down the quality of the feedback session. The impact of the results in enabling the client to achieve their goals depends on how well the client is helped to understand the implications, identify opportunities for new ways of behaving and making linkages between the outputs and their real-world concerns.

Which clients benefit most?

Psychometric instruments can be beneficial to a broad range of clients. However, as mentioned earlier in relation to the issue of scope, some tools are developed to have a breadth of application while others focus on a particular area of interest. It is probably fair to say that the widest choice of psychometric instruments is available for work-related applications, with a particular focus on understanding leadership skills and how people work together. Other tools which are generic may be equally useful examining issues in non-work settings.

The clients who gain the greatest benefit from psychometric tools are likely to be those who are open in their responses when completing them, open-minded and curious to understand themselves better and who do not take a defensive attitude to feedback which may challenge how they see themselves.

Some care should be taken when using psychometric instruments with adolescents in particular, as they may be at a relatively early stage of development and many attributes may still change significantly over the years ahead. In all cases, it is vital to ensure an instrument is only used for the purpose for which it is intended and that appropriate, representative norms are available to enable effective interpretation.

Case study

The following case study is intended to illustrate how the use of a psychometric instrument, in this case a personality questionnaire, was helpful in providing a client with greater insight into their own behaviour and how it was affecting their achievement of their desired goals.

David was a senior project manager in a global telecommunications business, primarily involved in managing the implementation of large infrastructure projects within the business. Having initially joined the business as an engineer, he had moved into junior operational management roles then worked in a number of successive project management roles.

Building on his reputation in the business as a successful project manager – someone who 'gets things done' – David was increasingly looking for a role where he could take broader operational responsibility in a 'head of' role for a business unit, with the aspiration of developing in time to a director level position.

In his own view, David felt he had been somewhat overlooked and been rather pigeonholed as a technical, project management specialist rather than having potential for more general roles. He described feeling that other, less experienced managers who spent more time on the 'people stuff' seemed to be getting better opportunities, while the business (and his manager) seemed to want him to carry on doing what he was doing well.

David was interested in coaching to help him explore how he could take the steps needed to advance his career in this way, and from this start to make some progress rather than continue doing the same thing but not developing further. It was suggested to David that he might find it useful to explore his style of working through a personality questionnaire, as this would help highlight both his strengths and potential areas for development that may be holding him back from achieving his objectives. The objective nature of a psychometric approach appealed to him as he wanted to get a clear view on how he compared to other managers, and was concerned that the results would be accurate and helpful to him.

The process

In order to gain useful insights into David's preferred styles of working and explore how this may be affecting how he is seen by others at work, it was appropriate for him to complete a work-based personality questionnaire specifically focused on behaviour in this context. A number of such tools are available in this regard, typically requiring BPS-accredited training to ensure users fully understand the tool and how to interpret and feedback results.

In this instance David completed the Dimensions personality questionnaire (Holdsworth, 2006) which covers three main domains: first, how the respondent works with others, second, their approach to tasks and projects and third, their drives and emotions. The resulting report covered 15 personality traits, which were fed back to David by a user trained in the tool to the required BPS standards. The following outlines some of the key insights drawn from the feedback, followed by the learning points and subsequent actions which David took away from the experience.

In relation to how David likes to work with others, an interesting and somewhat contradictory picture emerged. When asked to describe what he expected his results to be like, he indicated he was something of an extravert, always trying to engage others and move things forward. His profile suggested quite a strong preference for influencing others, as compared to most managers; however, his level of confidence in social situations was about typical in relation to the norm. When asked for examples in relation to this, it became apparent that while he often took the lead and sought to persuade others, there were at least two more senior or powerful stakeholders in the business with whom he sometimes felt a little out of his depth and found difficulty winning them over. One of the consequences had been some cutbacks on a project he had led where the sponsor appeared to lose interest in seeing it through to completion.

Related to the above and something of a surprise to David, his preference for networking and communicating was slightly lower than that of most managers. While David felt that he was close with his colleagues on all the projects he had worked on, and always focused on keeping his sponsors on board, it was apparent that he has to push himself to proactively network and spend time with others when there is not an immediate task at hand. In short, while he was outgoing in terms of seeking to influence things, he was somewhat less gregarious than he believed.

David's results indicated a preference for supporting others around him and maintaining a sense of harmony with colleagues; however, he also appeared to be less keen to consult with others when this would detract from 'getting the job done'. Overall, the results helped reinforce two key points for him. First, because he was very focused on delivering his own project and the team around him, he tended to shy away from building broader relationships across the business. As a result, he felt it was probably true that many colleagues in the organisation were aware of his reputation for delivering projects but were not so aware of him as an individual, and that he may be limiting his opportunities by not developing his network further. Second, while he had a strong desire to take the lead, David recognised that he may gain from reflecting on how he involved others and whether he was sometimes seen as preoccupied by colleagues or lacking confidence in front of senior stakeholders.

Perhaps unsurprisingly given his successes as a project manager, the results relating to how David managed his work and projects indicated that he was highly methodical and conscientious, with a strong analytical approach underpinning his decisions. He appeared to be about as conceptual and creative as most other managers. When asked what the implications of this might be, he acknowledged that this was probably the profile of 'a good project manager'. The qualities most important in the roles to which he was aspiring were then discussed, and he identified that he had previously had feedback suggesting he can sometimes get a bit too involved in the detail and would benefit from taking a broader, strategic view. This related back to his example of his recent project sponsor, who just wanted to see a brief summary of the key issues but was difficult to engage. David described thinking at the time that the sponsor was really not being supportive and not taking much interest; however, when it was suggested to him that this may be a difference of personality style, it was agreed there may be something to be gained from thinking about how to communicate more effectively with individuals who are very 'high level' in their approach.

In terms of looking at David's drive and emotions, the questionnaire results gave a clear indication that he had a great deal of day-to-day motivation to get things done, though he was fairly balanced in managing the impact of work on overall quality of life. David described himself as someone who is very active and ambitious, and was at first a little unsure of the veracity of the results. However, he described having been quite happy in project-focused roles over the last few years rather than putting career above all else, but had become more frustrated of late given his depth of knowledge and experience.

His profile indicated he can become frustrated fairly easily when under pressure, but has quite high levels of resilience compared to others when responding to this as well as a very flexible approach, adapting to changes around him when they occur. When this was explored further, it became apparent that at an emotional level David felt the organisation had perhaps not really supported him as much as he would like of late and that this had not particularly been recognised or taken on board by his line manager. It was suggested to David that perhaps because he had a high capacity for action and was resilient under pressure, these concerns may easily go unnoticed by others.

In summarising the key points to emerge from the feedback session, David was asked what he considered the most useful learning points from the session and what he might do to follow up on them. In relation to his style of working with others, he conceded he may not be quite as outgoing as expected and there was clearly some benefit to be had from getting to know colleagues and managers outside of his immediate area to strengthen his network and manage his reputation. More broadly there were a number of areas where David felt he could look at tailoring his communication style for certain individuals and importantly, that he should raise concerns earlier on with his line manager rather than letting pressure build up then appearing to get frustrated 'out of the blue' to others around him.

In David's case, the use of the personality questionnaire helped him move forward by providing an objective perspective on his behaviour, effectively holding a mirror up to his way of working and allowing him to reflect on it in a safe setting. While he was not always comfortable with the challenge from some of the results, the assessment allowed him to step out of his situation and having identified some pertinent issues, gave him a focus for further coaching and development.

References

British Psychological Society (2006) *Psychological Testing: A user's guide*. Leicester: BPS Psychological Testing Centre.

Cattell, R. B. (1965) *The Scientific Analysis of Personality*. Harmondsworth: Penguin.

Costa, P. T., Jr, and McCrae, R. R. (1992) Four ways five factors are basic. *Personality and Individual Differences* 13: 653–665.

Costa, P. T., Jr, and McCrae, R. R. (2006) Age changes in personality and their origins: comment on Roberts, Walton, and Viechtbauer (2006). *Psychological Bulletin* 132: 28–30.

Guilford, J. P. (1967) *The Nature of Human Intelligence*. New York: McGraw-Hill.

Holdsworth, R. F. (2006) *Dimensions Personality Questionnaire*. St Helier, Jersey: Talent Q Group.

Holland, J. L. (1973) *Making Vocational Choices: A theory of careers*. Englewood Cliffs, NJ: Prentice Hall.

International Test Commission (2001) International guidelines for test use. *International Journal of Testing* 1: 93–114.

Latham, G. P. (2007) *Work Motivation: History, theory, research and practice*. Thousand Oaks, CA: Sage.

Locke, E. A. (1976) The nature and causes of job satisfaction. In M. D. Dunnette (ed.) *Handbook of Industrial and Organizational Psychology* (pp. 1297–1349). Chicago, IL: Rand McNally.

McClelland, D. C. (1961) *The Achieving Society*. Princeton, NJ: Van Nostrand.

Maslow, A.H. (1943) A theory of human motivation. *Psychological Review* 50: 370–396.

Meyer, J. P. and Allen, N. J. (1991) A three-component conceptualization of organizational commitment: some methodological considerations. *Human Resources Management Review* 1: 61–89.

Schein, E. H. (1990) *Career Anchors – Discovering your real values*. San Diego, CA: Pfeiffer.

Spearman, C. E. (1904) General intelligence, objectively determined and measured. *American Journal of Psychology* 15: 201–293.

Stagner, R. (1958) The gullibility of personnel managers. *Personnel Psychology* 11: 347–352.

Sternberg, R. J. (1985) *Beyond IQ: A triarchic theory of human intelligence*. New York: Cambridge University Press.

Discussion points

- For the feedback from a psychometric instrument to be helpful it is first important that it is relevant and accurate. What key features would you look for in a psychometric assessment to ensure it is fit for purpose in this regard?

- While psychometric assessment can help develop useful insights for clients, the process of translating results into meaningful learning through the feedback process is critical. What do you see as the most important actions that should happen during feedback to ensure this occurs?
- What are the main benefits and limitations of using psychometric assessment as an approach to help clients in a coaching context?
- Why is client ownership of the results so important when using psychometric assessment? What are the risks to the coaching process if this is not generated?

Suggested reading

British Psychological Society (2006) *Psychological Testing: A user's guide*. Leicester: BPS Psychological Testing Centre.

Costa, P. T., Jr, and McCrae, R. R. (2002) *Personality in Adulthood: A five-factor theory perspective*, 2nd edition. New York: Guilford Press.

Rust, J. and Golombok, S. (1999) *Modern Psychometrics: The science of psychological assessment*, 2nd edition. Hove: Routledge.

Schein, E. H. (1990) *Career Anchors – Discovering your real values*. San Diego, CA: Pfeiffer.

Part IV

Sustainable practice

Concepts to support the integration and sustainability of coaching initiatives within organisations

Alison Whybrow and Vic Henderson

Introduction

The growth of coaching in organisations is a reflection of our ever strengthening belief in its potential to optimise individual and organisational performance and create a human capital advantage over competitors. The current estimate of the size of the coaching market is $2 billion per year (Fillery-Travis and Lane, 2006). Coaching is one of the top five development interventions for organisational executives and cases have been reported where it has had a hugely positive impact on performance (Corporate Leadership Council, 2003).

A word of caution; although coaching can create open dialogue, reduce defensiveness and allow individuals and organisations to learn, grow and perform it can also, as reported by the Corporate Leadership Council (2003), be fragmented and have limited impact on organisational performance.

The varied impact of coaching may be the result of any number of factors; differences in coach capability, the degree of match between the coach and coachee, how effectively coaching is integrated with organisational strategy or fits the organisation's culture. It may also be a result of the diversity in the practice of coaching in organisations (e.g. different policies about who has access to coaches, how coaches are accessed, what they are accessed for and how the coaching relationship develops and evolves).

Given the complexity of individuals and organisations it is not surprising that this variety in practice and impact is found. There are practical tools and techniques that can be used to maximise the effectiveness of coaching in your organisation.

First, recognise that the introduction of coaching is the start of a journey. Time is needed to embed new views and behaviours, and flexibility is required as the nature of coaching in your organisation evolves.

Second, adopt a systems based, managed change approach to understanding, implementing and integrating the coaching initiative. Change is complex and has multiple outcomes, some of which are expected, others can take us by surprise. Indeed, as many can testify it is a lot easier to get things started, to begin initiatives than it is to bring enduring changes into being (Senge et al., 1994).

Third, take heart in the fact that there are tools, techniques and safety nets that will ease the change process. This chapter outlines a number of managed change tools, concepts and techniques that will be useful when viewing the introduction of coaching from a systems perspective. Given that the biggest challenge is getting people to change the way they do things, the chapters in Part II provide useful insights into individual development and change.

This chapter presents frameworks, concepts and perspectives that you may find useful when considering the aims of coaching for your organisation and how these might be achieved. Perhaps some of the ideas presented here will assist you to effect a sustained change in the way people operate, improving overall performance in your organisation.

We start with a brief overview of a typology of coaching in organisations, and touching on some useful management change tools and techniques, we explore the implementation of your vision for coaching. We will introduce strategies, theories and concepts that are likely to support you in integrating and sustaining this vision, and include a set of self-assessment questionnaires to enable you to judge the level of support you have and additional support you may need. Finally, we end with a discussion as to why people might resist the introduction of coaching and what you might be able to do to overcome this.

A typology of coaching initiatives in organisations

Coaching in organisations is not a standard package, and what works well in one company or part of a company may not be successfully transferred elsewhere. However, our work has identified a number of approaches by which coaching may be introduced to an organisation. These include: the coach as expert, the manager as coach and/or specific individual coaching programmes. These are not mutually exclusive and can coexist happily within the same organisation. Indeed, in a survey of organisations, 51 per cent used external coaches, 41 per cent trained internal coaches and 79 per cent used manager coaches (Kubicek, 2002) to enhance individual, and organisational, performance.

The coach as expert

Here the organisation is encouraged to form a pool of expert coaches from a range of developmental and business backgrounds that can be drawn on to offer support to individuals as required. This pool may be made up of associates, independent of the organisation and/or full-time employees who may work solely as a coach or have additional responsibilities. A key challenge with this approach is getting individuals who are both competent as a coach and able to deliver within the context of the organisation. It might be expected that the expert coaches may be proficient in using one or more of the psychological frameworks outlined in Part II and have substantial coaching experience. The mix of coach capability is likely to be informed in part by the needs of individual coaching programmes within the organisation.

The manager as coach

This kind of coaching within the organisation may be used to assist the development of a culture where employees are supported to learn for themselves within a framework of guidance and facilitation, rather than a more traditional culture of command and control. Here the skills of coaching are seen as fitting into the existing repertoire of the manager. The aim is not to create coaching experts across the entire management team, but to provide a set of tools that the manager can use to enhance the performance within the organisation. This approach is key to building a learning organisation (Senge et al., 1994).

Individual coaching programmes

These programmes are typically tailored to meet individual performance requirements, or development themes that are priorities for the organisation. Grant and Cavanagh (2004) identify three generic levels of coaching programme:

- *skills coaching*, which requires the coach to focus on specific behaviours
- *performance coaching*, which focuses on performance improvement processes such as the coachee setting goals, overcoming obstacles, and evaluating their own performance
- *developmental coaching*, which takes a more holistic view, involving the creation of a personal reflective space; this might deal with more fundamental personal and professional development questions.

When introducing individual coaching programmes, different kinds of coaches may be brought in to the organisation to address specific individual requirements. For example, board members may have their own executive coaches, individual excellence coaches may be introduced as a proposition to engage the star performers, or performance coaches may be used for under-achievers.

Each of the three ways that coaching may be introduced to the organisation requires some level of change in people's behaviour as well as alignment of organisational structures, processes and culture. For example, there is no point in developing a pool of internal coaches who can be drawn on if the finance director will not allow you access to the necessary coach from within the finance team because of pressing departmental deadlines. Similarly there is no point in expecting managers to use their newly learned coaching skills if their own manager is not supportive, or they are rewarded in the short term purely for 'what' they deliver rather than 'how' they deliver. Finally, raising aspirations of star performers through the implementation of a coaching programme, only to find that the organisational structure does not allow the 'star' to move their career forward may have a negative rather than positive impact.

The prevailing culture in an organisation is likely to have an impact on the success of coaching initiatives. Clutterbuck and Megginson (2005) identified six characteristics of a culture that supports coaching (a coaching culture):

- Coaching is linked to business drivers.
- Being a coach is encouraged and supported.
- Coaches are provided with training.
- Coaching is recognised and rewarded.
- A systems perspective is adopted.
- The move to coaching is managed.

A systems thinking perspective and managed change

When introducing an initiative that requires people to change the way they think and do things within an organisation, a systems thinking perspective is useful. All living beings thrive on stability, continuity and predictability and have a natural tendency to oppose any force which attempts to upset this balance (Heller et al., 1998). Disturbances to this equilibrium, such as a requirement to change behaviour or thinking, are likely to be met with resistance in some form.

The strength of this resistance is understood when we explore systems theory a little more. Not only are we as individuals complex systems, but also we exist within any number of other systems. This creates a context where any action is embedded within a system of reactions, reciprocations and impacts and cannot be isolated from the system. Individual behaviour is seen as a response to the current demands of the system as a whole (Peltier, 2001). From this perspective it is easy to see that to bring about changes in behaviour, a pervading change in context is required.

More complexity is added when we see that within every system, there are subsystems, with more or less permeable and flexible boundaries between them. Within the system and subsystems behavioural expectations are defined to a certain extent by stories and images that hold us captive and prevent change, even when the external environment demands it. Peltier (2001) points out that to change behaviour at the individual and organisational level, the rigid expectations, individual roles, behaviours, hierarchies and coalitions that exist within the systems and subsystems of the organisation need to be examined and made more flexible. See chapter 14 for a discussion on systems.

Put simply, to integrate coaching effectively the organisation's systems need to change, providing a different context, an alternative system that people value and can engage with. To have a greater hope of success, detailed attention is required at the outset to enable a new context to be shaped. A holistic approach that proactively and reactively attends to people's behaviour as well as organisational systems, processes and culture is likely to be more successful.

The Managed Change™ framework developed by LaMarsh and Associates (2005) allows you, as an agent of change who is embedded in the existing system, to step out and establish a more objective understanding of it as you begin to shape the new context.

Using the Managed Change™ Framework to effectively integrate and sustain your coaching initiative

The Managed Change™ model, its ideas and guiding logic underpin the content of this chapter. Specific tools are referenced as they appear.

Right at the beginning – why change?

You think you know what sort of coaching initiative(s) would be helpful in furthering people development in your organisation and you know effort and attention are required to ensure coaching is integrated into business as usual. But have you really scoped the scale of the journey you are starting out on? What resources do you have and what more do you need? Where do you start? The following questions (adapted from LaMarsh and Associates, 2005) are designed to help you to clarify where you are and what you need to be successful.

- Why coaching?
- Why did you start the coaching journey?
- What are you trying to achieve through coaching?
- What happens if you do not introduce coaching successfully?
- What forces (internal and external) are driving your desire to integrate coaching into your business practices?
- Why didn't you take action earlier?
- How much time do you have before the impact of not doing this starts to negatively impact the organisation?

Together the answers to these questions provide the context within which coaching is being introduced, the expectations about what 'coaching' will deliver, the drivers behind implementation and the timescales for delivery (LaMarsh and Associates, 2005).

Already you might want to start challenging the remit of the coaching initiatives: What is realistic? By what time? What further input do you need right now?

The two scoping questions

- What is your vision for the coaching initiative(s)?
- Where are you now?

In your eagerness to start the journey, you may fall into the pitfall of answering the first question (often with some sketchiness around the detail) and forget about the second question altogether. The implication of this is that you may set off prepared for a very different journey to the one that you encounter. Taking time to answer both questions is essential to understand the scale and depth of the journey. Here we will focus on how you might answer the first question in more detail.

Setting clear, realistic, tangible goals is a challenge in itself, however research demonstrates the effort invested is worth it (for an early reference see Kahn et al., 1964). Basically, explicit, specific goals lead to a greater likelihood of success. Visioning is a very relevant and important part of goal setting in individual and organisational change. As with any visioning exercise, the more detailed, realistic and tangible you can make the vision the more it enables you to plan, ensure appropriate contingencies and reduce unpleasant surprises. At the same time, there's a balance between a highly detailed vision and remaining flexible in your thinking to accommodate changing circumstances.

When responding to the question 'what is your vision', you want to aim for a detailed understanding of the structures, processes, people and culture required to make your vision a reality. Simply stating 'to introduce coaching to address employee performance problems' is unlikely to deliver success. You may find Figure 21.1 particularly useful to assist you in mapping your vision for the coaching initiative(s). (The frameworks for mapping the vision of coaching and your starting point are adapted from LaMarsh and Associates, 2005.)

To get a really good understanding of the task ahead of you, the following critical areas need to be explored in relation to your coaching vision:

- communication
- employee involvement
- management style
- decision-making
- relationship with customers (internal and external)
- focus on quality
- use of technology

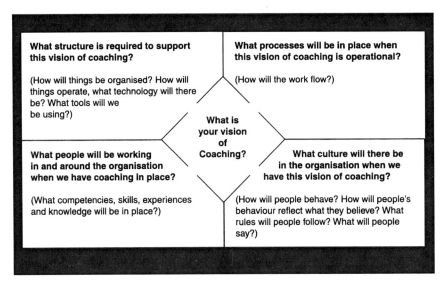

Figure 21.1 Framework for mapping your vision of coaching.

- teamwork
- reward and recognition
- change management.

Simply reword the question in the central diamond of Figure 21.1 to include the different critical areas, and explore this new question within each of the four quadrants. For example, with communication, the question in the diamond becomes: How will communication be when coaching is successfully integrated? Then, what structures and processes will be in place to support this communication, what competencies will people have, how will they behave and so on. In this way you can generate a full picture of what you are aiming at.

The visioning exercise gives you the end point. To understand the scale of the journey you also have to understand your starting point. Answering the question 'Where are you now?' provides the 'stake in the ground' from which your planning and implementation can begin. As with the first question, the response needs to be sufficiently detailed to be useful. See Figure 21.2 for a set of useful questions to help you understand where you are now.

Together, the answers to these questions provide you with a more rounded understanding of the gap between coaching as it is now in the organisation, where you would like it to be and what has to change.

Systems thinking reminds us that one change in any one part of the map of the current situation will have ripple effects and bring about change in the other elements of the framework. These planned (or more often unplanned)

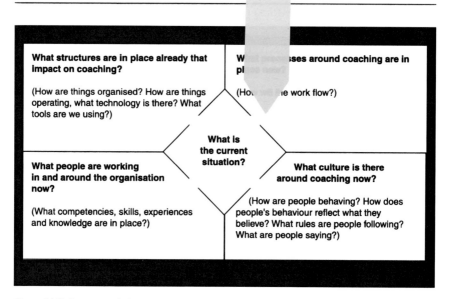

Figure 21.2 Framework for mapping your starting point.

changes will influence the development of the coaching initiative(s) within the organisation. The exact route you take to integrate coaching into the organisation is likely to feel a little hazy at times as unexpected obstacles as well as fantastic opportunities emerge along the way.

Strategies to navigate the journey

One certainty when making changes, even small ones, is that individual and organisational performance will dip. This is a completely natural response as people enter a period of uncertainty, where the rules of thumb that they followed in their day-to-day jobs change and their personal worldview of how the workplace operates is challenged. They will begin to ask themselves (or the organisation) questions – What does this change mean for me? How do I behave? Do I really need to change the way I have always done things? – and individual levels of stress may increase. Indeed, organisational change is one of the Health and Safety Executive's (HSE) key stress risk areas.

The challenge for organisations is how to minimise this performance dip. Clarity about why you are introducing coaching and the journey ahead will help. Additionally, there are strategies you can draw on and safety nets you can put in place to support people through the change. Based on our experiences, some of these follow here.

Understanding the key players

Some key roles need to be fulfilled for your coaching initiative(s) to be successful (LaMarsh and Associates, 2005); these include the change sponsors and change agents.

The change sponsors

The change sponsors include everyone in the management cascade to whom the targets of the change report. You need to have someone at the most senior organisational level to back you and effect the necessary organisational changes. Their behaviour has to match that required of others as described in your coaching vision. Sponsors have a number of key duties to fulfil to support the change. One of the key aspects is to make sure that you have the resources for your initiative, including financial as well as people. More details are outlined in the section on key roles assessment.

The change agents

The change agents can be an individual or group of individuals who have the responsibility to make change happen. The change agents have a different role from the main change sponsor. The change agents are focused on creating the change at an operational level, drawing on the change sponsor to enable things to happen at a more strategic level.

Targets of the proposed change

The targets are those who need to change (which often also includes the change sponsor), and are likely to experience at least some of the following:

- feeling awkward, uneasy and self-conscious
- thinking first about what they have to give up – not what they'll get
- feeling alone, even if everyone else is going through the same change
- believing that they can handle only so much change (readiness to change differs between individuals) and they don't have the resources to change
- knowing they will go back to doing things the 'right' way when the pressure is off.

Changing roles

The roles of change sponsor and change agent are *formally* given to only a few individuals during a change programme. However, the senior person (sponsor) who puts their full influence behind the coaching initiative(s) is often going to be a target as well. He or she may need to change his/her public and private behaviour to model the behaviour expected of others. The more individuals in the organisation that are prepared to sponsor and be an agent of change as well as align their own behaviour with that described in your coaching vision, the more successful integration will be.

Being effective as a change sponsor and/or change agent

To influence others to adopt or change a particular behaviour and commit to a new way or working, there are four basic components to consider:

- your behaviour and commitment
- how and what you and others communicate
- the extent to which you enable authentic participation
- your personal risk taking, and endorsement of risk taking in others.

Your behaviour and commitment

You'll need to pay close attention to aspects of your interpersonal style and behaviour. You may find it insightful to reflect for a moment on how it feels to be a 'target' of change. The vision of coaching has to be modelled from the top if it is to have integrity and be believed within the organisation. When employees are made aware of the need to change their behaviour, or to provide access to coaching support for those that they manage, they scrutinise the behaviour and attitudes of those at senior levels for a realistic understanding of what they are really expected to do. The rituals, actions and habits displayed by the top team, and especially by key change sponsors, are paramount.

Why is the behaviour of those at the top of the organisation so important? Psychological enquiry suggests that when situations are more ambiguous (during change), we rely more on other people to model how we are meant to behave (Aronson, 1984). We look to colleagues, peers, managers and leaders to provide the clues. If the leaders of the organisation are exhibiting behaviour in line with the coaching vision, others see that behaviour as important and follow suit.

Similarly, research on commitment suggests that the way your words and actions demonstrate your commitment to the coaching initiative(s) will work to generate appropriate beliefs and actions in others at three levels.

- If you behave in a certain way, you develop beliefs consistent with your behaviour, sustaining the behaviour in the future (Salancik, 1977).
- People do things because others do them, and they believe it's the right thing (Wiener, 1982).
- People do what is asked of them because they identify with part or all of the organisation whether it's a person, the team, the job, their manager (Mowday et al., 1979).

As the key sponsor and even as a change agent in the process, any deviation from the desired behaviour will indicate your underlying commitment is not there and the coaching initiative(s) is not really that important.

How and what you and others communicate

There is a vast amount of research on communication (see Hargie and Dickson, 2004 for a thorough overview): here is a brief snapshot of how we can make our messages more influential.

- The communicator needs to be seen to be trustworthy, with good judgement, to have nothing to gain, and potentially something to lose from the position they are presenting (Aronson, 1984; Hargie and Dickson, 2004). A highly credible communicator can persuade others even when their view differs substantially from that of the audience.
- The message needs to contain personal vivid examples that people have either witnessed or heard about (e.g. Nisbett and Ross, 1980). Presenting a two-sided perspective is more influential, especially where there is resistance to the message (Aronson, 1984; Hargie and Dickson, 2004).
- The message should include emotional content, together with clear, optimistic details of what needs to be done to bring about the required change. This is especially true if the message is one of fear (e.g. 'The company will fall behind the competition unless everyone takes responsibility for their performance. To achieve this, we need to change our management style to more of a coaching style.').
- The audience is more receptive if comfortable, and not expecting a hard sell.

The extent to which you enable authentic participation

The issue of participation is particularly relevant when introducing coaching initiatives to organisations. Coaching, as it is normally understood, involves a participative two-way relationship between the coach and the coachee, thus a participative change process is consistent with the basic tenet of coaching. While you may feel that encouraging employee participation in the change process is a challenge, and likely to increase uncertainty and conflict, the evidence suggests that participation gives substantive benefits for both individuals and organisations, including the following:

- Commitment, involvement, and greater personal responsibility for organisational outcomes (Heller et al., 1998).
- An increased perception of fairness of the decision-making process and outcome, leading to greater commitment to the final decision (McFarlin and Sweeney, 1992).

- Fulfilment of our need for environmental mastery and self-determination (e.g. White, 1959).
- The development of competence and improved performance.
- Avoidance of 'group think' (Janis, 1982). This occurs where a homogeneous, highly cohesive group is so concerned with maintaining unanimity that they fail to effectively evaluate their chosen course of action, the potential alternatives and other options, leading to suboptimal and at times damaging outcomes.

How do you make the opportunity to participate authentic? Trust is difficult to establish and easy to destroy and inconsistency between management's statements and actual practice will reduce the success of your coaching initiatives (e.g. Fucini and Fucini, 1990). Employees feel hostile, manipulated, frustrated and are likely to withdraw from the change process if they believe that decisions are made irrespective of their contribution to decision-making (Heller and Wilpert, 1981; Marchington et al., 1993). Inauthentic participation reduces the likelihood of people participating in the future.

First, make participation part of the culture, so it becomes business as usual, and ensure participative structures and processes exist. If people feel knowledgeable and skilled enough to participate, have an interest in the issues, believe in a personally positive outcome and can accommodate the additional work with their day-to-day jobs, participation is more likely to happen. Basically, to get people to participate, you need to make it easy and unthreatening for them.

Second, ensure people have a positive experience of participating and that their input is valued, and at the same time minimise inter-group politics and rivalries (Heller et al., 1998).

Your personal risk taking, and endorsement of risk taking in others

Changing the way that anything is done requires an element of personal risk. The first time you try to do a new thing, for example, to coach someone instead of telling them what you want them to do, it feels strange. You feel exposed, you do not know whether you have done what you intended and you are not sure what the response will be. By deviating from what is comfortable for you and what is expected by others, you take a risk. Given that risk taking is an element of change, there are a number of steps you can take as the change sponsor or change agent to facilitate risk taking and innovation in others.

- Publicly and proactively share the difficulties you personally encountered, or mistakes you made in trying to behave in line with the coaching initiative(s). This gives a message that getting it wrong is OK and manages others' expectations for immediate success.

- Work to free up individual and organisational defensive routines, focus on interpersonal interactions as well as the task of change (Argyris, 1985) – be prepared to challenge your own and others' habitual defence mechanisms.
- Ensure people feel safe trying out new and different ways of behaving. They need verbal and actual support, cooperation and tolerance of failure.
- Promote an aspirational performance standard, provide progress monitoring procedures, promote a climate of excellence and individual and team accountability.

Unsupportive behaviour or blame will lead people to do what they have always done, because it feels safe and more comfortable.

Key roles assessment

So how does the current behaviour of your key players match up to the ideals laid out above? The checklists outlined in Boxes 21.1, 21.2 and 21.3 enable you to assess what your change team need to do to ensure their approach and behavioural credibility is lined up to deliver, integrate and sustain the coaching initiative(s).

Box 21.1 Checklist for the key sponsor(s)

The key sponsor(s) of the coaching programme need to understand the change and move obstacles to enable it to happen throughout the organisation. They need to be openly committed to the vision of coaching and openly supportive of their change team even if errors occur. They need to

- be clear about what is required, financially and behaviourally, throughout the organisation to achieve the coaching vision
- gain support and build consensus for the coaching outcome throughout the organisation – not just at board level
- be passionate about the coaching programme – demonstrate commitment and belief in it, talk about the benefits it will bring
- be committed to addressing the obstacles and resistance that are inevitable when introducing the coaching programme
- support funding for the goal and allocate their personal time to it
- enable the change agents to manage the project
- identify the type and amount of dip in performance that will be tolerated as the change is brought about
- ensure the communication, learning and reward systems are used to

support the changes in behaviour required to realise the vision of coaching
- abide by any rules of confidentiality surrounding the coaching relationships established and uphold these if questioned by others
- empathise, and address line manager issues around coaching programmes
- provide people with the opportunity to express their concerns and fears about the coaching programme and support to break down barriers they are facing
- commit to the vision both publicly *and* privately
- take risks by changing their own behaviour, having their own coach and being open about this with others.

Source: adapted from LaMarsh and Associates, 2005; © LaMarsh and Associates, Inc.

Box 21.2 Checklist for the key change agent(s)

The key change agent(s) need to understand the coaching initiative(s) and its likely impact, manage the change process and deal with associated people issues. They may need to find the right sponsor and ensure the sponsor provides the appropriate level of sponsorship. They need to estimate the scale of likely resistance at a surface level and at a deeper level. They need to

- have a clear understanding of the coaching initiative(s) and have effectively implemented change in the past
- demonstrate a deep personal understanding of the personal, organisational, technical, customer and supplier dynamics of the coaching initiative(s)
- build effective sponsorship for the coaching initiative(s) – balancing ownership between the sponsors and themselves, educating the sponsors about the coaching initiative(s), key developments and what is required from them
- have the trust and respect of the sponsors **and** the targets of the coaching initiative(s)
- assess the variables that are critical to the successful implementation of the coaching initiative(s), the resistance, the current culture and the history of change in the organisation
- communicate effectively, getting the message across **and** actively listening to others, demonstrating patience when working with both sponsors and targets

- design a comprehensive plan to implement the coaching initiative(s) by:
  - surfacing business risks and recommending ways to reduce the risk
  - balancing the effective use of resources with the requirements of the change
  - building a communication plan, a learning and development plan and a reward and recognition plan
- be prepared to stop working on the initiative if not getting the necessary support.

Source: adapted from LaMarsh and Associates, 2005; © LaMarsh and Associates, Inc.

Box 21.3 Checklist for the targets

The targets are all those who are required to change their behaviour to fit with the coaching initiative(s). The ideal target behaviour includes targets who are

- willing to take risks
- willing to disrupt the status quo
- willing to fight for the coaching initiative(s)
- able to accurately assess and articulate feelings
- bored if things stay the same for too long
- able to live with a high level of disruption and lack of definition
- willing to adjust and negotiate the coaching vision
- willing to adjust and negotiate the process by which they will reach the coaching vision
- willing to spend time coming up with ways to change
- willing to spend time to make things happen.

Source: adapted from LaMarsh and Associates, 2005; © LaMarsh and Associates, Inc.

Thoughts on aligning systems and processes

Reward and recognition, learning and development and communication systems need to be scrutinised, altered and integrated to allow people to embrace the introduction of coaching and exhibit the behaviours detailed in your coaching vision (LaMarsh and Associates, 2005).

This integration provides employees with multiple points of reinforcement for the required changes in behaviour, clarifying what is expected of them in terms of work performance, everyday behaviours, and interactions with colleagues – what is acceptable and what is not. If you say that you want managers to adopt a coaching approach, but don't challenge the manager who bullies, blames, manipulates and shouts at her team, people will soon realise that a coaching approach is not that important.

Reward and recognition

Rewarding and motivating behaviours that are consistent with your coaching initiative(s) are key to sustaining the positive outcomes of coaching. Tangible rewards (pay, benefits, promotions etc.) *and* softer forms of recognition (celebrations, learning and development opportunities, day-to-day recognition by managers) need aligning, sometimes incrementally, to ensure you are

- rewarding desirable behaviours rather than undesirable behaviours
- rewarding those who constructively surface, or express resistance to the coaching initiative(s) especially early on
- rewarding achievement of new performance measurement levels
- penalising undesirable behaviours as the change becomes embedded

From a practical point of view it is far from straightforward to 'tweak' the formal reward system and much work and heartache is likely to be involved with such an emotive subject. Similarly, the inconsistencies that reward policies engender more often remain unseen, or unquestioned (Heller et al., 1998).

In order to understand how your current reward system is operating and maintaining existing behaviour, try identifying

- the current behaviours that are rewarded
- formal rewards
- informal rewards
- current performance measures
- the degree of difficulty of doing the job the old way (not in line with the coaching vision)
- the degree of difficulty of doing the job the new way (in line with the coaching vision)

(adapted from LaMarsh and Associates, 2005)

Learning and development

The learning and development system should focus on the behaviours required to support the coaching initiative(s). Employees need tools and opportunities to practise the required behaviours, gain constructive feedback and develop competence. A learning process that engages people in new behaviours at work as well as in more formal workshops is likely to lead to more consistent behavioural change in employees (Kirkpatrick, 1996).

A good learning and development system enables people to understand the philosophy of the coaching initiative(s), to practise and reflect on appropriate behaviours and apply these to everyday situations (e.g. Kolb, 1974). Day-to-day constructive feedback then gives employees an awareness of their progress and outlines the remaining gaps in their capability. As people develop new capabilities and enhanced awareness they start to see and experience the world differently. New beliefs and assumptions begin to form, which enables further development of skills and capabilities (Senge et al., 1994).

To ensure the formal learning and development system complements the coaching vision, you need to

- identify the behaviours and performance levels required in the coaching vision
- assess the gap between the current knowledge or skill level and the required performance level
- plan training and development to bridge the gap.

When introducing the coaching initiative(s), you need to

- bring in training and development at the right time
- bring in training in the right sequence to optimise skill development
- provide training in individual and organisational change and the change process
- provide people with constructive feedback skills
- constantly and consistently tie training and development to the coaching vision.

As progress is made, you need to

- ensure that people have the opportunity to maintain or improve their skills through refresher courses or 'advanced' programmes
- integrate the required capability into induction and career development programmes.

(adapted from LaMarsh and Associates, 2005)

Communication systems

Communicating the message about the coaching initiative(s) consistently and openly requires work. An organisation's communication system has formal components, and very powerful informal aspects, with the 'grapevine' often having a huge influence on employees' beliefs and behaviours. Indeed, where formal communication is so poor for a variety of reasons, informal network provides employees with their only information during periods of change.

Regardless of how good the formal communication system is, people listen to their peers and colleagues to make sense of what coaching is likely to mean on a personal level. Personal experiences are relayed in informal conversations and underpin the rumours that will be rife about your proposed coaching initiative(s).

How can you impact the message people are receiving? Basically, ensure a clear and consistent message about the coaching initiative(s) at every employee–organisational interface. People's personal experiences (through the reward and recognition, and learning and development systems) need to reflect the formal message. If this is the case then the formal and informal communication systems are likely to have more similar content. As Stacey and Griffin (2005) indicate, the quality of conversation in an organisation indicates the quality of the organisation.

There are roughly three phases (before, during and after the introduction of coaching) that require different emphases when planning your formal communication about the coaching initiative(s).

At the beginning:

- Establish your credibility either personally, or through endorsement from a trusted person (this person may change depending on your audience).
- Ensure that credible employee representatives are involved and identify credible change agents and sponsors.
- Explain why the change is necessary and focus the discussion on the outcomes.
- Explain the consequences of no change.
- Have the detail to hand that justifies the change (e.g. market research, surveys, case studies, cost-benefit analysis).
- Describe the coaching vision – and again, from the perspective of the person or people you are talking to.
- Identify and emphasise the external drivers.
- Be up front about personal outcomes that are known, for example, planned job cuts or organisational re-engineering (the grapevine will do this if you don't and the impact will be much more negative).
- Acknowledge the success or failure of previous attempts to introduce coaching initiative(s).
- Explain the changes people will see as you move towards the coaching vision.
- Identify what is not changing.
- Proactively develop and encourage two-way communication, taking on board suggestions and innovations where you can.
- Do not blame people, provide a structured, factual argument.

During the change:

- Repeat the message again and again – emphasise the need to change, and why the coaching vision is the right one.
- Clarify the coaching vision in many different ways – changing the words and the focus.
- Generate interest and enthusiasm by emphasising the personal and organisational benefits of the coaching initiative(s).
- Establish what people need to do to change in line with the vision and what resources they have.
- Create a variety of safe ways for people to express resistance to the change – assure them the change is not personal.
- Ensure you are rewarding the new behaviours, not the ones you want to eradicate.
- Grieve for the old ways of doing things – say goodbye to them and bury the old ways.

As progress is made:

- Show the distance people have come.
- Remind people why they are changing.
- Acknowledge the price people have paid.
- Present problems and issues today, don't wait (remember that grapevine).
- Identify future changes to keep you on course.
- Thank everyone for their efforts and for the results.

(adapted from LaMarsh and Associates, 2005)

It becomes clear that reward and recognition, learning and development and communications within an organisation interact at a number of levels and form the cornerstones of the prevailing organisational culture. Each of the systems holds the other in check. To change one element, such as learning and development, without the other two will ultimately lead to ineffective integration of your coaching initiative(s), and prolonged resistance.

Keeping your coaching initiative on track: understanding the change curve and negotiating resistance

You have got all the systems in place and aligned, detailed the vision, identified key sponsors and agents and understand where you are starting from – but people keep disagreeing with you, they do not do what you want them to. Why isn't it all going smoothly?

People go through a transition in attitudes and behaviour when they change. This might be something they hardly notice, or a change they struggle with for a number of years. Events affect individuals very differently. A change to a coaching culture might be met with a welcome embrace by some, while others are completely shocked by the change this requires in their way of working. Resistance occurs when people experience the discomfort and ambiguity associated with change. It may only be fleeting or it can become entrenched, it can be conscious or unconscious, people may not even be aware that they are behaving in a way that is incongruent with the coaching vision.

Resistance as part of the change process

During change, people go through a series of stages and emotions (Kubler-Ross, 1973). Typically this starts with the shock of being confronted with the need to behave differently or change their views in some way. During times of change, to avoid the discomfort associated with change, individuals may deny change is required. Strong emotions may characterise people's reactions as they move from shock into denial. The required change in behaviour and attitudes is too threatening to our sense of self. To maintain a positive self-image and affirm we are correct in our beliefs, information is processed in a biased way that fits our worldview. If in a state of strong denial about the need to change, individuals are strongly consciously resisting change and may experience stress and feel very angry, hurt and aggrieved at the situation.

Once over these initial stages, there is an acceptance that change is necessary and a shift in beliefs associated with the change. This change in beliefs often leads to a change in behaviour, and when people start engaging in new behaviours, their beliefs further shift and align with the new behaviours and changes are integrated and sustained. Ongoing maintenance is then enabled through the organisational systems and culture designed to support the coaching vision.

Some people never get through the transition, they remain in denial about the need to change, the required change is too uncomfortable, they may leave. Others oscillate between different stages in the transition curve as they deepen their self-awareness, their awareness of others and of the organisation.

Not surprisingly, a change in beliefs and behaviours is more likely if we feel our sense of self is threatened if we do not change. We are also more likely to change our beliefs and behaviours if we believe we are in control of changing them.

Dealing with resistance

It is easy to be fearful of resistance, to try to limit the opportunities for it to emerge, and to try to deny and destroy it when it does occur. Resistance is part of the territory of change, it will come up. Resistance has energy that can be directed and engaged with. It demonstrates people's commitment and loyalty. Resistance needs to be listened to, addressed and used in order to assist people to develop new behaviours and attitudes.

Using resistance can lead to a reduction in the effect of 'group think', to innovation and creativity and to a better coaching vision than the one that was originally suggested. Ignore it at your peril!

At the individual level, there are strategies and techniques to provide support that utilise resistance and enable people to change. These are outlined in Table 21.1 (adapted from LaMarsh and Associates, 2005).

At the organisational level, resistance is likely to stem from two main sources, the people and the systems within which they operate. From this, we see there are things you can do to address organisational level resistance.

First, deal with the resistance at the individual level as outlined above. Second, map out the systems of rewards and recognition, learning and development and communication and explore areas where they are working against each other and creating a block to integrating your coaching initiative. Where necessary, you may have to engage the change sponsor to make the necessary changes in the systems happen, to deliver the hard messages and to maintain people's focus on the goals of the coaching initiative.

Table 21.1 Strategies and techniques to move people through the change cycle

Stage	Strategies and techniques
Shock	Keep repeating the communication, changing the words and the method. Divide the change required into smaller steps and focus on the first step. Avoid confrontation and provide some space. Link their personal change to the change in the organisation as a whole.
Denial	Acknowledge and legitimise feelings Don't take other's feelings personally. Don't try to use logic and reason.
Awareness	Raise awareness of the parts of coaching vision that are flexible and negotiable. Clarify what is not changing. Support the individual and inform people what resources are available to them. Increase two-way communication and encourage employees to take responsibility for changing.
Acceptance	Support individual learning and development. Identify what has been learned and reward and acknowledge progress. Remind people how far they've come already.
Experimentation	Build employee confidence and provide constructive feedback.
Search for meaning	Enhance two-way communication and feedback and lay the ground for deepening the change still further.
Integration	Reward and acknowledge progress, maintain desired behaviour through constant monitoring and reshaping of organisational systems.

Summary

This chapter has described how creating the culture in which a coaching initiative can be integrated and sustained as part of the way things work in your organisation is not a particularly straightforward or quick process but, if managed thoughtfully and from a systemic point of view, can bring about substantial long-term performance gains.

The chapter has outlined a logical framework of the steps needed to create a culture where your coaching initiative can thrive and deliver performance improvements.

In summary, employees are more likely to actively engage in the change to integrate and sustain coaching in the organisation if you

- consistently use sound change management strategies and tactics
- define the coaching vision at the organisational and departmental levels
- reward only those who were good sponsors of change
- make sure communication, learning and development and reward and recognition systems are aligned
- provide people with the resources they needed to make changes
- admit failures and mistakes
- communicate the need for change throughout the organisation
- encourage the expression of resistance and respond to it
- involve employees at all levels in the change process
- recognise and celebrate small victories and the ultimate success.

People tend to make the best of something they know is bound to occur (Aronson, 1984). So if there is a history of successful change, systems are aligned with each other and the coaching vision, employees will gain a sense that this vision is going to happen.

References

Argyris, C. (1985) *Strategy, Change and Defense Routines*. Boston, MA: Pitman.

Aronson, E. (1984) *The Social Animal*, 4th edition. New York: Freeman.

Clutterbuck, D. and Megginson, D. (2005) *Making Coaching Work: Creating a coaching culture*. London: CIPD.

Corporate Leadership Council (2003) *Maximising Returns on Professional Executive Coaching*. Washington, DC: Corporate Leadership Council.

Fillery-Travis, A. and Lane, D. (2006) Does coaching work or are we asking the wrong question? *International Coaching Psychology Review* 1(1): 23–36.

Fucini, J. and Fucini, S. (1990) *Working for the Japanese: Inside Mazda's American auto plant*. New York: Free Press.

Grant, A. and Cavanagh, M. (2004) Toward a profession of coaching: sixty five years of progress and challenges for the future. *International Journal of Evidence Based Coaching and Mentoring* 2: 7–21.

Hargie, O. and Dickson, D. (2004) *Skilled Interpersonal Communication: Research, theory and practice*. London: Routledge.

Heller, F. and Wilpert, B. (1981) *Competence and Power in Management Decision-Making: A study of senior levels of organisation in eight countries*. Chichester: Wiley.

Heller, F., Pusic, E., Strauss, G. and Wilpert, B. (1998) *Organisational Participation: Myth and reality*. New York: Oxford University Press.

Janis, I. (1982) *Groupthink*. Boston, MA: Harcourt Press.

Kahn, R., Wolfe, D., Quinn, R. and Snoeck, J. (1964) *Organisational Stress: Studies in role conflict and ambiguity*. New York: Wiley.

Kirkpatrick, D. L. (1996) Great ideas revisited: revisiting Kirkpatrick's four-level model. *Training and Development* 50(1): 54–57.

Kolb, D. A. (1974) On management and the learning process. In D. A. Kolb, I. M. Rubin and J. M. McIntyre (eds) *Organizational Psychology*, 2nd edition (pp. 27–42). Englewood Cliffs, NJ: Prentice Hall.

Kubicek, M. (2002) Is coaching being abused? *Training* May: 12–14.

Kubler-Ross, E. (1973) *On Death and Dying*. London: Routledge.

LaMarsh and Associates (2005) *Master of Managed Change™ Handbook*. Chicago, IL: LaMarsh and Associates.

McFarlin, D. B. and Sweeney, P. D. (1992) Distributive and procedural justice as predictors of satisfaction with personal and organisational outcomes. *Academy of Management Journal* 35(3): 626–637.

Marchington, M., Wilkinson, A., Ackers, P. and Goodman, J. (1993) The influence of managerial relations on waves of employee involvement. *British Journal of Industrial Relations* 31: 553–576.

Mowday, R. T., Steers, R. D. and Porter, L. W. (1979) The measurement of organizational commitment. *Journal of Vocational Behaviour* 14: 224–247.

Nisbett, R. and Ross, L. (1980) *Human Inference: Strategies and shortcomings of social judgement*. Englewood Cliffs, NJ: Prentice Hall.

Peltier, B. (2001) *The Psychology of Executive Coaching*. New York: Brunner-Routledge.

Salancik, G. R. (1977) Commitment and the control of organizational behaviour and belief. In B. M. Staw and G. R. Salancik (eds) *New Directions in Organizational Behaviour* (pp. 1–54). Chicago, IL: St Clair.

Senge, P., Kleiner, A., Roberts, C., Ross. R. and Smith, B. (1994) *The Fifth Discipline Field Book: Strategies and tools for building a learning organisation*. London: Nicholas Brealey.

Stacey, R. and Griffin, D. (2005) *Complexity and the Experience of Managing in Public Sector Organisations*. London: Routledge.

White, R. W. (1959) Motivation reconsidered: the concept of competence. *Psychological Review* 66: 297–333.

Wiener, Y. (1982) Commitment in organisations: a normative view. *Academy of Management Review* 7: 418–428.

Discussion points

- When developing internal coaching experts in an organisation, what are the issues associated with confidentiality, responsibility and contracting that you might consider?
- What learning and development systems might in particular need to be reshaped when introducing coaching?
- How might you evidence return on investment having introduced coaching into an organisation?
- How might the introduction of coaching into an organisation be similar and different to other organisational development initiatives?

Suggested reading

LaMarsh, J. and Potts, R. (2004) *Managing Change for Success: Effecting change for optimum growth and maximum efficiency*. London: Duncan Baird.

This book provides more insight into the Managed Change™ model of LaMarsh and Associates, Inc. than that given here. It will assist in understanding the practical and effective strategies for gaining in-depth knowledge of the change process.

Megginson, D. and Clutterbuck, D. (2005) *Making Coaching Work: Creating a coaching culture*. London: CIPD.

Specifically focused on creating a coaching culture within an organisation in order to enhance the likely success and effectiveness of your coaching initiative.

Senge, P., Kleiner, A., Roberts, C., Ross. R. and Smith, B. (1994) *The Fifth Discipline Field Book: Strategies and tools for building a learning organisation*. London: Nicholas Brealey.

This provides a wealth of tools, techniques and strategies for creating a learning organisation. It deals with ways to map a system and to leverage change in a system. A useful book to have to hand when working with organisational change.

Fillery-Travis, A. and Lane, D. (2006) Does coaching work or are we asking the wrong question? *International Coaching Psychology Review* 1(1): 23–36.

A research paper published in the first edition of this international coaching publication that provides insight into how the added value of coaching can be usefully considered in organisations.

Chapter 22

Coaching psychology supervision

Luxury or necessity?

Michael Carroll

Introduction

Clinical supervision has been around for over a century. First devised as a support and reflective space for social workers in the late nineteenth century in the United States, it was slowly adopted by other helping professions – probation, advice and welfare programmes, employee assistance programmes and teaching. In the early days of Freud there is some evidence that small groups gathered to discuss and review each others' client work. Supervision was informal at this stage. Max Eitington is reckoned to be the first to make supervision a formal requirement for those in their psychoanalytic training in the 1920s. The second phase of supervision emerged in the 1950s with the introduction of other counselling or psychotherapy orientations besides the psychodynamic. The type of supervision emanating from these new developments has been called 'counselling-bound or psychotherapy-bound' models of supervision in that they allied their theory and interventions in supervision to the counselling or psychotherapy orientation they espoused. Watching Rogers, Perls or Ellis supervising would make an observer wonder what was different from the manner in which they supervised to the way they engaged in counselling. It was in the 1970s that supervision began to move away from counselling and make a bid for being more of an educational process than a counselling one. The focus moved from the person doing the work to the work itself. As a result the social role or developmental frameworks for supervision became more popular. Supervision now became centred on practice, the actual work done with a view to using that work to improve future work. This was quite a major shift in supervision theory and practice and the divide between counselling and supervision was firmly established. Supervision was unapologetically and unashamedly centred on practice and whatever impacted on that practice was the rightful subject of supervision (e.g. the person of the practitioner, the impact of the organisations involved).

By the 1970s supervision had been well and truly adopted by the US counselling psychology fraternity and there found its primary home for the next 20 years. From the US universities there emerged a wealth of supervision theory, models and research. There is little doubt that the main bulk of supervision research has come from and still comes from the USA and still, in particular, from counselling psychology. The emphasis from within counselling psychology on the 'reflective-practitioner' model as the best way of defining a counselling psychologist gave supervision its credibility. Supervision was the 'reflection on practice' aspect of the work.

Though it had been in Britain before 1980s (again in youth work, social services, teaching and probation), in the late 1970s and early 1980s clinical supervision made its journey across the ocean and settled here. It carried the US models and frameworks through the professions of counselling, counselling psychology and psychotherapy. Going even further than in the USA, the British Association for Counselling and Psychotherapy (BACP) not only adopted the new infant, but also made supervision mandatory and a requirement for all its practitioners. No longer an option or a recommendation, BACP was the first counselling organisation to require all its practitioner members to attend supervision for a minimum of 1.5 hours a month. This is still the case. Like the USA, counselling psychology in Britain saw supervision as an integral part of training and ongoing development and while stopping short of making it a requirement for those qualified (it is mandatory for those in training) has been forceful in recommending its use and usefulness.

Coaching psychology is currently reviewing its stance *vis à vis* supervision and few conferences on coaching psychology pass without supervision getting at least a mention and often centre stage. However, quite rightly, coaching psychology is wary of transferring models of supervision pertinent to other professions into the coaching arena. Pampallis Paisley (2006) asks the key question here: 'Whether the existing models of supervision are sufficient for the demands of coaching' and answers it with a 'both . . . and'. Coaching supervision can borrow elements and models from supervision as applied to other professions and there is room to look at coaching as 'a distinctive enough discipline to require a particular frame of supervision and a particular theory to support this'. This chapter wants to look at the added value supervision can give to coaching psychology as well as articulating how coaching psychology supervision can be implemented within a coaching psychology culture using existing models of supervision while recognising 'the need for multiple layers and levels of complexity that the executive coach finds him or herself in when working in organisations' (Pampallis Paisley, 2006).

Types of supervision

Before moving into coaching psychology supervision a few different types of supervision need to be outlined. In general there are four types of supervision (Hawkins and Shohet, 2000: 53):

- *Tutorial (research) supervision:* supervision here is characterised by a mentor relationship where a supervisor oversees (guides, advises) someone who is engaged in completing a research thesis or a work project. Clearly the supervisor needs to be more experienced than the supervisee and needs to know the pathways along which the new supervisee travels.
- *Trainee Supervision:* this type of supervision deals with those in training, those not yet qualified. The supervisor in this instance is also part of the assessment process that moves a trainee towards qualification. Evaluation takes on a major role in trainee supervision. The relationship here is a sort of 'apprenticeship' model with the experienced and qualified supervisor again guiding the novice into the profession and towards experience.
- *Consultative supervision:* this is called consultative because the supervisee is qualified (perhaps even more experienced than the supervisor in their area of work). Clearly this is more of a collegial relationship with less formal evaluation and more of a companion on a learning journey relationship than a hierarchical one.
- *Managerial supervision:* this is supervision where the supervisor is also the line manager of the supervisee.

By and large what we have called clinical supervision (or reflective or developmental supervision) pertains to circumstances where the work of the practitioner is the focus of the meeting between supervisee and supervisor and where the supervisor has no other relationship with the supervisee other than the supervision relationship. For this reason this chapter will look in detail at consultative supervision as the main agenda of coaching psychology supervision today. As training programmes in coaching psychology emerge then trainee coaching psychology supervision will need to be addressed more fully.

While most of what is written here will concentrate on executive coaching, life coaching shares many of the supervisory insights. What is usually different between the two is the existence of an organisation that sponsors executive coaching and wants a say in the coaching psychology agenda.

What is meant by supervision?

What is supervision in general, across professions? At its simplest, supervision is a forum where supervisees (in this case coaching psychologists) review and reflect on their work in order to do it better. Coaching psychologists bring their practice to another person (individual supervision) or to a group (small group or team supervision) and with their help review what happened in their practice in order to learn from that experience. Ultimately, supervision is for better coaching work. It is not the only help to better work but in the estimation of many it is one of the most effective interventions. In a relationship of trust and transparency, supervisees talk about their work and through reflection and thoughtfulness learn from it and return to do it differently. Supervision is based on the assumption that reflecting on work provides the basis for learning from that work and doing it more creatively (King and Kitchener, 1994; Moon, 1999; Bolton, 2001).

Ryan (2004) puts it well:

> Supervision is an inquiry into practice. It is a compassionate appreciative inquiry. . . . In supervision we re-write the stories of our own practice . . . supervision interrupts practice. It wakes us up to what we are doing. When we are alive to what we are doing we wake up to what is, instead of falling asleep in the comfort stories of our clinical routines.
>
> (Ryan, 2004: 44)

Coaching psychology supervision is a form of experiential learning. At its heart is practice, the actual work of the coaching psychologist supervisee. There is no such thing as supervision where work is not reviewed, interviewed, questioned, considered and critically reflected upon. Supervision that is not centred and focused on actual practice and work is simply another form of counselling or psychotherapy. Supervision is reflection-on-action or indeed, reflection-in-action to result in reflection-for-action.

Lane and Corrie (2006: 19) summarise what they see as the benefits of supervision for counselling psychologists. In my view, these benefits are equally true for coaching psychologists:

- It offers protection to clients (cases are reviewed).
- It offers reflective space to practitioners (so insights for improvement).
- It helps practitioners identify their strengths and weaknesses.
- It helps learning from peers.
- It offers the opportunity to keep up to date with professional developments.

I would add some further benefits to the above:

- It alerts practitioners to ethical and professional issues in their work and creates ethical watchfulness.
- It provides a forum to consider and hold the tensions that emerge from the needs of various stakeholders in the coaching psychology arrangement (the company, the coachee, the profession).
- It allows practitioners to measure the impact of their coaching work on their lives and to identify their personal reactions to their professional work.
- It offers a 'third-person' perspective (feedback) from the supervisor who is not part of the client system.

- It is ultimately for the welfare and better service of the client (the coachee).
- It creates a forum of accountability for those to whom the coaching psychologist is accountable (company, coachee, profession, etc.).
- It updates coaching psychologists to the best in psychological innovation, insights and research.

Lane and Corrie (2006) quite rightly point out that effective supervision should lead automatically to communities of practice (action-learning groups who work together to help each other provide better services). In such communities of practice developing excellent work becomes the project for all the members who use the community as a forum for reflection. Team supervision and small group supervision can easily become communities for the practice of coaching psychology.

Hawkins and Smith (2006) capture a number of these elements above in their definition of coaching supervision where they emphasise the systemic view of coaching psychologists:

> Coaching supervision is the process by which a Coach with the help of a Supervisor, who is not working directly with the Client, can attend to understanding better both the Client System and themselves as part of the Client-Coach system, and by so doing transform their work. It also allows the coach to discover where he or she is not currently creating the shift for the benefit of the client and client organisation.
>
> (Hawkins and Smith, 2006: 147)

As we will see, effective supervisors need to be systemic in their views and inclusive in holding a number of needs together (see www.bathconsultancy.com).

Coaching psychology supervisors

Supervisors are primarily facilitators of reflection (Hay, 2007). Above all they create a relationship and environment of safety and honesty where supervisees lay out their work and together (supervisor and supervisee) review it. Practice then becomes mindful involvement rather than mindless repetition (the opposite of reflection is mindlessness where work becomes routine, the same work reproduced again and again in a mindless way). Supervision creates mindful supervisees who think deeply and courageously about their work. Unapologetically they, supervisors and supervisees, want excellent work, quality work, and the best service for coachees. Bond and Holland (1998) capture the flavour of this in their definition of supervision as 'a regular, protected time for facilitated, in-depth reflection on practice'.

A group of 50 Maori psychologists, social workers and counsellors I worked with in 2005 devised their own definition of supervision as 'gathering the treasures of the past into the competencies of the present for the wellbeing of the future' (private communication, New Zealand, 2005). Supervision is not a given: it is culturally friendly, professionally adaptable and needs to be moulded to situations and supervisees. Coaching psychology supervisors are eminently flexible – they move towards supervisees and not the other ways around demanding supervisees accommodate to supervisors (as has been the tradition in supervision for so long).

In summary then, some of the central tenets that determine what coaching psychology supervision is are the following:

- Coaching psychology supervision is for the learning of supervisees (coaching psychologists).
- Experiential learning is the heart of supervision – the coaching work becomes the vehicle for learning (learning from doing).
- Supervisors facilitate supervisee learning.
- Learning in supervision is transformational (not just transmissional).
- Learning is for the future (what do we need to do the work better when we return to it?).
- Learning includes finding a voice so that coaching psychologist can articulate what they do and why they do it the way they do.
- Supervision is conversation-based learning – in a thoughtful and reflective dialogue learning takes place.
- Supervision moves from 'I-learning' to 'we-learning'.

Supervision is for the learning of the supervisee

The focus of coaching psychology supervision is the learning of the supervisee. Every supervision session could easily end with the same boring phrase: 'What have you learned from the last hour with me?' The learning involved is not just theoretical or simply head learning. It is learning from experience which results in doing the work differently. Supervision is about transformational learning (Mezirow, 2000). The very experience of working becomes the teacher; we sit at the feet of our own experience (Zachary, 2000). The American Military devised a form of this kind of supervision called the AAR (After Action Review) where after an operation, commanders gather their troops in small groups and face them with six questions (Garvin 2000) as follows:

- What did we set out to do?
- What happened?
- What went well?
- What went badly?

- What have we learnt from this exercise?
- What will we do differently next time?

This is genuine supervision and the same questions could be asked by coaching psychology supervisors in reflecting on a coaching psychology session. The last two questions summarise the future. We revisit the past to reflect on it, we move to the future to do it differently in the light of what we have learned from the past. In the present we review the past to learn for the future.

I am convinced we over-teach and, as supervisors, we are much poorer at facilitating learning than we are at teaching. The two (teaching and learning) are not the same and may not even necessarily be connected. Teaching does not necessarily result in learning and it certainly and often does not result in the learning I, the teacher, am hoping for. In teaching we ask the recipient to join us in our world: in learning we join them in their world. I am not saying that teaching is unimportant – I am just saying it is not as important as learning.

If 'all learning begins from the learner's frame of reference' then it does not make sense for coaching psychology supervisors to supervise as if all supervisees should be supervised in the same manner. Supervisors, understanding that one size does not fit all in learning terms, need to know the learning styles or intelligences of those we teach. How rarely we ask: before I teach you could you let me know your learning style?

Before beginning supervision it seems advisable to ask supervisees:

- How do you learn?
- What is your learning style?
- How can I facilitate your learning?
- What would I do that might block your learning?
- How might differences between us impact on your learning?
- How can we learn together?

Armed with this information coaching psychology supervisors become flexible and adaptable in gearing their style and interventions to the learning needs and the learning styles (and learning intelligences) of coach supervisees.

Systemic supervision

While the visible focus of coaching psychology supervision is usually two people (as in life coaching), or a small group of people (peer, team, group supervision), to ignore the systemic side of supervision is to miss the unseen but very active participants in the wider field who impact dramatically on the coaching psychologist, the coachee and their work together. Supervision inevitably involves a number of subsystems, even if they are invisible participants in the process. Not to consider them and keep them in mind and be aware of their impact is to create blindness, what Oshry calls 'system blindness' (Oshry, 1995). A systems approach to coaching psychology supervision keeps the big picture in mind as outlined in Figure 22.1.

In Figure 22.1 an organisation contracts with a coaching organisation for individual executives to engage in executive coaching with a designated coach employed by the coaching organisation. This coach is being supervised by an external supervisor or in some instances by a supervisor internal to the coaching organisation.

Sometimes the above five subsystems are all involved, sometimes four of them and less often in executive coaching three of them (executive, coach and supervisor). Imagine some of the dynamics needing consideration when an external supervisor is supervising the work of a coach psychologist who belongs to a coaching organisation or company which contracts with an organisation to provide coaching to individual executives. Maintaining professional boundaries, managing contracts and in particular the psychological contract (Carroll, 2005) and being aware of the needs and responsibilities of each of the players can become a minefield (Copeland, 2005, 2006; Towler, 2006).

It is here particularly that coaching psychologists and coaching psychology supervisors need knowledge, insights and skills in understanding and working with companies and within a business context. Many coaching psychologists do not have this background from their previous experiences even when they have worked in the public sector. Hawkins and Smith (2006) alert to this factor,

> hence the dangers of over-applying the theories and models of one group to the work of another. One of the dangers of a coach going for supervision to a counsellor, or counselling psychologist, is that the supervisor's professional focus will tend towards understanding the psychology of the client . . . . The biggest danger is when a fundamental orientation, that is more interested in individuals than organisations, tips over into an unrecognised tendency to see individuals as victims of 'bad' or 'unfeeling' organisation.
>
> (Hawkins and Smith, 2006: 148)

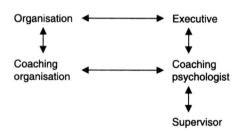

Figure 22.1 A systemic overview of coaching psychology supervision.

Coaching psychology supervisors add the organisational aspect (as well as the individual perspective) to their agenda.

Two PhD theses have looked at supervision within organisational context, one in particular reviewing the impact of the organisation on the supervision arrangement (Gonzalez-Doupe, 2001; Towler, 2006).

Towler (2006) is specifically interested in 'how the factor of context has influenced the process of supervision' and he uses the concept of 'organisation as client' to look at the impact and 'influence of the invisible client' (the company or organisation). Towler's qualitative research uncovers the psychosocial process of 'supervisees and supervisor assimilating and acculturating in the flux and flow of the supervisory field that is expressed in:

1 Supervisee wrestling with the perceived negative influences of the supervisor (multiple roles of supervisor, not being understood, power).
2 Supervisees wrestling with the perceived negative influences of the organisation (litigation, expectations, constraints, culture).
3 Supervisors wrestling with their role in relation to supervisee and the organisation (collusive stances, monitoring, three-way contracts).
4 Supervisees valuing and feeling valued by the supervisor (relationship, respect, protection, supervisor flexibility).
5 Supervisors valuing and feeling valued by the supervisees (respect, trust, clarity of roles).
6 Supervisors and supervisees valuing and feeling valued by the organisation (congruence in values, being held).
7 Supervisees and supervisors engaging in and co-creating a flexible space and relational focus for supervision (coping with organisational change, difficult clients, ethical issues).

Towler's conclusions are similar to those of Gonzalez-Doupe (2001), who concluded that supervisors act as buffers between supervisees and organisations. Her work centred on small group supervision within organisation settings and her core finding was that the work group functions as a boundary of protection against group, team and organisational pressure. This small group supervision has been referred to as a 'group as protection'. Her study shows the importance of supervision and supervisors 'supporting counsellors' attempts at self-advocacy within the organisational system' (Gonzalez-Doupe, 2001: 238).

Both these authors offer conclusions highly relevant to supervisors working with coaching psychologists who work within organisations where executive coaching is nested. Sue Copeland (2005) whose work is also with counsellors in organisations challenges us further to focus on the systemic (organisational side). Her model (very much for counsellors in organisations but very applicable to coaching psychologists who work with executives and teams in companies) is comprehensive and embedded in the organisation (see Figure 22.2).

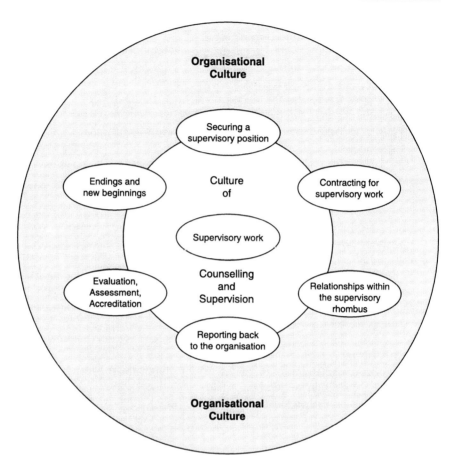

Figure 22.2 Copeland's (2005) model of coaching supervision in organisations.

Source: Copeland, 2005: 33, Figure 2.1.

Carroll has outlined ten tasks that supervisors need to fulfil when there is an organisation as part of the supervisory field, summarised as the ability to do the following:

1 Generate clear contracts with all (these will include two-way, three-way and sometimes four-way contracts).
2 Enable coaching psychologists to collaborate (without colluding) with companies and organisations.
3 Help coaching psychologists manage the flow of information with the whole system (confidentially, who talks to whom).
4 Assist supervisees to make appropriate ethical decisions in organisational contexts.

5 Work with coaching psychologists at the interface between the individual executive and the organisation (who is the client?).
6 Help coaching psychologists look after and support themselves as they work within organisations.
7 Help coaching psychologists deal with records, statistics, reports and how to communicate these to organisations.
8 Know how to deal with three-way meetings when appropriate.
9 Facilitate coaching psychologists' understanding and ability to manage the parallel process within organisations.
10 Evaluate, with supervisees, how coaching psychology can be a vehicle for understanding and facilitating organisational change (e.g. team coaching, coaching for culture change).

A number of authors have begun to look at how best to prepare for and implement executive coaching within origination contexts (see Hawkins and Shohet, 2000; Austin and Hopkins, 2004; Clutterbuck and Megginson, 2005; Copeland, 2005). However, little work has been done on coaching supervision itself. A recent doctoral dissertation tackles the issues of 'multiple triangulations one finds oneself in when supervising in an organisation and the main one for coaching is: the coach, the client and the organisation' (Pampallis Paisley, 2006). Effective coaching psychology supervisors hold these subsystems together, their needs and interactions, in a creative tension.

Holding and containing the paradoxes of supervision?

Coaching psychology supervisors have the unenviable task of sitting at crossroads and maintaining the tensions that come with holding opposites together. The following supervisory questions capture the dilemmas and struggles faced by all supervisors and ask of supervision:

- Is it surveillance or developmental?
- Is it about accountability or quality service?
- Does it curtail deficiency or maximise potential?
- Is it about assessment and feedback or self-evaluation?
- Is the focus on the supervisee or the client?
- Is it about the system or the individual?
- Is it teaching or learning?
- Is it collegial or authority based?
- Is it about experts or beginners?
- Is it counselling or education?

In almost all of these tensions the answer lies somewhere in the middle. Coaching psychology supervision is 'both . . . and', rather than an 'either . . .

or' stance. It is both evaluation and development, both learning and accountability. Quinn (2004) talks about categories melting when we begin to stop splitting opposites and polarities like love/hate, life/death, and making one good and one bad. He suggests combination such as: reflective action, responsible freedom, grounded vision and detached interdependence. Effective supervisors create combinations and make connections.

Holding and working creatively with such tensions can be difficult in relationships and organisations which pressurise coaching psychologist and coaching psychology supervisors to opt for one or other side of the dilemma. It is easy to get 'caught in the crossfire' of maintaining a neutral stance between the various parties involved (organisation, executive, executive coach).

Helping coaching psychology supervisees use supervision effectively

Many supervisees rightly complain that they have no training in being and becoming supervisees. Indeed there is little literature to guide them and few resources to help them understand what supervision is, how to choose a supervisor, contract within supervision, present coaching clients, deal with conflict, etc. One manual (Carroll and Gilbert, 2005) offers supervisees practical help in being an effective supervisee. Among other areas there are six sets of skills that help coaching psychology supervisees make the best use of supervision time. These are:

- learning how to reflect
- learning how to learn
- learning how to give and receive feedback to facilitate learning
- learning how to be emotionally aware
- learning how to self-evaluate realistically
- learning how to dialogue (see Carroll and Gilbert, 2005).

Carroll and Gilbert (2006) have translated their supervisee book into a manual for coaches (*On Being a Coachee: Creating learning relationships*) which adds another support to coachees who have little literature to guide them in becoming effective coachees.

Supervisees need help in using supervision to its maximum and time spent helping them do so will have valuable returns.

Models for understanding coaching psychology supervision

While not devised for coaching psychology, a number of existing models of supervision are very applicable to working with executive coaches (e.g. Page and Wosket, 1994; Holloway, 1995; Hawkins and Shohet, 2000; Inskipp and

Proctor, 2001a, 2001b). Hawkins and Shohet's Seven Eyed Supervisor is of particular help here where coaching psychology supervisors can use it to help supervisees prepare for supervision (Inskipp and Proctor, 2001b) or as a focus for what Hawkins and Smith call the Seven Modes of Coaching Supervision. These models will be used later in reviewing the example of Anthony.

Case study

Anthony is an executive coaching psychologist with Coach Supreme, a company that specialises in offering executive coaching to the banking industry. His company have a contract with Abell Investments and Anthony has been allocated two executives as his coachees. He has been working with both of them (Amelia and Jason) for almost four months now and meets with them once a month for an hour and half.

Gabrielle is Anthony's supervisor. She is external to Coach Supreme, who pays her as supervisor. Coach Supreme also has an internal accounts director (Adam) who offers day-to-day supervision on case management in respect of Coach Supreme, which is one of the accounts he manages.

Anthony has brought Amelia to Gabrielle in supervision twice now and in this last supervision session mentioned that he was quite worried about what was happening to her. Amelia is a producer-manager in that she manages her own investment account for clients but also oversees and line manages a team of 15 investment bankers. She is quite young to be promoted to this level, which is an indicator that Abell Investments see her as talented and having potential of going further with the company. Anthony has been working with her on her management style (which is what Abell also wanted), has met with Amelia and the HR director to agree the agenda for executive coaching and is expected to put in an interim report after six months.

However, Amelia has 'gone to pieces' in the past two months after a lively and involved start to her managerial career. It began with her need to confront and challenge poor performance on the part of one of her team. Anthony encouraged her to do this and coached her about how to intervene. It did not go as planned and after some acrimonious exchanges, the member of the team in question went to Amelia's boss, who seems to side with her (the member of Amelia's team) and while agreeing with Amelia about the need to tackle shoddy performance felt that she was handling it poorly and suggested he take over. The end result was that the member of staff resigned and the rest of the team have turned against Amelia – almost ostracising her. They are certainly sabotaging what she does, talk about her behind her back and on some occasions now she has not been invited to after work drinks or 'get togethers' when before she would have been an obvious choice. The impact on Amelia is quite devastating. She hates coming to work, she talks in her coaching sessions about going home and crying, about her partner at home who is fed up with her depressions and her incessant talk about work and about feeling constantly low and depressed. She feels isolated, unsupported and stuck. She has just recently returned to work after two weeks off due to stress.

Anthony is stuck too. He does not know how to handle this. He is getting two messages. His accounts manager (Adam) is recommending he go higher into the organisation to suggest team development and conflict resolution, his other supervisor (Gabrielle) thinks this would disempower Amelia and that Anthony should support her in tackling this. Amelia has pointed out similarities between this situation and her family of origin which Anthony has noted but not pursued. He is anxious that the coaching does not turn into quasi-counselling which focuses on Amelia's background and her transference of some of that into the present team situation. On the other hand he feels a need to help Amelia move out of 'survival mode' which results in her just getting through the day, getting to the end of the week but has no positive strategies for improving her role as manager. Anthony is worried that Amelia will have a 'breakdown' or will impulsively resign (it was her doctor who suggested she take two weeks off with stress).

In supervision, Gabrielle, using the seven eyed model (Hawkins and Shohet, 2000), reviews, with Anthony, possible avenues of enquiry and points out that they could work together on any of the following:

- The client – if we look at the team as client then we can concentrate on what is happening to them (e.g. why are they siding against Amelia?), try to understand the dynamics involved and make sense of this organisationally and in terms of the various relationships involved.
- The interventions: what can Amelia do to remedy the situation so that it does not get worse? What has she done that has triggered the events? What future strategies are needed to create a better atmosphere?
- Relationships: how do we evaluate the various relationships involved (Amelia and her boss, and the team, and the individuals in the team, the HR director)? Are there ways of building new improved relationships?
- What is happening to Anthony and why? Can we understand his reactions, thoughts and feelings to what is happening? How can we manage his reactions and his feelings of being stuck?
- Parallel Process: what is happening in the team that may be transferred into the supervision relationship (both systems seem stuck!)?
- What is happening to Gabrielle and what are her reactions as well as her intuitions, theories, hunches, etc?

- What is happening in the wider system of the organisation and how are the various parts of it impacting on Amelia?

Each and all of the above focus points make fertile material for the executive coaching psychology supervision session. The supervisory questions are the following:

- Who decides, with limited time, which of these avenues to pursue?
- What would best help Amelia just now and how would the various actors in the drama know?
- When should the supervisor intervene (if at all) other than simply provide supervision?
- Should the supervisor talk to the case manager (Adam) about what is going on?
- Should Adam feed back any information into Abell Investments (through the HR department)?
- Should Anthony take a more proactive role and involve himself more in the organisational side of what is happening?
- Should Anthony recommend that Amelia have counselling support alongside the executive coaching he is providing (he would not be the counsellor but he could make a referral so that it is set up confidentially for Amelia – he is certain the company would pay)?

In supervisor-led supervision, the coaching psychology supervisor would decide which of these 'eyes' to use: in supervisee-based supervision the question to the supervisee is: 'What would best help you? From the various options available which would you choose as the way forward for you and your learning?'

This example shows some of the individual, team, organisational and supervisory issues/problems/dilemmas/challenges that can pertain when executive coaching is implemented in an organisation.

Other areas

This chapter on coaching psychology supervision has traced the history of supervision and begun to apply supervision theory, research and practice to coaching psychology. Inevitably it has focused on a number of key areas and not considered others. Before ending it is worth mentioning some of these as areas coaching psychology supervisors need to pay attention to in setting up and maintaining an effective supervisory relationship – while other professions have frameworks and models for these, work has to be done on applying their conclusions to the coaching psychology field:

- Contracting for supervision (Inskipp and Proctor, 2001a, 2001b; Carroll and Gilbert, 2005). Getting contracts agreed, clear and written is fundamental where a number of subsystems are involved as in coaching psychology.
- Processes and stages that supervision goes through (Carroll, 1996; Hawkins and Shohet, 2000).
- Developmental stages of supervisor and supervisee progression (Skovholt and Rønnestad, 1992). Awareness that supervisees move through various stages of their own professional development allows coaching psychology supervisors to 'pitch' their interventions accordingly. It also allows room for looking at the type of supervision best needed by the supervisee and the kinds of relationships involved (Pauline Willis, private communication).
- Evaluation and feedback within supervision (Carroll and Gilbert, 2005) and how this works within an organisational setting.
- Small group and team supervision (Lammers, 1999; Proctor, 2000).
- Research into the effectiveness of supervision (Freitas, 2002).
- Good and bad supervision: what do effective supervisors do and what should they avoid doing (Ladany, 2004)?
- Ethical decision-making and legal issues in supervision (Carroll, 1996) especially when there is an organisation as part of the system.

Conclusion

Coaching psychology has begun its journey to becoming professional with a concentration on codes of ethics, accreditation, training and research. Part of that professionalism is supervision – the forum where practice is reviewed, learnings are gleaned and then applied to future practice. Coaching psychology is asking what supervision models, frameworks and strategies are pertinent to experiential learning for coaching psychologists. Moves are afoot to take existing theory and research in supervision in general and translate those into frameworks pertinent to coaching psychology. Coaching psychology also needs innovative thinkers, theorists and researchers who will begin to create coaching psychology supervision as a learning intervention in its own right. Interesting times loom ahead!

References

Austin, M. J. and Hopkins, K. M. (eds) (2004) *Supervision as Collaboration in the Human Services*. Thousand Oaks, CA: Sage.
Bolton, G. (2001) *Reflective Practice*. London: Paul Chapman.
Bond, M. and Holland, S. (1998) *Skills of Clinical Supervision for Nurses*. Buckingham: Open University Press.
Carroll, M. (1996) *Counselling Supervision: Theory, skills and practice*. London: Cassell.

Carroll, M. (2005) The psychological contract in organisations. In R. Tribe and M. Morrissey (eds) *Professional and Ethical Issues for Psychologists, Psychotherapists and Counsellors*. London: Brunner-Routledge.

Carroll, M. and Gilbert, M. (2005) *On Becoming a Supervisee: Creating learning partnerships*. London: Vukani.

Carroll, M. and Gilbert, M. (in press) *On Becoming a Coachee: Creating learning partnerships*. London: Vukani.

Clutterbuck, D. and Megginson, D. (2005) *Making Coaching Work: Creating a coaching culture*. London: CIPD.

Copeland, S. (2005) *Counselling Supervision in Organisations*. Hove: Routledge.

Copeland, S. (2006) Counselling supervision in organisations: are you ready to expand your horizons? *Counselling at Work* 51(winter): 2–4.

Freitas, G. J. (2002) The impact of psychotherapy supervision on client outcome: a critical examination of two decades of research. *Psychotherapy* 39(4): 354–367.

Garvin, D. A. (2000) *Learning in Action: A guide to putting the learning organisation to work*. Boston, MA: Harvard Business School.

Gonzalez-Doupe, P. (2001) The supervision group as protection: the meaning of group supervision for workplace counsellors and their supervisors in organisational settings in England. PhD dissertation, University of Wisconsin-Madison.

Hawkins, P. and Shohet, R. (2000) *Supervision in the Helping Professions*, 2nd edn. Buckingham: Open University Press.

Hawkins, P. and Smith, N. (2006) *Coaching, Mentoring and Organizational Consultancy: Supervision and Development*. Maidenhead: Open University Press.

Hay, J. (2007) *Reflective Practice and Supervision for Coaches*. Maidenhead: Open University Press.

Holloway, E. (1995) *Clinical Supervision: A systems approach*. Beverly Hills, CA: Sage.

Inskipp, F. and Proctor, B. (2001a) *Making the Most of Supervision, Part 1*, 2nd edition. London: Cascade.

Inskipp, F. and Proctor, B. (2001b) *Making the Most of Supervision, Part 2*, 2nd edition. London: Cascade.

King, P. and Kitchener, K. S. (1994) *Developing Reflective Judgment*. San Francisco, CA: Wiley.

Ladany, N. (2004) Psychotherapy supervision: what lies beneath? *Psychotherapy Research* 14(1): 1–19.

Lammers, W. (1999) Training in group and team supervision. In E. Holloway and M. Carroll (eds) *Training Counselling Supervisors*. London: Sage.

Lane, D. and Corrie, S. (2006) Counselling psychology: its influences and future. *Counselling Psychology Review* 21(1): 12–24.

Mezirow, J. (2000) *Learning as Transformation: Critical perspectives on a theory in progress*. San Francisco, CA: Jossey-Bass.

Moon, J. (1999) *Reflection in Learning and Professional Development*. London: Kogan Page.

Oshry, B. (1995) *Seeing Systems: Unlocking the mysteries of organizational life*. San Francisco, CA: Berrett-Koehler.

Page, S. and Wosket, V. (1994) *Supervising the Counsellor: A cyclical model*. London: Routledge.

Pampallis Paisley, P. (2006) Towards a theory of supervision for coaching – an integral approach. DProf. thesis, Middlesex University, UK.

Proctor, B. (2000) *Group Supervision: A guide to creative practice*. London: Sage.
Quinn, R. (2004) *Building the Bridge as You Walk on It*. San Francisco, CA: Jossey-Bass.
Ryan, S. (2004) *Vital Practice*. Portland, UK: Sea Change.
Schon, D. (1987) *Educating the Reflective Practitioner*. San Francisco, CA: Jossey-Bass.
Skovholt, T. M. and Rønnestad, M. (1992) *The Evolving Professional Self*. New York: Wiley.
Towler, J. (2006) The influence of the invisible client. PhD dissertation, University of Surrey, UK.
Zachary, L. (2000) *The Mentor's Guide: Facilitating effective learning relationships*. San Francisco, CA: Jossey-Bass.

Discussion points

- What contribution does supervision make to the quality of the work done by coaching psychologists?
- What concept of learning should underpin effective supervision for coaching psychologists?
- What do you see as the difference between effective and ineffective supervision?
- How can supervisors help supervisees make the best use of supervision time?

Suggested reading

Carroll, M. (2006a) Key issues in coaching psychology supervision. *The Coaching Psychologist* 2(1): 4–8.
Carroll, M. (2006b) Supervising executive coaches. *Therapy Today* 17(5): 47–49.
Hawkins, P. and Smith, N. (2006) *Coaching, Mentoring and Organizational Consultancy: Supervision and Development*. Maidenhead: Open University Press.
Hay, J. (2007) *Reflective Practice and Supervision for Coaches*. Maidenhead: Open University Press.

Afterword

Stephen Palmer and Alison Whybrow

When we first started this project at the beginning of 2004, coaching psychology was still in its infancy and was developing fast. It still is! With the publisher's permission, we've attempted to keep up with the developments and hence the *Handbook of Coaching Psychology* is different from our original book proposal. This has been an exciting and rewarding project to work on. We hope that the *Handbook* will contribute to the subject of coaching psychology and firmly believe that it complements the available academic literature in the field.

We would be interested in receiving your feedback and possible suggestions for new topics in later editions. We can be contacted on:

Stephen Palmer: dr.palmer@btinternet.com
Alison Whybrow: alison.whybrow@btinternet.com

Coaching and coaching psychology professional bodies

Key: Coaching psychology body = *

Association for Coaching
www.associationforcoaching.com

Association for Professional Executive Coaching and Supervision (APECS)
www.apecs.org/

Australian Psychological Society, Interest Group in Coaching Psychology*
www.groups.psychology.org.au/igcp/

British Psychological Society, Special Group in Coaching Psychology*
www.sgcp.org.uk/

Danish Psychological Association, Society for Evidence-based Coaching
(Selskab for Evidensbaseret Coaching)
www.sebc.dk

European Mentoring and Coaching Council
www.emccouncil.org/

Federation of Swiss Psychologists, Swiss Society for Coaching Psychology*
www.coaching-psychologie.ch/

International Association for Coaching
www.certifiedcoach.org/

International Coach Federation
www.coachfederation.org/ICF/

Worldwide Association of Business Coaches (WABC)
www.wabccoaches.com/

Coaching and coaching psychology related journals

International Coaching Psychology Review (*ICPR*)
Published by the BPS Special Group in Coaching Psychology in association with the Australian Psychological Society, Interest Group in Coaching Psychology. The *ICPR* is an international publication focusing on the theory, practice and research in the field of coaching psychology. It publishes academic articles, systematic reviews and other research reports which support evidence-based practice. It is peer reviewed.
www.sgcp.org.uk/coachingpsy/publications/icpr.cfm

International Journal of Evidence Based Coaching and Mentoring
Published by Oxford Brookes University. The journal is a free access, international peer-reviewed journal, which is published bi-annually online in February and August. The aim of the journal is twofold: first, to provide evidence-based, well-researched resources for students, professionals, corporate clients, managers and academic specialists who need to be at the forefront of developments in the field; and second, to offer an accessible yet powerful discussion platform for the growing number of coaching and mentoring practitioners seeking to validate their practice.
www.brookes.ac.uk/schools/education/ijebcm/home.html!

The Coaching Psychologist (*TCP*)
Published by the BPS Special Group in Coaching Psychology. *The Coaching Psychologist* publishes articles on all aspects of research, theory, practice and case studies in the arena of coaching psychology. Contributions from related disciplines are welcome. *TCP* is available through Open Access and requires no registration. It is peer reviewed.
www.sgcp.org.uk/coachingpsy/publications/thecoachingpsychologist.cfm

Coaching: An International Journal of Theory, Research and Practice
Published by Routledge in affiliation with the Association for Coaching. The journal aims to develop novel insights and approaches for future research. Broad and interdisciplinary in focus, articles published include

original research articles, review articles, 'interviews', technique reports and case reports. It offers an international forum for debates on policy and practice. The journal considers publishing special sections or special issues on particular topics.
www.informaworld.com/rcoa

University-based coaching psychology units and centres

Coaching Psychology Unit, City University, UK
www.city.ac.uk/psychology/research/CoachPsych/CoachPsych.html

Coaching Psychology Unit, University of Sydney, Australia
www.psych.usyd.edu.au/psychcoach/

Coaching Psychology Institute, Harvard Medical School
www.coachingpsychologyinstitute.com

Index